The Business of Gaming: Economic and Management Issues

Edited by

William R. Eadington

Professor of Economics and Director
Institute for the Study of Gambling and Commercial Gaming
University of Nevada, Reno

Judy A. Cornelius

Associate Director
Institute for the Study of Gambling and Commercial Gaming
University of Nevada, Reno

ISBN 0-942828-38-0

Published by
Institute for the Study of Gambling and Commercial Gaming
College of Business Administration MS 025
University of Nevada, Reno
Reno, Nevada 89557 USA

Library of Congress Catalog Card Number 97-77847

Dust jacket artwork and design by
Michael Eadington
High Mountain Imagery
Crystal Bay, Nevada

Book design and layout based on design by
Diane Chester Berg
Computer Support Services of Northern Nevada
Carson City, Nevada

Printed in the United States of America

In memory of Nigel Kent-Lemon
Our good friend and colleague

The Business of Gaming:
Economic and Management Issues
Contents

Section 1
Economic Dimensions of Commercial Gaming Industries

Section 2
Casino Management Issues

Section 3
Casino Operations Issues

Section 4
Casino Design and Ambience

Section 5
Studies of Casinos and Competition

Contributors

Randolph Baker, J. D., APR

President, Thompson & Baker
Memphis, Tennessee
Harrah's Visiting Professor of Gaming Studies
University of Nevada, Reno 1995–1996.

George W. Borden

Community Development Specialist
Nevada Cooperative Extension
University of Nevada, Reno

John T. Bowen

Professor and Director of Graduate Programs and Research
William F. Harrah College of Hotel Administration
University of Nevada, Las Vegas

William J. Callnin

Managing Director
Spectrum Gaming Group
Lawrenceville, New Jersey

Felicia F. Campbell

Professor of English
College of Liberal Arts
University of Nevada, Las Vegas

David H. Ciscel

Senior Economics Researcher
Bureau of Business and Economic Research
The University of Memphis

Lynn D. Constan

Urban Systems, Inc.
New Orleans, Louisiana

William J. Corney

Professor of Management
College of Business
University of Nevada, Las Vegas

Lawrence Dandurand

Professor of Marketing
College of Business
University of Nevada, Las Vegas

Robert R. Fletcher

Professor of Applied Economics and Statistics
Center for Economic Development
College of Agriculture
University of Nevada, Reno

John E. Gnuschke

Director
Bureau of Business and Economic Research
The University of Memphis

Deborah M. Goebel

Research Assistant
William Blair & Company, L.L.C.
Chicago, Illinois

Leonard E. Goodall

Professor of Management and Public Administration
College of Business
University of Nevada, Las Vegas

Fredric E. Gushin

Managing Director
Spectrum Gaming Group
Lawrenceville, New Jersey

David Kranes

Professor of English
University of Utah
Salt Lake City

Robert G. Lawrence

Director
Equine Industry Program
College of Business and Public Administration
University of Louisville

Jeffrey A. Lowenhar

President
Gaming Research, Inc.
Las Vegas, Nevada

Andrew MacDonald

Executive General Manager
Risk Management
Crown Limited
Melbourne

Dean M. Macomber

President & Chief Operating Officer
Casino Niagara and General Manager
The Navegante Group

James C. Makens

Associate Professor
The Babcock Graduate School of Management
Wake Forest University

Mary Alice Maloney

Research Assistant
Department of Marketing
University of Nevada, Las Vegas

Christian Marfels

Professor of Economics
Dalhousie University
Nova Scotia

John R. Mills

Professor of Accounting
College of Business Administration
University of Nevada, Reno

Merwin C. Mitchell

Associate Professor of Economics
College of Business Administration
University of Nevada, Reno

Mary Ann Perkins

The Perkins Corporation
Reno, Nevada

J. Kent Pinney

Professor of Marketing (*retired*)
University of Nevada, Las Vegas

Brian Repsher

Management Consultant
Las Vegas

Jack B. Samuels

Program Coordinator
Recreation, Tourism and Hospitality Programs
Montclair State University
Upper Montclair, New Jersey

John A. Schibrowsky

Associate Professor and Chair
Department of Marketing
College of Business and Economics
University of Nevada, Las Vegas

Robert J. Simonson, CFA

William Blair & Company, L.L.C.
Chicago, Illinois

Yvonne Stedham

Associate Professor of Management
College of Business Administration
University of Nevada, Reno

Derek Syme

formerly Senior Lecturer
School of Nursing, Health & Environmental Sciences
Wellington Ploytechnic—New Zealand
Recipient
1994 JOHN ROSECRANCE GAMBLING RESEARCH PAPER COMPETITION

Laurens Tan

Lecturer
School of Design
University of Western Sydney Nepean

Lawrence X. Taylor

Director of Investor Relations
Grand Casinos, Inc.
Minnesota

Contributors

Richard Thalheimer

Associate Professor
Equine Industry Program
College of Business and Public Administration
University of Louisville

Jannet M. Vreeland

Assistant Professor of Accounting
College of Business Administration
University of Nevada, Reno

Jeff Wallace

Senior Research Associate
Bureau of Business and Economic Research
The University of Memphis

Preface

Looking back at Nevada in the old days, before corporate ownership became the standard for casino companies there and elsewhere, one confronts considerable romanticism and folklore about the business of gaming and the nature of casino operations. First and foremost, authorities—especially those outside of Nevada—viewed casinos with a very suspicious eye. The gaming industry came from illegitimate roots, and at mid-century casinos were illegal in most jurisdictions in America and throughout the world. Indeed, Nevada had been widely criticized when in 1931 it legalized casino gaming. By so doing, it provided a safe haven for an "outlaw" industry and its "outlaw" managers and owners.

The old days for casinos were before 1969. That was the year the State of Nevada passed the Corporate Gaming Act, and permitted publicly traded companies to become casino license holders (Eadington, 1982). It was also a year after the passage of the British Gaming Act and a year before it was implemented, creating a highly regulated and controlled—but nonetheless legitimate—casino industry in that country. And it preceded by three years the legalization of the Wrest Point Casino in Tasmania, the first legal casino in Australia.

Casino management in the old days and in the early "new" days—more often than not—had gained their casino experience in legal or illegal gambling joints in faraway places such as Havana, the Bahamas, the French Riviera, Steubenville, or Saratoga Springs. The formal education achieved by most casino managers was limited. Casino management was certainly not considered a respectable way to make a living, especially for those who had other options.

Within the industry, a belief prevailed that the only way a person could learn the gaming business was from the ground up, starting on the casino floor, learning every game and every scam, keeping one's eyes open, and constantly observing. After ten or twenty years of such apprenticeship, a person would be ready to run a joint of his own. Being friends with the Boss also helped.

Employees were hired on the basis of whom they knew rather than what they knew. "Juice" was the name of the game, especially in Las Vegas. Organizational structures were characterized by a "monopoly on brains," a steep pyramidal hierarchy where orders and directions flowed in only one direction—downward. Only the Top Man or the "inner circle" had the vision to steer the organization in the right direction (Macomber, 1994). The buck—and the bucks—stopped there. For everyone else, it was "dummy up and deal," and the less one knew about what was going on, the better (Solkey, 1980).

Customer relations were often developed on a very personal basis. A player was sought after as long as he had the means with which to gamble. If he tapped out, he was no longer welcome. Because gambling debts in the old days were not legally collectible in Nevada or in most other jurisdictions, the trump card of the casino industry was the threat of cutting a player off from further play. Thus, debt collection, a by-product of credit play, involved a combination of carrot and stick strategies to threaten or encourage players to pay up so they could get back to the tables at the casino once again.

And the players were for the most part serious—some would say *degenerate*—gamblers. They were predominantly male and played table games, especially craps. Slot machines and roulette were for the ladies or the novices. Serious action players wanted to roll the dice. The more cerebral players were attracted by the challenges of blackjack.

Most casino operations were guided by a philosophy that the only profit center for the entire operation was the casino itself. Everything else—hotel rooms, restaurants, lounge shows, headliner showrooms, golf courses—were loss leaders expected to generate business for the casino as the ultimate cash cow. This was based on the belief that gamblers loved bargains, and casinos certainly did offer very good value for money in most of their ancillary products. Then—as now—casinos understood that many gamblers did not look at casino losses as expenditures, but rather as bad luck. Thus, compared to other leisure and entertainment industries, casinos had a hidden psychological advantage, and their pricing strategies took full advantage of providing lots of excuses to the player who wanted into the action.

Competition in the old days was, for the most part, limited to the State of Nevada. In Las Vegas, market segmentation was bifurcated between the "sawdust joints" of downtown Las Vegas and the "carpet joints" of the Strip. Northern Nevada was perhaps even more homogeneous, with

Reno drawing more of a working class clientele, and Lake Tahoe casinos aiming slightly up-market from that. Nonetheless, there was strong competition within each market, and by the late 1960s, it was clear that Nevada's destination resort casinos were dominated by positive economies of scale. As a result, new gaming properties in the 1960s and early 1970s—such as Caesars Palace, Circus Circus, the Las Vegas International (now the Las Vegas Hilton), and the MGM (now Bally's)—were each built more expansively and more expensively than their predecessors.

By modern standards, investment decisions often were seemingly undertaken based on "back of the envelope" calculations, frequently pursuing untested themes and outlandish ideas. (Occasionally, white elephants were constructed, as with the Landmark in Las Vegas.) But the effect of economies of scale made financing a far more important part of the overall picture. The illegitimate status of casinos in the eyes of the establishment—especially Wall Street—foreclosed the industry from traditional debt and equity markets. As a result, sources of financial capital were wherever one could find the money. This occurred through partnerships, the selling of ownership "points" of the casino (sometimes to parties hidden from authorities), or through such questionable sources as the Teamsters Central States Pension Fund. The reception of most casino owners and managers at most banks and financial institutions prior to the 1970s—with the notable exception of Nevada National (later Valley) Bank—was a near total absence of interest.

The relationship of casino operators to regulatory authorities was also somewhat strained. Nevada created its regulatory structure in the 1950s and 1960s in response to the perceived Federal threat of intervention, brought about by such exposés as the Kefauver Committee hearings of 1951 or the McClellan Committee hearings in 1961 (Skolnick, 1978; ch. 9–11). In effect, the State of Nevada was attempting to protect its sovereignty at least with respect to the gaming industry. (Parallels to this situation have arisen in the 1990s with regard to Indian gaming in America.)

However, because of the nefarious backgrounds of many of Nevada's early gaming owners and operators, it was difficult, especially prior to the 1970s, to establish a credible degree of regulatory authority over the casino industry. Casino owners and managers who had operated outside the law before coming to Nevada were not the easiest candidates to persuade that regulation was something to which they should submit, even though the casino industry in Nevada had given them legal status. (Many of them were also not keen on paying taxes.) Thus, the old days of casino operations and regulation in Nevada—and well into the transition period—had more than their share of *bona fide* scandal. From the 1950s through the 1970s, Nevada's casino industry had lots of scandals to cope with, including hidden ownership, threats by casino owners against regulators, systematic skimming, and, on numerous occasions, an active presence of organized crime (Reid and Demaris, 1962; Glass, 1981; Skolnick, 1978; Spanier, 1994, ch. 9).

How much has casino management changed in the past thirty years? Have the changes been for the better? Often, the retrospective view still heard is that ". . . they knew how to run casino operations in the old days, not like the accountants and attorneys today." Is that really true, or just a romantic notion of a time not so long past?

The casino industry has indeed evolved at warp speed, in comparison to most other industries of the late 20th century. It has moved out from the gray shadows of illegitimacy and become a major and visible presence on Wall Street and Main Street. Much of this is a direct result of extensive growth. Casinos and casino-style gaming—limited to Nevada and Atlantic City as recently as 1989—could be found in nearly 30 states by 1999. The venues and forms for casinos also multiplied (riverboats, racetracks, mining towns, Indian reservations, urban and suburban casinos, etc.). Furthermore, casinos exist under a variety of market structures (competitive, exclusive franchise monopoly, regional monopoly, oligopoly) and ownership regimes (private sector with low tax rates; private sector with high tax rates; government owned and privately managed; government owned and managed).

Ownership of casinos in America is now characterized by publicly traded corporations with broad-based institutional participation. The biographical profiles of modern casino executives and managers look much like those of executives and managers in the hotel, airline, or insurance industries. Various universities offer courses or even degrees in gaming management. The mainstream business press—as well as specialized casino trade publications such as *International Gaming and Wagering Business, Casino Executive,* and *Casino Journal*—report on, evaluate, and critique gaming industry trends and performance on a regular basis.

This volume reflects these trends: in a nutshell, the growing science of gaming management. Articles contained herein deal with a wide variety of topics that challenge the modern casino executive. Part of the evolution of casino gaming has been recognition that, as with other industries, one could apply broad management principles to casinos and gain insights that would improve overall performance. Rather than spending ten to twenty years on the casino floor looking for scams and glad-handing customers, the new generation of casino executives has been formally trained in the disciplines and subtleties of human resource development, customer service, strategic planning, market segmentation, feasibility analysis, compliance, and public relations. He—or she—is well versed in EBITDA, win per unit per day, theoretical win percentage, incremental returns from various promotions, currency transaction reporting, and meeting probity. He—or she—is becoming increasingly aware of community concerns over issues such as localized crime, underage gambling, and problem gambling.

Modern casino management is not as unique as the old school may have believed, though it is far from generic; running a casino is far more complex than running, say, a hotel or a restaurant. Much can be learned by cross-fertilizing concepts, ideas, and strategies from other industries. Successful initiatives from elsewhere can generate considerable gain in casinos' operating performance. Parallels between the airlines' frequent flyer programs and casinos' player tracking programs or between *cast members* at Disney World and *cast members* at Treasure Island are good illustrations of such cross-fertilization.

Many analysts and observers have claimed that casino industries are evolving from selling gambling to selling entertainment (e.g. Christiansen and Brinkerhoff-Jacobs, 1997). At the same time, competition for the leisure dollar, for the entertainment dollar, is becoming increasingly keen. As the third Millenium becomes a reality, the demands on the casino executive to become more systematic, more scientific, more conceptual, can only increase. Volumes such as this one will provide the basis for the continued transformation and education of the gaming manager.

William R. Eadington
July 1998

REFERENCES

Christiansen, Eugene and Julie Brinkerhoff-Jacobs (1997), "The relationship of gaming to entertainment," in William R. Eadington and Judy A. Cornelius (eds.), *Gambling: Public Policies and the Social Sciences,* pp. 11–48. Reno: Institute for the Study of Gambling and Commercial Gaming, University of Nevada.

Eadington, William R. (1982), "The evolution of corporate gambling in America," *Nevada Review of Business and Economics,* reprinted in Kathryn Hashimoto, Sheryl Kline and George Fenich (eds.) (1996) *Casino Management for the 90s,* pp. 52–65. Dubuque, Iowa: Kendall/Hunt.

Glass, Mary Ellen (1981). *Nevada's Turbulent '50s : Decade of Political and Economic Change.* Reno: University of Nevada Press.

Macomber, Dean (1984), "Management policy and practices in modern casino operations," *The Annals of the American Academy of Political and Social Sciences,* July, Vol. 474, pp. 80–90.

Reid, Ed and Ovid Demaris (1963). *The Green Felt Jungle.* New York: Trident Press.

Skolnick, Jerome (1978). *House of Cards: Legalization and Control of Casino Gambling.* Boston: Little, Brown & Co.

Solkey, Lee (1980). *Dummy Up and Deal.* Las Vegas: GBC Press.

Spanier, David (1994). *Inside the Gambler's Mind.* Reno: University of Nevada Press.

Acknowledgements

The University of Nevada, Reno has been the sponsor and organizer of the International Conferences on Gambling and Risk-Taking since their inception in 1974. Since the university formed the Institute for the Study of Gambling and Commercial Gaming in 1989, the coordination of the conferences has been a primary activity of this department along with the production of publications such as *The Business of Gaming: Economic and Management Issues.* This volume represents professional and academic papers that were presented at the 9th International Conference held in Las Vegas in 1994 and the 10th International Conference held in Montreal in 1997.

While the Institute assumes responsibility for organizing the International Conferences on Gambling and Risk-Taking, it is an undertaking that involves the efforts of many. We receive substantial support from our colleagues and friends from around the world. The support comes to us in a variety of forms.

Both the 9th and 10th International Conferences on Gambling and Risk-Taking were exhilarating experiences for those involved. We were fortunate to have chosen The Queen Elizabeth Hotel in Montréal as the site for the 10th International Conference. We arrived in Québec for the beginning of spring weather and a week of gracious hosting by Vincent Trudel, Président, Société des Casinos du Québec Inc. and his staff. The Société des Casinos du Québec Inc. not only graced us with a generous financial donation, but also treated everyone at the conference to a tour of the Casino du Montréal followed by a party that no one will ever forget. From an organizers' viewpoint, we could not have had a better site for a major conference.

We want to acknowledge and thank the following individuals and organizations for their financial contributions for events during the 10th

International Conference on Gambling and Risk-Taking, all of which helped make the conference a success:

- Mr. Vincent Trudel, Président
  Société des Casinos du Québec Inc.
- Mr. Ron Sheppard, President
  International Hospitality Casino Corporation—Toronto
- Señor José Luis Guirao de Parga, Chief Operating Officer
  Inverama, S. A. (Casinos de Catalunya)—Barcelona

The 9th International Conference was held in Las Vegas at the MGM Grand Hotel, Casino and Theme Park, which at that time had only been open for six months. Larry Woolf, who is also co-chair of the Institute's Advisory Board, was serving as President and Chief Executive Officer. Larry and his staff helped to make the conference run smoothly and efficiently.

We want to thank the following organizations who provided financial support for conference related events during the 9th International Conference on Gambling and Risk-Taking:

- MGM Grand, Inc.—Las Vegas
- Resorts International, Inc.—Atlantic City
- Casinos du Montréal
- Société des Casinos du Québec
- International Gaming Technology—Reno
- Harrah's Entertainment, Inc.—Memphis

An expression of gratitude is extended to the staff of the Institute who, during both conferences, worked tirelessly to produce a smooth running conference. For the 10th International Conference, thanks go to Tara Riley and Aaron Fox, both program assistants to the Institute. While in Montreal, we had additional assistance from Phoenix Wilson, a student at UNLV, Angela Caszatt of UNR, and several graduate students from McGill University who volunteered their time. Thanks to everyone for the time and effort put forth.

During the 9th International Conference the Institute's staff included Jennifer Crawford, Ingrid Yocum, Teri Case, Krishna Kumar, and Scott Evans, all of who were students at the University of Nevada, Reno. They know how much their help was appreciated.

We are grateful to Diane Chester Berg and Larry Berg of Computer Support Services of Northern Nevada who have assisted with the International Conferences since 1990. They both work long hours during the conferences to keep up with the flood of paperwork. In addition, Diane has put forward extraordinary effort in designing and producing the books that are ultimately the permanent record of the conferences. Her computer expertise is substantial, and her advice on these publications has been invaluable.

The concept and layout for the dust jackets for this and a previous volume is credited to Michael Eadington of High Mountain Imagery. Michael—the truly free spirit of the Eadington clan—is proof that the dismal science of economics is not genetically or environmentally passed on to offspring.

The primary objective in producing these compendiums is to build upon the body of competent published research related to gambling. To this end we thank the contributors to this and the other publications produced by the Institute. They include friends and professional colleagues from throughout the world. Many of them have supported the conferences and these publications for well over a decade—some for much longer. They share in the ideal of finding the truth regarding this controversial and inherently ambiguous topic of gambling. They have generated high quality research, opinion and information that will contribute significantly to future policy and practices. Their continued support of the efforts pursued by the Institute is appreciated and valued.

Judy A. Cornelius
William R. Eadington
July 1998

Economic Dimensions of Commercial Gaming Industries

Section 1

Recreation, Leisure, and Gaming Expenditures: Exceptional Long-Term Growth Prospects©

Robert J. Simonson, CFA and Deborah M. Goebel

The first baby boomers turned 50
in 1996, and over the next 20 years the percentage of "elderly" people (55 and older) will skyrocket, from 16% of the total population in 1945 and 21% currently, to 23% in 10 years and 29% in 25 years. While each generation experiences different income breakdowns and spending patterns, one observation might be true always: People dispose of personal income in different ways as they grow older. Consumption has averaged 63.2% of gross domestic product (GDP) since 1946; it troughed at 60.2% of GDP in 1966 and now appears to be peaking at 67.4%, a rate reached in 1986 and 1993 as well. The dramatic aging of the population is very likely to result in significantly slower growth in consumption. In addition, because consumption constitutes two-thirds of the total economy, slower overall economic growth should result as the prime consuming age group declines sharply as a percentage of the population. Moreover, this moderating trend will affect the three principal components of consumption—durables, non-durables, and services—quite differently. In turn, these larger consumption trends will affect absolute and relative segment growth rates and market valuations. The following conclusions appear consistent with these observations.

- Relative valuations of consumer-related stocks probably have crested, as the contribution to aggregate GDP growth from consumption declines.
- Companies that produce and distribute durable and non-durable goods are likely to face slowing growth rates.

Editor's Note: This paper was produced on March 19, 1996. Selected data has been updated.

- Consumer-service-related entities should not only buck this overall trend but be positioned to experience accelerating growth both absolutely and relatively.

An important caveat to these fundamental and valuation-related conclusions is that very important exceptions to the basic conclusion will offer significant investment opportunities. Those consumer companies with proprietary market positions and established market share positions should be very well rewarded since overall economics growth is likely to slow, and, therefore, fewer companies will grow as rapidly as in the past. Also, the more favorable outlook for consumer-service-related companies will not guarantee superior stock market performance, since individual companies still could underperform, particularly if they do not demonstrate a capability to increase market share.

Over the longer term, it appears likely that the hunt for excellent growth stocks in the consumer sector will be significantly more difficult, especially in the durable and non-durables areas, while becoming appreciably more satisfying in consumer services.

Changing Consumption: Products Down, Services Up

In 1994, personal consumption accounted for 67% of total economic output (excluding foreign trade), dwarfing the contribution from private investment (18%) and government purchases (17%). This contribution appears likely to decline considerably over the next 10 to 20 years as the percentage of the population in the "high-consuming" age group declines sharply as a percentage of the total population. Perhaps the most critical factor in determining the magnitude of this deceleration will be the degree to which accelerating consumer spending on services offsets the slowing pattern in consumption of durable and non-durables products. This is difficult to assess since spending on services is nearly equal to that spent on goods. Most important for investors, however, is to recognize that one-half of all consumer spending is slowing while the other half is accelerating.

Consumption has risen as a percentage of GDP from the mid-50% range in the early 1950s, as shown in Table 1, to the mid-60% area for the last 15 years. The contribution troughed at 56.8% in 1952, shortly after the 1950–51 recession ended, and now appears to be peaking 10 percentage points higher, at the 67% level, where it has remained for the last 10 years.

This surge in consumption since 1960 is due principally to strong growth in durable spending and services' offsetting declining spending on non-durables. As shown in Table 2, consumer spending on durables has

TABLE 1

Gross Domestic Product and Components (Billions of seasonally adjusted 1987 dollars)

Year	Gross Domestic Product	Personal Consumption Expenditures	Private Domestic Investment	Government Purchases	Personal Consumption as % of GDP	Investment as % GDP	Government as % GDP
1947	$1,252.8	$793.3	$198.8	$218.9	63.3%	15.9%	17.5%
1949	1,305.5	831.4	187.4	269.3	63.7%	14.4%	20.6%
1952	1,624.9	923.4	231.6	467.6	56.8%	14.3%	28.8%
1964	2,340.6	1,417.2	371.8	549.1	60.5%	15.9%	23.5%
1967	2,685.2	1,622.4	418.6	667.9	60.4%	15.6%	24.9%
1986	4,404.5	2,969.1	735.1	855.5	67.4%	16.7%	19.4%
1994	5,344.0	3,579.6	951.6	922.8	67.0%	17.8%	17.3%

Least Squares Growth Rates

	GDP[a]	PCE	Investment	Government			
1947–64	3.5%	3.4%	3.0%	4.7%			
1949–67	3.5%	3.6%	3.7%	3.5%			
1967–86	2.5%	3.0%	2.8%	1.0%			
1986–94	2.1%	2.1%	1.7%	1.0%			

(a)Includes imports/exports.
Source: Bureau of Economic Analysis

5

TABLE 2
Consumption Categories as a % of GDP and
Total Personal Consumption Exp.

% of GDP	1950	1960	1970	1980	1990	1994
Consumption	61.6%	61.4%	63.1%	64.8%	66.8%	67.0%
Total Durables	6.7%	5.9%	6.0%	7.0%	9.0%	10.0%
Furniture	2.2%	1.9%	2.2%	2.6%	3.5%	4.5%
Motor Vehicles	3.6%	3.1%	3.4%	3.0%	3.9%	3.9%
Total Non-durables	28.2%	26.7%	25.0%	22.8%	21.7%	20.8%
Food	16.6%	15.5%	13.8%	11.9%	10.7%	10.0%
Clothing/Shoes	3.5%	3.0%	2.8%	3.3%	3.8%	3.9%
Total Services	26.7%	28.8%	31.8%	35.1%	36.1%	36.3%
Medical Care Serv.	4.1%	5.0%	6.3%	8.0%	8.7%	9.0%
Recreation	3.1%	2.7%	3.2%	3.9%	5.3%	6.2%
As a % of Consumption						
Total Durables	10.9%	9.5%	10.1%	10.7%	13.5%	14.9%
Furniture	3.5%	3.1%	3.6%	4.0%	5.2%	6.7%
Motor Vehicles	5.9%	5.1%	4.7%	4.6%	5.9%	5.8%
Total Non-durables	45.8%	43.5%	39.5%	35.2%	32.4%	31.0%
Food	26.9%	25.3%	21.9%	18.3%	16.0%	15.0%
Clothing/Shoes	5.6%	4.9%	4.5%	5.2%	5.7%	5.8%
Total Services	43.3%	47.0%	50.3%	54.1%	54.0%	54.1%
Medical Care Serv.	6.6%	8.1%	15.3%	25.6%	36.0%	40.6%
Recreation	5.3%	4.4%	5.0%	6.1%	8.0%	9.3%
Source: U.S. Bureau of Economic Analysis						

increased 4 percentage points as a percentage of total personal consumption since 1950, to nearly 15%, while spending on consumer services has risen nearly 9 percentage points, to 54%. The loser in the growth race was spending on non-durables, declining from nearly 46% to 31%, due principally to a sharp decrease in the percentage spent on food.

The Effects of Demographics

Analysis of total population growth can be as exciting as watching paint dry or grass grow; the rates of change are numbingly consistent. But, because the base on which these changes occur is so large, shifts in age groups within the total population can prove to be as subtle as a train wreck. These age-group changes are both dramatic and predictable. For example, in just 15 years beginning in 1955, the 5-to-14-year-old segment of the population rose from 18.3% to 20.1%. Sellers of goods to this segment saw the number in the group increase by 35%, from 30.2 million to 40.8 million between 1955 and 1970. However, after its peak, the group declined 13% within just five years, to 35.4 million in 1975. This rapid change in the number of 5-to-14-year-olds—both up and down—created dramatic changes in the market for seats in school rooms and traffic in junior apparel retail stores, to name but two entities affected by this change. In 1949, the total number of elementary and high school students (both public and private) was 28 million. Twenty years later, that number nearly doubled, to 51 million in 1969. (Forty-five-year-olds may remember how crowded their senior class was.) Then, just as quickly as the overcrowding brought on a surge in bond offerings to build new, larger schools, the problem began to recede, with the total number of students declining 10% over the next 20 years. The total student enrollment in 1994 was still 3% less than at its peak 25 years earlier.

Just as this dramatic change in the number of students has altered educational requirements since the early 1950s, the aging of this group has the potential to just as dramatically alter the demand for goods and services for "old" people. There still may be Muzak played in nursing homes now, but within 20 years it is a safe bet it will be replaced by the Beatles and the Righteous Brothers. In 1945, the percentage of the population over 65 years old was only 7.5%. This figure is now 12%, where it has hovered for nearly 10 years and could remain for another 15 years. By 2030, this group will have risen to 20% and constitute the largest segment of the population by more than 50%. In 1945 it was the smallest segment of the population.

During the last 45 years, the U.S. population grew 1.2% annually. This rate is projected to slow to 0.6% in the next 45 years. While these appear to be modest differences between historical and prospective population growth, the impact of changes by age group will certainly create dramatic new opportunities, as well as dislocations.

An Aging Population and Shifts in Consumption

A wardrobe for the new job, furniture for the apartment, a second car, setting up the nursery, supplies for school, a rocker for retirement: As each individual passes through the distinct stages of life, new and different kinds of "stuff" are required. While no two generations necessarily share the same priorities in how they consume or experience identical income breakdowns within their generation, a basic reality is that most individuals and families (except members of the lowest income groups) have most of what they "need" by age 45. (Of course, replacement demand partially mitigates this trend, since a sofa can be upgraded, an old suit replaced and a finer car parked in the garage.) What seems to be obvious but also very critical is that beyond middle age, most individuals are simply consuming new items at the margin of an existing portfolio of assets, both durable and non-durable. Over the next 5–15 years, a significant portion of the total population will move beyond their peak consuming years. While the next generation may succeed in sustaining spending patterns similar to their parents', there simply will not be as many of them. This dramatically changing demographic constraint suggest some very powerful shifts in what types of business will have the wind at their back, with ample opportunity for growth, as opposed to those that will face slowing growth and concurrent intense market share battles that can harm profitability.

The correlation between the rise and fall of consumption in the U.S. economy and the percentage of the population in their high-consumption years (ages 25–34) is very powerful. When actual consumption is smoothed for the negative impact of recessions, the correlation is even closer. The sharp decline in this age group's importance to the total population over the next 10 years is likely to slow overall consumption, especially of non-durable and durable goods.

A changing age-composition of the population affects not only growth in consumption, but also total economic growth, because consumption is such a big part of the total economy. From 1949 to 1967, the percentage of the population in the high-consuming 25-to-34 group declined from 16% to 11%, with a commensurate decline in personal consumption as a percentage of the economy from 63% to 60%. Then, as the baby boomers came of age between 1967 and 1986, this group increased from a low of 11% to a high of just less than 18%, creating a surge in personal consumption as a percentage of GDP, to a new post-World War II high of 67%. Since 1986, the 25–34 group has declined back down to about 16%, and consumption has stagnated at 67% of GDP. As shown at the bottom of table 1, personal consumption was the real engine of economic growth in 1967–1986, expanding a half percentage point faster than the overall economy (3.0% versus 2.5%). However, as the prime consumers in the 25-to-34 group began declining as a percentage of the economy in 1986, so did consumption and overall growth. Since 1986, personal consumption growth has decelerated, from 3.0% to 2.0%, while total GDP growth has slowed more moderately, from 2.5% to 2.1%. Thus, consumption went from the relatively strongest part of the economy to merely a moderate component. The implication of the correlation, shown in Figure 1, below, seems clear—consumer spending is likely to decline in its importance to overall economic growth at least for the next 10 years.

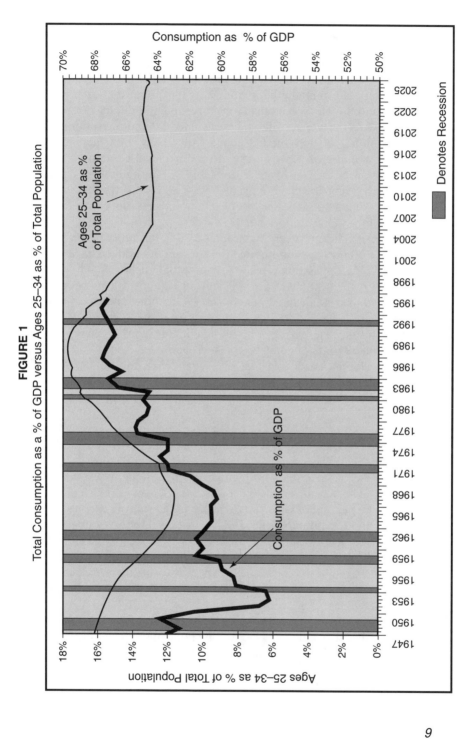

FIGURE 1
Total Consumption as a % of GDP versus Ages 25–34 as % of Total Population

Consumption Patterns: Winners and Losers

Although the contribution to total economic growth from personal consumption is likely to recede over the next 10 or more years, the impact is likely to vary substantially by sector. We believe that the losers will be durables (automobiles sooner than furniture) and non-durables (especially apparel), while the winner will be services (medical and recreation).

Consumption of non-durable goods (principally food, apparel, and shoes) has declined as a percentage of total personal consumption from 46% to 31% over the last 45 years (see table 2). The clothing component essentially has remained in a range of 4.5%–6.0%. while the food component has declined dramatically (people are not necessarily eating less, but their need for more food does not grow over long periods of time as does their income). There is a very tight, long correlation between the relative growth of clothing expenditures and the rise and fall of the number of 25-to-44-year-olds. Population forecasts suggest that apparel could be a major loser over the next 10–15 years. The front end of the baby boomers is now beyond its peak demand period for new clothing, and its continuing aging is likely to have a detrimental impact on demand growth, which is likely to sustain the current margin-debilitating market share battles. Those about 50 years old may be considering the following: In the 1970s and 1980s, clothes "made" the man or woman. Now, you call Goodwill to pick up another box of closet rejects. The baby boomers have become the generation that buys new clothes by the item and disgorges them by the closetful.

In durables, the outlook is not totally dissimilar to non-durables, but it is not quite as negative (since it does not include the persistently declining food component). The correlation between changes in the prime consuming age group of 25 to 44 is not as tight as in clothing, but nonetheless significant. The variability of year-over-year changes is higher than for non-durables because of recessions, which have a much greater short-term impact on big-ticket-durable sales and production. The two principal components of durable consumption are furniture and motor vehicles. Since growth in furniture demand appears to correlate more closely to an older age group than motor vehicles, it is expected to be a stronger category until the 35-to-44 age group begins declining as a percentage of the population in 2000.

Spending patterns on consumer services do not seem to be vulnerable to the same negative influences of an aging population; therefore, this subset appears to be the clear winner—the graying of America may increase spending on services. Since 1980, total personal consumption has risen 2 percentage points as a percentage of overall GDP, from 65% to 67%. Gains in consumption of services (1 point) and durables (3 points) more

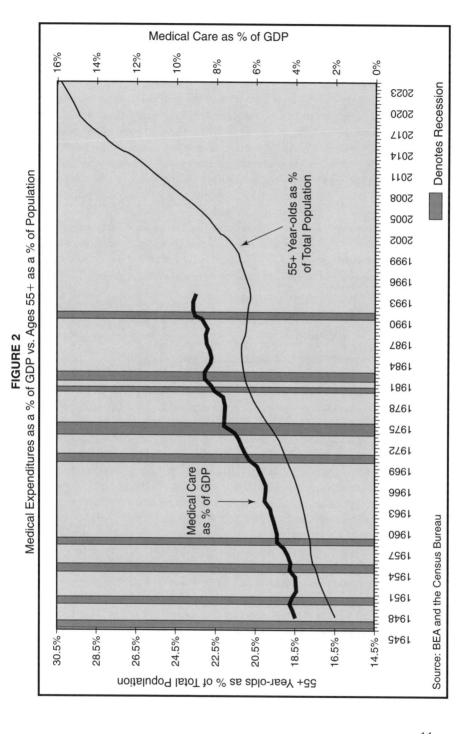

FIGURE 2

Medical Expenditures as a % of GDP vs. Ages 55+ as a % of Population

Medical Care as % of GDP

55+ Year-olds as % of Total Population

Medical Care as % of GDP

Denotes Recession

Source: BEA and the Census Bureau

11

than offset a 2-point decline in non-durable demand. It is interesting that with all the discussion of increased health costs (see Figure 2), spending on medical care services has risen only 1 percentage point as a percentage of GDP over the last 15 years, a slower pace than the 2-point rise in recreational spending (which is from a 1980 base half as high as medical services.) This conundrum can be resolved by recognizing that while the big population bulge of baby boomers is aging, the majority of them still do not need a walker or a visiting nurse. The percentage of the population over 55 has remained stagnant for 15 years—20.9% in both 1980 and 1995. However, one might begin thinking about walkers and nurses, because in 15 years this group will rise constituting 24.8% of the population, and 29.4% in 20 years—a nearly 50% rise.

Recreation expenditures do not seem to correlate with any specific age group. Rather, the only correlation to ever-increasing recreation expenditures as a percentage of GDP (except during recessions) is total population. We believe, therefore, that this sector is inevitably a long-term winner.

RECREATION/LEISURE: A GROWTH COMPONENT OF CONSUMER SPENDING

Consumer expenditures for recreational pursuits has outpaced the growth of total consumption expenditures, on both a current and constant dollar basis, in every five-year period for the last 35 years. This above-average growth has increased recreational spending from 5.6% of total personal consumption in 1959 to 8.0% in 1994. However, not only has this subset of spending enjoyed superior relative growth over the long term, but these expenditures have not experienced a single annual decline, in current dollars, during the entire 35-year period, which included six discrete recessions. The demographics of an aging population suggest that, over the next 5 to 15 years, personal consumption expenditures for both durables and non-durables will decline as a percentage of not only total consumption but also of the economy overall. These two components were only a slightly lower percentage of the economy in 1994, at 31% (see Table 2).

Offsetting these expected declines is a probable rise in spending on services. A rise in spending on medical care services is almost entirely a function of older individuals' needing more medical services as well as this group's sharp rise as a percentage of the total population. Our expectations that spending on recreational activities will continue to rise at a faster-than-average pace are based on the following factors:

• A continuing revolution in the ability of suppliers to bring new forms of entertainment and information into the home.

- The introduction of new products and services subsets—for example, there was no VCR rental business in 1975.
- Accelerating growth in the number of individuals completing the furnishing of homes, filling their closets, and nearing their peak earnings capacity.
- Over time, state governments are likely to intensify the revenue-producing capacity of entertainment facilities from sporting teams, amusement parks, and even casinos as the shift in consumption patterns from goods (and associated state sales tax revenue) to recreational and amusement expenditures unfolds.

During the last 35 years, total annual spending on recreation has grown a full percentage point faster than total personal consumption: 9.7% versus 8.7%, respectively. This above-average growth over such an extended period has resulted in a sharp rise in recreational spending as a percentage of total consumer spending, from 5.6% in 1959 to 8.0% in 1994. These very-long-term trends have been sustained in the more recent 5- and 10-year periods, with the difference in relative growth rates continuing to widen. These growth rates and shares of spending are shown in Tables 3 and 4.

Historically, consumer spending on recreational services has grown more rapidly than on recreational products. This, however, has at least temporarily reversed in the most recent five-year period because of the rapid growth of home computer purchases. Despite this recent switch in growth, we expect spending on services to continue rising, from 41% of total recreation spending (up from 36% in 1959), to perhaps 45% within the next 5–10 years. Again referring to Table 3, several important observations can be made:

- The fastest-growing segments of the products side of recreational spending are technology-oriented, including home computers, VCRs, TVs, and audio equipment. The slower-growing segments are low-tech, including books, newspapers, and sporting equipment. With high technology doing for entertainment what it formerly did for the defense industry, the relative growth of high-tech products should continue to rise at a faster relative pace.
- On the service side, the fastest-growing major sector is casino gaming, followed by VCR rentals and live entertainment (excluding spectator sports). Casinos have sustained double-digit growth in every five-year period measured since 1959. Casino growth, however, has been less dependent on rising prices than most entertainment services. During the last 10 years, the growth rate of casino spending in nominal terms was 23% faster than combined spending on recreational services, 10.2% ver-

TABLE 3

Recreation Expenditures (Dollars in Millions)

Year	Total PCE (in Billions)	Total Recreation Exp.	Combined Recr. Products	Sporting Goods and Toys	VCRs, TVs, Audio Equipment	Books, Magazines, Maps, Newspapers	Home Computers	All Other Products
1959	318.11	17,651	11,308	3,852	3,056	3,224	—	1,176
1964	412.47	24,555	15,455	5,305	4,309	4,145	—	1,696
1969	603.68	39,940	26,182	9,038	7,991	6,001	—	3,152
1974	927.70	63,579	41,093	15,152	12,095	9,073	—	4,773
1979	1583.08	109,707	71,160	25,023	18,876	16,600	100	10,561
1984	2460.29	172,844	104,384	35,356	26,762	26,126	2,370	13,770
1989	3523.07	266,032	156,244	50,455	42,460	37,856	4,860	20,613
1994	4628.44	371,193	220,374	71,929	67,048	50,282	9,166	21,949
Least Square Growth Rates-Current Dollars								
5-Year	5.51%	6.64%	6.76%	7.00%	9.30%	5.61%	13.25%	0.31%
10-Year	6.46%	7.79%	7.45%	7.15%	8.85%	7.21%	15.34%	3.51%
15-Year	7.36%	8.59%	7.94%	7.27%	8.94%	7.71%	28.88%	5.65%
20-Year	8.36%	9.24%	8.55%	7.80%	8.59%	9.11%	NA	7.30%
30-Year	8.95%	9.74%	9.21%	8.96%	8.79%	9.30%	NA	9.24%
35-Year	8.73%	9.68%	9.34%	9.14%	9.20%	9.03%	NA	9.72%
Least Square Growth Rates-Constant Dollars								
5-Year	2.07%	5.68%	7.47%	5.01%	10.76%	1.44%	38.59%	−2.12%
10-Year	2.40%	5.72%	6.80%	4.45%	10.75%	2.79%	35.01%	1.07%
15-Year	2.77%	5.75%	6.25%	4.50%	10.82%	2.32%	53.00%	2.77%
20-Year	2.79%	5.44%	5.60%	4.41%	9.38%	2.49%	NA	3.22%
30-Year	3.01%	5.36%	5.40%	5.61%	8.89%	2.35%	NA	4.24%
35-Year	3.22%	5.39%	5.61%	6.11%	9.46%	2.79%	NA	4.54%

Year	Combined Recr. Services	Casino	Lottery	Pari-mutuel	Cable TV	Amusement Parks	VCR rentals	Live Entert.	Movie Admissions	Spectator Sports	All Other Services
1959	6,343	139	1	503	9	213	—	324	1,043	311	3,800
1964	9,100	272	4	769	67	417	—	390	1,038	587	5,556
1969	13,758	446	35	1,035	245	688	—	506	1,507	1,053	8,243
1974	22,486	1,050	428	1,559	643	1,612	—	702	2,022	1,249	13,221
1979	38,547	2,640	1,104	2,121	1,878	3,014	—	1,529	2,823	2,070	21,368
1984	68,460	6,304	3,462	2,954	7,030	4,507	1,473	2,471	3,452	3,436	33,371
1989	109,788	9,427	8,323	3,627	13,569	7,800	5,532	3,936	3,884	4,260	49,430
1994	150,819	15,972	11,306	3,818	18,685	10,380	8,612	6,285	5,830	5,895	64,036
Least Square Growth Rates-Current Dollars											
5-Year	6.47%	10.98%	6.51%	0.73%	6.92%	5.56%	9.60%	9.09%	7.58%	6.37%	5.22%
10-Year	8.28%	10.20%	11.59%	2.55%	10.99%	8.80%	15.99%	9.98%	6.39%	0.02%	6.62%
15-Year	9.60%	11.62%	17.86%	3.98%	15.97%	9.17%	NA	9.39%	5.31%	7.14%	7.45%
20-Year	10.33%	14.42%	19.28%	4.85%	19.66%	9.56%	NA	10.96%	5.09%	8.17%	8.23%
30-Year	10.62%	16.15%	30.92%	6.08%	22.31%	12.07%	NA	10.53%	5.50%	7.90%	9.10%
35-Year	10.24%	15.81%	35.11%	6.41%	23.78%	12.40%	NA	9.67%	5.32%	8.40%	8.96%
Least Square Growth Rates-Constant Dollars											
5-Year	2.78%	7.14%	2.83%	-1.95%	0.07%	1.75%	NA	4.80%	3.34%	2.18%	1.87%
10-Year	4.05%	6.09%	7.44%	-1.33%	3.32%	4.87%	NA	4.43%	1.02%	0.03%	2.98%
15-Year	4.98%	6.96%	12.94%	-1.17%	9.08%	5.14%	NA	3.53%	-0.33%	1.42%	3.43%
20-Year	5.19%	8.34%	12.94%	-0.63%	12.95%	4.87%	NA	5.01%	-0.66%	2.24%	3.64%
30-Year	5.30%	9.48%	23.23%	0.37%	15.99%	6.46%	NA	4.51%	-0.50%	2.52%	4.35%
35-Year	5.09%	9.65%	27.70%	0.94%	17.76%	6.99%	NA	3.55%	-0.80%	3.45%	4.45%

Source: U.S. Bureau of Economic Analysis

TABLE 4

Recreation Expenditures Mix

Year	Total Recr. as % of PCE	Products as a % of Recr.	Toys/ Sporting Equip. as % of Recr.	VCRs, TVs, Audio as % of Recr.	Books, Mag., Maps, Newspapers as % of Recr.	Home Computers as % of Recr.	Combined Recr. Services as % of Recr. Exp.	Casino Gaming as % of Recr.	Lotteries as % of Recr.	Pari- mutuels as % of Recr.	Cable TV as % of Recr.	Amuse- ment Parks as % of Recr.	VCR Rent- als as % of Recr.	Live Enter. as % of Recr.	Movie Admiss. as % of Recr.	Spec- tator Sports as % of Recr.
1959	5.55%	64.06%	21.82%	17.31%	18.27%	0.00%	35.94%	0.79%	0.01%	2.85%	0.05%	1.21%	0.00%	1.84%	5.91%	1.76%
1964	5.95%	62.94%	21.60%	17.55%	16.88%	0.00%	37.06%	1.11%	0.02%	3.13%	0.27%	1.70%	0.00%	1.59%	4.23%	2.39%
1969	6.62%	65.55%	22.63%	20.01%	15.03%	0.00%	34.45%	1.12%	0.09%	2.59%	0.61%	1.72%	0.00%	1.27%	3.77%	2.64%
1974	6.85%	64.63%	23.83%	19.02%	14.27%	0.00%	35.37%	1.65%	0.67%	2.45%	1.01%	2.54%	0.00%	1.10%	3.18%	1.96%
1979	6.93%	64.86%	22.81%	17.21%	15.13%	0.09%	35.14%	2.41%	1.01%	1.93%	1.71%	2.75%	0.00%	1.39%	2.57%	1.89%
1984	7.03%	60.39%	20.46%	15.48%	15.12%	1.37%	39.61%	3.65%	2.00%	1.71%	4.07%	2.61%	0.85%	1.43%	2.00%	1.99%
1989	7.55%	58.73%	18.97%	15.96%	14.23%	1.83%	41.27%	3.54%	3.13%	1.36%	5.10%	2.93%	2.08%	1.48%	1.46%	1.60%
1994	8.02%	59.37%	19.38%	18.06%	13.55%	2.47%	40.63%	4.30%	3.05%	1.03%	5.03%	2.80%	2.32%	1.69%	1.57%	1.59%

Source: Bureau of Economic Analysis

sus 8.3%, respectively. However, adjusted for inflation, growth in casino spending has been 49% faster than this total: 6.1% versus 4.1%, respectively.

- A significant shift is occurring between categories. In 1959, casino gaming accounted for less than 15% of what Americans were spending on moviegoing. In 1994, it was nearly 175% greater. Even if VCR rentals are added back to movie admissions in 1994, casino spending was still 10% greater than "total" movie revenue.
- New categories have contributed significantly to recreational spending. During the last 35 years, lotteries and VCR rentals, which did not exist in 1959, accounted for nearly 15% of the combined growth in recreational services spending.

In the future, the fastest-growing segments of recreational spending are likely to share at least some of the following characteristics.

- The appeal of the product or service can be enhanced or broadened with technological advancements.
- The current level of acceptance of the product or service can be expanded by broadening the distribution capacity of the sector, such as bringing more parks (sporting and amusement), casinos, and theaters nearer a greater percentage of the population. The spectacular growth of shopping malls during the 1970s and 1980s turned shopping into a national pastime.
- Those products or activities whose appeal is high regardless of age of the consumer and which will not be constrained by the demographic shift to over-55 consumers should grow quickly.

Investors historically have been well rewarded investing in companies that grow over intermediate-to longer-term timeframes. The screening process for finding growing companies is made easier when an industry is expanding faster than all others on average, since the risk of profit-debilitating market share battles is lower. Since we believe consumer spending on recreational products and services is likely to remain above-average for a very long time, the search for market outperformers among recreation/ entertainment companies should prove rewarding.

GAMING

The casino industry, at $15.9 billion in 1994, is nearly as large as movie admissions, live entertainment, and spectator sports combined. This is also true for the number of visits, which, according to "Harrah's 1995 Survey of Casino Entertainment," total 125 million to casinos and 102 million combined to all NFL and NCAA football games, arena and symphony concerts, and Broadway and touring shows. A lot of people like to go to casinos, and they are willing to pay for it. Over the last five years, no form of entertainment service of at least $5 billion has grown as fast as the 11%-growth in casinos. Casino revenue (which excludes room, food and beverage, and other related revenue) has increased from 0.8% of total consumer spending on recreation in 1959, to 4.3% in 1994. If consumer spending on state lotteries and parimutuels are included, consumers spend 8.4% of their recreational dollars on gaming, up from 3.6% in 1959. This growth occurred because of rising, but still moderate, participation rates; the opening of new jurisdictions, which brought the experience much closer to an increasing percentage of the population; and a reduction in the still-high-but-declining percentage of people who not only do not participate but also do not want anyone else to play, either. Attitudes are changing and availability is increasing; both factors are likely to continue to improve over the next 5 to 10 years, which suggests that casino revenue will continue to be among the fastest-growing categories of consumer expenditures.

Gaming Industry Characteristics and Structure

Excluding gaming on Indian reservations, casino gaming is currently legal in eight states and on a limited basis in two others. The opening of new state jurisdictions has been an important contributor to industry growth. From 1984 to 1994, casino revenue rose from $6.3 billion to $16.0 billion, as shown in Table 5. New jurisdictions that have opened since 1990 accounted for $3.6 billion, or 62%, of this aggregate growth. While these new states enhanced the overall revenue growth rate, it should be noted that Nevada and New Jersey combined accounted for 38% of the total incremental industry revenue. Those states still accounted for 78% of industry revenue in 1994. We believe that a confluence of pressures and opportunities will expand the number of legal gambling jurisdictions over the next 5 to 10 years and, in tandem with continuing growth in existing jurisdictions, will sustain a high rate of industry growth. The magnitude will be influenced by the timing of new state approvals, which cannot be predicted with confidence.

The majority of casino revenue is generated by slot machines, which enjoy extremely high, consistent profitability, as they have a predictable payout (gross margin) and a low expense ratio (labor expense to operate is much lower than for table games). Slot revenue was 60% and 67%, respectively, of Nevada and New Jersey casino revenue in 1995. While slot revenue is predictable, baccarat winnings are the most volatile. On the Las Vegas Strip, baccarat accounts for 16% of total casino win. In 1994 and 1995, baccarat win on the Strip advanced 27% and 32%, respectively, while

TABLE 5

Revenues by Geographic Location (Dollars in Millions)

	Nevada	New Jersey	Illinois	Mississippi	Louisiana	All Other[a]	Combined
1995	$7,366,807	$3,749,580	$1,177,268	$1,725,632	$1,128,619	$1,127,071	$16,274,977
1994	7,000,726	3,422,616	979,548	1,462,795	603,688	586,508	14,055,881
1993	6,247,508	3,301,360	605,684	787,834	16,234	340,176	11,298,796
1992	5,864,228	3,215,969	226,337	123,808	0	272,144	9,702,486
1991	5,510,747	2,991,562	14,943	0	0	88,858	8,606,110
1990	5,238,721	2,951,582	0	0	0	0	8,190,303
1989	4,590,199	2,807,018	0	0	0	0	7,397,217
1988	4,270,073	2,734,774	0	0	0	0	7,004,847
1987	3,925,147	2,495,676	0	0	0	0	6,420,823
1986	3,482,097	2,281,206	0	0	0	0	5,763,303
1985	3,314,433	2,138,651	0	0	0	0	5,453,084
10-Year							
LSGR	8.5%	5.3%					11.1%

[a]Includes all other states, but excludes Indian and charitable gaming.
Source: Individual state gaming commissions.

total casino win rose 20% and 4%, respectively. In 1995, the year-to-year percentage change in monthly baccarat win on the Strip ranged between a decline of 49% (July) to a gain of 123% (August).

The mix of revenue varies dramatically between operators on the basis of location. Casinos in Nevada, a destination location, derive substantial revenue (15% to 20% of the total) from rooms. No other market is as exposed to room revenue. In fact, the total number of hotel rooms in 12 Atlantic City casinos totals only 8,960. One casino in Las Vegas, the MGM Grand, has 5,005 rooms itself, and, in total, Las Vegas has ten times as many rooms (88,560) as Atlantic City.

The principal source of growth in a casino company is new units and, to a much lesser degree, the physical expansion of existing units. Unlike retail stores, which often have first-year sales volume of 65% to 75% that of mature (four-to-five-year-old) stores, casinos open with a burst, often with revenue in excess of 90% of volume achieved in the fifth year. This differentiates the growth and profitability of a casino from a retailer in two ways. Casinos enjoy higher levels of initial profitability than a retailer, but also produce less growth in subsequent years. Growth in retailing is a combination of expansion in new stores plus growth in existing stores. In casinos, the majority of growth derives from new units, which puts a premium on a company's ability to open new units successfully.

The Cyclicality of Gaming

The gaming industry is cyclical, but a lot less so than many other consumer businesses. Except for individuals plagued by compulsive behavior or blessed with substantial wealth, most individuals consider gaming a discretionary item that follows the demands of housing, food, and other necessities. Therefore, when aggregate income growth slows, so does casino revenue. It may be fun, but it can be postponed. The second half of 1995 exhibited a measurable slowing in a number of consumer areas, including sluggish general merchandise retail sales, increasing usage of rebates to keep car sales moving even at only a fairly flat rate, and declining rates of gain in casino revenue in most states. Does the slowing to date in these and other consumer areas capture the full extent of this cycle's slowdown in consumer spending, or does it have further to go? We do not know that answer, but we do know that if this slowdown intensifies and is extended, it will further slow casino and related revenues.

Slowdowns impact revenue and profitability in a number of ways. Any change in average room rates has an immediate impact on the top and bottom lines, but only on room revenue. However, changes in the occupancy rate also affect casino revenue (estimates vary, but each room occupied generates between $50 and $120 in downstairs casino revenue) and

TABLE 6
Las Vegas Occupancy and Room Rates

	1990	*1991*	*1992*	*1993*	*1994*	*1995*
Occupancy						
Hotel	89.1%	85.2%	88.8%	92.6%	92.6%	91.4%
Motel	69.8%	62.6%	66.1%	69.7%	73.2%	72.4%
Average Room Rate[a]	$45	$49	$44	$48	$52	$54

[a]Based on double occupancy.
Source: Las Vegas Convention and Visitors Authority

food-and-beverage demand. We estimate that a 1% change in occupancy has a somewhat greater impact on profitability than a $1 change in room rates.

Las Vegas enjoyed several years of strong and rising room and occupancy rates through 1994 (see Table 6). Occupancy rates moderated slightly in 1995, but most room rates remained firm or risen. The negative risk to estimates of a weakening in room rates largely has been ignored, due to an extended period of overall economic prosperity, as well as Las Vegas' ability to sustain high occupancy rates even as a substantial number of new hotel rooms (12,000, or 16% of the 1992 base) came on stream in 1995 and 1996. This will continue to be an issue into the millenium.

Casino Revenue—Stimulants to Growth

We believe a number of demographic and political considerations are likely to contribute to the gaming industry's remaining one of the fastest-growing segments of consumer spending over an extended period. None of these considerations would be of much importance if it were not for one very basic consideration: A growing percentage of the population seems to enjoy going to casinos. This growth is predicated on the following.

- Demographics suggest that a sharply rising percentage of consumers are approaching an age when they will slow their consumption of "stuff" (durable and non-durable) and shift toward services and saving.
- Budgetary realities will result in more states' legalizing gaming. These realities will develop and intensify only over time. This suggests that the process may be slow in developing, but, once begun, could well become an accelerating trend.

Legally, individuals under age 21 cannot participate in casino gaming in most major markets. Moreover, gaming has been found to be most attractive to an older audience. The aforementioned Harrah's gaming study indicates that the median age of a player in Las Vegas and New Jersey was 48 in 1994, up from 46 in the prior year. The "1995 Las Vegas Visitor Profile Study" indicates that 49% of casino patrons in Las Vegas were 50 years old or older, up from 44% in 1982. This same study indicates that those patrons 60 years old or older are 30% of total customers, up from 27% in 1992. Between 1990 and 1995, the population of 55 and older grew 7%, or 3.7 million people. In the next three five-year periods (ending 2010), this age group will increase respectively by 8%, 12%, and 13% on a percentage basis and 4.2 million, 6.8 million, and 8.8 million on a unit basis. This dynamic suggests a not only rising but accelerating market of potential casino patrons.

In addition to this long-term trend of an increasing potential market is a rising participation rate as attitudes toward gaming changes. The Harrah's 1995 survey found that 41% of those surveyed in 1994 thought casino gaming was not acceptable for them or anyone else. While still a high number, which suggests that casino gaming remains an intensely controversial subject, this ratio has declined from 45% in 1992. As a consequence, this same survey indicates that the percentage of households that have visited a casino in the last year has risen from 17% in 1990 to 30% in 1994, a near doubling of the participation rate. The combination of an acceleration in the growth of a key age group along with rising participation rates should result in a sustained rise in the number of people desiring to go to a casino.

These are extremely positive potential conditions for both casino operators and investors. There is, however, one problem: capacity. It is debatable whether Las Vegas and Atlantic City or the existing and already approved new riverboats will be able to accommodate the potential growth of new gaming participants over the next 10 to 15 years. The rich (operators) will get richer, and the customers will be faced with very crowded casinos if the base of casinos is not significantly expanded. This leads logically to the highly controversial subject of new jurisdictions' legalizing gaming.

For most state governors, putting the approval of gaming up to a vote of their constituents has about as much appeal as getting poked in the eye with a blunt stick. However, not having enough revenue to fund existing programs (much less new initiatives) without significantly raising the deficit (an option that some states legally do not have) may make it equally difficult to get elected. While a number of states currently enjoy budget surpluses, a number of dynamics likely to unfold over the next three to five years and beyond could dramatically change this condition.

The growth of total state revenue has trailed the growth of expenditures in both the last 5- and 10-year periods. Given the new political reality of the likelihood of the federal government forcing states to accept responsibility for a growing number of programs, a number of states are likely to find that the attendant block grants they receive simply may be insufficient to fund existing services fully. Further complicating this situation is that states may well be faced with a slowdown in a key revenue source—the state sales tax—which currently accounts for 14% of total state revenue. If our earlier premise that a changing demographic landscape is likely to result in a slowdown in consumer expenditures for a variety of goods, the relative growth of states' tax revenue will slow, further pressuring the budgeting process.

Casinos have the potential to generate very large amounts of tax revenue. In 1994, Nevada generated $520 million, not including room, food, or beverage taxes. Illinois generated $230 million, and Mississippi, after being in the business only three years, generated $166 million. These are direct taxes and do not include the additional benefit of jobs created directly and indirectly by casinos or, on the other hand, the costs associated with the increased needs created by the casinos. Logic suggests that, over time, the solution to a state's predicament of slowing growth in revenue (federal grants and sales taxes, which, combined, accounted for 37% of total state revenue in 1994) and rising expenditures as the federal government sends the management of an increasing number of programs to states will be to look for new sources of revenue. Casinos certainly can provide that.

Deterrents and Risks to Growth

The principal risks that interrupt growth in any industry are either cyclical and therefore tend to be temporary in their impact, or secular and longer-term, and prove to be truly problematic. While no single issue appears important enough to influence the above-average long-term growth potential of gaming, a number of developments could preoccupy investors at least temporarily.

In the cyclical or "temporary" area of concern is the aforementioned impact that a softening economy and slowing disposable income growth can have on the casino industry. Any sign of weakening room rates in Las Vegas may well be recognized by investors as a sign that an overall slowdown of sufficient duration to affect earnings expectations sectorwide has begun.

While some people view all concerns or risks as simply opportunities in disguise, it may be worthwhile to enumerate these "opportunities." One is increased taxes. In Illinois, the Governor Jim Edgar is proposing to raise the levies on the nine currently operating riverboats. The wildly successful riverboat in Elgin will begin profit sharing with the municipality around mid-1996. There also is the potential for a federal tax on gaming receipts;

Congress periodically proposes setting up a national commission to study gaming. However, increases in tax rates on casinos would be difficult to pass on to consumers due to the currently competitive nature of the industry, and, therefore, there is the potential for a degradation in the return on investment for the industry (if a federal tax were imposed) or individual companies (depending on which states were to raise tax rates). Several factors could offset the negative impact of rising tax rates, at least partially. First, the companies potentially affected at the state level are likely to request changes in existing regulations to offset the higher taxes. These could take the form of elimination of betting limits, cruising requirements, and others. Second, the effect of an increased tax burden on the marginal industry participants could prove a death knell that forces closures or sales of properties. While increasing tax rates, even if at the federal level, would affect the *level* of profitability, as dollar profit declined, the potential *growth* of profit following a shift likely would be maintained.

A second concern is gaming on the Internet. This potential outlet for gaming is still in its infancy and has many hurdles to clear before it is positioned to account for a meaningful percentage of gaming revenue. First, gaming is illegal for individuals under 21 years of age, which introduces a potentially expensive problem of insuring that junior isn't using dad's code word to make a wager. Second, the security of deposits or credit card numbers given by participants must be guaranteed. Third, the integrity of the arrangement must be maintained. In sporting events, casinos, and the stock market, effective, unquestioned regulation is key to the confidence of participants. Fourth, should states or the federal government be the regulating authority? Most of these issues will be resolved only over time and probably in the courts.

While entrepreneurs may be the first to try to capitalize on the Internet's possibilities, the existing major companies have some built-in advantages. First, they already possess a level of integrity and visibility that could attract customers. Second, they have the financial capacity to afford the development and legal expenses of such a venture. Lastly, the potential market for gaming on the Internet may prove, over time, to be limited. Assuming a full range of casino games ultimately are offered electronically, what would their appeal be? To the compulsive gambler, it would be a boon. To the casual participant who views a trip to a casino as either entertainment or a vacation and almost always goes with friends or relatives for the social aspects, the Internet may not fill the need. Currently, a number of "casino" software programs are available for "play" that simulate various games but do not include wagering. One may question how often would a non-compulsive individual sit at home and lose money playing blackjack or video poker until he or she realizes that gaming on the Internet has a much higher component of "gambling" and a much lower component of social interaction than going with friends to a casino? They may still play, but how often and how much will they be willing to lose remains unanswered. Perhaps the greatest growth potential for gambling on the Internet will be lotteries. While issues regarding security and regulation are similar, the "entertainment" content of playing a lottery is low, while the "gambling" content is high, which is considerably different from casino gaming. It, therefore, seems likely that opportunities for growth via the Internet will be greater for lottery than casino operators.

Gaming on Indian reservations is becoming a major competitive threat as well as an opportunity. Gaming on Indian reservations began with the passage of the Federal Indian Gaming Regulatory Act of 1988. Currently, there are approximately 550 federally recognized tribes and 300 Indian reservations, of which approximately 35%, or 200 tribes, are located in sparsely populated Alaska. Approximately 23% of the tribes currently have compacts with state governments to operate Class III casinos, which can include blackjack, baccarat, craps, roulette, other casino games, slot machines, parimutuel wagering, and wagering on sporting events.

In 1994, total gaming on reservations totaled an estimated $3.4 billion, or 20% of total U.S. gaming revenue, excluding charitable gaming. Tribal gaming is successful. Foxwoods, operated by the Mashantucket Pequot Indians in Connecticut, is the largest casino in revenue in the United States. More than a dozen Indian casinos now operate in the Phoenix area, which has been a significant factor in the major slowdown in the Laughlin, Nevada, market.

Regardless of who owns the casino, it needs to be near a relatively large population base. Since many tribal reservations are in extremely rural areas, a substantial number of tribes will be unable to establish a viable casino. Indian casinos do enjoy one important comparative advantage. Since they are recognized as sovereign nations, earnings are not taxable by federal or state governments (except in separate arrangements, as in Connecticut). While Congress occasionally has suggested levying a tax on Indian gaming, this is not likely to become effective in the foreseeable future since substantial legal issues would tie the issue up in the courts for a long time. This insures that existing Indian casinos and proposed units in potentially attractive locations will enjoy a strong comparative advantage in generating coverage of debt or return on equity, and all but guarantees their proliferation. Assuming this assessment is relatively accurate, a principal risk for Nevada-based operators would be the initiation of Class III Indian gaming in California. There are approximately 100 tribes in California that have federally recognized sovereign lands. We estimate as many as 50% of these are in areas that could sustain a successful casino. However, to date, the State of California has been unwilling to sign operating compacts with the tribes, greatly limiting activity. If, at some point, either by litigation or change in political attitude, Class III gaming is allowed on Indian reservations, the potential competitive impact on Nevada is likely to be significant. According to a survey by the Las Vegas Convention and Visitors Authority, in 1995, 35% of visitors to Las Vegas were from California. Indian gaming in California would not stop Californians from going to Nevada, but it almost certainly would have an impact on the frequency of visits.

While the further growth of Indian gaming presents a risk to certain existing properties, there is also the opportunity for existing companies to participate in the growth by signing management contracts with tribes. These contracts have to be approved by an agency of the federal government and are limited to terms of five to seven years and cannot exceed fees of more than 40% of gaming revenue. A number of companies currently are entering into these agreements. There is potentially good and bad news in such contracts. Capital requirements of these management contracts are modest. Therefore, over time, income generated from the agreements will tend to raise comparative return on total equity and investment. Conversely, the risk of these contracts is their renewable feature. After a contract expires in five to seven years, we estimate that a casino could be generating, on average, $5 million-$10 million in management income. A question then arises: Would the contract then be extended or would the tribe be willing to hire its own managers and save a portion of the fee? The issues in each contract will vary, but will include an estimate of savings by self-management, the loss of association and customer recognition of the partner, and the need to replace sophisticated services such as customer tracking systems, the costs of which typically are spread across an entire family of casinos. Not all contracts will be renewed nor will they all lapse; this uncertainty creates its own risk.

Another issue with aspects that generate both positives and concerns is the opening of new jurisdictions. As discussed earlier, the geographic expansion of legal gaming has enhanced industry growth not only in new jurisdictions, but in the destination market of Nevada. While gaming is expected to grow at an above-average rate over an extended period and continue to rise as a percentage of recreational spending, the actual rate of growth will depend on the opening of new state jurisdictions. This is a political and controversial process, and it is difficult to predict either the date or name of the state that next will legalize gaming. While we previously detailed the reasons why we believe that over the longer term a growing number of states will legalize gaming, the current political environment suggests little progress will be made over the next 12–24 months. Political scandals reinforce the existing level of sentiment against casinos and can jeopardize the future proliferation of legalized gaming.

A separate issue regarding new jurisdictions is their potential impact on existing markets. If either New York or Pennsylvania approves gaming, the impact on Atlantic City revenue would be significant. Likewise, legalization in California would have a substantial impact on Nevada. Offsetting this risk would be the opportunity to participate in new jurisdictions with major projects in major markets.

Another risk attendant to new jurisdictions is the probity of the efforts by companies to win licenses in those states, new and existing, where limited gaming licenses are available. In a number of incidents, licensing has been denied, postponed, or resulted in management changes. The larger, publicly traded companies, especially those with operations in Nevada and/or New Jersey, are more likely to avoid these difficulties, but even they are not immune.

CONCLUSION

We expect gaming to be one of the fastest-growing segments of consumer spending over the next 5 to 10 years. We base this favorable industry conclusion on:

- A long-term acceleration in the growth of consumer spending on recreation as an aging U.S. population shifts spending from goods to services;
- An increasing share of recreation expenditures' shifting to gaming, a subset that will benefit from an aging population;
- Strong growth in casino industry revenue due to the expansion, over time, of legal gaming jurisdictions and rising individual participation rates;
- Highly predictable, above-average earnings growth potential;
- An ability to participate in the growth of new markets as well as continue to grow aggressively in the Las Vegas market; and
- Strong balance sheets and below-average cost of capital.

Concentration, Competition and Competitiveness in the Casino Gaming Industry

Christian Marfels

The U.S. casino gaming industry has undergone a series of profound changes during the past 20 years. When Resorts International opened its casino in Atlantic City in 1978, Nevada's monopoly gave way to a duopolistic market configuration. This event provided a welcome dose of competition inasmuch as the lopsided orientation of the gaming industry was corrected with the creation of another center of gravity on the East Coast. Perhaps the most important contribution of Atlantic City to the gaming industry was the final breakthrough into the corporate era for the industry. Along with corporatism came reliability and integrity that have given shape and form to the new gaming industry.[1]

The subsequent introduction of limited-stakes gaming in Deadwood, South Dakota, and in the former mining towns of Blackhawk, Central City, and Cripple Creek in Colorado between 1989 and 1991 added a few more spots on the U.S. gaming map, but they were only of minor importance. In stark contrast, the emergence and rapid expansion of riverboat gaming and of gaming on Indian lands changed the industry dramatically, especially in view of the rapid proliferation of gaming destinations and opportunities.

What does this all mean for the economics of the gaming industry, an industry which, with an average annual growth rate of 15% from 1992 to 1996, is among the fastest growing industries in the United States? What about concentration in the industry, scale economies of operations, and rent-seeking behavior created by restriction of entry through the licensing process? This study is an attempt to provide some answers.

TABLE 1

Casino Gaming Revenues by Jurisdiction 1992 and 1996[a]

Jurisdiction/Year	1992		1996	
	$Million	*%*	*$Million*	*%*
Nevada[b]	5,864.2	60.3	7,426.5	43.0
New Jersey[c]	3,216.0	33.1	3,825.3	22.2
Mississippi[d]	122.0[g]	1.3	1,861.8	10.8
Louisiana[d]	—	—	1,211.6	7.0
Illinois[d]	226.3	2.3	1,131.5	6.6
Missouri[d]	—	—	571.1	3.3
Colorado[e]	180.0	1.9	411.7	2.4
Iowa[d]	69.5	0.7	395.4	2.3
Indiana[d]	—	—	372.0	2.2
South Dakota[f]	40.3	0.4	43.0	0.2
Total	9,718.3	100.0	17,249.9	100.0

[a]Excluding Indian Reservation Gaming.
[b]Nonrestricted operations > $1 Million gaming revenues.
[c]Atlantic City.
[d]Riverboats.
[e]Black Hawk, Central City, Cripple Creek.
[f]Deadwood.
[g]Five months.
Sources: Ernst & Young LLP, *Compilation of Gaming Data,* 1992 and 1996 ed.

FIRM SIZE AND CONCENTRATION

Excluding gaming on Indian lands, casinos were in operation in 10 states at the end of 1996 (see Table 1). Nevada and Atlantic City, the traditional centers of gravity, still accounted for close to two-thirds of nationwide gaming revenues in 1996. Nevertheless, their combined market share had declined by 28 percentage points from 1992 levels because of the rapid growth of riverboat gaming.

Firm size by scale of casino operations provides a full spectrum of dimensions, ranging from mega-casinos in Atlantic City and the Las Vegas Strip to mini-casinos in Colorado and South Dakota to predominantly medium-sized casinos in much of Nevada and in riverboat jurisdictions.

The market configuration in Atlantic City can be clearly described as an oligopoly consisting of a few large casinos. In fact, the average 1996 gross gaming revenue of the 12 casinos of $316 million was almost 10 times higher than the Nevada average of $32 million for all non-restricted

TABLE 2
Distribution of Gaming Revenues in Nevada
by Major Markets/Locations FY1996

	No. of Casinos	Gaming Revenue $Million	% of NV Total	Gaming Revenue per Casino $Million
Statewide:				
All Casinos[a]	229	7,390.4	100.0	32.3
Large Casinos[b]	30	4,329.2	58.6	144.3
Las Vegas Strip Area:				
All Casinos[a]	40	3,629.7	49.1	90.7
Large Casinos[b]	19	3,194.5	43.2	168.1
Downtown Las Vegas Area:				
All Casinos[a]	18	654.4	8.9	36.3
Large Casinos[c]	12	623.8	8.4	52.0
Reno/Sparks Area:				
All Casinos[a]	36	896.7	12.1	24.9
Large Casinos[d]	9	633.8	8.6	70.4
Laughlin Area:				
All Casinos[a]	10	504.7	6.8	50.5
South Shore Lake Tahoe Area:				
All Casinos[a]	5	328.0	4.4	65.5

[a]Gaming Revenue > $1 Million
[b]Gaming Revenue > $72 Million
[c]Gaming Revenue > $12 Million
[d]Gaming Revenue > $36 Million
Source: State of Nevada Gaming Control Board, *Nevada Gaming Abstract 1996*, Carson City, December 1996.

operations with gaming revenues of $1 million and over.[2] Even in a comparison with the peer group of the 19 largest casinos on the Las Vegas Strip which had gaming revenues of $72 million and over, Atlantic City casinos were, on average, still almost twice as big. In contrast to Atlantic City's few-firm market, Nevada is a many-firm market because of its statewide dimensions with some 229 non-restricted licenses in FY 1996–97. Even some of its local markets, and most notably Las Vegas, resemble this polypolistic structure.

An overview of the distribution of larger nonrestricted operations in major Nevada markets is presented in Table 2. It shows that the 30 largest casinos (13% of the total) accounted for almost 60% of statewide gaming revenues in 1996. In specific local markets the dominance of the largest casinos is much greater: in the Reno/Sparks area, the largest casinos took 70% of gaming revenues, and in the Las Vegas Strip and Downtown markets 88% and 95%, respectively. Nevertheless, the medley of firms of all sizes in Nevada markets makes for a low overall average firm size, and it would appear that less than a handful of casinos, which would include Caesars Palace, Las Vegas Hilton, MGM Grand, and The Mirage, recorded 1996 gaming revenues in excess of $200 million. Yet this threshold has become the norm in Atlantic City since the late 1980s, and by 1996 only the Claridge was left with a lower gaming revenue.

At the other end of the spectrum are the mini-casinos in Colorado and South Dakota which are small-scale operations because of limited-stakes gaming ($5 maximum bet) and a restriction to 30 gaming devices for individual licensees in South Dakota. Moreover, gaming activities are confined to rather small localities: Deadwood in South Dakota (97 casinos), and Cripple Creek (25), Black Hawk (19), and Central City (12) in Colorado. This makes clearly for atomistic market configurations with average 1996 gaming revenues in the Colorado mining towns of $7.3 million, and in Deadwood of about $0.44 million.[3] Similar estimates for the riverboat jurisdictions show an average of $113 million in Illinois, $87 million in Louisiana, $63 million in Missouri, $62 million each in Mississippi and Indiana, and $44 million in Iowa. These levels indicate medium-sized to large scales of casino operations.

Concentration levels in Table 3 are based on gaming revenues of casino operators, and they extend from moderate-to-high levels in riverboat jurisdictions to moderate levels in Atlantic City to low levels in Nevada. To begin with the Nevada market, the estimated lead-firm market share (CR1) increased slightly between 1992 and 1996, and so did the four-firm ratio (CR4). In 1996, the leading casino operators were Mirage Resorts, Hilton, Circus Circus, and MGM Grand. A minimum estimate of the Hirschman-Herfindahl-Index (HHI) reflects very low levels of concentration.[4] This is not surprising in view of the multitude of firms in the Nevada market as a whole. It also reflects the character of the gaming industry to be regional, if not local.[5]

A case in point is the Atlantic City market, where concentration is moderate (see Table 3). From a structural point of view this market provides an interesting microcosm of a gaming industry in a self-contained local market. Furthermore, with the individual casinos being large enough operations, they clearly qualify for the classical "competition among the few" scenario. During the early years of formation of the Atlantic City industry from the late 1970s to the mid-1980s concentration levels in terms of HHI declined from very high levels to the lower end of the range of

TABLE 3

Concentration in the Gaming Industry by Gaming Revenues
of Casino Operators 1992 and 1996

Jurisdiction/Measure	CR1		CR4		HHI	
	1992	1996	1992	1996	1992	1996
Nevada	9.1[a]	10.1[a]	32.2[a]	34.0[a]	261[b]	297[b]
New Jersey[c]	28.4	30.0	69.1	65.3	1,509	1,596
Iowa[d]	50.2	17.4	92.8	65.2	3,301	1,322
Illinois[d]	34.8	20.6	92.7	65.3	2,489	1,382
Mississippi[d]	26.4	n.a.	85.4	n.a.	2,083	n.a.
Louisiana[d]	—	14.1	—	47.6	—	897
Missouri[d]	—	18.0	—	57.7	—	1,243
Indiana[d]	—	28.5	—	90.2	—	2,223

[a]Estimate.
[b]Minimum estimate based on CR4.
[c]Atlantic City.
[d]Concentration by riverboats.
Note: In the Mississippi and Nevada jurisdictions data on gaming revenues by casino operator are not available.
Sources: Calculated from data from the New Jersey Casino Control Commission, Ernst & Young, and *Moody's Industrial Manual.*

moderate concentration. This movement was mainly caused by a rush of newcomers. Fueled by a series of spectacular mergers and acquisitions involving the Trump Organization, the Griffin Company, and Bally Manufacturing, concentration has since risen steadily to reach the upper end of the moderate range. External growth lifted Trump Hotels & Casino Resorts Company (THCR; formerly Trump Organization) into the lead position in 1985 with a 15% market share. By 1996, this share had risen to 33%, and with gaming revenues of $1.14 billion in the Atlantic City market, THCR was among the nation's top three casino operators along with Harrah's Entertainment and Hilton.

In the early 1990s, concentration in the riverboat jurisdictions was very high, which is a typical feature of the gaming industry in its early stages, comparable to the 1978–81 period in Atlantic City. However, with an influx of newcomers, high concentration levels declined thereafter.

SCALE ECONOMIES

Casinos in the traditional markets of Nevada and New Jersey operate in a very competitive environment, and the fight for market share makes it essential to maintain a cost-efficient operation. In the production economy efficiency is related to the concept of scale economies. Empirical studies have shown that in many industries long-run average cost curves decline for low levels of capacity/output, then remain constant over a considerable range of output and, thus, resemble a tilted L-shaped form. This curve can be used to determine a minimum efficient scale of operations (MES) which must be achieved to realize the cost savings at higher output levels. However, this concept cannot be directly applied to the gaming industry because of an absence of physical capacity/output levels. What can be done is to employ the size of the casino floor space in terms of casino square footage as a substitute measure of capacity to generate gaming revenue from table games and slot machines.

Does a greater casino floor space lead to greater efficiency in terms of lower average total cost? In order to trace such evidence, an analysis of the relation between the total costs and expenses per square foot of casino floor space (average total cost) and casino square footage was conducted for the 12 casinos in Atlantic City for the period from 1980 to 1996. Total costs comprise the entire annual expenses to operate the casino-hotel establishment as reported to the New Jersey Casino Control Commission. The main reason for selecting total costs rather than casino costs as the dependent variable in the present context relates to the nature of modern American casinos, which make casino, hotel, restaurant, and recreational facilities a self-contained entity of their marketing strategy.

In Figure 1 a total of 167 observations have been plotted in a scatter diagram. A curve fitted through the observations indicates a gradual decline of average total costs at greater casino floor spaces.[6] While this curve lacks the kink of an L-shaped curve its convex curvature nevertheless indicates a decline at a diminishing rate which suggests a stronger decline of average total costs at smaller casino sizes than at larger ones. Furthermore, the diagram suggests an MES of about 60,000 square feet of casino floor space below which potential cost savings appear not to have been fully exploited. This advantage of size in terms of cost efficiency gains momentum from the fact that there exists a marked negative correlation between casino floor space and average total cost, i.e., the greater the floor space the lower the average total cost.[7]

A few cases may highlight this issue. In the early 1990s the Taj Mahal was the *largest* casino in Atlantic City with 120,000 square feet of casino floor space, but it recorded the *lowest* average total cost at an annual average of $3,095 per casino square foot. Likewise, TropWorld (now Tropicana)— as Atlantic City's second largest casino—recorded the third lowest average annual costs of $3,493. In contrast, Bally's Grand (now the Atlantic City Hilton) was second to last in terms of casino floor space, but it recorded the highest average total cost at an annual average of

FIGURE 1

Scale Economies in the Atlantic City Gaming Industry, by Casino Floor
Space and Deflated Total Costs of Casino-Hotel Operations, 1980–1996

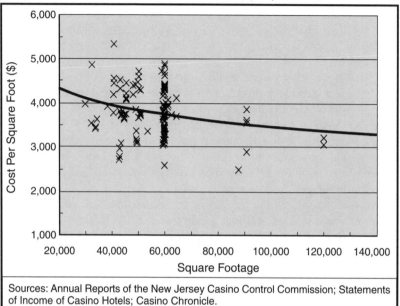

Sources: Annual Reports of the New Jersey Casino Control Commission; Statements
of Income of Casino Hotels; Casino Chronicle.

$4,275. Using the 60,000 square foot threshold as a benchmark for MES,
nine of the 12 casinos in Atlantic City had a greater casino floor space
than the threshold at the end of 1996. Consequently, they were in the range
to potentially realize the scale economies needed to remain cost efficient.

It would appear very likely that similar relationships between casino
size and total cost exist in Nevada markets. However, it must also be noted
that the dimensions of the Nevada gaming industry make for a multitude
of casinos of all sizes. Thus, it is not surprising to see only 32 of a total of
230 larger casinos with gaming revenues in excess of $1 million to exceed
the aforementioned benchmark of 60,000 square feet.[8] However, as a caveat, it must be noted that Nevada casinos operate in a lower-cost environment than their New Jersey counterparts, which means that their MES
would most likely be lower.

COMPETITION: PLAY OUR MACHINES

The casino gaming industry is fiercely competitive. This competitive spirit
prevails in virtually every potential structural setting, ranging from oligop-

olistic to polypolistic markets. As long as there are at least two firms in the market they will fight for the player's attention—*Play our machines (not theirs)*. Thus, it is hard to imagine a scenario of collusion or other anti-competitive behavior among casino operators. Rather, casino operators in the United States prefer to gain competitive advantage through innovative efforts to differentiate their product in what is largely a "look-alike industry."[9]

The competitive spirit makes for a dynamic industry of profound structural changes, product innovations, and marketing wizardry. However, dynamism was different in different regional and local markets from 1990 to 1996. Among the six major traditional markets, the Las Vegas Strip assumed a clear lead with an average annual growth rate of gaming revenues of 5.4%. This put it ahead of Atlantic City with 4.4%, Laughlin with 3.6%, Reno/Sparks with 3.3%, Downtown Las Vegas with virtually no change, and South Shore Lake Tahoe with −1.2%.

However, growth in the traditional markets is paltry in comparison to the rapid expansion of riverboat gaming. In the first months of operation in 1991—spanning nine months in Iowa and four months in Illinois to be precise—riverboats made a total of $80 million in gaming revenues. In 1992, riverboats in Mississippi joined with five months of operations, and combined revenues increased more than fivefold to $418 million. The rapid pace of growth of riverboat gaming accelerated even more in subsequent years when Louisiana (1993), Missouri (1994), and Indiana (1995) joined the ranks. Based on full-year operations during 1990–96, average annual rates of growth of gaming revenues showed a double-digit performance in riverboat jurisdictions, *viz.* 55.8% in Iowa, 41.5% in Louisiana, 34.1% in Mississippi, 23.1% in Illinois, and 22.5% in Missouri.[10] Consequently, the share of national gaming revenues generated in riverboat jurisdictions jumped from 4.3% in 1992 to 32.2% in 1996 (see Table 1).

The competitive spirit of the industry is fueled by an intricate network of efforts of casino operators to enhance customer relations and service, a system referred to as "Lagniappe" by William Thompson and Michele Comeau.[11] The most important instrument of product differentiation in the gaming industry in order to gain and maintain customer loyalty is the system of complementaries, which include free food and beverages, accommodation, cash coupons, and the like. In fact, there is no other industry in the production and service economies which has developed promotional allowances to the degree of perfection as a marketing tool as the gaming industry.

In order to provide a perspective for the magnitude of complementaries, Atlantic City casinos spent 30 cents per dollar of gaming revenue on promotional measures in 1996 to attract players.[12] By casino operation, the ratio of total promotional costs and gaming revenues ranged from a low of 22% for Bally's Park Place to a high of 36% for the Atlantic City Hilton. When a lower ratio is regarded as a more efficient, i.e., less costly, way to attract gaming revenue, a differential of $14 per $100 of gaming revenue represents, indeed, an important competitive advantage. This gains momentum in a high-cost environment such as the Atlantic City market. On the other hand, in a mature market with declining rates of growth, a casino may very well adopt a strategy of a more generous rather than frugal disbursement of complementaries in the expectation of short-term expenditures for long-term gains.

The competitive spirit of the gaming industry is an important ingredient for casino operators' competitiveness, which refers to a firm's ability to maintain sustained growth in a rapidly changing environment. How did the competitive environment in the gaming industry enhance the competitiveness of gaming corporations? An analysis of selected competitiveness indicators was conducted for the six leading gaming corporations: Aztar, Boyd, Circus Circus, Harrah's Entertainment, Hilton, and Mirage Resorts. Measures of competitiveness were the growth rate of gaming revenues, profitability, and rate of return on equity, and the time period covered was from 1992 to 1996.[13]

Annual averages of the group composite show that:

- gaming revenues increased by 13.3%
- the profit margin stood at 6.1%, and
- the rate of return on equity was 10.8%.

Sustained growth of gaming revenues is the cornerstone of success in the gaming industry. Four of the six corporations experienced double-digit growth, with Hilton, Boyd, and Harrah's Entertainment in the lead. When it comes to the all-important bottom line, Circus Circus set a standard of solid performance for the industry with double-digit ratios, on average, in both profitability and rate of return on equity. Tight cost control also helped to build their flagship property, Luxor Casino Hotel & Resort, on the Las Vegas Strip, entirely from retained earnings.[14] However, a closer inspection of the stellar performance at Circus Circus reveals a steady decline of profitability and of the rate of return on equity over the five-year period. In contrast, the trend was up at Mirage Resorts for the entire period under investigation. In fact, profitability at 15.1% in 1996 was twice as high as at Circus Circus which still posted a respectable 7.5%.

This strong upward trend at Mirage Resorts has made the company the showcase of the industry. Mirage Resorts is clearly the most dynamic gaming company. This performance was duly recognized in *Fortune's* survey of America's Most Admired Companies where Mirage Resorts made it into the ivy league of the Top Ten in 1995 and 1996 alongside luminaries such as Microsoft, UPS, and Coca Cola. In summary, it would appear that Mirage Resorts and Circus Circus together with the solid performers Harrah's Entertainment and Hilton and the much smaller Aztar and Boyd are well positioned to face the challenges in the most competitive of all entertainment industries.

COMPETITIVE RENT-SEEKING

The gaming industry can be classified as an industry with a considerable extent of rent-seeking behavior. In microeconomic theory an economic rent is defined as those payments to a factor of production over and above the minimum payment necessary to have the factor supplied.[15] Usually, this applies to factors that are available in fixed supply in the long run. A typical illustration would be non-renewable resources such as coal, oil, and metals that are available in limited amounts only. Beyond these natural limitations, which give rise to economic rents, there are artificial limitations in terms of entry barriers via licenses and permits. In such cases, economic rents are created by restricting entry. Firms compete to become beneficiaries of such rents. In this process of "competitive rent seeking," expenditures are made to achieve and to preserve the monopoly position.[16] The licensing procedure in the gaming industry generates such economic rents. State governments participate in rents through taxes on gaming revenues, and casino operators devote considerable resources in order to preserve their sheltered status.

State governments have made gaming taxes, licensing fees, and other gaming-related fees a primary source of revenue. Tax rates on gaming revenues in the ten states where casino gaming is legal range from lows of 6.25% in Nevada and 8% in Mississippi, New Jersey (plus a 1.25% fee on gaming revenues to a redevelopment authority), and South Dakota, to double-digit rates of 18% in Colorado, 18.5% in Louisiana, and 20% in Illinois, Indiana, Iowa, and Missouri.[17] At least partly to preserve government's share of economic rents, entry is tightly controlled by state gaming control commissions. Likewise, some of the jurisdictions of the rapidly expanding riverboat markets have set upper limits for the number of licenses to be issued, *viz.* Illinois (10), Indiana (11), and Louisiana (15).

For casino companies, competitive rent-seeking means intensive lobbying to secure and preserve their privileged rent status. There have also been numerous cases of efforts of rent-preserving. In New Jersey, Atlantic City casino operators effectively put pressure on the state government to prevent the introduction of VLTs elsewhere in the state. In Minnesota, Indian gaming lobbyists worked hard against the passage of a bill in the state legislature that would have allowed VLTs into bars and taverns in the state. In Federal Court, Mr. Trump brought a lawsuit concerning the unequal treatment of Indian and non-Indian casino operations; and in Congress, Senator Reid from Nevada introduced a bill "to clarify" and "to close loopholes" in the Indian Gaming Regulatory Act.[18]

However, the textbook case of rent-seeking is the Foxwoods casino. This casino is an Indian gaming facility on Mashantucket Pequot tribe land in southeastern Connecticut, which opened in 1992 with table games and high-stakes bingo. In order to get authorization for slot machines, the casino's management struck a deal with the state government. In return for being allowed to operate slot machines they offered to pay the princely sum of 25% on gross annual gaming machine revenues or $100 million (later raised to $113 million), whichever was greater. However, the offer was linked to the condition that Foxwoods would remain the sole operator of such machines in the state, and should the state government hand out gaming machine licenses elsewhere Foxwoods' payments would stop immediately.[19]

The state government under former Governor Weicker—who was known to be opposed to casino gaming—seized the golden opportunity and thus got the best of two worlds. There was a windfall to state coffers— to which the state was arguably not entitled—and furthermore the state received "well-funded" arguments to oppose a further spread of casino gaming.

At the time, this latter aspect gained momentum in view of the intense lobbying of Mirage Resorts for a license to operate casinos in Hartford and Bridgeport. In fact, these lobbying efforts could be viewed as the lever for Foxwoods' rent-seeking efforts. As a classical rent-seeker, Foxwoods decided to make the payments in exchange for the guarantee to preserve its monopoly. What a monopoly! Until October 1996, when another tribal casino, the Mohegan Sun Casino, commenced operations, Foxwoods had not only been the sole casino operator in Connecticut but in all of New England.

To put the annual payment for the maintenance of the monopoly into proper perspective it would have required $1.8 billion of gaming revenues in the Nevada jurisdiction and $1.4 billion in the New Jersey jurisdiction to achieve $113 million in gaming taxes. To put it differently, the initial payment in 1992 represented no less than 44% of the gaming taxes paid by all of the 12 casinos in Atlantic City in 1992. As a consequence of the competition from the Mohegan Sun Casino, the former guarantee was lowered for both casinos to $80 million or 25% of the slot revenues whichever was higher.[20]

Is rent-seeking in the public interest? Economists deny that and denote the presence of a rent as a deadweight loss, which means that resources spent on rent-seeking are pure wastes from a societal point of view. This is true for most of the industries with restricted entry. But the gaming industry is different inasmuch as the licensing process is primarily in place to maintain the integrity of the industry. It is very unlikely that the industry would have earned the recognition and approval of an overwhelming majority of respondents in the recent Harrah's surveys on casino gaming entertainment were it not for the high standards set for the process of issuing a gaming license and the subsequent monitoring by the state gaming control commissions.[21] Consequently, it is felt that rent-seeking and preserving in the gaming industry as a cost factor is clearly outweighed by the benefits of having the barrier to entry to maintain its integrity.

OUTLOOK: WHAT IS IN THE CARDS?

The two major vehicles for the growth of gaming revenues are the rapid proliferation of gaming and society's ever-increasing acceptance of gaming. How will this development affect traditional markets and, specifically, Las Vegas and Atlantic City?

If anything, this position was strengthened in the 1990s. It was strengthened through the development of larger and larger casino hotel properties on the Las Vegas Strip. This process began in 1989/90 with the opening of the Mirage (Mirage Resorts) and the Excalibur (Circus Circus). It continued in 1993 with the MGM Grand, Luxor (Circus Circus), and Treasure Island (Mirage Resorts), and in 1996/97 with the Monte Carlo (Mirage Resorts/Circus Circus), and New York New York (MGM Grand/Primadonna). To understand the dimensions of this rapid expansion, the 1989/90 "supply shock"[22] added 7,000 rooms and 5,800 gaming positions to the market, the one in 1993 contributed another 12,000 rooms and 10,000 gaming positions, and the one in 1996/97 5,000 rooms and 5,500 gaming positions.[23]

These are enormous dimensions that put pressure on existing casinos in an already crowded market. Victims of the intra-market competition were aging properties, such as the El Rancho, the Dunes, the Aladdin, the Hacienda, and the Sands. Yet, this very cycle of "creative destruction" gives the Las Vegas market its unique image of being a place of innovation and ingenuity to provide the best product to gaming patrons. And there is no end in sight for further expansion. In 1998, Bellagio (Mirage Resorts) and Mandalay Bay (Circus Circus/Four Seasons Resorts) will join the crowd to be followed in 1999 by Paris (Hilton) and the Venetian (Adelson Group). Altogether, this greatest "supply shock" of them all will add at least another 14,000 rooms and 12,000 gaming positions to Las Vegas's already rich gaming menu.[24] Time will tell whether this unprecedented new supply of hotel-casino venues will create enough new demand to justify the enormous capital investment of the new properties.[25]

In contrast, the Atlantic City market has been and will be affected by both inter-market and intra-market competition. The emergence of Indian casino gaming in Connecticut made more than a dent in Atlantic City's gaming revenues since 1993, and more trouble may be looming if significant casino gaming comes to New York City and/or Philadelphia, or other East Coast venues. But, then, Atlantic City has something unique to offer: the presence of twelve casinos, ten of which are in easy walking distance from each other on the famous Boardwalk, and the two other casinos conveniently reachable by car or shuttle-bus service. In an era when consumers in general and gaming patrons in particular want choices, Atlantic City offers them. Another strong asset is the oceanside location of the casinos which provides the most spectacular environment for gaming anywhere.

Intra-market competition is fierce as the gargantuan expenses on complementaries indicate. However, the impact of these valiant marketing efforts appeared to be minimal in view of the 1996 and 1997 Atlantic City growth rates of gaming revenues of 1.8% and 2.4%, respectively.[26] Against this background it is somewhat reassuring to see the confidence of Mirage Resorts and MGM Grand in the vitality and viability of the market. Assuming political hurdles will be overcome, Mirage Resorts will build the 4,000-room "Le Jardin" in the Marina District next to the Harrah's and Trump Marina properties, and MGM Grand has earmarked a $700 million project at the northern end of the Boardwalk. The newcomers will further increase the level of competition. Yet, Atlantic City casinos have always been committed to the competitive spirit, and they certainly have the experience to stay ahead.

ACKNOWLEDGEMENT

I am indebted to Melvin Cross for his helpful suggestions and comments, as well as to James Sawler for the design of the graph on scale economies.

---

1. For a detailed account of the historical and institutional background of the industry see Marfels, C., "Casino Gaming," *The Structure of American Industry,* 9e., ed. by W. Adams and J. W. Brock, Englewood Cliffs: Prentice Hall, 1995, pp. 223–245; see also Eadington, W. R., "The Casino Gaming Industry: A Study of Political Economy," *The Annals of The American Academy of Political and Social Science,* Vol. 474, July 1984, pp. 23–35.

2. New Jersey Casino Control Commission, *1996 Annual Report,* Atlantic City, 1997; State of Nevada Gaming Control Board, *Nevada Gaming Abstract 1996,* Carson City, December 1996.

3. Data from Ernst & Young.

4. According to the Horizontal Merger Guidelines of the Department of Justice and of the Federal Trade Commission, concentration levels in terms of HHI are classified as "low" for values below 1,000, "moderate" from 1,000 to 1,800, and "high" in excess of 1,800.

5. Marfels, C., "Casino Gaming," *loc. cit.,* pp. 228–232.

6. The curve was fitted according to the formula

$$Y = \beta_0 + X^{\beta_1} + \mu$$

where Y represents the total cost of casino-hotel operations per square foot of casino floor space, X is the size of the casino floor space, b_0 the y-intercept of the regression line, and b_1 the slope of the regression line; m is a random term.

7. Spearman's rank correlation between the 1980–96 average casino square footage and the overall average of the total costs per casino square foot is -0.45.

8. Nevada Gaming Control Board, *Listing of Financial Statements Square Footage, 1996 Data,* Carson City, n.d. (Mimeograph).

9. *Standard and Poor's Industry Surveys—Leisure Time,* March 11, 1993, p. L36.

10. Bear Stearns, *Global Gaming Almanac 1997,* New York, 1997.

11. Thompson, W.N./Comeau, M., *Lagniappe: The Key to Casino Survival in a Buyers' Market,* Eighth International Conference on Gambling and Risk Taking, London/England, August 16, 1990.

12. Communication from the New Jersey Casino Control Commission.

13. Financial data from *Moody's Industrial Manual;* for a more-comprehensive assessment of competitiveness during the 1988–1992 period, see Marfels, C., "Casino Gaming," *loc. cit.,* pp. 239–341. The analysis includes gaming corporations with 1996 gross gaming revenues in excess of $500 million. Trump Hotels & Casino Resorts and ITT were excluded since the former became a public company only in 1995 and the latter had an insignificant gaming segment prior to the acquisition of Caesars World in 1995.

14. Fine, A., "Luxor: The Wonder of Discovery," *New Jersey Casino Journal,* November 1993, pp. 38–39.

15. Varian, H., *Intermediate Microeconomics,* 3e., New York: Norton, 1993, p. 390.

16. Krueger, A., "The Political Economy of the Rent-Seeking Society," *American Economic Review,* June 1974, p. 291.

17. Rates for Colorado, and Iowa are maximum rates (Data from Ernst & Young).

18. Fine, A., "1993—The Year in Review," *loc. cit.,* pp. 15–16; *The Boston Globe,* September 29, 1993, p. 24.

19. Gros, R., "Following Foxwoods," *New Jersey Casino Journal,* July 1993, p. 12.

20. Bear, Stearns, *Global Gaming Almanac 1997,* New York, 1997, p. 65.

21. *The Harrah's Survey of U.S. Casino Gaming Entertainment,* Memphis, Annual.

22. Salomon Smith Barney, *Food for Thought Revisited,* Industry Report, January 30, 1998.

23. *Id.,* p. 12; Bear Stearns, *Gaming Industry,* December 1997, p. 9.
24. Bear Stearns, *Gaming Industry,* p. 9.
25. Salomon Smith Barney, *Food for Thought Revisited,* pp. 22–23.
26. *Atlantic City Action,* January 1997 & 1998 issues.

Structural Dynamics in the Las Vegas Casino Gaming Market

Lawrence Dandurand and J. Kent Pinney

The casino gaming business is dynamic. It is changing as never before. The supporting economic, political, legal, social, and technological environments are in transition. Casino customers are coming from different socio-demographic backgrounds. They are behaving differently in the market. Concurrently, the structure of the casino industry is being adjusted. New corporate and marketing strategies are being developed.

In a general business environment characterized by mass media, mass entertainment, mass information systems, telecommunications networks, liberated consumers, global competition, strategic alliances, global capital movements, computer-based decision support systems, total quality management techniques, business re-engineering philosophies, dynamic markets, short product life cycles, product proliferation, competitive organizations, and efficient operations, the casino industry is no exception. The magnitude of change affecting casino gaming is indicated in the 1994 *Harrah's Survey of U.S. Casino Entertainment.* The Survey states that "with 92 million annual visits, casino entertainment ranks ahead of attendance at many other popular forms of entertainment including Major League Baseball games, arena concerts and Broadway shows. . . . By the year 2000, 97% of all Americans will most likely live in a state with legal casino entertainment."

RESEARCH OBJECTIVES

The underlying purpose of this research project is to determine the nature of the dynamics of the casino gaming business during the last ten years, and, consequently, to consider implications of the dynamics for future public and private policy development. The research objectives are concerned with the basic components of the dynamics of the casino gaming business. The research objectives are to identify, describe, analyze, and understand the nature of change in the Las Vegas market, the Las Vegas gaming industry, the Las Vegas product/service mix, Las Vegas corporate and marketing strategies, Las Vegas financial impacts, and Las Vegas capital investments. Emphasis is placed on the Las Vegas casino gaming market and the Las Vegas casino gaming industry.

Las Vegas is the best known and the single largest and most dynamic component in the casino gaming industry. Thus, research findings of this study are applicable to other casino gaming markets and casino gaming industries.

The model used for this study assumes that the Las Vegas market is a function of its environment, its external task circumstances. It postulates that the Las Vegas market will change as its environment changes. The model is composed of seven components, including the environment. Each component, excluding the environment, is a basic structure, a situation, of either the demand or supply side of the Las Vegas casino market.

The environment affects both the demand and supply components of this market. The seven components of the model are:

1) the environment;
2) the Las Vegas market structure;
3) the Las Vegas industry structure;
4) the Las Vegas product/service structure;
5) the Las Vegas marketing strategy structure;
6) the Las Vegas financial impacts structure; and
7) the Las Vegas capital investments structure.

These seven structures are arranged in a hierarchical scheme. Each structure, in a logical sequence, is seen as a function of a previous structure and a determinant of a subsequent, or subordinate, structure. The initial Las Vegas structure—the Las Vegas market structure—is linked to the external environment. All structures are linked across variables and time.

THE LAS VEGAS MARKET STRUCTURE

Las Vegas is a major tourist and convention destination. In 1993, 23.5 million visitors came to Las Vegas. This was an increase of about 8% compared to the previous year. Ten years before, in 1983, there were 12.3 million visitors, an increase of 11.2 million or 91%. This represents an annual increase of about 1 million or 9%. During this rapidly growing period from 1983 to 1993, the socio-demographic profile of the Las Vegas visitor changed dramatically. For example, females now represent the majority of the Las Vegas customers. Table 1 indicates, that in Fiscal Year 1993, females constituted 51% of the Las Vegas visitor population. This was an

TABLE 1
Las Vegas Visitor Population

Sex	1983	1993	Change
Male	52%	49%	−3%
Female	48%	51%	+3%
Total	100%	100%	

increase of 3% compared to Fiscal Year 1983. In 1993, there were about 12 million female person-trips to Las Vegas. In other words, in 1993, there were about 500,000 more female then male person-trips.

VISITOR SOCIO-DEMOGRAPHICS

An analysis of *Las Vegas Visitor Profile Studies* (Las Vegas Convention and Visitors Authority 1983–1993) indicates that other Las Vegas visitor socio-demographics, behavioral fashions, and expenditure patterns have also changed significantly during the last ten years from 1983 to 1993. Table 2 illustrates visitor socio-demographics. It shows that:

- the proportion of single (including separated, divorced and widowed) visitors increased by 4%;
- the proportion of retired workers increased by 13%;
- the proportion of high school or less educated visitors increased by 6%;
- the proportion of visitors aged 65 or more increased by 10% (the median age increased from 46 to 47 years of age);
- the proportion of Hispanic and Asian visitors increased by 5%;
- the median income in real terms (adjusted forward for inflation using the CPI [1982–1984=100; end of 1992=141.9]) declined from $50,000 to $44,000—a decline of 12%;
- the proportion of visitors from the Western Region declined by 12%;
- the proportion of visitors from California declined by 9%;
- the proportion of foreign visitors increased by 11%; and
- the proportion of Southern California visitors declined from 38% to 27%—a decline of 11%. The Southern California market decline is equivalent to 2,585,000 person-trips in terms of the 1993 Las Vegas market.

VISITOR BEHAVIOR

Table 3 contains statistics regarding visitor behavior. It indicates that:

1) the proportion of first time visitors increased by 4% from 1983 to 1993;

47

TABLE 2

Visitor Socio-Demographics

		1983	1993	Change
Marital Status				
	Married	72%	68%	−4%
	Single	28%	32%	+4%
Occupation				
	Employed	77%	67%	−10%
	Retired	14%	27%	+13%
	Homemaker	7%	4%	−3%
	Student	2%	2%	0%
Education				
	High School	35%	41%	+6%
	Some College	30%	25%	−5%
	College Graduate	35%	34%	−1%
Age				
	Less than 65	92%	82%	−10%
	65 or More	8%	18%	+10%
	(Median Age)	46	47	+2%
Ethnicity				
	White	86%	85%	−1%
	Black	8%	4%	−4%
	Hispanic	2%	5%	+3%
	Asian	3%	5%	+2%
	Other	1%	1%	0%
HH Income				
	(Median/Real)	$50k	$44k	−12%
Residence				
	East	8%	8%	0%
	Midwest	16%	17%	+1%
	South	11%	11%	0%
	West	61%	49%	−12%
	Foreign	4%	15%	+11%
Western States				
	California	41%	32%	−9%
	Arizona	6%	6%	0%
	Others	14%	11%	−3%
Southern California*				
		38%	27%	−11%

*(Based on a geographical dividing line at the southern extremity of Monterey and Fresno.)

TABLE 3
Statistics Regarding Visitor Behavior

		1983	1993	Change
Type of Visit				
	First Visit	21%	25%	+4%
	Repeat Visit	79%	75%	−4%
Visit Frequency				
	Ave. # Visits	2.1	2.5	+19%
Length of Stay				
	Average	4.5	3.1	−31%
	Most Frequent	3.0	2.0	−33%
Party Size				
	Average	1.8	2.9	+61%
	Most Frequent	2.0	2.0	0%
With Families*				
	Yes	6%	8%	+2%
	No	94%	92%	−2%

*(Base: visitors staying in a hotel or motel [92%]. Excludes RV park, friends and not staying overnight.)

2) the average visit frequency increased from 2.1 (FY1984) to 2.5 (FY 1993) visits—an increase of 19%;

3) the average length of stay declined from 4.5 to 3.1 nights—a decline of 31%;

4) the most frequent length of stay declined from 3 to 2 nights—a decline of 33%;

5) the average party size increased from 1.8 to 2.9 persons—an increase of 61%; and

6) the proportion of visitors traveling with families increased from 6% to 8%—an increase of 2%.

The number of children (persons under 21 years of age) visiting Las Vegas in 1993 was 1.7 million; 7% of the Las Vegas visitor market (based on a party size of two persons and assuming two children in parties traveling with children). Parties traveling with children are estimated at 3% of total parties (based on an average party size of two visitors—equivalent to 50% of the 6% of visitors with families). Assuming, on average, a family visiting Las Vegas with children consists of two adults with two children, the combined size of the Las Vegas visitor family market is 14% of the Las Vegas visitor market. In 1993, this was 3.3 million persons (i.e., 14% of 23.5 million). In 1994, the family market increased to about 3.8 million persons

TABLE 4
The Dynamics of Gambling and Non-Gambling
Expenditures from 1983–1993

	1983	1993	Change
Yes	93%	90%	−3%
No	7%	10%	+3%
(Average/Real)	$1,216	$445	−63%
(Most Fr./Real)	$710	$200	−72%
(Average/Real)	$122	$112	−8%
Gambling Visitors			
Gamling Budget*			
Non-Gambling Expenditures**			

*(Trip gambling budget per person.)
**(Daily expenditures per person.)
Note: All real values based on the CPI [1982–84=100; 12/92=141.9].

(i.e., 14% of 28 million)—an increase of 500,000 visitors. These are conservative estimates because demand dynamics and new mega-resort facilities produced a greater proportion of gambling-prone, family-oriented visitors.

GAMBLING AND NON-GAMBLING EXPENDITURES

Table 4 depicts the dynamics of gambling and non-gambling expenditures from 1983 through 1993. It shows that:

- the proportion of gambling visitors declined from 93% to 90%—a decline of 3%;
- the average trip gambling budget declined 63% in real terms;
- the most frequent gambling budget per person declined 72% in real terms; and
- the average daily expenditures per person declined 8% in real terms.

FUNCTIONAL DYNAMICS

Changes witnessed in the Las Vegas market are a function of the dynamics of the external environments, such as the socio-demographic changes in Southern California, affecting the Las Vegas market. In turn, the dynamics of the Las Vegas market are determining the structure and strategies of the Las Vegas casino gaming industry. The perspective in this model is that demand creates supply. In the long run, supply is a function of anticipated opportunities and demand. Regardless of the creativity and innovativeness of supply management, the industry will falter and fail if it does not meet the real needs of consumers and other "stake holders" in the external environment.

The focus on demand—actual and potential consumers—does not negate the importance of creativity and innovativeness in the casino industry, the supply side of the market. The industry would not always want to rely on consumer surveys or customer complaints for creative ideas. As Hammer and Champy in *Reengineering the Corporation* (1993) indicate, consumers cannot be expected to be a direct source of new-product ideas when they have not been exposed to—or know how to—process relevant environmental information. An industry's objective is to create new products that redefine how consumers satisfy articulated and latent needs. The Sony Walkman was such an example in the consumer electronics industry. Examples in the Las Vegas casino industry in the 1990s include the Mirage, the MGM Grand, the Luxor, Treasure Island, the Las Vegas Hilton's Star Trek—The Experience, Rio's Masquerade Village, Caesars Forum Shops, and Caesars Magical Empire.

THE LAS VEGAS CASINO INDUSTRY STRUCTURE

The dynamics of the Las Vegas casino industry structure in the 1990s can be characterized as more casino locations, more publicly held corporations, more publicly held casinos, growth in total casino assets, growth in total casino capital, and growth in total casino employment. Casino industry dynamics include new corporations, new public corporations, new corporate ownership, and new corporate names. It is not unusual in the current Las Vegas marketplace to see advertisements that reflect new corporate names, new complex organizations, and an awareness of the changing nature of the new market.

Table 5 indicates specific time values and percentage changes in the Las Vegas casino industry. In the ten year span 1983 to 1993, casino locations increased from 70 to 98 locations—an increase of 40%; publicly held firms grew 8%; publicly held casinos grew 86%; total casino assets grew 150%; total capital grew 157%; and casino employees grew 92%.

THE LAS VEGAS PRODUCT/SERVICE STRUCTURE

The Las Vegas MSA (Metropolitan Statistical Area, i.e., Clark County) casino product/service structure also changed significantly during the decade between 1983 and 1993. The Las Vegas casino industry developed more casino space, more guest rooms, more casino games, more casino tables, more slot machines, more race books, and more sports pools.

TABLE 5

Time Values and Percentage Changes in the Las Vegas Casino Industry

	1983	1993	Change
Casino Locations*	70	98	+40%
Corporations**	12	13	+8%
Casinos**	14	26	+86%
Total Assets*	$2,794m	$6,990m	+150%
Total Capital*	$1,232m	$3,162m	+157%
Total Employees*	53,259	102,186	+92%

*(Casinos in Clark County with revenues of $1 million plus.)
**(Publicly held corporations in Clark County with FY1983 revenues of $10 million plus and FY1993 revenues of $12 million plus.)
Note: (m=million).

TABLE 6

The Dynamics of the Product/Service Structure

	1983	1993	Change
Casino Space*	1,537k	2,982k	+94%
Guest Rooms**	52,529	86,053	+64%
Games/Tables***	2,687	3,201	+19%
Slot Machines***	58,974	100,703	+71%
Race Books/Sports Books***	46	108	+135%
Total Games/Tables/Slots/Books***	61,707	104,012	+69%

*(Casino space in square feet; k=1,000; Casinos in Clark County with revenues of $1 million +.)
**(Guest rooms; CY1983; CY1993.)
***(Clark County; all licenses; FY1983; FY1993.)

Table 6 presents details showing the dynamics of the product/service structure. Over the decade in question, casino floor space increased 94%; guest rooms increased 64%; games and tables increased 19%; slot machines increased 71%; race books and sports books increased 135%; and total games, tables, slots, and books increased 69% (*Marketing Bulletin* 1993; Gaming Control Board 1993; *Las Vegas Review Journal* January 26, 1994).

Changes in the Las Vegas casino industry structure and the Las Vegas product/service structure reveal strategic decisions made by industry executives over this period. These decisions were formulated based on situation analyses of the Las Vegas visitor market, the Las Vegas casino industry, the internal environments (such as objectives, skills, and resources) and external environments (such as economic realities, socio-demographic shifts, "off-shore" gaming developments, and changes in cultural values). In general, the nature of the expansion decisions—such as public stock offerings, more casino locations, and more slot machines—reflect the dynamics of the external global environment, including opportunities and threats, and the changing needs and wants of the consumers who constitute the Las Vegas market. Many marketing strategies associated with past operations, and these strategic choices, remain. Others are new.

THE LAS VEGAS MARKETING STRATEGY STRUCTURE

Elements of past Las Vegas business and marketing strategy, namely, those in common use in the early 1980s, were still being used in the mid-1990s. New marketing strategies have been developed during the later 1980s and early 1990s.

BUSINESS AND MARKETING STRATEGIES—1983

Table 7 is a listing of selected business and marketing strategies in effect in 1983. These strategies reflected an increasing sophistication on the part of the Las Vegas casino gaming industry. The key attractions of gambling, entertainment, dining, parties, "bright lights," lodging, recreation, sightseeing, warmth, blue skies, sun, and "sin" were there as before. Las Vegas was referred to as the gambling capital, the entertainment capital, the convention capital, the rodeo capital, and the boxing capital of the world. It was a favorite site for multi-media coverage. It was frequently seen as a setting for movies and television programs. Las Vegas—along with Disneyland, New York, Washington DC, and the Grand Canyon—was recognizable around the world.

Gambling was seen as the catalyst for other non-gaming activities. It was the total expected experience that was the basic consumer motivator. Activities, such as star performances in theatre showrooms or lounge shows, were still seen as "loss leaders" for gambling.

Specific promotional appeals also focused on identified consumer needs and wants. These appeals included associating Las Vegas with fun, excitement, escape, change of pace, a vacation, excellent climate, clean, relaxation, feeling comfortable, passive entertainment, limited challenge, limited risk, quick returns, potential windfalls, selective socialization, feeling special, and enhanced awareness of self. Las Vegas was seen by the majority of visitors and locals as a place of entertainment. Customers might win, but did not expect to.

TABLE 7
Business and Marketing Strategies—1983

1)	Reorganizations
2)	Major Remodelings
3)	Marketing Research
4)	Scientific Management
5)	Profit Centers
6)	Product Markets
7)	Target Markets
8)	Gaming Tournaments
9)	Special Events/Meetings
10)	Conventions/Trade Shows
11)	Junkets/"Comps"
12)	Charters (Air and Bus)
13)	Local Gamblers
14)	Product Lines and Mix
15)	Courteous Service
16)	Distribution Channels
17)	Liberal Paybacks
18)	Progressive Jackpots
19)	Coordinated Promotion Programs
20)	Implementation and Control Strategies

BUSINESS AND MARKETING STRATEGIES—1993

Table 8 contains a list of additional business and marketing strategies implemented by the Las Vegas casino gaming industry in 1993. By this time, there was clear evidence of more scientific and professional management, and public ownership. Business practices within the industry more and more resembled those of other industries. *The Economist* (1994) stated that: "some of the older casinos are being driven out of business by their grand new rivals, but this has happened each time Las Vegas reinvented itself. . . . Now it is a theme-park for adults." Popular press outlets, as *Time* magazine, the *Christian Science Monitor* and the *Wall Street Journal* regularly ran articles on the industry, specific companies in the industry, and gaming personalities.

TABLE 8

Additional Business and Marketing Strategies Implemented
by the Las Vegas Casino Gaming Industry in the 1990s

1)	Professional Management
2)	Public Corporations
3)	Public Stock Offerings
4)	Off-Shore Operations
5)	Multinational Operations
6)	Multiple Business Units/Casinos
7)	Joint Ventures and Consortia
8)	Mega-Resort Destinations
9)	Theme Hotel/Casinos and Parks
10)	High-Tech Special Effects
11)	Casino and Shopping Malls
12)	Sports Books/Race Books
13)	Multiple Target Markets and Market Niches
14)	Positioning Strategies: a) The Best in the World b) The Most Unique Location c) Greatest Value for Money d) Something for Everyone
15)	Players Clubs
16)	High Technology Product Lines
17)	Global Distribution Systems
18)	Multiple-Level Pricing Strategies
19)	Multi-Media and High Profile Promotion Strategies
20)	Automation
21)	High Technology Planning and Management Support Systems

THE LAS VEGAS GAMING INDUSTRY FINANCIAL IMPACTS STRUCTURE

The Las Vegas casino gaming industry generated significant financial gains between 1983 and 1993. Total revenues increased 183% while net operating income grew 554%.

Table 9 illustrates details of the growth from FY1983 through FY1993. In this decade, the casino industry increased its net operating income efficiency from 5.3% to 12.3 %. The casino industry also increased its absolute return on average assets employed about 11%, its return on invested capital about 14%, and its return on stock equity about 17%.

TABLE 9

Las Vegas Casino Gaming Industry Growth from FY1983–FY1993

Variable*	FY1983	FY1993	Change
Total Revenue	$2,565m	$7,263m	+183%
Net Operating Income (NOI)	$136m	$891m	+554%
NOI Percentage	5.3%	12.3%	+7.0%
Return on Ave. Assets	4.9%	16.1%	+11.2%
Return on Invested Capital	6.0%	19.5%	+13.5%
Return on Stock Equity	11.1%	28.2%	+17.1%
*(Casinos in Clark County with revenues of $1 million plus.)			

TABLE 10

Illustrates National (USA) Potentials and Penetration Ratios for FY1993

Variable*	Conservative	Optimistic
Domestic Potential	32.9m	82.2m
Domestic Penetration	24%	10%
*Sources: *Market Statistics, Harrah's Survey of U.S. Casino Entertainment, Marketing Bulletin, Las Vegas Visitor Profile Studies,* and the *Las Vegas Review-Journal.*		

MARKET POTENTIALS AND PENETRATION RATIOS

A. The Domestic Market

Table 10 estimates national potentials for casino customers, along with penetration ratios, for FY1993. The conservative estimated market potential in FY1993 for the 315 Metropolitan Statistical Areas (MSA's) of the U.S.A. was 32.9 million customers. The optimistic estimated potential was 82.2 million persons. The FY1998 projected conservative potential is 34.7m persons, and the projected optimistic potential is 86.7m persons. From this framework, the Las Vegas market FY1993 national penetration rates were 24% and 10% based respectively on the conservative and optimistic potentials.

The conservative market potential is estimated based on the total adult population (the proportion of persons aged 18 or older—73%) of the 315 MSA's (204.9 million persons) multiplied by the proportion (22%) of American adults that had a casino experience in 1993. The optimistic estimate is based on the MSA's adult population modified by the proportion (55%) of American adults who feel that gambling is acceptable for themselves as a form of entertainment.

TABLE 11
The Southern California Market

Variable*	Conservative	Optimistic
Southern California Potential	2.9m	7.2m
Southern California Penetration	73%	29%
*Southern California is based on the following five MSA's: Los Angeles-Long Beach, Orange, Ventura, Riverside-San Bernardino, and San Diego.		

The conservative national penetration rate is based on the proportion of domestic visitors (85%) of the Las Vegas visitor market (23.5m visitors in 1993) divided by the average number of trips (2.5) divided by the conservative market potential (32.9m persons). The optimistic penetration rate is determined by dividing the number of domestic visitors, modified by the number of trips, by the optimistic market potential (82.2 million persons).

B. The Southern California Market

Table 11 indicates the market potentials and penetration rates for the Southern California market. The 1993 conservative market potential for the Southern California market was 2.9 million gambling prone adults. The conservative penetration ratio was 73%. The optimistic potential was 7.2 million persons. The optimistic-based penetration rate was 29%. The projected FY1998 conservative market potential for Southern California was 3.1 million persons, and the optimistic projection was 7.8 million potential customers. The conservative potential was calculated by multiplying the population of Southern California (18m persons) by the national adult percentage (73%) by the national proportion of adults having a casino experience in the last year (22%). The optimistic potential was determined by multiplying the number of Southern California adults by the "gambling is acceptable" percentage (55%).

The conservative penetration ratio was derived by multiplying the number of Las Vegas visitors (23.5 million persons, i.e., person-trips) by the Southern California market share (27%) divided by the annual number of trips for Southern California (3 trips) divided by the conservative market potential (2.9 million persons). The optimistic penetration rate was calculated by dividing the actual number of Las Vegas visitors from Southern California (2.1 million persons) by the optimistic potential for Southern California (7.2 million persons).

TABLE 12
Winnings, Taxes, and Fees for the Last Decade

Variable	CY1983	FY1993	Change
Taxable Winnings	$1.9b	$4.7b	+150%
Percentage Fees	$105m	$263m	+151%
Room Taxes	$22m	$52m	+140%
Entertainment Taxes	$12m	$19m	+68%

LAS VEGAS PUBLIC FINANCIAL IMPACTS STRUCTURE

The Nevada casino gaming industry is the primary revenue producer for the State of Nevada. Las Vegas (Clark County—including the Laughlin/Colorado River gaming area), with a metropolitan population of about 983,000 residents in 1992 (*Market Statistics* 12/31/92), was—and is—Nevada's key tax revenue source. For example, in calendar year 1993, the gross gaming win in Clark County was $4.7 billion, including the Laughlin component of $540 million—equivalent to 11% of the total county gaming win. This was an increase of $2.8 billion or 150% compared to the 1983 base.

The primary gaming tax—the *percentage fee*—is based on the gross gaming win. Gross taxable winnings are taxed at multiple rates. A rate of 6.25% is applied on net casino gaming winnings exceeding $134,000. This generated percentage fees from Clark County of approximately $294 million for 1993.

Table 12 indicates specific winnings, taxes, and fees for the last decade. In some cases, calendar year (CY) data are used. In other cases, fiscal year (FY) figures are shown (*Marketing Bulletin* 1983, 1993 and *Las Vegas/Laughlin 1993 Summary: 10 Year Review* 1994). It should be noted that during this 10 year period, sales/use tax taxable transactions increased from $3.8 billion to $8.7 billion—an increase of 129%. However, in Nevada in 1993, sales taxes represented only 20.8% of state and local governments revenue receipts (*The Council of State Governments* 1993).

THE LAS VEGAS CASINO GAMING STOCK MARKET STRUCTURE

Casino gaming stocks are considered consumer cyclicals. Publicly owned and traded casino gaming stocks performed quite well during the five years from 1988 to 1993. They were expected to outperform the S&P 500 stocks during the next five years from 1994 to 1998. For example, an analysis of industry group performances in the Dow Jones World Stock Index report (*Wall Street Journal,* 1994) indicated a domestic (USA) perfor-

TABLE 13
Casino Gaming Stocks: Industry Performance Index Values

Variable*	Domestic	Global
Casinos	1,318	186
Consumer Cyclicals	595	129
DJ Equity Market	437	114
*(Domestic: 6/30/82=100; Global: 12/31/91=100)		

mance index of 1,318 for listed casino gaming stocks (using the base June 30, 1982 = 100). This is a significantly stronger performance than the consumer cyclical group, which had an index value of 595 and the DJ equity market index of 437.

Table 13 highlights selected index values for casino gaming stocks, consumer cyclicals, and the DJ equity market on a domestic and global scale. The domestic index value of the casino gaming stocks had increased about 12 times or 1200% when compared to the base value of 100 in 1982—a span of about 12 years.

CONCLUSIONS AND IMPLICATIONS OF THE RESEARCH FINDINGS

Las Vegas has become a renowned global attraction. It offers multiple product lines to multiple markets. The modern mercurial amorphous consumer, the contemporary Las Vegas visitor, mixes with several target markets during the short stay as he or she searches for morsels of psychic satisfaction across the myriad product offerings.

The Las Vegas product has changed. It had to change in response to a changing environment (cultural, social, political, legal, economic, competitive, and technological). It will continue to change. For example, as consumer socio-demographics, attitudes, values, life-styles, needs, and wants evolve, the Las Vegas casino gaming industry has had to anticipate the appropriate infrastructures, facilities, strategies, and programs that would be attractive to the different target markets.

Las Vegas continues to focus on gambling as the catalyst of its endeavors. Gambling is its key competitive advantage. The mega-resorts, with their gambling complexes forming the basis of the total Las Vegas experience, exert a strong conglomerate pull on the average entertainment-prone consumer throughout the world. Las Vegas in the 1990s has not finished reinventing itself.

Conventions, junkets, tournaments, high-rollers, grind clients, and families—to mention just some product-markets—are all viable parts of the Las Vegas market. None of these diverse markets are inherently contradictory, disruptive, or unprofitable to the others. They all represent attractive business opportunities, especially when the broad product-markets are segmented into viable target markets and market niches. This will be more tenable as technological developments and skills lead to more "atomistic" (smaller and smaller) markets, redefined markets, and more focused and adaptable marketing strategies and programs.

A quarterly report of the time issued by Circus Circus Enterprises, Inc. (Circus Circus 1994) illustrates the opportunities, threats, complexities, and policies that were challenging casino industry management in the 1990s. The report considered new projects in Las Vegas and Reno, Nevada, other states (e.g., Louisiana and Mississippi), and other countries (e.g., Australia and Canada). It also discussed joint ventures, a consortium (including a government partnership), a climate-controlled theme park, and "participatory adventures." It finished by saying that "the Company also remains committed to seek out new opportunities in order to maintain its growth track well into the future."

REFERENCES

The Christian Science Monitor (1994). "Survey: Americans Bet on Chance." (April 13): 9.

Circus Circus (1994). *Third Quarter Report.*

Compact Disc (1994). *Corporate Reports.*

Council of State Governments (1993). *The West Comes of Age Hard Times, Hard Choices.*

The Economist (1994). "Fifty Ways to Lose Your Wallet." (March 26): 31.

Hammer, Michael and James Champy (1993). *Reengineering the Corporation.* New York: HarperCollins Publishers.

Harrah's Casinos (1994). *The Harrah's Survey of U.S. Casino Entertainment.*

Las Vegas Convention and Visitors Authority (1983). *Las Vegas Visitor Profile Study—1983.*

Las Vegas Convention and Visitors Authority (1993). *Las Vegas Visitor Profile Study-1993.*

Las Vegas Convention and Visitors Authority (1984). *Marketing Bulletin—1983 Summary.*

Las Vegas Convention and Visitors Authority (1993). *Marketing Bulletin-Fourth Quarter 1992 Summary.*

Las Vegas Convention and Visitors Authority (1994). *Las Vegas/Laughlin-1993 Summary-10 Year Review.*

Las Vegas Review-Journal (April 15, 1994): 1E-20E.

Market Statistics (1993). *Demographics USA 1993.*

Pledger, Marcia (1994). "Tourism Expected to Stay Strong." *Las Vegas Review-Journal* (January 26): 9E.

State Gaming Control Board (1983). *Quarterly Report.* Carson City, NV: Gaming Control Board.

State Gaming Control Board (1994). *Nevada Gaming Abstract-1993.* Carson City, NV: Gaming Control Board.

Whitney, Glenn (1994). "World Stock Markets." *The Wall Street Journal* (March 28): C1.

Parimutuel Wagering and Video Gaming: A Racetrack Portfolio©

Richard Thalheimer

Parimutuel wagering has been declining for several decades due, in part, to increased competition from state lotteries and casino gaming. In recent years, an attempt has been made to integrate video lottery terminal (VLT) gaming into a parimutuel racetrack's product portfolio. Daily data are used to develop product demand equations for parimutuel horse-race wagering and video lottery gaming at a thoroughbred racetrack. It is found that introduction of VLTs into the product mix results in decreased parimutuel wagering and revenues. However, the additional revenue generated from the VLTs is found to more than offset the decline in parimutuel revenue and the increased expense associated with the VLTs, given that a sufficient number of terminals are made available. When revenue from the combined parimutuel and VLT gaming product increases, if the respective shares of the VLT revenue distributed to the racetrack, to the horsemen who race horses at the racetrack and to the government are the same as their distributive shares from parimutuel wagering, all will enjoy an increase in revenue. To the extent that the respective shares of these participants differ from their share of parimutuel wagering, all participants may or may not enjoy an increase in revenue, depending upon the magnitude of the revenue increase. An additional finding of importance is that patrons who attend and wager on horse racing also wager on the VLT games while patrons who attend for the VLT gaming are less likely to wager on horse racing.

©1998 Routledge. This article was previously published as: Thalheimer, R. (1998). Parimutuel wagering and video gaming: a racetrack portfolio, *Applied Economics,* vol. 30, pp. 531–544. Permission to reprint has been granted by the author and publisher.

I. INTRODUCTION

Parimutuel horse-race wagering has been in a state of decline over the past several decades. For example, average daily wagering on all types of horse racing declined by 61% in real dollars from 1960 through 1994.[1] This decline has been caused, in part, by increased levels of competition from other gaming venues. Recent studies by Ali and Thalheimer (1996), Gulley and Scott (1989), Simmons and Sharp (1987), Thalheimer and Ali (1995b, c) and Vasche (1990) have found that state-run lotteries have resulted in significant decreases in parimutuel horse-race wagering. Casino gaming was also found to have resulted in a significant decrease in parimutuel wagering (Ali and Thalheimer, 1996; Thalheimer and Ali, 1995a).

In recent years, video gaming devices have become an alternative product offered by a limited number of state lotteries in an attempt to increase stagnant or declining state lottery revenues. Video gaming devices, which offer games such as keno and poker, are available in most casinos and are functionally equivalent to slot machines.[2] When video gaming devices are placed under the auspices of a state lottery they are referred to as video lottery terminals (VLTs). VLT gaming was first introduced in the United States in South Dakota (1989). Subsequent states in which VLT gaming was introduced were West Virginia (1990), Oregon (1992), Rhode Island (1992) and Delaware (1995). In three of these states VLT wagering is restricted to parimutuel facilities; West Virginia (horse and dog), Rhode Island (dog and jai alai) and Delaware (horse). In these instances the restrictive licences were granted not only to increase state revenues but also to increase total revenues to the racetracks and to the horse and dog owners who raced there.[3]

In this paper, the potential for increasing revenues generated at a parimutuel horse racetrack by integrating the competing product, VLT gaming into the portfolio mix, is investigated. The net effect on combined parimutuel and VLT wagering, revenue and profit is estimated. Specifically, the effect of integrating VLT gaming with parimutuel wagering at Mountaineer Park, a thoroughbred racetrack in West Virginia, is examined. VLT gaming was introduced at this racetrack in 1990 on an experimental basis.

Recent studies which have analysed determinants of parimutuel horse-race wagering include those of Gruen (1976), Coate and Ross (1974), Suits (1979), Morgan and Vasche (1979, 1982), Pescatrice (1980), Simmons and Sharp (1987), DeGenarro (1989), Gulley and Scott (1989), Church and Bohara (1992), Ali and Thalheimer (1997), Thalheimer and Ali (1992, 1995a, b, c). None of these studies has examined the *net effect* of the substitution between parimutuel revenues and other gaming revenues when they are combined in one location. Since casino gaming and a state lottery have been found to be substitutes for parimutuel wagering, it is expected that the video gaming devices at the racetrack will lead to reduced parimutuel wagering. Of particular interest is whether wagering on video games can produce enough revenue to more than replace the loss from the expected decrease in parimutuel revenue. Another issue of importance is the potential change in revenues to the state, racetrack and horsemen who race horses at the racetrack, after the introduction of VLTs.

The model specification is given in Section II together with a discussion of the data, variable definitions and functional form. Model estimation and its implications are given in Section III. Summary and conclusions are given in Section IV.

II. MODEL SPECIFICATION

Mountaineer Racetrack and Resort (Mountaineer Park), a thoroughbred racetrack in West Virginia, was chosen as the subject for the analysis. The racetrack is located in northern West Virginia near the Ohio and Pennsylvania borders. Mountaineer Park includes, in addition to the racetrack with its grandstand and clubhouse areas, a separate lodge with hotel rooms and a restaurant located a short distance from the racetrack.

On 9 June 1990, a limited number of video gaming devices, under the auspices of the West Virginia Lottery, were introduced on an experimental basis at the racetrack. Mountaineer Park acted as agent for the lottery. This was the first instance in US history where casino-type gaming devices were located in a state and restricted to a parimutuel wagering facility. Initially, 70 machines were installed. The video terminals were placed at a variety of locations around the racetrack and at the hotel facility. On days when live racing was conducted, VLTs were available at all locations. On days when there was no live racing, the number of VLTs available for play was restricted to those at the lodge.

In addition to the introduction of VLTs in 1990, full-card simulcasting on races from out-of-state locations was begun on 29 September 1990. Full-card simulcasting involves the simultaneous running of a full day (card) of live races at an out-of-state location and the simulcast of those races, via satellite, to receiving locations in another state, Mountaineer Park in this instance. Patrons at the receiving location may simultaneously view the races of the out-of-state 'host' track on television monitors as they are being conducted and bet on those races through the parimutuel totalizator system. Simulcast races were received at Mountaineer Park from Arlington Park and Hawthorne thoroughbred racetracks in Illinois for the remainder of 1990. The racetracks conducted back-to-back schedules so that Mountaineer Park received only one racetrack per day of full-card simulcast wagering. In 1991, full-card simulcasting was again conducted on the two Illinois racetracks and, in addition, on two California racetracks, Santa Anita and Hollywood Park. As in 1990, only one race-track's signal was imported on any given day of simulcast wagering. This can be considered as a very limited full-card simulcast product since in later years the number of out-of-state racetracks from whom full-card simulcasts were received was increased to many more than one per day. It should also be mentioned that on days when both live racing at Mountaineer Park and simulcast racing from out-of-state were jointly conducted, there was only limited overlap between them.

The data are daily over the period 1989, the year before the introduction of the VLTs, through 1991, the first full year after their introduction. The number of VLTs was increased from 70 to 150 over this period. After its introduction, VLT wagering was offered every day except Christmas and days when wagering was cancelled due to bad weather. In 1991, the first full year of full-card simulcast and VLT wagering, there were 361 days of VLT wagering. There were 39 days of VLT wagering with no parimutuel wagering in the sample. In that same year, there were 95 days of full-card and VLT wagering with no live racing, 49 days with live racing and no full-card racing, and 178 days with both.

Average daily live race wagering was $217441 in 1989, $162675 in 1990 and $112938 in 1991. In real dollars, average daily wagering declined 36% over this period. Average daily full-card simulcast wagering was $19545 in 1990, when it was first introduced, increasing to $32478 in 1991. Average daily VLT wagering (credits played) was $43198 in 1990, when VLT gaming was first introduced, increasing to $76254 in 1991. On a per machine basis, average daily VLT wagering was $502 in 1990 and $650 in 1991.

Three wagering product demand equations were estimated: one for live race wagering, one for full-card simulcast wagering, and one VLT wagering. Following Thalheimer and Ali (1995b), standard consumer theory was used in specifying each of the three demand equations. Each of the demand equations is specified not only as a function of its own demand factors but also as a function of those of the other two products in the three-products portfolio. On a given day, total demand is the sum of the three separate product demands, one or more of which might not be offered. As in earlier studies of the demand for parimutuel wagering (Ali and Thalheimer, 1996; Thalheimer and Ali, 1992, 1995a, b, c), the logarithms of real daily wagering were specified as linear functions of their determinants. The demand equations were then specified as:

$$\ln(W_{Lt}) = f(L_t, F_t, V_t, X_t) + u_{Lt} \tag{1}$$

$$\ln(W_{Ft}) = g(L_t, F_t, V_t, X_t) + u_{Ft} \tag{2}$$

$$\ln(W_{Vt}) = h(L_t, F_t, V_t, X_t) + u_{Vt} \tag{3}$$

W_{Lt}, W_{Ft} and W_{Vt} are live race, full-card simulcast, and VLT wagering demands, respectively, on day t when such product was offered. The sample size is 668 in Equation 1, 328 in Equation 2 and 417 in Equation 3. L_t, F_t and V_t are sets of own-product determinants of live race wagering, full-card simulcast and VLT wagering demands, respectively. The same set of variables is used in each equation. In Equation 1, L_t is a set of own-product demand factors and F_t and V_t are sets of cross-product demand factors. In Equation 2, F_t is a set of own-product demand factors and L_t and V_t are sets of cross-product demand factors. In Equation 3, V_t is a set of own-product demand factors and the L_t and F_t are sets of cross-product demand factors. In Equations 1, 2 and 3, X_t is a set of factors which affect tastes and the market environment and are common to each of the product demands. The error terms in Equations 1, 2 and 3 are denoted by u_{Lt}, u_{Ft} and u_{Vt}, respectively.

Once wagering demand has been estimated for each wagering product, revenue is computed as wagering demand times price according to the following three equations:

$$R_{Lt} = p_L W_{Lt} \tag{4}$$

$$R_{Ft} = p_F W_{Ft} \tag{5}$$

$$R_{Vt} = p_V W_{Vt} \tag{6}$$

where p_L and p_F are the prices of live and full-card simulcast parimutuel wagering, respectively and p_V is the price of VLT gaming.

Wagering Demand Variable

A description of the demand variables in this analysis now follows. Daily total wagering over a day was taken as the demand variable for each wagering product. Wagering demand was converted to its real dollar equivalent using the consumer price index for all urban consumers.[4] Live race wagering (W_L) is defined as the total amount wagered on all live races conducted by Mountaineer Park and offered at that racetrack in a day of racing. Full-card simulcast wagering (W_F), is defined as the total amount wagered at Mountaineer Park on every imported simulcast race from a given racetrack over one full day ('card') of racing at the out-of-state host track location.[5] VLT wagering (W_V) is defined as credits played and is the VLT equivalent to horse-race wagering. Credits played is the total amount of plays in a day which include the credits played on the cash deposited in the VLT (cash-in) plus additional games played from credits won but not cashed in.

Demand Determinants

The major variable of interest in this analysis, indicated by V_t in Equations 1–3, is the number of available VLTs. These may be taken as a measure of the opportunity cost of VLT wagering. As the number of machines is increased, the time spent waiting to play is reduced and thus the opportunity cost of playing is reduced. The number of VLTs available to players varied over the sample period from a minimum of 5 machines to a maximum of 150 machines.[6] The number of machines available to players varied according to whether or not there was live racing on a given day. On days when there was live racing, VLT wagering was available, both at the lodge and at the racetrack. On days when there was no live racing, VLT wagering was restricted to those machines located in the lodge. In 1990, the number of VLTs at the lodge ranged from a minimum of 5 to a maximum of 47, the number at the track ranged from 0 to 87, and the total number ranged from 5 to 134 on a given day. In 1991, the number of VLTs at the lodge on a given day ranged from 46 to 69, the number at the track ranged from 0 to 86 and the total number ranged from 46 to 150. It is expected that as the number of VLTs is increased, VLT wagering will increase and live and full-card horse-race wagering will decrease.

L_t and F_t in Equations 1 and 2 contain measures of racing quality defined by the number of stakes races offered on a given day, the value of the largest stakes offered by races on a given day, and special event days such as the simulcast of the Kentucky Derby, the Preakness Stakes and the Belmont Stakes. It is expected that higher-quality live races will result in increased live race wagering and higher quality full-card simulcast races will result in increased wagering on that product. The effect of higher-quality purses of one product on the other products is an empirical question. Factors included in L_t and F_t which measure product characteristics are the number and type of exotic wagers offered on a given day and special characteristics of full-card simulcast races. Exotic wagers are those where, for the price of a single ticket, a racetrack patron may wager on various combinations of more than one horse to finish in a particular order rather than on a single horse to finish first, second or third in a race. Certain exotic wagers have 'carryover' pools which were also included as demand determinants. For these wagers, if no one has the winning combination on a given day, a designated percentage of the pool is paid as a 'consolation' to those patrons with winning tickets. The remainder of the pool is carried forward and added to the pool for that wager on the following day. This process continues until someone holds a winning ticket, at which time all the proceeds in the pool are paid out to the patron(s) who holds the winning ticket. Exotic wagers with carryover pools are similar to state lottery lotto games. The effect of exotic wager opportunities on wagering demand is an empirical question. Finally, the effect of particular racetracks providing the full-card simulcast may not be captured entirely by the set of variables enumerated above. The presence of a particular full-card simulcast racetrack is included as a product characteristic for the full-card simulcast demand determinant set.

Factors included in X_t in Equations 1–3 are: day of the week, weather and holidays.[7] It is expected that wagering on weekends and holidays will increase since the opportunity cost to attend is reduced. The relationship of the other variables to wagering demand is an empirical question.

The individual demand determinants, a brief definition and their data sources are given in Table 1.[8] A detailed description of each is given in Appendix A. Summary statistics of the dependent and independent variables are given in Appendix B.

Revenue Determinant-Price

In revenue Equations 4 and 5, the price of parimutuel horse-race wagering, p_L and p_F, is referred to as the takeout rate. The takeout rate is set by state statute as a percentage of total wagering and is deducted before any winnings are returned to the patron at the conclusion of each race.[9] The takeout rate may vary between types of wagers. Generally, the rate is higher on exotic wagers than on one-horse ('straight') wagers to win, finish second or finish third. Revenues from the takeout rate are distributed by statute to the state (parimutuel tax), racetrack (commissions), and horsemen with horses at the racetrack (purses).[10]

The effective takeout rate for live racing (p_L) at Mountaineer Park was 20.5%.[11] The effective takeout rate for the import of out-of-state full-card simulcast racetracks (p_F) to Mountaineer Park over the sample period was 19.3%.[12] Both live and full-card takeout rates were unchanged over the sample period and so were not included in the demand estimation models.[13]

The price of VLT gaming, p_V, is the win percentage. This is similar to the takeout rate for parimutuel wagering in that it is the amount remaining after payout of winning bets. However, while the takeout rate is known and set by state statute, the takeout rate for VLT wagering is not a fixed deduction from each wager. Rather, it is based on the long-run probability of winning and the payoffs associated with that probability. The expected payoff for lottery-run video gaming terminals is generally set by state statute and determined by a random number generator (rng) in the machine. The price of wagering for VLTs, win percentage, is computed as win divided by total wagering, where win, or net terminal revenue, is defined as credits played less credits won. Credits won is the amount of credits won by the player and either replayed on additional games or taken as cash.[14]

TABLE 1

Variable Definitions and Data Sources

Dependent Variables	Definition	Source
W_L and W_F	Live and full-card simulcast wagering	West Virginia Racing Commission daily wager sheets
W_v	VLT wagering measured as credits played	West Virginia Lottery Commission daily sheets Available 11/90–12/91
Independent variables General (X)		
TEMPAV	Average daily temperature	US Department of Commerce, National Oceanic and Atmospheric Administration, National Climatic Data Center, Asheville, North Carolina. The observation site was Montgomery Lock and Dam in Pennsylvania
Precip Holiday Sun Mon Tue Thu Fri Sat	Average daily precipitation (inches) Holiday (1=yes, 0=no) Sunday (1=yes, 0=no) Monday (1=yes, 0=no) Tuesday (1=yes, 0=no) Thursday (1=yes, 0=no) Friday (1=yes, 0=no) Saturday (1=yes, 0=no)	US Department of Commerce, National Oceanic and Atmospheric Administration, National Climatic Data Center, Asheville, North Carolina. The observation site was Montgomery Lock and Dam in Pennsylvania
Video lottery (V)		
VLTNO	Number of VLTs	West Virginia Lottery Commission daily sheets Available 6/90–12/91

DERBYSIM	Simulcast of Kentucky Derby on live race day	Daily Racing Form Chart Book
PRKNSSIM	Simulcast of Preakness Stakes on live race day	Daily Racing Form Chart Book
BELMTSIM	Simulcast of Belmont Stakes on live race day	Daily Racing Form Chart Book
STKNO	Number of stakes races	Daily Racing Form Chart Book
STKMAX	Value of highest-stakes race on a stakes race day	Daily Racing Form Chart Book
EXOT2	Number of exotic wagers—two-horse (doubles, exactas)	West Virginia Racing Commission daily wager sheets
EXOT3	Number of exotic wagers—trifectas	West Virginia Racing Commission daily wager sheets
CARRYTRISU(-1)	Trifecta-superfecta exotic wager carryover pool from prior day	West Virginia Racing Commission daily wager sheets
CARRYTWTRI(-1)	Twin trifecta exotic wager carryover pool from prior day	West Virginia Racing Commission daily wager sheets
Full-card (F)		
STKNO	Number of stakes races	Daily Racing Form Chart Book
STKMAX	Value of highest stakes race on a stakes race day	Daily Racing Form Chart Book
EXOT2	Number of exotic wagers—two-horse except quinella (doubles, exactas)	Daily Racing Form Chart Book
EXOTQUI	Number of exotic wagers—two-horse (quinellas)	Daily Racing Form Chart Book
EXOT3	Number of exotic wagers—three-horse (trifectas)	Daily Racing Form Chart Book
CARRYTRISU(-1)	Trifecta-superfecta exotic wager carryover pool from prior day	Daily Racing Form Chart Book
CARRYTWTRI(-1)	Twin trifecta exotic wager carryover pool from prior day	Daily Racing Form Chart Book
EXOTP6	Number of exotic wagers—pick 6	Daily Racing Form Chart Book
CARRYP69(-1)	Pick 6 plus pick 9 exotic wager carryover pool from prior day	Daily Racing Form Chart Book
HAWSIM	Day when full-card simulcast is taken from Hawthorne racetrack (1=yes, 0=no)	West Virginia Racing Commission daily wager sheets

Win percentage for the VLTs at Mountaineer Park, as set by the West Virginia Lottery, averaged 11.9% in 1991. As was the case for parimutuel takeout rates, the expected win percentage was constant over the sample period. For this reason, the price of VLT wagering was not included as a determinant of demand.

III. MODEL ESTIMATION AND IMPLICATIONS

The demands for live, full-card and VLT wagering were estimated using standard linear regression analysis and a common variable set.[15] Demand model estimation results are given in **Appendix C**. The adjusted coefficients of determination for live, full-card and VLT wagering demands were 0.71, 0.52 and 0.80, respectively. All the regression equations were statistically significant. Following is a brief discussion of individual equation results.

Live Race Wagering

Seventeen of the 29 variables in the live race wagering model were significant at the 10% level or lower. Of particular interest is *VLTNO,* which was statistically significant and negative as expected. All but one of the significant live race variables were positively related to live race wagering. The trifecta wager (*EXOT3*) was negatively related to live race wagering. This result was also found in an earlier study (Thalheimer and Ali, 1995a). There were no significant full-card simulcasting variables, possibly due to the limited amount of simulcasting (limited to one out-of-state race per day when offered) over the period and the limited overlap between post-times of live and full-card simulcast wagering. The only full-card simulcast variable that was found to be significant was *HAWSIM.* It was found to have a negative relationship with live wagering demand. One explanation for this is that patrons who bet on full-card simulcasts attend less on days when the Hawthorne races are being simulcast to Mountaineer Park, leading to a reduction in betting on the live races on those days.

Full-Card Simulcast Wagering

Nine of the 28 variables in the full-card wagering model were significant at the 10% level or lower. *VLTNO* was statistically significant and negative as expected. Each of the significant full-card simulcast variables was positively related to full-card wagering. With the exception of the tri-superfecta carryover pool, none of the live race variables were significant with respect to full-card simulcast wagering. It was found that on days when there was a live race tri-superfecta carryover pool, wagering on full-card racing increased.

Video Lottery Terminal Wagering

Ten of the 27 variables in the VLT wagering model were significant at the 10% level of significance or lower. *VLTNO* was significant and positively related to its own wagering demand, as expected. None of the live race variables was found to have a statistically significant relationship to VLT wagering. With respect to the full-card simulcast variables, the number of two-horse exotic wagers and the pick-6 wager were found to be significant and positively related to VLT wagering. Since two-horse exotic wagers were offered each day there was full-card simulcasting, this indicates that, on days when there is full-card simulcasting, patrons attending the track to wager on full-card simulcasts are likely to also wager on the VLT games. *HAWSIM* was found to be significant and negative, as it was for live race wagering.

Additional Model Implications for Wagering Demand and Revenue

In order to estimate the effect of VLT gaming on parimutuel wagering, a simulation was performed using the 1991 data set. To determine the impact of introducing VLT gaming on parimutuel wagering, W_L and W_F were first estimated using the 1991 values of all variables included in Equations 1 and 2, respectively. W_L and W_F were then recomputed substituting the value of 0 for *VLTNO* to simulate its absence over the sample period. In 1991, parimutuel wagering from live racing and full-card simulcasting combined ($W_L + W_F$) was estimated to have declined by 24% as a result of VLT gaming at the racetrack and lodge.[16] The net effect on total wagering was determined by adding W_V to $W_L + W_F$, estimated using actual 1991 values of all variables, and comparing this total to $W_L + W_F$, computed with *VLTNO* set to zero. The addition of W_V to $W_L + W_F$ was enough to offset the estimated reduction of $W_L + W_F$ in 1991 due to the introduction of the VLTs and to have added an additional 21% to total wagering. The computation results for 1991 is given in Appendix D, Table D1.

Using Equations 4 and 5, revenue from parimutuel wagering ($R_L + R_F$) was estimated to have declined by 23.9% in 1991, equal to the decline in wagering.[17] On the other hand, total revenue ($R_L + R_F + R_V$) for the 320 days when there was parimutuel wagering was estimated to have increased by 2.7%. When VLT wagering on the 39 days with no parimutuel wagering is also accounted for, total revenue was estimated to have increased by 3.9%. The estimated increase in total revenue in 1991 is seen to be much smaller than the increase in total wagering. This is explained by the lower takeout rate for VLT wagering ($p_V = 11.9\%$) versus that for parimutuel wagering ($p_L = 20.5\%$, $p_F = 19.3\%$). Each one dollar of parimutuel wagering lost at a combined live plus full-card simulcast parimutuel revenue rate of 20.3 cents is replaced by a dollar of VLT wagering at 11.9 cents. Computation of the change in revenue for 1991 is given in Appendix D, Table D2.

In 1992, the maximum number of VLTs was increased from 150 to 165 and remained at this higher level until the autumn of 1994. To test the model, an out-of-sample wagering demand simulation was performed using the 1992 values for *VLTNO*.[18] These were substituted into the three wagering demand equations to generate estimates of wagering for each. Estimated VLT and parimutuel revenues differed from corresponding actual revenues by 0.4% and 0.6%, respectively.[19] The impact of VLT gaming in 1992 was estimated to have reduced parimutuel wagering by 27.3% and to have increased total wagering by 34.8%. Parimutuel revenues were estimated to be 27.3% lower due to the presence of VLT gaming while total revenue was estimated to be 9.2% higher.

To determine the effect of a large increase in the number of VLTs above the 1991 and 1992 experimental levels, a simulation was performed to estimate parimutuel and VLT wagering using an arbitrary 20% increase in the level of VLTs over their 1992 levels.[20] In this scenario, the maximum number of VLTs available on a given day is increased from 165 to 198, the minimum is increased from 78 to 94, and the average from 133 to 159. Using this configuration of VLTs, parimutuel wagering was estimated to decrease by 31.7% while total wagering would have increased by 62.0%. The decrease in parimutuel revenue would have been 31.7% and total revenue would have increased by 23.3%. Table 2 summarizes the effect on wagering and revenue due to the presence of VLTs in the various scenarios.

Although revenues were positive at the 1991 levels of VLTs, the cost of the operating lease for the VLTs must be deducted from gross revenue to obtain net revenue.[21] In 1991 and 1992, the lease and operating expense of the VLT operation was paid as a percentage of VLT revenue. The cost of the operating lease for the VLTs from a commercial vendor to Mountaineer Park in 1991 and 1992 was 23% of VLT revenue. In 1991, the maximum percentage of VLT revenue that could be paid for lease and operating expenses with no loss in revenue was 14%.[22] Therefore, even though the VLTs contributed to an increase in revenue, *profit* was reduced due to the unfavourable lease agreement with the VLT vendor. The maximum lease expense that could have been incurred at the 1992 level of VLTs was 25% of VLT revenue, yielding an approximate break-even profit situation for that year. Finally, if the number of VLTs had been 20% greater than their 1992 levels, the maximum lease expense that could have been incurred was 42% of VLT revenue, which would still yield a profitable outcome.

TABLE 2
Change in Wagering and Revenue from VLTs

	VLTs at 1991 levels (1)	VLTs at 1992 levels (2)	VLTs at 20% over 1992 levels (3)
Wagering			
Parimutuel wagering	−23.9%	−27.3%	−31.8%
Total wagering (4)	23.5%	34.8%	62.0%
Revenue			
Parimutuel revenue	−23.9%	−27.3%	−31.7%
Total revenue (4)	3.9%	9.2%	23.3%

(1) Maximum VLTs = 150, Minimum VLTs = 46, Average VLTs = 114
(2) Maximum VLTs = 165, Minimum VLTs = 78, Average VLTs = 133
(3) Maximum VLTs = 198, Minimum VLTs = 94, Average VLTs = 159
(4) Total = Parimutuel + VLT

IV. SUMMARY AND CONCLUSIONS

The results of this analysis indicate that VLT gaming at a parimutuel race-track results in significant decreases in both live race and full-card simulcast wagering. The order of magnitude of the decrease in parimutuel wagering is consistent with that estimated for the New Jersey racetracks when faced with competition from casinos located in their market area but not at the racetracks (Ali and Thalheimer, 1997).[23] The availability of full-card simulcast wagering opportunities appears to result in increased wagering on VLT games. This finding of complementarity is consistent with the practice of many casinos which include space for a race book (full-card simulcast area) in their casino even though they do not yield as much profit as video and slot machines or table games. One can conclude from this analysis that patrons who attend the racetrack to wager on parimutuel racing also wager on VLTs. On the other hand, patrons who attend and wager on the VLT products are less likely to wager on the parimutuel races.

Revenue from video lottery terminals placed at a parimutuel racetrack facility may more than offset the loss in parimutuel revenue and cover the lease cost of the VLTs if a sufficient number of machines are made available. To the extent that additional revenues from the VLTs more than offset the loss in parimutuel revenue, and cover the expense associated with leasing the machines, the racetrack, the horsemen with horses at the racetrack, and the government all benefit, given that their respective share of VLT revenue is the same as that of parimutuel revenue. To the extent that their respective shares of VLT revenue differs from their share of parimutuel revenue, at least one and possibly all three participants will benefit from having VLTs at the racetrack, depending upon the magnitude of the increase in VLT revenue.

Finally, it should be noted that to the extent that VLT revenues are allocated to quality purses to increase them above their pre-VLT levels, parimutuel wagering and revenues are likely to increase.[24] This is especially likely in the case of racetracks which simulcast their live races to out-of-state wagering sites where they compete with other racetrack simulcasts for the patron's wagering dollars.

ACKNOWLEDGEMENTS

This article is based on a research project prepared for the Equine Industry Program, University of Louisville, Kentucky. The author would like to thank Mukhtar M. Ali for his helpful comments and suggestions. Thanks are also due to J. Shannon Neibergs for his comments. As is customary, the author assumes full responsibility for the analysis and the remaining errors.

---

1. Computed using data from Association of Racing Commissioners International, Inc. (1995), Parimutuel Racing 1994, A Statistical Summary, Lexington, KY.
2. To illustrate the importance of slot machines in the overall casino gaming mix, in 1994 slot machines accounted for 65% of gross gambling revenues in Las Vegas and New Jersey casinos (Christiansen and Cummings, 1995).
3. For example, the VLT legislation in Delaware (HB 628) states that: "This Act Shall Be Known As The 'Horse Racing Redevelopment Act.'"
4. The base year period of the CPI is 1982–84.
5. The wagering pool at Mountaineer Park was combined ('co-mingled') with that at the host track location and the quoted odds and payoffs were identical at both locations.
6. The maximum number of machines that could be installed from 1990 through March of 1994 was 165. In September 1994, the number of machines was increased to 400 with an unlimited amount available upon approval from the West Virginia Lottery.
7. To avoid the problem of perfect collinearity the contribution of each day of the week variable was measured against the excluded variable *WED*.
8. To distinguish between days when live race simulcasting was offered and days when it was absent in Equations 2 and 3 a dummy variable indicating the presence of full-card simulcasting was constructed and set to 1 when full-card simulcasting was offered; otherwise it was set to 0. In addition to the dummy variable, an interaction term of the product of each full-card simulcast vari-

able times the simulcast dummy was implicitly constructed. This procedure accounts for days when full-card simulcasting is absent (dummy variable and all interaction terms are 0) and days when it is present (dummy variable is 1 and interaction terms may or may not be 0). Since live race *EXOT2* was present every day that live racing was offered over the sample period, it was highly collinear with the live race dummy variable and so the live race dummy variable was dropped from the estimated equations. The same procedure was followed for full-card simulcast racing in Equations 1 and 3 where, due to the high collinearity between the full-card simulcast dummy variable and full-card *EXOT2* which was present each day that full-card simulcasting was offered, the full-card simulcast dummy variable was dropped from Equations 1 and 3. The presence of VLT wagering in Equations 1 and 2 was accounted for using the same procedure as that for live and full-card simulcast racing. In this case the VLT dummy variable was highly collinear with *VLTNO* and was dropped from Equations 1 and 2.

9. A second, much smaller component of the price of wagering is called breakage. This is amount retained from winning wagers due to rounding down of payoffs to the nearest even number which is typically the nearest nickel or dime. This, too, is determined by state statute. For the tracks examined over this sample period, the statutory breakage was to the nearest dime.

10. In various instances, the share going to the racetrack and horsemen (purses) is designated in total by state statute and the distribution between the racetrack and horsemen is determined by contract.

11. The statutory takeout rates were 17.25% on one-horse wagers, 19% on two-horse wagers and 25% one three- or more horse wagers. Effective takeout rate was computed as a weighted average of these takeout rates where the weights were the respective share of handle of each type of wager. Breakage of 0.5% was added to the takeout rate.

12. See Thalheimer (1995) for a detailed explanation of the computation of effective takeout rate for full-card simulcasting. The procedure was identical to that followed for live race takeout rate with 0.5% breakage.

13. Attendance-related prices such as entrance fees may also affect the demand for wagering. These prices were constant over the sample period and so were not included in the wagering demand equations.

14. Alternatively, win can be computed as cash-in less cash-out.

15. There is one less variable in the full-card equation than in the live race wagering equation due to perfect collinearity between *STKNO* and *STKMAX* since there was only one such live race offered when full-card simulcasting was available. For this reason, live race *STKNO* was dropped from the estimating equation.

    The variable *STKNO* was eliminated from the full-card equation due to its high collinearity with *STKMAX*. The live race variables *STKNO* and *STKMAX* were absent over the period prior to the introduction of the VLTs and so were not included in the VLT equation.

16. W_L and W_F were estimated to have decreased by 23.2% and 26.9%, respectively.

17. This is expected since parimutuel revenue is computed using the takeout rate, t as a constant percentage of handle.
18. The configuration of VLTs remained unchanged after 1992 until the experiment was ended in 1994. At that time statutes were adopted permitting VLTs at the racetrack, subject to a local referendum, and the number of VLTs was increased from 165 to 400. Daily VLT data were not available for 1993 onwards.
19. Actual VLT revenues in 1992 as reported in the financial statement of Mountaineer Park, Inc. and Subsidiary on file with the West Virginia Racing Commission were $4250307. The estimated value of $4142023 in 1991 dollars adjusted for inflation from 1991 to 1992 is $4266698, where the inflation rate from 1991 to 1992 as measured by the CPI was 3.01. Estimated parimutuel revenue of $8249920 in 1991 dollars adjusted for inflation is $8498243. Actual parimutuel revenue of $8448616 was reported on the 1992 financial statement.
20. The simulated level of VLTs was computed as $1.2 VLTNO$.
21. It should be noted that there is a likely decrease in expenses associated with parimutuel wagering as wagering is decreased due to the introduction of the VLTs.
22. Computed using the formula: $R_{L+F}(VLT = 0) = R_{L+F}(VLT) + (1 - x)R_V$, where $R_{L+F}(VLT = 0)$ is parimutuel revenue with no VLTS, $R_{L+F}(VLT)$ is parimutuel revenue with VLTs, and R_V is net terminal revenue from VLTs. X is the fraction of VLT revenue which is the maximum that can be paid for expenses with no loss in revenue relative to revenue without VLTs.
23. The estimated decline in parimutuel wagering due to the presence of casino gaming in the market areas was 32% in 1988.
24. In 1991 purses were estimated to have actually decreased. In that year 48% of parimutuel revenue was allocated to purses. In that same year only 10% of VLT revenue was allocated to purses. This change in distribution of revenue, coupled with the fact that the VLT revenues just barely replaced the reduction in parimutuel revenue, led to a decrease in the amount allocated to purses.
25. The double and exacta bets were highly collinear and so were combined as one two-horse wagering opportunity.

REFERENCES

Ali, M. M. and Thalheimer, R. (1997) Transportation costs and product demand: wagering on parimutuel horse racing, *Applied Economics,* 29, 529–42.

Association of Racing Commissioners International, Inc., *Parimutuel Racing, A Statistical Summary,* Lexington, KY, various issues.

Christiansen, E. M. and Cummings, W. E. (1995) The United States 94 gross annual wager, *International Gaming and Wagering Business,* 6(8), 29–68.

Church, A. M. and Bohara, A. K. (1992) Incomplete regulation and the supply of horse racing, *Southern Economic Journal,* 58, 732–42.

Coate, D. and Ross, G. (1974) The Effect of off-track betting in New York City on revenues to the City and State Governments, *National Tax Journal,* 27, 63–9.

Daily Racing Form, *Chart Book,* Hightstown, NJ, various volumes.

DeGennaro, R. P. (1989) The determinants of wagering behavior, *Managerial and Decision Economics,* 10, 221–8.

Gruen, A. (1976) An inquiry into the economics of race track gambling, *Journal of Political Economy,* 84, 169–77.

Gulley, D. and Scott, F. (1989) Lottery effects on parimutuel tax revenues, *National Tax Journal,* 42, 89–93.

International Gaming and Wagering Business, *North American Gaming Report, 1994* (supplement), New York, NY.

Morgan, W. D. and Vasche, J. D. (1979) Horseracing demand, parimutuel taxation and state revenue potential, *National Tax Journal,* 32, 185–94.

Morgan, W. D. and Vasche, J. D. (1982) A note on the elasticity of demand for wagering, *Applied Economics,* 14, 469–74.

Pescatrice, D. R. (1980) The inelastic demand for wagering, *Applied Economics,* 12, 1–10.

Simmons, S. A. and Sharp, R. (1987) State lottery effects on thoroughbred horse racing, *Journal of Policy Analysis and Management,* 6, 446–8.

Suits, D. B. (1979) The elasticity of demand for gambling, *Quarterly Journal of Economics,* 9, 155–62.

Thalheimer, R. (1995) Parimutuel Horse Racing and Video Gaming, working paper, Department of Equine Administration, College of Business and Public Administration, University of Louisville, Louisville, KY.

Thalheimer, R. and Ali, M. M. (1992) Demand for parimutuel horse race wagering with special reference to telephone betting, *Applied Economics,* 24, 137–42.

Thalheimer, R. and Ali, M. M. (1995a) Exotic betting opportunities, pricing policies and the demand for parimutuel horse race wagering, *Applied Economics,* 27, 689–703.

Thalheimer, R. and Ali, M. M. (1995b) Intertrack wagering and the demand for parimutuel horse racing, *Journal of Economics and Business,* 47, 369–83.

Thalheimer, R. and Ali, M. M. (1995c) The demand for parimutuel horse racing and attendance, *Management Science,* 41, 129–43.

Vasche, Jon David (1990) The net revenue effect of California's lottery, *Journal of Policy Analysis and Management,* 9, 561–4.

West Virginia Lottery, *Video Lottery Project,* Mountaineer Park, Chester, WV (various), West Virginia Lottery, Charleston, WV.

West Virginia Lottery, Charleston, WV (daily video lottery data sheets).

West Virginia Racing Commission, Charleston, WV (daily wagering data sheets).

West Virginia Racing Commission, *Annual Report,* Charleston, WV.

APPENDIX A

Demand Determinants

Number of available VLTs.   The number of VLTs ($VLTNO$) available on a given day.

Day of the week and holiday.   The day of the week ($SUN, MON, TUE, THU, FRI, SAT$) or holiday ($HOLIDAY$) is assigned a value of 1 if live wagering, full-card wagering or VLT wagering occurs on that day, otherwise it assumes a value of 0.

Weather.   Two variables, average temperature ($TEMPAV$) and precipitation ($PRECIP$), represented weather conditions.

Product quality.   Racing product quality is measured by the number of stakes races offered in a given day and by the maximum stakes race value on that day measured in real dollars. Stakes races are races which have the highest purse values over a race meet. They generally require the owner of each horse desiring to participate in the race to pay an entry fee ('stake') to enter that race. Stakes race information was defined for both live racing and full-card simulcasting.

In addition to the quality variable being defined as the number ($STKNO$) and value of the largest stakes race ($STKMAX$) offered on a given race day, this information is supplemented with individual quality races of national interest simulcast from out-of-state racetracks to Mountaineer Park. These races were, the Kentucky Derby ($DERBYSIM$) in Kentucky, the Preakness Stakes ($PRKNSSIM$) in Maryland, and the Belmont Stakes (*BELMTSIM*) in New York, all of which were simulcast into Mountaineer Park when it was conducting live racing.

Product characteristic: two- and three-horse exotic wagers. The number of two- and three-horse exotic wagering opportunities offered at the live meet over a given day is an aggregate of two-horse betting opportunities (double, exacta, quinella) and three-horse betting opportunities (trifecta). A double is a wager on the winner in two successive races for a single ticket. An exacta is a wager on two horses in a given race to finish first and second, in order, for a single ticket. A quinella is similar to an exacta except that order doesn't matter. A trifecta (*EXOT3*) is a wager on three horses to finish first, second and third, in order in a given race for a single ticket. The number of two-horse exotic wagering opportunities offered in a given day is highly correlated with the number of races offered on that day, since every race had at least one two-horse wagering opportunity. For purposes of estimation, the number of double and exacta bets were combined into one variable (*EXOT2*).[25] The quinella bet was not available for the live races but was available for full-card simulcast races and was included as a separate two-horse wager (*EXOTQUI*).

Product characteristic: four- or more horse exotic wagers. A superfecta bet is one in which the patron must pick four horses in order of finish in a given race from first to fourth for a single ticket. The other forms of four- or more horse wagers offered at racetracks over the sample period involved a 'carryover' pool. The tri-superfecta ('tri-super') exotic wager is one in which the patron must pick a trifecta in a given race (i.e., three horses in order from first to third) and if that combination wins, the ticket must be used on a subsequent designated race in the two race series to select a superfecta. If no one has the tri-superfecta winning combination on a given day, a designated percentage of the pool is paid as a 'consolation' to those patrons with winning trifecta tickets. The remainder of the pool is carried forward and added to the tri-superfecta pool (*CARRYTRISU*) on the following day. This process continues until someone holds a winning ticket at which time all the proceeds in the pool are paid out to the patron(s) who hold(s) the winning ticket combination. Exotic wagers with carryover pools are similar to state lottery lotto games. *CARRYTRISU* is computed in real dollars and assigned the value of the prior day's carryover pool if there was one, otherwise it takes the value of 0.

The twin-trifecta ('twin-tri') exotic wager is similar to the tri-superfecta except that if the patron wins on the first trifecta offered for the wager, the ticket must be redeemed for a second trifecta, rather than a superfecta as for the tri-superfecta, in the two race series. The payout and carryover procedures are the same as for the tri-superfecta, although the percentages paid as 'consolation' and carryover may vary. The twin-tri carryover pool (*CARRYTWTRI*) is computed in real dollars and assigned the value of the prior day's carryover pool if there was one, otherwise it takes the value of 0. The presence or absence of the tri-superfecta or twin-trifecta wagers was not included due to their high degree of correlation with their associated carryover pools.

The pick-6 (pick-9) exotic wager is one in which the patron must select the winner of six (nine) successive races for a single ticket prior to the first race in the series being run. As with the tri-superfecta and the twin-trifecta wagers, a carryover pool is associated with the pick-6 (9). Due to the frequency with which the pick-6 wager (*EXOTP6*) was won relative to the other carryover pool types of wagers, its presence was not as highly correlated with the carryover pool as was the case for the other carryover pool wagers discussed earlier. For this reason, it was included in the analysis. This variable assumes the value 1 when present and 0 when absent. The pick-9 wager was seldom correctly selected and thus was highly correlated with its associated carryover pool. Because of their high degree of correlation, the pick-6 and pick-9 carryover pools from the previous race day were combined into one variable (*CARRYP69*). Each of the carryover variables is defined in the same fashion as for the live race exotic carryover wagers.

Product characteristic—full-card simulcast racetrack. Initial experimentation with each of the out-of-state full-card simulcast racetracks lead to inclusion of a binary variable for Hawthorne racetrack in Illinois (*HAWSIM*) in the final demand models. *HAWSIM* is assigned a value of 1 if the Hawthorne races are being received at Mountaineer Park, otherwise it assumes a value of 0.

Competition. Mountaineer Park faced parimutuel competition from greyhound racing at Wheeling Downs in West Virginia and from harness racing at Ladbroke at the Meadows in Pennsylvania. These racetracks were already in place over the sample period, and raced year-round. Initial experimentation indicated that there was no significant effect on wagering at Mountaineer Park over the study period, as expected, and these variables were excluded from the final demand models.

APPENDIX B

Summary Statistics

Variable	OBS	Mean	Median	Min	Max
		Entire Sample			
CPI	881	131.5	133.4	121.3	138.3
TEMPAV	881	54.42	56.50	6.00	82.50
PRECIP	881	0.102	0.000	0.000	3.060
HOLIDAY	881	0.017	0.000	0.000	1.000
SUN	881	0.171	0.000	0.000	1.000
MON	881	0.159	0.000	0.000	1.000
TUE	881	0.135	0.000	0.000	1.000
THU	881	0.094	0.000	0.000	1.000
FRI	881	0.172	0.000	0.000	1.000
SAT	881	0.177	0.000	0.000	1.000
		Live race model			
CPI	668	130.4	130.6	121.3	138.3
$LN(W_L)$	668	11.86	11.84	10.87	12.98
General variables					
TEMPAV	668	53.96	55.50	6.00	82.50
PRECIP	668	0.101	0.000	0.000	2.720
HOLIDAY	668	0.022	0.000	0.000	1.000
SUN	668	0.196	0.000	0.000	1.000
MON	668	0.205	0.000	0.000	1.000
TUE	668	0.126	0.000	0.000	1.000
THU	668	0.007	0.000	0.000	1.000
FRI	668	0.224	0.000	0.000	1.000
SAT	668	0.231	0.000	0.000	1.000
VLT variables					
VLTNO	668	71.4	85.0	0.0	150.0
Live race variables					
DERBYSIM	668	0.004	0.000	0.000	1.000
PRKNSSIM	668	0.004	0.000	0.000	1.000
BELMTSIM	668	0.003	0.000	0.000	1.000
STKNO	668	0.024	0.000	0.000	2.000
STKMAX	668	385.2	0.000	0.000	80256.8
EXOT2	668	11.3	11.0	10.0	16.0
EXOT3	668	6.5	6.0	5.0	12.0
CARRYTRISU(-1)	668	51556	0.000	0.0	498348.0
CARRYTWTRI(-1)	668	6363.5	0.0	0.0	82036

(*continued*)

APPENDIX B (continued)

Summary Statistics

Variable	OBS	Mean	Median	Min	Max
			Entire Sample		
Full-card variables					
STKNO	668	0.254	0.000	0.000	7.000
STKMAX	668	25781.3	0.000	0.000	740740.7
EXOT2	668	4.045	0.000	0.000	24.000
EXOTQUI	668	1.045	0.000	0.000	15.000
EXOT3	668	0.880	0.000	0.000	11.000
EXOTP6	668	0.199	0.000	0.000	1.000
CARRYTRISU(-1)	668	335.0	0.000	0.000	48796.7
CARRYTWTRI(-1)	668	683.9	0.000	0.000	66844.1
CARRYP69(-1)	668	17610.2	0.000	0.000	827910.2
HAWSIM	668	0.057	0.000	0.000	1.000
Full-card model					
CPI	328	135.9	136.0	132.6	138.3
$LN(W_F)$	328	9.92	9.91	8.51	11.40
General variables					
TEMPAV	328	54.6	55.2	14.5	82.5
PRECIP	328	0.081	0.000	0.000	3.060
HOLIDAY	328	0.012	0.000	0.000	1.000
SUN	328	0.177	0.000	0.000	1.000
MON	328	0.073	0.000	0.000	1.000
TUE	328	0.006	0.000	0.000	1.000
THU	328	0.180	0.000	0.000	1.000
FRI	328	0.189	0.000	0.000	1.000
SAT	328	0.192	0.000	0.000	1.000
VLT variables					
VLTNO	328	110.6	133.0	46.0	150.0
Live race variables					
DERBYSIM	328	0.003	0.000	0.000	1.000
PRKNSSIM	328	0.003	0.000	0.000	1.000
BELMTSIM	328	0.003	0.000	0.000	1.000
STKNO	328	0.006	0.000	0.000	2.000
STKMAX	328	17.2	0.000	0.000	5656.1
EXOT2	328	6.8	10.0	0.0	16.0
EXOT3	328	4.2	6.0	0.0	12.0
CARRYTRISU(-1)	328	19049.2	0.0	0.0	151225
CARRYTWTRI(-1)	328	19049	0.000	0.000	151225

(continued)

Summary Statistics

Variable	OBS	Mean	Median	Min	Max
			Entire Sample		
Full-card variables					
STKNO	328	0.637	1.000	0.000	7.000
STKMAX	328	59559.0	30257.4	0.000	740740.7
EXOT2	328	12.0	18.0	0.0	24.0
EXOTQUI	328	3.3	0.0	0.0	15.0
EXOT3	328	2.6	1.0	0.0	11.0
EXOTP6	328	0.649	1.000	0.000	1.000
CARRYTRISU(-1)	328	2022.5	0.0	0.0	73053.6
CARRYTWTRI(-1)	328	1966.5	0.0	0.0	91311.6
CARRYP69(-1)	328	61883.8	0.0	0.0	1472895
HAWSIM	328	0.223	0.000	0.000	1.000
VLT model					
CPI	417	136.0	136.0	133.9	138.3
$LN(W_v)$	417	10.59	10.64	7.61	12.27
General variables					
TEMPAV	417	52.90	51.50	14.00	82.50
PRECIP	417	0.091	0.000	0.000	3.060
HOLIDAY	417	0.014	0.000	0.000	1.000
SUN	417	0.146	0.000	0.000	1.000
MON	417	0.144	0.000	0.000	1.000
TUE	417	0.137	0.000	0.000	1.000
THU	417	0.144	0.000	0.000	1.000
FRI	417	0.144	0.000	0.000	1.000
SAT	417	0.144	0.000	0.000	1.000
VLT variables					
VLTNO	417	112.0	133.0	46.0	150.0
Live race variables					
DERBYSIM	417	0.002	0.000	0.000	1.000
PRKNSSIM	417	0.002	0.000	0.000	1.000
BELMTSIM	417	0.004	0.000	0.000	1.000
STKNO	417	0.000	0.000	0.000	0.000
STKMAX	417	0.000	0.000	0.000	0.000
EXOT2	417	6.85	10.0	0.00	16.00
EXOT3	417	4.17	6.00	0.00	12.00
CARRYTRISU(-1)	417	19036.9	0.0	0.0	112436.9
CARRYTWTRI(-1)	417	457.7	0.0	0.0	19733.9

(*continued*)

Summary Statistics

Variable	OBS	Entire Sample			
		Mean	Median	Min	Max
Full-card variables					
STKNO	417	0.480	0.000	0.000	7.000
STKMAX	417	45259.7	0.0	0.0	740740.7
EXOT2	417	6.3	6.0	0.0	14.0
EXOTQUI	417	2.1	0.0	0.0	12.0
EXOT3	417	2.9	3.0	0.0	10.0
EXOTP6	417	0.511	0.000	0.000	1.000
CARRYTRISU(-1)	417	1570.2	0.0	0.0	73053.6
CARRYTWTRI(-1)	417	1546.8	0.0	0.0	91311.6
CARRYP69(-1)	417	48676.0	0.0	0.0	1472895.0
HAWSIM	417	0.165	0.000	0.000	1.000

APPENDIX C

Demand Models

	Live race wagering		Full-card simulcast wagering		VLT wagering	
Variable	$LN(W_L)$ Coefficient	t-statistic	$LN(W_F)$ Coefficient	t-statistic	$LN(W_V)$ Coefficient	t-statistic
General variables						
C	9.9892E+00	53.95	8.1853E+00	27.61	8.3993E+00	59.54
TEMPAV	2.6572E-03	5.45	-1.4790E-03	-0.86	7.2872E-04	0.49
PRECIP	-1.9631E-02	-0.68	6.1851E-02	0.91	1.5164E-02	0.24
HOLIDAY	2.9444E-01	5.38	-1.5509E-01	-0.92	1.7165E-01	1.12
SUN	2.0654E-01	2.78	1.4028E-01	1.71	3.1309E-01	3.81
MON	1.5991E-01	2.20	3.5895E-01	3.61	4.3657E-01	4.71
TUE	6.3156E-02	0.85	-7.2949E-02	-0.31	5.9232E-01	6.62
THU	1.2614E-01	1.16	1.1159E-01	1.94	1.9072E-01	2.87
FRI	1.9027E-01	2.59	6.0300E-02	0.68	4.8909E-01	5.59
SAT	2.9128E-01	3.83	1.2678E-01	1.26	7.6718E-01	7.83
Video lottery terminal variables						
VLTNO	-1.8596E-03	-11.24	-2.6080E-03	-1.89	1.3408E-02	9.54
Live race variables						
DERBYSIM	4.3416E-01	4.08	3.8102E-01	1.23	1.9437E-01	0.54
PRKNSSIM	2.1833E-01	2.04	2.9492E-01	0.95	6.1126E-02	0.17
BELMTSIM	3.7203E-01	2.83	1.1747E-01	0.38	-6.3561E-02	-0.18
STKNO	4.0434E-02	0.78	—		—	
STKMAX	7.0319E-06	3.82	-7.1547E-05	-1.30	—	
EXOT2	1.6090E-01	7.09	-5.2702E-03	-0.16	-1.7337E-02	-0.54
EXOT3	-3.2660E-02	-1.78	4.5830E-02	1.02	-1.7958E-02	-0.40
CARRYTRISU(-1)	1.2222E-06	9.36	3.3436E-06	3.58	-1.0512E-06	-1.23
CARRYTWTRI(-1)	3.9802E-06	5.30	1.5192E-05	1.62	1.1291E-05	1.27

(continued)

APPENDIX C (*continued*)

Demand Models

Variable	Live race wagering		Full-card simulcast wagering		VLT wagering	
	$LN(W_L)$ Coefficient	t-statistic	$LN(W_F)$ Coefficient	t-statistic	$LN(W_V)$ Coefficient	t-statistic
Full-card simulcast variables						
STKNO	-2.1936E-02	-1.07	4.2030E-03	0.12	-1.9393E-02	-0.47
STKMAX	4.0216E-08	0.30	3.7923E-07	1.65	1.1099E-07	0.42
EXOT2	-1.4624E-03	-0.28	2.3663E-02	3.00	2.9239E-02	2.94
EXOTQUI	-4.8150E-03	-0.64	1.5654E-01	5.39	6.5663E-03	0.51
EXOT3	8.8692E-03	0.80	-1.0909E-02	-0.60	2.9652E-02	1.35
EXOTP6	-3.2669E-02	-0.51	1.5783E+00	5.78	4.8982E-01	4.43
CARRYTRISU(−1)	2.5886E-06	0.94	1.8896E-06	0.75	-2.2132E-06	-0.73
CARRYTWTRI(−1)	2.6510E-01	0.15	1.0791E-06	0.48	1.8936E-06	0.71
CARRYP69(−1)	4.9247E-08	-0.32	1.0312E-06	6.46	9.2206E-08	0.50
HAWSIM	-1.1605E-01	-2.16	-7.7148E-02	-0.91	-4.7099E-01	-5.29
Sample statistics						
Number of observations	668		328		417	
Mean dependent variable	11.86		9.92		10.59	
R-squared	0.72		0.56		0.82	
Adjusted R-squared	0.71		0.52		0.80	
Standard error of regression	0.18		0.30		0.35	
Sum squared residual	20.47		27.05		47.51	
F-statistic	57.40		13.45		63.82	

APPENDIX D

TABLE D1

Comparison of Wagering and Revenue by Product; Estimated Impact of VLTs on Wagering—1991
(Maximum VLTs = 150, Minimum VLTs = 46, Average VLTs = 114)

Wagering source	Days	Wagering no VLTs*	Wagering with VLTs*	Percentage change Due to VLTs
Impact for days with at least one type of parimutuel racing				
Live race (W_L)	225	$44 554 500	$34 216 200	−23.2%
Full-card simulcast (W_F)	272	$11 450 384	$8 368 080	−26.9%
Total Parimutuel ($W_L + W_F$)	320	$56 004 884	$42 584 280	−23.9%
VLT (W_V)	320	$0	$25 342 720	**
Total (parimutuel + VLT) − racing days	320	$56 004 884	$67 927 000	21.3%
Impact for days with parimutuel wagering and days with no parimutuel wagering				
VLT − non-parimutuel days (W_V)	39	$0	$1 212 471	**
Total (parimutuel + VLT) − all days	359	$56 004 884	$69 139 471	23.5%

*Wagering in nominal dollars
**Undefined

89

TABLE D2
Estimated Impact of VLTs on Revenue—1991
(Maximum VLTs = 150, Minimum VLTs = 46, Average VLTs = 114)

Revenue source	Days	Takeout rate	Average revenue no VLTs*	Average revenue with VLTs*	Percentage change due to VLTs
Impact for days when there was parimutuel racing					
Live race (R_L)	225	20.5%	$9 133 650	$7 014 375	−23.2%
Full-card simulcast (R_F)	272	19.3%	$2 210 000	$1 615 136	−26.9%
Total parimutuel ($R_L + R_F$)	320	20.3%	$11 343 650	$8 629 511	−23.9%
VLT (R_V)	320	11.9%	$0	$3 015 680	**
Total (parimutuel + VLT) – racing days	320		$11 343 650	$11 645 191	2.7%
Impact for days when there was both racing parimutuel and no parimutuel racing					
VLT – non-parimutuel days (R_V)	39	11.9%	$0	$144 300	**
Total (parimutuel + VLT) – all days	359		$11 343 491	$11 789 491	3.9%

*Revenue in nominal dollars
**Undefined

A Global Market Analysis of Casino Gaming on the Internet

Lawrence Dandurand

Casino gaming on the Internet has arrived. It is an interactive, on-line, high-tech form of commercial gambling. It occurs in an electronic medium called cyberspace. It can be played alone, with another person, or in a group. Other players do not have to be physically together. It can occur anywhere in the world. It is available to anyone, at anytime, and at anyplace—provided that the gambler has appropriate hardware, software, computer skills, and access to the Internet system.

Internet gaming is a rapidly evolving and significant market niche of the global casino gaming market. Internet gamblers represent new target markets. Some of the Internet gamblers will be new gamblers. Other Internet gamblers will be regular gamblers who are gambling in a new situation. This is especially the case for those non-resident gamblers who travel to gambling destinations such as Las Vegas or Atlantic City in order to gamble. However, it would also apply to resident, i.e., local, gamblers.

Internet gaming is a small part of the overall global gaming market (perhaps about one percent of legal global wagering by the year 2000). It is not likely to significantly threaten or displace significant amounts of revenue from traditional casino gaming. However, it might produce a relatively low-cost, new stream of revenue and expand the overall casino gaming market in terms of consumers, organizations, handle, revenues, and profits.

Internet gaming will be a significant market opportunity for some new organizations, and for certain existing firms in the casino gaming industry. It is a new form of competition and could be considered as a product-line extension. It could—along with such products as hotel in-room gambling or special facilities gambling—become another commonly provided service line item in the total hotel-casino offering. It could also be used in relationship marketing programs with existing casino customers. At the same time, Internet gaming will create new management challenges such as integrity, security, licensing, regulation, transaction processing, integration of management systems, and operations control.

The Internet gaming product, the technology, the supply, the task environment, and the demand already exist, and they are all very dynamic. On the other hand, certain aspects of the task environment—such as legal structures and the regulatory systems—are confusing, contradictory, inadequate, and outdated. They need to be reviewed, clarified, developed, and modernized to fit current market needs.

THE "CASINO GAMING ON THE INTERNET" PROJECT

This study is a multinational marketing analysis of an important emerging market and industry. It uses marketing theory concepts, such as product life cycles and the diffusion of innovation, and focuses on basic research—as opposed to applied research—in order to produce fundamental knowledge. The orientation is micro-marketing from the perspective of industry and government, rather than from the consumer. The study presents the results, implications, and conclusions of a comprehensive primary and secondary investigation and analysis of the controversial Internet casino gaming market (consumers, i.e., demand) and the casino gaming industry (organizations, i.e., supply).

The study focuses on an analysis of the on-line, cyberspace, wide-area Internet, intranet, and extranet video-graphic-text modes of traditional table and machine-type casino gaming operations—such as video-poker, slots, roulette, and blackjack—as well as race-book and sports-book betting. The analysis includes wire and wireless communications networks, cable systems, and satellite systems, as well as systems utilizing other combination technologies (such as CD's/PC's).

PURPOSE AND OBJECTIVES

The primary purpose of this study is to articulate the nature of the global Internet gaming phenomenon. Its findings are relevant to the purpose of managerial decision science, i.e., to improve private and public knowledge and decision making regarding Internet gaming. This is not an advocacy study for any given position; there is no hidden or moral agenda involved, nor are there any pre-determined hypotheses.

The specific objectives of the study are to determine, describe, and analyze:

- the nature of casino gaming on the Internet;
- the structure of the Internet gaming industry;

- the competitive environment of Internet gaming;
- the character of the Internet gaming market;
- the marketing opportunities of Internet gaming;
- the marketing threats of Internet gaming;
- the product-markets of Internet gaming;
- the market segments of Internet gaming;
- the target markets of Internet gaming;
- the market niches of Internet gaming;
- the market positioning strategies, marketing strategies, marketing programs, and marketing tactics of Internet gaming;
- the market demand of Internet gaming;
- the market potentials of Internet gaming; and
- the market trends of Internet gaming.

THE NATURE OF CASINO GAMING ON THE INTERNET

Casino gaming on the Internet is an intangible, commercial, consumer service. It is immediate, private, and interactive. It offers real time variety—in terms of games, locations, and gaming environments—on a global basis. It provides the gambling consumer with personal control of the gaming situation (e.g., game selection, turn-over speed, and playing information). It can be linked to other intangible activities, such as news, movies, chat rooms, video games, electronic mail, virtual reality, and real casino environments. It retains certain aspects of voluntary social interaction, such as personal interaction and group play. It eliminates or reduces psychological, physical, time, and economic risks associated with traditional casino gaming. Internet gaming might be "the Web's first killer" application (Hower 1997).

THE PRODUCT CONCEPT

The core Internet gaming product concept is: *a virtual casino located in cyberspace where people can engage in wagering in a gambling environment.* The environment could include sensory attributes associated with casino gaming. The total product concept could incorporate patronage dimensions associated with a modern, megastore casino at a resort destination.

The product concept is based on wide-area communications networks, client and server hardware and software, secure and private transmissions, on-line cash and credit systems, currency transaction-conversion-transfer mechanisms, independent verification controls, credible brands, attractive packages, and meaningful warranties.

Alternative communications networks can be based on any technologies that enable digital transfer of data, graphics, sound, and video. They can use different wire and wireless technologies, including cables, radio, satellites, and telephone lines.

INTERNET GAMING MARKET OPPORTUNITIES

Internet gaming market opportunities are substantial and growing. Commercial possibilities resulting from the merger of Internet technologies and gaming are significant. More consumers are gambling and more consumers are using the Internet. Any form of gambling can be placed on the Internet. The Internet provides consumer access at the household level.

Global Internet usage by adult home users will exceed 50 million persons by 1997. World-wide Internet usage will increase to 170 million users by the year 2000. Over half—about 56 percent—of the usage by the year 2000 will be offshore from the United States and Canada (Sinclair 1997).

Internet gaming is a new form of gambling. It is a new place—a location in cyberspace. Most people enjoy gambling in one form or another. Most people do not perceive gambling as harmful to individuals or society. Gambling is perceived as a unique form of entertainment. It is a catalyst for other entertainment activities. It provides real economic value, i.e., psychic satisfaction. It satisfies similar needs across the world.

The global gambling market is currently wagering well over $1 trillion per year. Over 50 percent of the global gambling market is located outside of the United States (VentureTech 1997). In the United States, 91 percent of the adults accept casino gambling entertainment as appropriate either for themselves or for others (Harrah's 1996).

INTERNET GAMING MARKET THREATS

The biggest threat to global Internet gaming is the legal and political environment. It is considered by many to be illegal in the United States under Federal Law—18 U.S.C. 1084, The Wire Act. The objective of the Act was "to attack the financial base of organized crime's horse racing and sports betting" (Barry 1997). It is possible that ". . . whether Internet gaming is legal is irrelevant because government can do little to prevent it. . . . Regulators may soon have no choice but to tolerate Internet gaming. When this happens, as it did in Nevada, the focus must shift from prohibition to regulation and the creation of a parallel universe" (Cabot 1996).

Other major internal and external environment threats to the successful development and maintenance of a viable Internet gaming industry include a relatively weak global Internet infrastructure, unsatisfactory applications of hardware and software technology, problems of system security, undercapitalized financial structures, generic product competition, potential corporate fraud, unexpected jackpot payoffs, lack of staying power, organized crime infiltration, casino gaming market saturation, more attractive product substitutes, consumer dissatisfaction, and lack of industry credibility. The trans-national, cross-cultural, and diverse nature of the Internet business poses even greater challenges to decision makers in the industry.

These internal and external threats to the Internet gaming industry exist, and they are serious, but their realization is neither inevitable nor insurmountable. The industry needs to formulate and administer a "good"—viable and sustainable—strategy. Good strategy is "one that neutralizes threats, exploits opportunities, takes advantage of strengths, and avoids or fixes weaknesses" (Barney 1997).

THE STRUCTURE OF THE INTERNET GAMING INDUSTRY

The current structure of the global Internet casino gaming industry is embryonic and dynamic. The scope, character, and product-market domain of the industry are yet to be determined. It is global, high-tech, competitive, and controversial.

The nature of the industry can be analyzed in terms of the Cravens Industry Analysis Model. Cravens Model focuses on the following five industry characteristics:

- industry size, growth, and composition;
- typical marketing practices;
- industry changes that are anticipated;
- industry strengths and weaknesses; and
- strategic alliances among competitors (Cravens 1997).

INDUSTRY SIZE, GROWTH, AND COMPOSITION

As of 1998, Internet gaming companies tend to be new, relatively unknown, "small-cap" companies (i.e., less than $5 million investment), subsidiaries operating in off-shore jurisdictions such as Antigua, Honduras, Turks and Caicos, British West Indies, and British Virgin Islands. There were over thirty (government authorized) legal sports books operating off-shore, about 50 percent operating on the Internet.

By the end of 1997, there were already over fifty commercial casino and sports book sites operating on the Internet. There were also legal sports book operations in Australia and Austria, and an international Internet lottery in Liechtenstein, as well as Internet bingo and Internet lotteries in some states of the United States (such as Oklahoma, Idaho and Washington).

FIGURE 1
Internet Gaming Operations (Representative Listing)

- Caribbean Casino (Turks & Caicos Islands)
- Casinos of the South Pacific (Cook Islands)
- Galaxi World (Tortola)
- Global Casino (Grenada)
- World Wide Web Casinos (Antigua)

Most Internet gaming companies offer only sports books. However, some are full service, multi-game casino gaming operations. At least fifteen major multi-game Internet casino competitors exist in 1997. Figure 1 contains a representative list of five major Internet casino gaming competitors and their locations. The number of operators has increased at a significantly high rate. An expected eventual shakeout and consolidation of firms could occur relatively quickly and rapidly, especially if there is a major scandal, or if the legal environment is clarified.

TYPICAL MARKETING PRACTICES

Existing Internet gaming marketing programs are not sophisticated or well supported. The industry does not exhibit any good examples of integrated communication strategies focusing on achieving realistic objectives. Typical Internet casinos currently offer a service line of table games, slot machines, and tournaments, and also provide chat facilities. Some companies are in the process of developing encrypted communications and on-line debit and smart cards. Barring legal impediments, new hardware, software, network, WebTV, PC-TV, and communications technologies will be integrated into existing operations on a continuous basis.

The resort destination superstore/megastore approach of Las Vegas could conceivably go on-line. The customer would be able to do almost anything on-line that could be done in a casino. Eventually, the customer would be able to enter an actual land or sea-based casino on-line. Intranets, extranets, internets, the casino floor, and the megastore could merge. In addition, the Internet player could have access to anything else on the Internet on a real time basis. This would be an advantage over regular casinos, but it would be offset if regular casinos offered their customers connections to the Internet.

The Internet virtual casino could be a part of a real casino. Gaming machines located on a casino floor could also be a part of an Internet casino. Internet gaming could be an extension of a casino. It could also be used as a test market for new casino services.

ANTICIPATED INDUSTRY CHANGES

There is no global, multinational, or international authority for regulating Internet gaming; such an international jurisdiction does not exist. Thus, reliable industry-wide statistics are not available. As of the late 1990s, major existing, land-based, water-based, and Native-American-based casino companies are not directly involved in Internet gaming.

The Internet gaming industry situation could change quickly and dramatically if Federal law were to allow states to determine the legality and regulation of Internet gaming. If a state—such as Nevada—were to license and regulate Internet gaming, the composition, nature, and potential of the Internet gaming industry would change dramatically.

INDUSTRY STRENGTHS AND WEAKNESSES

The Internet gaming industry has several strengths. It has access to infrastructure, facilities, technology, gaming knowledge, capital, and skilled personnel. The global demand for gaming services, personal computers, Internet products, and Internet entertainment services, such as non-commercial casino games on the *TV Guide Entertainment Network,* is substantial and growing.

The industry also has many weaknesses, including unfamiliar names, off-shore locations, product newness, weak brands, lack of credibility, and inadequate marketing programs. It is opposed by the premiere United States casino industry trade group—the American Gaming Association— ". . . because it isn't regulated, which threatens the integrity of the game." At present, traditional casinos could lose their licenses if they engaged in unregulated gaming (Quick 1997).

In summary, Internet gaming is a new, dynamic, high risk transaction situation for service providers, investors, gamblers, casinos, and government officials. It offers low-cost synergy and great business potential for the participants. It has been characterized by new corporations, new subsidiaries, mergers, strategic alliances, personnel changes, off-shore operations, foreign jurisdictional licensing, credibility measures, software development, stock speculation, technology licensing, litigation, political posturing, uncertainty, and lack of reliable, relevant information.

STRATEGIC ALLIANCES

Internet gaming competitors are forming strategic alliances.

"A strategic alliance is more than a joint venture. . . . In a true strategic alliance, two firms collaborate in a far more complete way by exchanging some key resources (although new entities may also be formed) to enable both parties to enhance their performance. . . . Alliances involve exchanges of. . . . new product technology, production technology and capacity, [and] access to sales and distribution networks" (Guiltinan and Paul 1994).

Internet suppliers and service providers are cooperating in the development of customers, client-server locations, software, transaction processing, secure communications, credibility measures, and financing.

COMPETITIVE MARKET SITUATION

The present Internet gaming competitive market situation can be characterized as *monopolistic competition*. The industry contains several firms, and each firm is providing differentiated services. The initiation of the Internet offering is occurring at a time when the traditional casino industry is becoming more competitive, is being politically scrutinized, and is growing more slowly.

Traditional competitors are searching for a competitive advantage. Some experts believe that ". . . in a more competitive environment, new technology will be an important dynamic to enhance casino profitability" (Ader 1997). New slot machines, such as Silicon Gaming's computer-based *Odyssey*™, are one application of new technology. Internet gaming is another.

The Internet market exhibits characteristics of both the introduction and growth stages of the product life cycle. Product strategy is experimental and lacks uniformity. However, model product lines and product mixes already exist. Product ideas are being copied from existing casino formats.

Distribution strategy is intensive at the start of the product life cycle. Every firm Internet site anywhere in the world is potentially available to every household in the world that has a PC, a modem, and an Internet access provider. This coverage will increase as personal computers and televisions merge.

Pricing strategy has not been at a premium level; it is not a "profit skimming" strategy. Rather, it has followed a penetration policy by setting prices and betting minimums at relatively low or economical levels.

Internet gaming follows the economy market, price model—in terms of coin denominations and minimum bets—found in many regular casinos. Promotional strategy, especially advertising strategy, has stressed *primary information* such as product information and availability, as opposed to *selective information*, such as one competitor versus another.

MARKETING STRATEGY

Strategic global marketing theory suggests that the appropriate marketing strategy for the pioneering firms of Internet gaming, given the expected nature of competition and the market, is a policy of strategic alliances and rapid diffusion. This would enable the pioneers to "ride the revenue curve" and achieve strong market share and high return on investment.

Potential advantages of a rapid diffusion strategy include economies of scale, experience curve effects, defining the rules of the game, distribution advantages, influence on consumer choice criteria and attitudes, preempting scarce resources, preempting competition, and high switching costs (Boyd, et. al., 1995).

TARGET MARKETS

There are many product markets and target markets in the traditional business of casino gaming. Each product market —such as slot machines in Las Vegas—is composed of market segments (e.g., premium players and grind players). A casino can elect to compete in one or more of the market segments in a defined and segmented product market. A market niche is a narrowly defined market segment, or a sub-segment of a specified market segment. A strategic business unit —such as an individual casino operation—is composed of a set of product markets, and many sets of target markets.

Internet gaming forms another strategic business unit. It will eventually contain product markets, target markets, and market niches. Each market would be reflected in a corresponding profile or databank. A separate marketing program could be developed for each target market, and for each market niche. Within a given organization, operating synergies could be identified across all strategic business units, product markets, market segments, and market niches. This would include traditional casino strategic business units and a new Internet gaming unit.

One combined target market perspective sees the typical traditional casino customer as a natural target market for Internet gaming. Another perspective sees a convergence of the typical casino gambler and the typical Internet user. The model profile is an adult male, 45 years of age, college educated, and earning $45,000 (Bellehumeur 1997).

An alternative perspective can be based on the typical gambler reported in the annual *Harrah's Survey of Casino Entertainment*. In 1995, Harrah's gambler's profile consisted of an adult male/female, 47 years old, some college/college graduate, earning $39,000, and a blue collar/retired/military/homemaker occupation (Harrah's 1996). One interpretation of

Harrah's report sees "... the typical casino gambler [as] the classic boomer" (Duff 1997).

In all of these perspectives, the cited customer profile, or relationship, is either too broad or questionable to make meaningful forecasts for future Internet gaming markets. For example, more research needs to be conducted to determine what proportions of casino customers use the Internet, purchase products on the Internet, and would gamble on the Internet. Also, there is probably a significant difference between local (resident) and visitor (tourist) casino customers with respect to Internet usage, purchase behavior, and propensity to gamble on the Internet. Furthermore, a meaningful Internet gaming target profile would include more consumer dimensions covering socio-demographics, attitudes, life-style, and consumption behavior.

CONSUMER NEEDS

The basic consumer needs associated with the Internet gaming service (such as convenience) are the same as those attributed to traditional casino gaming. However, these needs will have to be met given the heightened market sensitivity, the market success requirements, and the nature of the new medium.

Figure 2 indicates some specific identified consumer needs relevant to casino gaming in this new environment. The results of Internet product launch—and eventual market success or failure—will be dependent on

FIGURE 2
Consumer Needs

- Convenient
- Simple
- Fast
- Credible
- Exciting
- Fair
- Secure
- Easy
- Fun
- Worthwhile
- Available
- Different
- Variety
- Low Risk
- Safe
- Rewarding

managerial understanding of relevant consumer behavior, and the ability to meet articulated and sub-conscious consumer needs and concerns, to provide consumer experience and satisfaction, and to navigate the legal and regulatory environments.

INTERNET GAMING PRODUCT LIFE CYCLE

Internet gaming is in the initial phase of the introductory stage of the product life cycle.

> "The introductory stage of the product life cycle occurs when a product is first introduced to its intended target market. During this period, sales grow slowly, and profit is minimal . . . The marketing objective for the company at this stage is to create consumer awareness and stimulate trial—the initial purchase of a product by a consumer" (Berkowitz, et. al. 1997).

Internet gaming services are just now being commercialized. Members of the industry are still testing network software and other aspects of the service offering. Most potential consumers are not aware of the product or how to access it.

The competitive situation at market introduction is generally characterized by monopoly or monopolistic competition—one or a few firms. The product line consists of one or a few items—the set of desired features is not yet clear.

Distribution strategy focuses on building channels of distribution, and exclusive or selective distribution. Price strategy is either skimming oriented (high) or penetration oriented (low). Promotion strategy stresses primary demand as well as informing, and educating the market (Perreault and McCarthy 1996).

Figure 3 suggests an estimated market position of the Internet service in 1997 and the year 2000. Crossover from market growth to market maturity could occur by the fourth year of the product life cycle.

DIFFUSION OF INNOVATION

The diffusion of the innovation of Internet gaming across product adopter groups (e.g., innovators—2.5%; early adopters—13.5%; early majority—34%; late majority—34%; and laggards—16%) comprising the long-run market potential could be relatively quick, notwithstanding relatively slow and frustrating communications connections, privacy worries, security concerns, legality threats, fraud fears, and unfamiliar, confusing local, state, federal, foreign, and international legal environments. Innovators and early adopters are considered opinion leaders. It is assumed that 10

FIGURE 3
Internet Gaming—Product Life Cycle

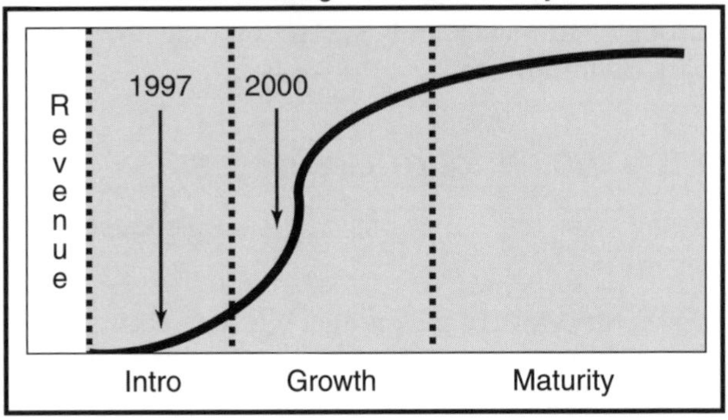

percent of the potential market—the opinion leaders—will try Internet gaming in the first year of its introduction.

If the opinion leaders are satisfied, Internet gaming could diffuse relatively quickly. In a credible and open market, free of artificial constraints, Internet gaming could diffuse more quickly. Diffusion is a function of the perceived relative advantage of the product over existing products, the perceived product compatibility with current consumption behavior and cultural values, the perceived level of complexity, the perceived trialability of the product, and the easy observability of product benefits (Cateora 1996).

Internet gaming exhibits relative advantages. It is compatible with current consumption behavior and cultural values; it is relatively simple to use for the targeted market; it can be tried on an experimental basis; and its benefits are readily observable and can be easily communicated. Furthermore—given the state of Internet technology in 1998—there are many competitors, international trade barriers are low, the capital cost of entry is low, the technology is widely available and easily accessible, marketing policies are penetration oriented, and consumers have the resources and easy access to a variety of retail locations.

The nature and type of the gaming innovation will affect the rate of diffusion. Internet gaming is an innovative product. It is as innovative to casino gaming as the microwave oven was to cooking. It meets the dictionary definition of innovation as ". . . the introduction of something new . . . a new idea, method, or device." "From a sociological viewpoint, any idea perceived as new by a group of people is an innovation" (Cateora 1996).

Internet gaming is a significant change from existing casino gaming services. It could be described as a discontinuous type of innovation. This type of change, as compared to a continuous innovation, such as disposable razors, is the most difficult to diffuse across a population. Such an innovation "involves the establishment of new consumption patterns and the creation of previously unknown products. It introduces an idea or behavior pattern where there was none before" (Cateora 1996).

Household consumers in the potential market are—more and more— familiar with and have been involved in both the Internet and casino gaming. It is assumed that there is a positive relationship between this past Internet and casino related behavior, and recognized service advantages, consumption patterns, cultural values, lack of complexity, trialability, and observability of the new product.

DIFFUSION OF INTERNET GAMING

The velocity of diffusion of Internet casino gaming innovation will be determined by corporate policies affecting:

- the level of market awareness of the product concept;
- the degree of market understanding of the product operating system;
- the ease of use of the computers, software, procedures (e.g., cash transfers) and network;
- the level of credibility (trustworthiness, financial security, privacy, and expertise) of the system providers and stakeholders;
- the ability to try out the system;
- clear product benefits for the consumer;
- obvious advantages over alternative forms of entertainment for the consumer;
- the amount of system compatibility with customer use habits with complementary products and systems; and
- the degree of compatibility with customer social and cultural values.

REPEAT USE OF INTERNET GAMING WEB SITES

Realization of Internet gaming market potential, and diffusion of the gaming service across the target market, is also dependent on repeat use of gaming web sites. Internet gaming web sites will experience the same challenges as any other commercial web site. Retaining desired gaming customers will be a challenge for marketing and web site managers.

A study by the marketing research firm, SurveySite, of visitors to web sites located in the United States and Canada indicated the relative attractiveness (in descending order) of the following factors of a web site: interesting content, enjoyable, layout quality, uniqueness, ease of finding information, exciting, visually attractive, easy to navigate, and the speed of moving around the site. Graphics quality was not considered ". . . an important consideration when compared to the other factors" (Rice, 1997).

MARKET POTENTIAL AND MARKET DEMAND

Market potential is a future estimate of "what a whole market segment might buy" (Perreault and McCarthy 1996). It is a feasible—realizable—objective for an industry. In the case of Internet gaming, the forecasted market potential is substantially higher than the forecasted market demand. The difference between the two forecasts would be like the relative difference between the number of households actually gambling in the past year and the number of households that are prone to gamble. The number of gambling prone households would be more than double those households actually gambling.

The market forecast (estimated market demand) is the expected demand, the revenue which would be generated for a future period for an industry, given specified economic and legal environments, marketing mixes, and marketing budgets. The global market demand—the expected demand—for the Internet gaming market has been estimated from about $9 billion to $40 billion—a range of $31 billion—for the year 2000 (Sinclair 1997; VentureTech 1997; and Walker 1997).

SEBASTIAN SINCLAIR'S MODEL

Figure 4 indicates a global Internet casino gaming market potential of about $25 billion and an optimistic market demand forecast for the global Internet casino gaming industry of about $9 billion for the year 2000 based on Sebastian Sinclair's forecasting model. Sinclair's model assumes 170 million Internet users, gaming revenue of $150 per adult, and a market penetration rate of 34 percent by the year 2000 (Sinclair 1997).

In 1996, the realized world market demand for Internet gaming was probably less than $200 million. A $200 million base growing to $9 billion would be over a 40-fold increase in a four year period. However, consider-

FIGURE 4
Internet Gaming Demand Forecast
Year 2000
(Sebastian Sinclair's Model)

Adult Home Internet Users (Global)	170M
US Casino Gaming Revenue	31B
US Adult Population	204M
Market Potential Penetration Rate	34%
Forecast: (170M × $150 = $25B × 34% = $9B)	

Sources: Christiansen/Cummings Associates, CommerceNet Consortium, Find/SVP, Morgan Stanley, Nielsen Media Research, Sebastian Sinclair, US Census Bureau

ing the recent declines in the growth rate of casino gaming in the late 1990s, along with the increasingly unfavorable political climate in the United States for casino gaming, the unclear legal environment for Internet gaming, and the lack of resources devoted to marketing Internet gaming, it seems even the low end estimates of the market forecast range are unlikely to be realized in such a short time frame.

BASS DIFFUSION MODEL

Figure 5 provides a forecast of the Internet gaming market potential using the Bass Diffusion Model (Calentone and Di Benedetto 1993; Bass 1969). The functional notation of the Bass Model is:

$$s_t = (p_0)(m) + (q - p_0)(y_{(t-1)}) - (a)(y_{(t-1)})^2$$

where s = sales, p = innovation rate, q = diffusion rate, m = market potential, y = cumulative sales, t = time period, a = slope coefficient, and $a = q/m$.

The Bass Model was applied to the Internet gaming problem using an innovation or trial rate of 10 percent, a diffusion or imitation rate of 50 percent, and a market potential of $25 billion, where year 1 is 1997, and year 4 is the year 2000. The resulting curve is a typical "s-curve" associated with marketing phenomena, including diffusion of innovation.

The Bass Model used in Figure 5 predicts accumulated first time sales of $14.5 billion for the year 2000, and the annual forecast first time sales

FIGURE 5
Market Potential Cumulative Forecast (Millions)

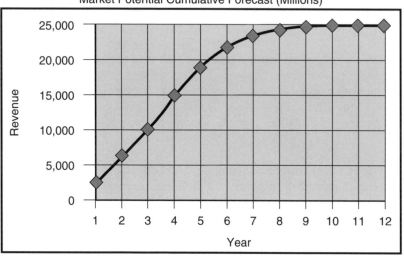

of $4.5 billion for the year 2000 (determined by subtracting accumulated sales of $10 billion for 1999 from the $14.5 billion accumulated by the year 2000).

Assuming that the repeat sales rate is 50 percent by the year 2000 (which would be expected to eventually rise to about 70 percent based on the experience in the Las Vegas casino market), the forecasted market demand would be about $9 billion for the year 2000. This forecast is consistent with that indicated by the Sinclair Model. A lower diffusion rate—such as 40 percent—would produce a flatter "s-curve" resulting in a lower demand forecast.

The model as demonstrated in Figure 5 indicates new revenues increasing at a decreasing rate after the year 2000 and stabilizing about the year 2006. However, the potential used in this model is based on the estimated potential in the year 2000.

This estimated market potential figure could change significantly depending on political, technological, legal, regulatory, cultural, competitive, and economic variables. Nonetheless, the Bass Model provides a dynamic working model of the industry, and its parameter values could be easily adjusted to reflect experience and changing environments.

AMENDED SINCLAIR MODEL

Figure 6 presents an optimistic market demand forecast for the global Internet gaming industry of about $3 billion for the year 2000 based on an amended version of Sinclair's model. It assumes a free market where traditional, regular casinos, as well as new, Internet casinos, participate in Internet gaming, licensed and regulated by credible, experienced state agencies, such as the Nevada Gaming Control Board.

In Figure 6, the number of Internet gamblers world-wide is estimated as the product of the global number of adult home Internet users times the percent of United States households visiting a casino in 1995. A global Internet casino market potential of $8 billion is calculated by multiplying the number of global Internet users times the average gaming revenue per adult in the United States. The number of potential global Internet gamblers is multiplied by the average gaming revenue per adult in the United States times the penetration rate to produce a global Internet gaming forecast of $3 billion.

The $8 billion Internet gaming potential estimate could be considered overstated because the number of adult home Internet users could be overstated. For example, research by the Yankee Group indicates that only 43 million United States homes will have Internet access by the year 2000—compared to the assumed 75 million United States and Canadian adult

FIGURE 6
Internet Gaming Demand Forecast
Year 2000
(Amended Sinclair Model)

Adult Home Internet Users (Global)	170M
Gamblers (USA %)	31%
Internet Gamblers (Global)	53M
US Casino Gaming Revenue	31B
US Adult Population	204M
Gambling Revenue per Adult	$150
Potential Forecast: (53M × $150 = $8B)	
Penetration Rate	34%
Demand Forecast: (53M × $150 × 34% = $3B)	

Sources: Christiansen/Cummings Associates, CommerceNet Consortium, Find/SVP, Morgan Stanley, Nielsen Media Research, Sebastian Sinclair, US Census Bureau

home users used in the Sinclair model. Furthermore, only 3 percent of these homes will have high-speed Internet access, greater than 28,800 BAUD.

On the other hand, the market potential could be understated because 61 percent of United States adults consider casino entertainment as acceptable for anyone, including themselves, whereas only 31 percent of United States households actually visited a casino in 1995 (Harrah's 1996).

It could be reasonably assumed that with the appropriate legal environment and marketing incentives, anyone who accepts the legitimacy of casino gambling as entertainment represents latent demand and could become an active customer. This would increase the number of Internet gamblers to about 104 million, resulting in a gaming market potential of about $16 billion, and a market demand forecast of about $5 billion for the year 2000.

Sinclair assumes that the United States' share of the global Internet usage will be about 45 percent—about 75 million adult home users—in the year 2000 (Sinclair 1997). Data from Jupiter Communications, Inc., indicates a lower forecast, predicting that there will be only 35 million on-line United States households (without considering the number of adult home users per household) by the year 2000 (Sandberg 1997). Also, the percent of Internet gamblers could be significantly less than the 31 percent of the United States household population that gambled in a casino during 1995 (Harrah's 1996).

FIGURE 7
Annual New Sales by Year ($ Millions)

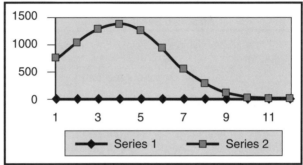

FIGURE 8
Accumulated Sales by Year ($ Millions)

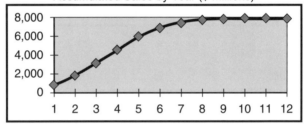

BASS MODEL APPLIED TO THE AMENDED SINCLAIR MODEL

Figure 7 indicates the shape of the annual Internet gaming revenue curve when the Bass Model is applied to the market potential produced by the Amended Sinclair Model, and where the innovative rate and the diffusion rate are kept equivalent to the original Sinclair Model (i.e, a market potential of $8 billion, an innovation rate of 10 percent, and a diffusion rate of 50 percent).

Series 1 data represent years into the future, with year 1 as 1997. The Series 2 data represent the annual new sales forecasts. The forecasted revenue for first time customers peaks at about $1.5 billion. Based on a repeat customer factor of 50 percent, Internet gaming revenue is forecasted at about $3 billion for the year 2000, which agrees with the forecasted demand in Figure 6 (the Amended Sinclair Model).

Figure 8 shows accumulated first time sales based on the Bass Model and the same data used in Figure 7 (market potential of $8 billion, innovation rate of 10 percent, and diffusion rate of 50 percent).

Cumulative sales in 1999 were $3.2 billion, and in the year 2000 they were $4.7 billion (resulting in the annual increase in the year 2000 of $1.5 billion).

DIFFERENT MARKET ASSUMPTIONS

Figure 9 provides conservative estimates of global market demand under different market assumptions. These assumptions are consistent with a more controlled market situation, where Internet gaming is considered by mainstream authorities as illegal and illegitimate, and where Internet gaming is not licensed and regulated in the traditional major gaming jurisdictions with established casinos.

In the first scenario, as shown in Figure 9, market demand for Internet gaming is projected at $1.2 billion for the year 2000. This assumes a global wagering handle of about $1 trillion in 1996, increasing to $1.5 trillion by the year 2000 for all forms of legalized, commercial gaming (where casinos

FIGURE 9
Internet Gaming Demand Year 2000 (Different Market Assumptions)

SCENARIO I

World Gaming Handle 1996 = $1 Trillion
10% Annual Compounded Growth Rate
1% Share of Market
8% Historical Hold Rate
($1T × 1.10 × 1.10 × 1.10 × 1.10 × .01 × .08 = $1.2B)

SCENARIO II

U.S. Gross Casino Revenue 1995 = $16B
10% Annual Compounded Growth Rate
5% Share of Market
($16B × 1.10 × 1.10 × 1.10 × 1.10 × 1.10 × .05 = $1.3B)

SCENARIO III

U.S. Gross Casino Revenue 1996 = $22B
10% Annual Compounded Growth Rate
5% Share of Market
($22B × 1.10 × 1.10 × 1.10 × 1.10 × .05 = $1.6B)

Sources: Duff, Harrah's, and La Fleur

---

and sports books are the dominant share at about 87 percent), and an historical 8 percent average hold rate (Christiansen 1996).

In the second scenario, market demand is projected to be about $1.3 billion in the year 2000, under the assumption of a 10 percent annual compounded growth rate of United States gross casino revenues ($16 billion in 1995), and the equivalent of a 5 percent share of the market for world-wide Internet gaming (La Fleur 1996).

In the third scenario, market demand is projected at $1.6 billion for the year 2000—assuming a 10 percent annual growth rate, a 5 percent share of market, and a 1996 base of $22 billion (Duff 1997 and Harrah's 1996).

SUMMARY AND CONCLUSIONS

Internet gaming is a new technological development in the global casino gaming industry, an on-line consumer service provided in the medium of cyberspace. Technically speaking, any household in the world equipped with a computer and a communications device can access any Internet gaming service provider on the globe.

There are many business opportunities in the global Internet gaming market. The product could replicate the offerings at existing casinos and casino-hotel megastores in real-time, multi-media, virtual reality. It could be integrated with casino intranets, casino floor facilities, and back-room operations. It could also be used as a test market to test new services.

Internet gaming could be implemented by new and existing casino organizations as a completely new offering, or a relatively low-cost, synergistic product line extension or product line flanker into new and existing target markets. It could be used as an element of competitive advantage, to enrich relationship marketing programs, or simply as a new stream of revenue for industry participants.

The global Internet gaming market potential is large and growing. With the exception of its legality, most of the underlying forces affecting the market potential are positive. Global computer usage, Internet usage, alternative Internet access modes, communications infrastructures improvements, Internet commerce, Internet financial transaction processing, casino gaming, and casino gaming acceptance are increasing. Relevant new hardware and software technology are being developed and gaming applications of new technology are rapid.

The overall global Internet gaming market is composed of several product-markets. Each product-market would consist of a specific set of Internet gaming services and a relatively heterogeneous group of identified customers. Each product-market would contain a set of relatively homogeneous market segments. One or more segments of each product-market could be selected as target markets, as product-market entries.

Each target market could be identified by a specific customer profile and supported by a specific marketing database. A specific marketing mix could be developed for each target market although many marketing mix elements could be standardized across product-markets and target markets. Each Internet gaming business could use its resource base to develop a set of marketing objectives and marketing mixes integrated across product-markets and target markets. These integrated sets of strategies could be significantly correlated with strategy sets of competitors in traditional casino gaming markets.

REFERENCES

Ader, Jason N. and Christine J. Lumpkins, 1997. *Global Gaming Almanac.* New York: Bear, Sterns & Co. Inc.

Barney, Jay B., 1997. *Gaining and Sustaining Competitive Advantage.* Reading: Addison-Wesley Publishing Company.

Barry, Glenn, 1997. "Haven't We Been Here Before?" *RGTonline. Internet.* March 6, 1997.

Bass, Frank M., 1969. "A New Product Growth Model for Consumer Durables." *Management Science,* 15, January 1969, pp. 215–227.

Bellehumeur, Michael, 1997. "Canadian Bill on Internet Gambling Introduced." *Internet,* March 16, 1997.

Berkowitz, Eric N., Roger A. Kerin, Steven W. Hartley, and William Rudelius, 1997. *Marketing.* Chicago: Richard D. Irwin, Inc.

Boyd, Harper W. Jr., Orville C. Walker, and Jean-Claude Larreche, 1995. *Marketing Management.* Chicago: Richard D. Irwin, Inc.

Cabot, Anthony, 1996. "Internet Gambling Report." *Internet,* November 26, 1996.

Calentone Roger J. and C. Anthony di Benedetto, 1993. *The Product Manager's Toolbox.* New York: McGraw-Hill, Inc.

Cateora, Philip R., 1996. *International Marketing.* Chicago: Richard D. Irwin, Inc.

Christianson, Eugene Martin, Sebastian Sinclair, and James S. J. Liao, 1996. "The United States Gross Annual Wager 1995." *International Gaming & Wagering Business,* August 1996, 17, 8, pp. 53–92.

Cravens, David W., 1997. *Strategic Marketing.* Chicago: Richard D. Irwin, Inc.

Duff, Christine, 1997. "Indulging in Inconspicuous Consumption." *Wall Street Journal.* April 14, 1997, B1-B2.

Guiltinan, Joseph P. and Gordon W. Paul, 1994. *Marketing Management.* New York: McGraw-Hill, Inc.

Harrah's, 1996. *Harrah's Survey of Casino Entertainment.* Memphis: Harrah's Entertainment, Inc.

Hower, Paul, 1997. "Gambling on the Internet: A Modest Proposal for Service Providers." *The Business Tech Guest Column, Internet,* April 15, 1997.

La Fleur, Teresa and Bruce La Fleur, 1996. *La Fleur's 1996 World Gambling Abstract.* Boyds: TLF Publications, Incorporated.

Perreault, William D. Jr. and E. Jerome McCarthy, 1996. *Basic Marketing.* Chicago: Richard D. Irwin, Inc.

Quick, Rebecca, 1997. "Web Gambling Faces Hurdle of Gaining Gamblers' Trust," *The Wall Street Journal Interactive Edition: Internet,* April 10, 1997.

Rice, Marshall, 1997. "What Makes Users Revisit a Web Site." *Marketing News.* March 17, 1997, p. 12.

Sandberg, Jared, 1997. "Talk, Talk, Talk." *The Wall Street Journal,* March 20, 1997, R4.

Sinclair, Sebastian, 1997. "Internet Casino Growth Predicted." *International Gaming & Wagering Business,* March 17, 1997.

VentureTech Inc., 1997. "VentureTech Executive Summary." *Internet,* March 8, 1997.

Walker, Terri C. and Richard K. Miller, 1997. *The 1997 Casino and Gaming Business Market Research Handbook.* Norcross: Richard K. Miller & Associates.

An Analysis of Sociological Factors Involved in the Decline of the New Zealand Racing Industry

Derek Syme

Since the late 1960s, and particularly in the 1990s, the New Zealand racing industry has experienced a marked decline in both attendance and turnover. This analysis discusses a number of social factors that have contributed to this decline. The reasons for racing's current downturn are complex, and they have their origins in cultural trends that have overtly and covertly shaped the betting behaviors of New Zealanders since the time of European settlement. Furthermore, there is little the racing industry can do in terms of altering the current values and attitudes of a predominantly non-betting New Zealand population.

During the final three years of the 1980s unemployment and inflation grew in New Zealand, and the country slipped deep into a state of recession. The years 1987 to 1990 are crucial ones in the context of New Zealand's gambling history. Not only were new forms of gambling introduced to the public; their introduction was to foster considerable societal debate concerning the nature and extent of gambling in New Zealand. By the end of the 1980s it was also quite obvious that the racing industry in New Zealand, like others overseas, was suffering from a marked decline in both crowd interest and turnover.

Prior to the introduction of Lotto in 1987, the Totalisator Agency Board (T.A.B.), along with other sectors of the racing industry, took steps by way of commissioned empirical research to learn more about both their actual and potential client base. The aim was no doubt to utilize the information gained to develop future marketing strategies.[1] These surveys also indicated that the racing industry itself was seeking clues as to why the interest in racing was waning, particularly in a climate where, until 1987, racing held a virtual gambling monopoly. After 1987, whether the racing industry was consciously looking for scapegoats for its decline or not, it found two in the form of the introduction of new forms of gambling and the October 1987 stock market collapse. Lotto, gaming machines and Instant Kiwi did indeed capture a share of the gambling dollar after 1987. It is also true that the October 1987 market crash signaled the beginning of an economic recession which four years later would appear to still be keeping the fashionable and 'big spenders' away from the course.[2]

The downturn in the economic circumstances of this group, and their direct effect on the racing industry has not been confined to their dwindling on-course spending. It is predominantly the members of the affluent middle class who make up the 40,000 registered owners of racehorse and breeding stock, either as individuals or as members of partnerships and syndicates.

Comprehensive analysis undertaken elsewhere by the writer argues that the racing industry was beginning to decline long before the advent of Lotto and the collapse of the New Zealand stock market.[3] While these two factors obviously affect the racing industry to some degree, for the industry to place all the blame only on these two particular happenings is being both simplistic and naive. This discussion develops the thesis that many other societal based factors are also involved in the general demise of the New Zealand racing industry.

A number of such factors are examined in the course of this analysis. First, the amount of discretionary income available for betting has always been limited and governed by priorities that have been dictated by marital status, household necessities, role performance and stigma. Second, the racing industry has relied on the family for the socialization of its new members—a process that, for a number of reasons, has been declining since the late 1960s. Third, the notion of *closure,* which involves the ritual and language of horse race gambling, operates to repel rather than attract potential spectators and customers. Fourth, a role is played in racing's decline by demographic factors such as age, gender, class and religion. Fifth, there are observable effects of new entertainment alternatives on the racing industry. Finally, the New Zealand racing industry has been grounded in a unique New Zealand cultural milieu whose emerging values and social behaviors have never been conducive to encouraging widespread and extensive gambling by all sectors of the population. Moreover, the many factors that have been instrumental in the recent gradual decline of this particular industry lie outside the sphere of its control.

REASONS FOR THE DECLINE OF HORSE RACING

Data from the study conducted by Wither (1985) indicate that the major reason for non-gambling participation in horse racing in 1985 was given as 'not interested.' Those most likely to have given such a response were high school graduates in the 45–49 age group, earning either less than

$N.Z.20,000 or more than $N.Z.40,000 per year. When it is considered that a host of factors inherent in the social structure constantly operate—both overtly and covertly—in developing the leisure and other interests pursued by any individual, the term 'not interested' becomes extremely complex as a reason for non-participation. Gidlow, et al. (1990) elaborate on this complexity by citing Cushman (1983).

"Leisure participation and demand is dependent on a host of changing social and economic factors. These include: personality and gender; family and peer group; age; lifecycle stage; educational, financial and class background; residential history; experience in childhood; ethnicity; influence of the media; the content of school curricula; and value positions and changes in the allocation of time to work and leisure" (p. 246).

Three themes emerge from the above quote. First, any theoretical explanation for racing's decline must take into account one hundred and fifty years of economic, demographic and social behaviors and attitudes. Second, the term 'not interested' can now be considered facile in terms of being any sort of explanatory mechanism for gambling at all or for non-participation in particular forms of gambling. Third—and the most problematic—one must decide on the most meaningful way of presenting the various social factors that have been mentioned by Cushman. A discussion framework is needed that not only identifies the many social factors involved but also explores the connections between them.

The author's solution to this challenge of complexity and clarity has been to construct and present the flow chart, as shown in **Figure 1**. The subsequent discussion of each element in the flow chart provides insight into why an individual has or has not gambled and—in the case of the former—the form that such a gamble may take.

Four points need to be made for ease of interpretation. First, the 'dotted' box on the left of line A is the recognition that several psychological factors may be involved in the gambling behaviors exhibited by any individual. However—as this study is grounded in sociological theory and explanation—no attempt is made to discuss these factors in this context. Second, two sets of percentages are presented with each type of gambling. Those identified with an asterisk are weekly participants while the percentage figures without an asterisk relate to those who have never participated in the named activity. The percentages are taken from phase one of a national survey on gambling and problem gambling in New Zealand undertaken by the research unit of the Department of Internal Affairs.[4]

Using a sample of 4,053 people, the survey's significance as a study is enhanced by the fact that it was the first survey in New Zealand to include data on participation rates in the "new" forms of gambling: Lotto, gaming

FIGURE 1
Social Factors that Underlie an Individual's Decision to Gamble
and the Form that Gambling Will Take

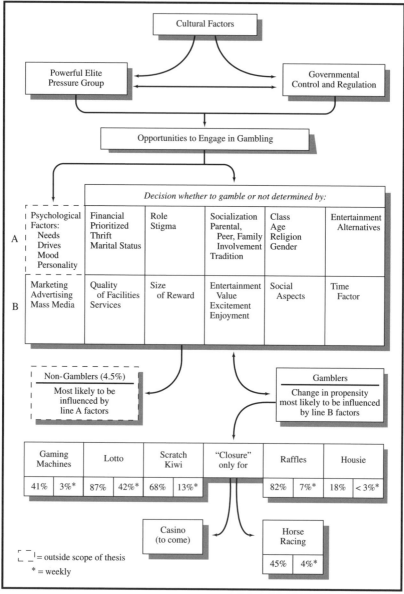

machines, and Instant Kiwi. The exception here of course is the 4.5 percent who have never gambled at all.

The third point is the social factors that may affect an individual's gambling behavior have been deliberately presented in two rows. Those factors in Row A are those that have tended to be overlooked by the hierarchy of racing in their search for the reasons for racing's downturn. Those in Row B, however, have been recognized and in all cases attempts have been made by the racing industry to address them.

The virtual gambling monopoly enjoyed by the racing industry ended in 1987 when the first of the three new gambling forms—Lotto—was sanctioned. However, long before this event, both the T.A.B. and racing clubs were aware of an industry downturn, particularly as manifested in on-course attendance. By 1979 this awareness had turned to the concern that was to prompt the first of several industry initiated surveys. The prime purpose of these surveys was twofold: to update the profiles of existing betting customers, and to give some indication of the wants and needs of such customers. A common feature of these surveys was that they all dealt with existing racing patrons and as such the information they yielded revealed no information about the non-horse race gambler. The findings of such surveys were to be later used in the formulation of racing industry marketing strategies.

Initially, the racing industry focused their ensuing marketing strategies on specific sections of the established betting market base in an attempt to get these individuals to increase their betting outlays. For example, the upgrading of T.A.B. offices and the introduction of new services appear to have been specifically motivated by the feelings of the discontenteds, a 16 percent segment of the T.A.B.'s established betting market identified in the commissioned McNair Survey (1987).

During the 1980s, and more specifically since the introduction of Lotto, the New Zealand racing industry at both a local and national level focused on the elements outlined in the cells of Row B in Figure 1 in their marketing strategies. However it is obvious from turnover figures and crowd attendance, which both continued to decline, that such strategies were not proving successful.[5] Such results are not surprising if one accepts the hypothesis that the social factors outlined in the cells in Row A of Figure 1 are those which primarily determine which individuals wager on horse racing and to what extent.

FINANCIAL CONSIDERATIONS

Crucial to the racing industry's economic viability is the issue of the level of punter expenditure. Elsewhere it has been advocated that, with the exception of the wealthy and the single male, punting expenditure by the average New Zealander has always been both measured and controlled.[6] Expenditure on racing has been governed by what can be called the *prioritized thrift ethic,* where initially necessity, and then other emerging cultural factors, dictate the nature of the priorities.

One of the major attractions of New Zealand as a place to settle has always been the ethos that—with hard work, good management, and thrift—one could come to own one's home. Hall, et al., (1984) indicate owner-occupier trends since 1911:

> "In 1911, for example, over 50 percent of New Zealanders were owner-occupiers. These figures have fluctuated during the course of the present century with a dip during the depression years of the 1930s when difficulties in obtaining finance and the generally depressed state of incomes increased the proportion of rental dwellers. The number of owner-occupiers, however, has always been greater than half the number of all households. At the 1981 Census in New Zealand the proportion of owner-occupiers had increased to just under 70 percent of all households" (p. 206).

A home of one's own offered tenure and hence, security. Furthermore, as Hall et al. point out, home ownership became not only: ". . . the crucial determinant of life chances in the city and, therefore, the clearest index of class position but (it) also provided an opportunity for owner-occupiers to generate wealth" (p. 206).

For those not yet in the position of owning their own homes, putting aside the weekly rent money became the number one household budget priority. Not only did the house itself become an index of class but so also did the furnishings and the other household items it contained.

A further financial priority—along with ingenuity and sewing skill—was the maintenance of a household dress code. What one wore in public contributed to one's respectability. Considerably more was spent by the individual on what was worn to a race meeting than was ever spent on actual betting.

The huge array of labor saving and recreational items that technological development introduced became further status symbols, and in many households a weekly budgeting item was the hire purchase installment which ultimately paid for such items. The extent of hire purchase on a national basis can be seen in data presented in *New Zealand Yearbook,* (1967, p. 612). At the end of 1966, $N.Z.64.3 million was owed nationally under hire purchase agreements. For example, average amounts on three categories of agreement were:

- television sets $204;
- other household and personal goods $60, and
- motor vehicles $766.

Another New Zealand cultural feature is a high level of private car owner-ship. In 1989 there was one car for every 2.3 persons (*New Zealand Year-book,* 1990, p. 549).

The expenditure on sports and amusements—which presumably in-cludes any household money spent on horse racing—has traditionally been low: two percent in 1910 and 1930 and rising to five percent in 1989. However, it must be remembered that this three percent increase now in-cludes a host of home centered technological leisure equipment, such as high quality stereos, video players, and camcorders, as well as computer equipment.

New Zealanders have traditionally had a high percentage of savings accounts per head of population.[7] Data from the *New Zealand Yearbook* (1990, p. 630) outline the development and progression of a savings bank system that encouraged regular deposits after New Zealand's first savings bank was established in Wellington in 1846. This habit of weekly savings with the Post Office was further fostered in the nation's primary schools in 1934 with the introduction of the school's savings bank scheme that was aimed at both encouraging early habits of thrift and capturing further potential adult savings customers. The success in retaining these young savings customers can be evidenced by the fact that by the mid-1950s, the Post Office savings bank controlled over eighty percent of the personal banking market.

More recently, changing social attitudes and practices has meant that the term *household* has undergone many changes, such as changing trends in living arrangements; parents now occupying two households; blended families; and de facto relationships. All these alternatives can imply a double paying of some basic costs, or a tighter budget for households primarily reliant on some form of government benefit.

Traditionally New Zealand women have had a major say in household expenditure and, perhaps apart from motor vehicle expenditure, have "called the shots" in terms of household purchase priorities.[8] "The home over the last few decades instead of being a retreat and bastion against the outside world, has become the center of consumption with women the prime caretaker of the household budget" (Banwell, 1991).[9]

Prioritized thrift underlies the order and speed with which larger con-sumer items are acquired. For example, once a couple know that the ar-rival of a first child is expected there is generally a conscious effort to save for the household items that a young child will require. In many family households, it was the tradition for all or most of the working male's weekly pay packet to be handed to the wife with the husband retaining a small portion for pocket money.

It has been illustrated that most New Zealand households prioritized expenditure from their weekly income. Furthermore, it can be argued that government and the moneyed elite, who were employers for the most part, ensured a system of wage control that never allowed the accumulation of a large cash surplus in the majority of households. Moreover, both the skill of budgeting and a set of expenditure priorities have been handed down from generation to generation as an element of the socialization process.

Unfortunately for the racing industry, in most household budgeting priorities, money to gamble on horse racing has always had a low priority. The level of New Zealand household expenditure in 1988/89 on gambling activity continued to remain small when compared with other forms of household retail spending, even when the new forms of gambling are included. Data from the *Review of Gambling in New Zealand* puts such expenditure into a perspective:

> "In 1988/89, expenditure on major forms of gambling averages $8.42 for each household per week compared with $14.50 for alcohol, $10.44 for sweets, spreads and beverages; $7.50 for takeaways, and $10.67 for meals out" (p. 28).

Data from *Gambling and Problem Gambling in New Zealand* (1991, p. 26) indicate that of all money spent on gambling, only 20 percent was spent by males on horse race gambling while women spent 6 percent. The racing industry, while feeling that this level of spending on horse racing is too low, may have to accept a reality that prioritized spending traits established over several generations cannot be changed easily, if at all.

The National Government in the early 1990s, once a staunch ally of the racing industry, unwittingly made the financial situation worse for the industry through certain policy changes. For example, the amount available for discretionary spending shrunk in many households when government support of youth in tertiary institutions and user pay health care were added to the household essential spending list.

ROLE AND STIGMA

Smith and McMath (1988, p. 53) stated that in their rural district, women of the 1950s generation:

> ". . . were seen to hold moral responsibility for the behavior of their husbands. Two women reported that people had congratulated them on the good influence they had been. In both cases this related to having a moderating effect on the husband's drinking. The women took these remarks as compliments, and felt proud that the effect was noticed" (cited in Park, 1991, p. 118).

Such thinking of women as moral guardians was not a new one as Dalziel (1986, p. 57) notes E. G. Wakefield's views of the 1840s that women were the key to the success of the colony:

> "They (women) were to create and care for house and home, thus freeing men for the work of production and would act as moral guardians for the men and children in their families" (cited in Park, 1991, 28).[10]

The wife's role as the *guardian of family morals* would appear to have a direct link with the budgeting role discussed in the previous section. Any limitations that could be placed on the amounts spent on gambling and drinking obviously meant more for the household budget. Perhaps the key word in the last sentence is 'limitation' as it suggests that the aim was not to completely eradicate both gambling and drinking behavior. It is likely that most women, at least until the late 1960s, were aware of the part played by a day at the races, an afternoon at the rugby, and an hour in the pub as elements in the phenomenon of male *mateship*. To persist in insisting that these activities be stopped completely would have placed the wife in the role of *henpecker* or *wowser*. Drinking and gambling could therefore be curbed in two ways, either by restricting the behaviors to certain times and occasions, or by restricting the amount to be spent on each occasion.

Anecdotal information provided to the author suggest that women consult with other women in order to decide what is a fair and reasonable amount to allocate to their husbands for expenditure on such 'male pleasures.' Often a combination of both strategies applied. Such an arrangement ensured that the male did not lose face among his male peers and the weekly household budget remained reasonably intact. The unattached male however, has always found himself free of such 'moral' restrictions. Statistical data from the Le Heron study, (1980) and the McNair survey (1987) also illustrate the point that the great majority of bettors—when betting—do so with a predetermined and fixed amount on each betting occasion.

One of the features of early gambling practices, particularly in the smaller rural community, was its visibility. Part of the attraction of betting with the local bookmaker was the greater degree of anonymity he could offer. Ticket selling outlets on the local race course were clearly marked "ten shillings," "one pound" and "five pound" and were usually sited adjacent to the totalisator odds indicator where virtually all at the course gathered to read the odds before betting. Those who bet, and how much they bet, were very visible to the local community who came to support the annual or bi-annual race meeting. In later years, those entering and leaving the community's only T.A.B. could be similarly observed. Once it was considered 'not the done thing' for women to be seen in such betting queues. Nor would people such as the local clergy, school teachers and other 'pillars of the community' have enhanced their role image by being seen constantly in the five pound betting queue. However such situations were probably infrequent as those just mentioned were also subjected to the constraints of both the prioritized thrift ethic and the moral constraints imposed by spouses.

This was a form of informal sanctioning. Conforming or not conforming to such middle-class community norms made the difference in being classified as 'deserving' or 'undeserving' poor. Such class-based distinction frequently had social consequences long before this. Richard John Seddon's 1898 old age pension of six shillings and eleven pence a week was only to be paid to those over the age of 65 ". . . who were of good moral character and led a sober and reputable life" (Stitch, 1971, p. 38). In 1926 the Coates Government introduced a family allowance of two shillings per week for the third and every subsequent child under the age of fifteen. Such an allowance however would not be paid if either of the parents was of 'notoriously bad character' or did anything "dishonorable in the public estimation" (Stitch, 1971, p. 39).

Clearly visible excessive betting (and drinking) could generate potential future economic consequences for both the individual concerned and their family. Erving Goffman (1963) perceptively remarks that such persons were viewed by the evaluating public as having a 'spoiled identity.'

From its inception, racing by its very nature created a milieu where stigma could be readily attached. Two aspects of this milieu—both with particular potential for stigma attachment—have already been mentioned: "responsible" gambling and gambling by women. Other facets of the racing milieu that have attracted stigma and have not yet been mentioned include race 'fixing,' illegal bookmaking, horse doping and corrupt practices.

The negative beliefs and suspicions that stigmatization generate are still deeply ingrained in many sectors of the New Zealand population. For example, many women still would not enter a T.A.B. on their own. This 'stigma factor'—in conjunction with the other factors discussed in this analysis—serves to discourage rather than encourage individuals to wager heavily on horse races.

SOCIALIZATION FACTORS

Prior to the 1960s, on-course attendance at race meetings tended to be both a traditional and a family occasion. Both factors have important implications for the current levels of spectator turnout. Such traditions were established at a time when few other forms of family entertainment were available, when the population was less mobile and the family was more united than at present. In recent years, many factors have contributed to the breakdown of such traditions, particularly with respect to adolescent family members. Since the 1960s, for a variety of reasons, adolescents have left small New Zealand rural communities and headed for the cities in increasing numbers. *Push* factors include the lack of opportunities in declining rural economies and the mechanization that has taken away much of the need for unskilled 'muscle power' in traditional rural based occupations. *Pull* factors include the need to attend boarding school or a tertiary institution, to seek employment, or simply to respond to the lure of the 'bright lights' of the city. The ownership of transport and the relaxation of social norms with regard to living arrangements (i.e., mixed flatting or simply living together) have also facilitated such movement. To this urban migration factor must be added the obvious fact that the rapid increase in family breakup through divorce or separation implies a reduction in the numbers who attend any event as a complete family.

Consequently, for various reasons, the tradition of attending the races as a family has been eroded in recent years. This change in the tradition of family attendance has an important implication for the socialization of new members into the racing milieu.

At another level, *tradition,* or what might be aptly named as 'habit' or 'routines,' is also operative. These routines underlie the behaviors that could be recorded in most households, and apply to such everyday happenings as the timing and nature of meals, the place and time of completing family shopping and even to the viewing of television programs. Routines are also established with activities that take place outside the home, such as the time one leaves for work, or has beer with work mates on a Friday night. Conversations with numerous T.A.B. patrons revealed that routine or habit governed their betting behavior. Most of the T.A.B. punters interviewed visited a particular T.A.B. agency at a set time each week, with a set amount of betting money, for reasons discussed above. Such inquiries indicated that the amounts bet and the types of bets taken have remained stable for years. If this is the case among the general public, then the many recent marketing innovations introduced by the racing industry may have done little, if anything, to change these established and habitual patterns of gambling behavior.

Such traditions, whether on or off course, consciously or unconsciously play a major role in the socialization process. More importantly, these 'traditions' were manifested in the setting of the most powerful agent of socialization, the family. A family day at the races had the potential to transmit many 'middle class' messages to children: that appearances were important, that betting should be measured and controlled, that one should be a 'good' loser, and—at least prior to the 1950s—'nice' women did not bet. More importantly, such a visit introduced the young person to the bet types, jargon and processes of horse racing and made considerable inroads on the concept of 'closure,' discussed in the following section. No doubt there were some children who saw a day at the races as a negative experience, a drawn out occasion which offered them little opportunity for participation and whom regarded the money they saw their father spend as being wasted. Such children possibly decided at this early point in their lives that horse racing was never going to be of serious interest to them.

By the end of the 1960s, for reasons that centered around suburban home ownership and alternative activities, the family day at the races began to decline. Or, if the family did attend, it was more likely that the adolescents of the family would not be present because of the 'push' and 'pull' factors mentioned previously. The decline in the socialization process began to take from the racing industry its virtual sole mechanism for inducting enthusiastic new members to participate fully in its specialized activities.

Other major elements in the socialization process, except perhaps for peer groups, were not in a position to do what the family had once done. The government and its agencies, along with the church, certainly did not encourage horse race gambling. Until paid advertising by the racing industry made an appearance from the 1980s onward, the mass media agencies had played little part in explaining the rituals of racing.

Many new recruits to sporting and leisure pursuits are first socialized into these activities by a major agency of socialization: the schools. Schools have never been involved with organizing class visits to the races or the T.A.B. and in all likelihood they never will. Thus, the racing industry, unlike most other organizations, had relied virtually solely on the family to undertake the induction of new participants on its behalf. The intergenerational process of socialization into the world of horse racing is in decline. Unfortunately for the racing industry, the dynamics of this process create a situation, which given the existing circumstances, will only get worse in the future.

CLOSURE

Wither (1987, p. 17) presents data to show that 68 percent of her sample did not participate in gambling on horses because they were 'not interested.' It can be hypothesized that among the 'disinterested' in Wither's sample there are those who believe that, to be a successful punter, the individual requires a knowledge of both racing procedures and horse form. In other words there is a high level of disinterest because many potential bettors feel they lack the necessary knowledge to bet effectively.

The diminishing influence of the family in inducting new generations to horse racing and its associated gambling can be linked with the concept of *closure.*

Sociologists utilize the concept of 'closure' in their analysis of social relationships. Weber (*Economy and Society,* vol. 1, pp. 43–46) states:

"A social relationship, regardless of whether it is communal or asso-ciative in character, will be spoken of as "open" to outsiders if and insofar as its system of order does not deny participation to anyone who wishes to join and is actually in a position to do so. A relation-ship will, on the other hand, be called "closed" against outsiders so far as, according to its binding rules, participation of certain persons is excluded, limited or subjected to conditions. Whether a relation-ship is open or closed may be determined traditionally, affectionally, or rationally in terms of value or expectations" (Cited in Giddens and Held, *Classes, Power and Conflict,* 1982, p. 77).

The particular type of social interaction discussed here is that of a specific monopolistic economic association and its relationship with actual and potential clients. The four percent of those who bet on a regular weekly basis can be identified as a specialized customer group. These 'regulars,' who are avid customers of the T.A.B. as well as race courses, are volunta-rily pursuing an activity which they themselves would perceive as being specialized. 'Regulars' do not see themselves as being deviant and carry out their activity in a largely informal but existing and normative social structure (Rosecrance, 1985, p. 132). The 'regulars' would consider their relationship with the racing industry to be 'open' where non-participants are likely to perceive their relationship with the same industry as a 'closed' one.

Three of the four social mechanisms of closure that Weber outlines (op. cit. 78) can be applied to non-participation in gambling.[11] Closure on a traditional basis, where family relationships with gambling and horse rac-ing involvement determines interest, operates because of the decline in socialization into the racing world by the family.

A second type of rational closure operates on the grounds of expedi-ency, a concept that is coming to have more relevance in a computer driven electronic age. Another variation of closure operates on a basis of *value rational commitment,* such as those who hold an explicit religious belief that any form of gambling is wrong or deviant.[12] Successful participation in horse race gambling, unlike some other forms of gambling, is more susceptible to the operation of a variety of closure mechanisms. In the racing milieu context, closure is more than just the lack of perceived knowledge thought to be required in order to participate effectively and with full understanding.

Of the gambling types listed in Figure 1, only two—racing and casino activity—appear susceptible to closure mechanisms. The individual can participate in various instant forms of gambling by simply asking for a ticket or dropping a coin in a slot. This, however, is not the case with horse racing and casino gambling. While horse racing can be reduced to simply picking a horse number, the mechanics of actually betting are more complicated, and a knowledge of betting type options is required. Many find the T.A.B. betting slip complicated, a fact recently recognized by the T.A.B. and is no doubt the rationale behind the introduction of *lucky dip* type tickets, where all the customer has to do is hand over their money in order to receive a pre-selected ticket.

Closure also operates at other levels of the racing industry. Those who feel that a knowledge of the runner's prior race form is the first prerequisite to successful betting are often unable to interpret the host of coded and jargon filled information that is contained in the specialized form guides. The race commentary itself generates closure for some through its use of jargon and many have difficulty making sense of such phrases as 'the executive sit,' 'buried' or 'facing the breeze.'

At various points, the very nature of racing and the betting process tends to discourage rather than encourage prospective betting customers. The nature of the more sophisticated and complicated casino games that were introduced to New Zealand in the 1990s generate similar problems of closure for potential customers.

An added closure factor regarding casinos may be that of required dress. If the high standards of customer presentation that is demanded by some overseas casinos—such as those in London—had been adopted in New Zealand, then those who do not own formal or semi-formal dress would not gain admittance to the gambling facilities, or would be put off by the expected standard. In contrast, part of the success of Lotto and Instant Kiwi as gambling activities lies in their simplicity and the obvious ease with which the customer can participate.

CLASS, AGE, RELIGION, GENDER

Religious belief is most likely to have an affect among those who choose not to gamble. Data from the Wither Survey (1985, p. 70) indicates that only eight percent will not bet money on horses or dogs for religious reasons. The discussion on stigma indicated that those of the middle and upper classes still do not see the T.A.B. as a desirable place and are reluctant to be seen there. Those of the middle and upper classes—with the highest amounts of disposable income for discretionary spending—choose to spend their money on other items (i.e., on overseas travel, which was listed as an expenditure item for the first time in 1989 New Zealand household expenditure figures). It is also this group which is the most likely to have the added burden of financially supporting children who are undergoing tertiary education. (The 'failure to socialize' argument can also be applied to this group.)

In an effort to retain this particular sector of the gambling market, some of the more larger and affluent urban racing clubs have attempted to upgrade facilities and incorporate events that may have status appeal, such as fashion shows and 'champagne' lunches. While this group's income may be higher than average, expenditures by members of the middle and upper classes may be governed by the concept of prioritized thrift. Middle and upper class women are also influenced by gender and age factors.

The lower participation rate by women in gambling activities is in part explained by adherence to a long established role expectation that 're-spectable' women do not gamble, at least not in public. For generations of women, the key question on a local race day was not "Who was going to win?" but rather "What clothes should be worn?" Until recently, few women had money that they could call their own, as what was left after the wage earner had taken his 'pocket money' each week was viewed as 'housekeeping' money with all in the household dependent on the matriarchal wisdom that lay in its thrifty spending. While the male could bet with his money, most women could only bet with the 'family' money, a course of action that was declined by most. By the 1960s—although social, economic and technological change had brought real changes to the role of married women, which often meant a wage of their own—earlier socialization factors had internalized attitudes and values which continued to dictate current spending behaviors. In spite of women having more money at their disposal than at any other time in New Zealand's history (*New Zealand Yearbook,* 1990, pp. 363–366), the potential income for the racing industry in effect had been lost by social processes that had taken place several decades ago. In the 1980s and 1990s, a generation of women over 30 were virtually lost as potential customers to the racing industry.[13]

The problem for the racing industry is how to attract the next generation—those in the eighteen to thirty age group—as future customers. However, the oldest women in this cohort were pre-adolescent when some of the changes discussed above rooted in the 1970s. They have been socialized in an era that has seen New Zealand's women's movement reject activities and values that were perceived as being central to the "male mateship" syndrome, such as rugby, racing and beer. It is perhaps not just a coincidence that along with diminishing racing crowds and turnover, rugby attendance figures and beer consumption have also fallen.

The final factor for discussion is that of age and betting behavior, as presented in Table 1. While 45 percent of the population have placed a bet

TABLE 1
Involvement in Horse/Dog Racing by Age

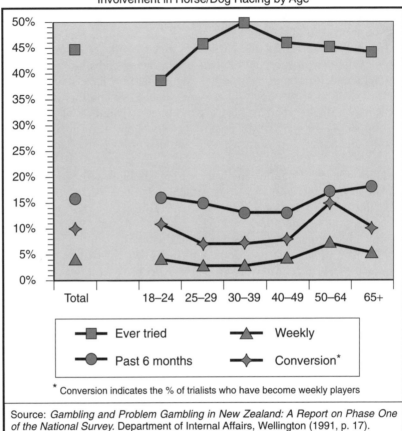

* Conversion indicates the % of trialists who have become weekly players

Source: *Gambling and Problem Gambling in New Zealand: A Report on Phase One of the National Survey.* Department of Internal Affairs, Wellington (1991, p. 17).

on a horse or dog race, only 15 percent indicated that they had done so in the six months preceding the survey. Only 10 percent of those who have tried this form of gambling have become weekly participants. Comparing additional data from the same survey, the finding emerges that the younger generation is not overly interested in horse racing. Only 36 percent in the 18 to 24 age group have tried horse race gambling compared with the 62 percent who have tried gaming machines, the 76 percent who have tried Instant Kiwi and the 84 percent who have played Lotto. Between the ages of 21 and 27, gambling on horse racing by the more regular group shows a decline.

At least two factors may account for this downward trend. First, some of this age group will be completing tertiary education and will have prioritized what little money they have for expenditure on necessities such as food and rent. Second, others in this age group who are establishing households, or who have become parents, will have other monetary priorities.

Although there are no raw data to prove it, it is likely that those in the 21–27 age group who continue to gamble on a regular basis are single males. Approximately 10 percent of those who tried horse race gambling earlier return after the age of forty to continue betting on a regular basis for at least ten years. Data from the Abbott and Volberg (1991, p. 17) study indicate a marked increase in the involvement in horse and dog racing by those in the 45 to 60 age group. That the number of regular weekly bettors should be at its highest between the ages of 50 and 64 is not coincidental. Still earning, and probably by now with a freehold home, a vehicle, and no longer tempted to purchase the current technological gadgetry, this age group would possibly have the greatest amount of discretionary income. The fall-off in gambling participation after the age of sixty is possibly influenced by the decrease in income on retirement.

Perhaps of more importance, however, is the socialization factor. The 50 to 64 year old age group represents the last group of financially viable males who not only grew up with—but who were well socialized into— the world of 'male mateship.' Members of this cohort would have been between the ages of 10 and 24 when the first T.A.B.s opened in the early 1950s, a decade when rugby and racing drew record crowds and *the six o'clock swill* prevailed in hotels. Not only were such behaviors tolerated by women, they were expected if one were to be considered 'a real man' and 'one of the boys.' For those who were self-conscious about this 'macho' image, even in the 1950s, they often still attended such fixtures simply because there was little else to do in New Zealand on a Saturday.

The opening of T.A.B. agencies in hotels in the 1980s and 1990s appears to be directed at this particular group. However, such a measure in terms of a marketing strategy would appear to have a limited life as, like R.S.A. members, over the next decade or two their numbers will dwindle markedly. What is even worse for the racing industry is that the numbers in this particular cohort would have been exaggerated by the fact that many were members of the post World War II 'baby boom' population bulge. When this factor is linked with the decrease in family size, the racing industry, like many other commercial enterprises, is faced with the task of selling its product to a shrinking market.

ENTERTAINMENT ALTERNATIVES

The last two decades have brought with them a host of new entertainment options, particularly for young people. Whereas there was little competition for the racing industry until the late 1960s for both a person's time and entertainment dollar, this situation has changed markedly. The falling race day attendance figures and totalisator turnover are an indication that the population—and particularly younger segments—are finding other things to do with their time and money in the 1990s. Approximately one third of those in the 18–24 age group in *Gambling and Problem Gambling in New Zealand* (1991, pp. 14–18) state that they purchase a Lotto ticket weekly, while approximately 14 percent purchase Instant Kiwi tickets and 6 percent use gaming machines on a weekly basis. With the exception of Lotto, which rises to approximately 45 percent, participation in the other two gambling forms tapers off until the 'baby boomers' cohort is reached when participation rises slightly. These data suggest that even when the new forms of gambling were introduced, approximately two-thirds of the 18 to 24 age group are simply not interested in participating on a weekly basis in any form of gambling. While the optimist may see this group as a potential market base for the racing industry, it may prove to be exceedingly difficult.

DISCUSSION

The purpose of this study has been to closely examine the reasons for the current downturn in racing's on-course attendance and betting turnover. The reasons most often cited by the industry—the introduction of Lotto and the Instant Kiwi, and the 1987 collapse of the New Zealand stock market—may have had some part to play, but placing the blame for racing's present situation on these two factors was both simplistic and naive.

Other social, historical, and economic factors demonstrated that spending on gambling in New Zealand was, and is, governed by the prioritized thrift ethic which varies according to one's financial circumstances. Single males traditionally spend more until marital status and family obligations create new priorities for household income, with rent or mortgage payments assuming the highest expenditure priority. When distinctions between the 'deserving' and 'undeserving' poor became socially and economically important, excesses in drinking and gambling became stigmatized. Such attitudes, particularly among the middle class, persist into the 1990s.

The racing industry, unlike many other leisure forms, has always been heavily reliant on the family for the socialization of new members into its activities. Since the 1960s in particular, this intergenerational process—highly motivated by habit and tradition—has rapidly broken down.

Women have played, even if somewhat covertly, a key role in the regulation of betting turnover. Since the time of settlement women were socialized into rarely betting themselves in order that 'respectability' might be maintained. As traditional keepers of the household purse, and more recently in their rejection of those activities associated with 'male mateship,' it is not likely that they will become racing industry customers. While in earlier times there was never much money left in the household purse for leisure and entertainment, the current political philosophy of *user pays* for such social items as health care and tertiary education may mean that there will be even less discretionary money in the future.

A numerically inflated cohort of post-World War Two 'baby boomers'—who were socialized into horse racing when the industry was at its zenith—are now at a stage in the life cycle where their numbers can only continue to dwindle. The major task facing the racing industry is the recruitment of a new generation of gambling customers. However, data were presented which indicated that up to two-thirds of the 18 to 24 year old age group are not interested in any form of weekly gambling participation. Finally, *closure* operates against, rather than for, the recruitment of new horse racing customers.

It would appear that the racing industry is in a 'no win' situation as there is little it can effectively do to change the existing demographic, social and economic factors which overtly and covertly influence betting behavior. The industry cannot take away entertainment alternatives, and it cannot alter the life cycle stages and rites of passage that underlie and ultimately dictate spending priorities. The racing industry is rapidly losing its century old socialization agent and has nothing with which to replace it.

The New Zealand racing industry must accept that it exists in a societal environment that is the result of a unique interplay of social, economic and political forces. While such forces have provided a cultural context for the racing industry, they have also socially shaped the values and attitudes of those who were—and are—active within it. The values of industry, thrift and respectability quickly emerged in New Zealand society, where they acted covertly and overtly as regulators of individual betting expenditure. It appears unlikely, after one hundred and fifty years, that these values will be abandoned in order that New Zealanders can actually live out the clichéd fantasy that they are a nation of compulsive and excessive horse race gamblers.

---

1. In 1979 the National Research Bureau carried out a survey for the Auckland Trotting Club. In 1980 the New Zealand Racing Authority commissioned Dr. R. B. Le Heron to analyse several central North Island racing crowds. In 1987 A. G. B. McNair completed a survey for the Totalisator Agency Board.
2. The figures from a Wellington Racing Club meeting held in January 1991,

which was staged as an 'up-market' event featuring a 'Magic Millions' one million dollar race, illustrate this. Despite increased advertising, attendance figures were down 37 percent, T.A.B. takings were down 800.000 dollars and on-course turnover was down for the previous year's meeting.

3. Syme, D. A. "The Social Context of Horserace Gambling in New Zealand. An Historical and Contemporary Analysis." Unpublished Ph.D. Thesis, Victoria University of Wellington, 1992.

4. Ibid.

5. *New Zealand Official Yearbook,* 1990, p. 167.

6. Syme, op. cit.

7. See *Women and Money,* (1981, pp. 29–39) for a detailed analysis of the frequency and nature of household savings in New Zealand in the late 1970s.

8. Data from *Women and Money* (p. 36) show that nearly a quarter of males in the sample controlled the car buying decision. In the remaining cases the decision tended to be shared between husband and wife.

9. In only 9 percent of surveyed households did the women have no say in the household budget. The survey findings suggest that it was the women who were influential when it came to budgeting (p. 89).

10. See Anne Summers (1975, Chapter 3) *Damned Whores and God's Police* for a discussion on how overt and covert 'rules and conventions' have dictated the sporting, drinking and gambling attitudes and behaviours of Australian women.

11. The fourth social mechanism outlined by Weber is 'affectional closure' which has a greater degree of application in situations involving erotic relationships or those where personal loyalty is involved.

12. Wither (1987, p. 17) records that 8 percent of her sample did not gamble on horse racing for religious or moral reasons.

13. This is not to say that all women are educated and subscribe to 'middle class' values. Nor should the discussion imply that women do not bet at all. The Abbott-Volberg Report (1991, p. 26) indicates that of the total money spent by New Zealand women on gambling, only 6 percent is wagered on horse and dog racing. The McNair Survey (1987) identifies two small groups of women who bet on horse racing. The first (approximately 6 percent of the population), are described as women who are mainly 'homemakers,' who are unadventurous in their betting behavior and are unlikely to bet on-course. The second defined group (less than 2 percent of the population), are identified as young women who bet infrequently when they attend on-course as a social occasion.

REFERENCES

Abbott, M. and Volberg, R. (1991). *Gambling and Problem Gambling in New Zealand.* Wellington: Department of Internal Affairs.

Banwell, C. (1991). "I'm not a Drinker Really: Women and Alcohol," in Park, J. (ed.), *Ladies A Plate.* Auckland: Auckland University Press.

Census and Statistic Department (1967–1990). *New Zealand Official Yearbook.* Wellington: Department of Statistics.

Department of Internal Affairs (1990). *Review of Gambling in New Zealand.* Wellington: Department of Internal Affairs.

Gidlow, B., Perkins, H., Cushman, G., and Simpson, C. (1990). "Leisure" in Spoonley, P., Pearson, D., and Shirley, I. (eds.), *New Zealand Society.* Palmerston North: Dunmore Press.

Le Heron, R. (1980). "Summary of Research into Racegoers and Race Attendance Patterns." Palmerston North: Massey University.

McNair, A.G.B. (1987). "Survey Report on T.A.B. Customer Behavior." Wellington: A.G.B. McNair.

National Research Bureau (1979). "Attendances and Attitudes to Night Trotting at Alexandra Park." Consumer Research Report prepared for the Auckland Trotting Club, Auckland.

Rosecrance, J. (1985). *The Degenerates of Lake Tahoe.* New York: Peter Lang.

Sutch, W. (1971). *The Responsible Society in New Zealand.* Christchurch: Whitcombe and Tombs.

Syme, D. (1992). "The Social Context of Horserace Gambling in New Zealand. An Historical and Contemporary Analysis." Unpublished Ph.D. Thesis, Victoria University of Wellington.

The Society for Research on Women Inc. (1981). *Women and Money.* Johnsonville: Society for Research on Women.

Weber, M. (1982). "Selections from Economy and Society," vols. 1 and 2; and "General Economic History" in A. Giddens and D. Held (eds.), *Classes, Power and Conflict.* London: Macmillan Education Ltd.

Wither, A. (1987). "Taking A Gamble: A Survey of Public Attitudes towards Gambling in New Zealand." Wellington: Department of Internal Affairs.

Casino Management Issues

Section 2

Developing a Target Guest Entertainment Experience Delivery System

Dean M. Macomber

Gaming is a business.

As a business, gaming has a product. The product is a set of leisure time services which includes but is not limited to gaming. The goal for casino executives is to initially conceptualize and accurately align the services with consumer needs, wants and expectations. Thereafter, the goal shifts to consistently producing those services at predetermined target levels of performance. The challenge is to achieve these goals in a business which has a complex set of production and consumption variables. One approach is to utilize a systematic approach to conceptualizing the service and then a systems approach to produce and maintain the service.

Not all organizations will be capable of taking a true and total systems approach to the challenge. Standing in the way will be ingrained cultural objections, built-in organizational impediments and/or limited financial resources (real or perceived). For those gaming companies who choose to do so, however, the rewards could be meaningful in both competitive positioning and raw financial terms.

DESCRIPTION OF THE GAMING "PRODUCT"

A. The Casino Industry and the Product It "Sells"

Casinos are part of the leisure time industry seeking to attract consumers' discretionary, disposable income. While gaming may be the focal point of a visit to a casino, the gaming product has expanded to mean much more. Today, a gaming visit certainly includes enjoying the roller coaster excitement created by the win-loss cycles at the blackjack table or slot machine. But equally important, a trip to a casino also means having dinner near a waterfall, vicariously engaging in the social sport of people watching people at a bar, seeing a high-tech pyrotechnic extravaganza, relaxing by a Caribbean inspired pool or purchasing *haute couture* at a Romanesque mall.

The "product" which customers come to buy—and therefore what casinos sell—is an experience, a gaming related entertainment experience. It is the responsibility of casino management to conceptualize, produce and deliver entertainment experiences that meet the needs, wants and expectations of the guest at a price that creates a perceived value.

This responsibility does not exist in a vacuum, however. Competitively this experience must be executed in a manner that results in the business capturing its fair share or greater than fair share of the existing or future demand. Under capitalism, the final test is financial. The experience must be manufactured and sold at a ratio of revenues to costs that results in operations meeting or exceeding target financial returns.

B. The Key Element To Success—Consistency

Any product that is successful over the long term depends upon the initial alignment of the customer's expectations for the product with the actual delivery of the product. This evaluation first extends to the experience qualitatively ("Did I get what I wanted?") and, if that criteria is satisfied, to an evaluation of whether the price paid for the experience created a perceived value ("Did I get what I paid for?").

Thereafter, long term success is built upon generating a steady flow of new customers and converting a target core group into loyal repeat customers. Admittedly, such marketing programs as advertising and promotions can generate demand, but it is far more effective to build demand upon a foundation of a solid, positive reputation.

Consistency is the key element to creating and maintaining both loyalty and a positive reputation. The initial quality levels set for opening day must be consistently reproduced every day thereafter. It is this "average" experience that a customer has with the business that determines reputation. Great companies are not generally characterized by peaks of excellence in product and delivery. Rather, they consistently deliver average experiences that materially exceed the experience created by the competition. Consistency is also important for the repeat customer because they need to know that each time they visit they will have the same great time they had on their first visit

The challenge in a service industry is that a great deal of the production of the experience is from human beings and is thereby subject to an infinite number of human driven variations each time the service is delivered. This is in stark contrast to far more predictable and precise machine produced commodities such as retail and hard goods. Aggravating the situation is the reality that no two customers are alike, and they often bring considerably different expectations and valuation criteria. Indeed, the same customer may have different experiential expectations and valuation criteria from one trip to another.

The first goal is to create a viable product or service. The second, perhaps more difficult goal, is then to sustain the product or service to target levels. Finding a way to deal with the production-consumption variables is the key to maintaining an all important degree of consistency.

C. Giving Structure to the Gaming Entertainment Experience

The casino experience is "manufactured" by utilizing a number of elements, tangible and intangible. An impulse driven walk-in visit or an overnight vacation to a casino is an experiential accumulation of contacts with the bricks and mortar, design, environment, employees, products and services offered by the casino. The total time-space continuum that defines each visitor-trip is actually a compilation of a large number of ongoing contacts with the casino.

This stream of contact events has been referred to as the "service cycle," each node on the cycle constituting a major service. Within each major service node category are the services that comprise that category. Each service may then be broken down into tasks, tasks into procedures and so on, until the entire customer experience is depicted by a model of all the elements which produce the customer experience.

The ingredients which comprise the experience include tangible and intangible, human and facility/system elements, conscious and subconscious stimuli. These range from the hard, tangible aspects of the customer visit such as the mix of services offered, quality of the food purchased and the types of slot machines on the casino floor—to the soft, intangible aspects such as employee courtesy, ambiance of the building and perceived chance of winning. And, despite attempts to label what is trying to be created for certain casinos, there is an indescribable "x-factor" that separates the experience of each customer from the others.

Wrapping around this multi-dimensional, experiential "cube" is the price (or cost) of the experience. The consumer will evaluate price/cost of individual services as well as the overall cost of the experience to determine if they received value.

BEGIN WITH THE END IN MIND—DEVELOPING A TARGET GUEST ENTERTAINMENT EXPERIENCE

A casino visitor's experience is comprised of a complex matrix of elements, some of which are static while others are dynamic, variable and only semi-controllable on both the production and consumption side of the equation. To cope with such complexity, the contention is that to create a predetermined customer experience in the first place and then to consistently maintain the quality of that experience over time requires a systems approach. For convenience, such a system might be labeled a "TGEED System," a TARGET GUEST ENTERTAINMENT EXPERIENCE DELIVERY SYSTEM.

The definition of any "system" is a set or arrangement of things so related or connected as to form a unity or organic whole. The system must not only produce the target experience to preset standards; it must also be capable of monitoring results and self-correct itself when sub-performance is identified.

The primary components of such a system are:

1. Define the Target Guest Entertainment Experience (the TGEE).
2. Develop standards and expectations for the TGEEs.
3. Draft written policies and procedures which result in the delivery of the TGEEs to the predetermined standards and expectations.
4. Develop hiring criteria that result in employees being hired who are best suited to deliver the TGEEs.
5. Develop orientation, training and probationary programs designed to prepare the employees to deliver the TGEEs on their first day of work and thereafter.
6. Develop monitoring and evaluation programs to identify when standards and expectations are not being achieved.
7. Develop remedial programs that "re-calibrate" the defect, be it an equipment, supply, system or employee problem.
8. Develop sanction programs to purge the system of elements that can not be corrected.
9. Develop reward and award programs that reinforce the goals of the system.

Each of the nine major components are major subject areas unto themselves. The focus of this article is on the system, not each of the elements, per se. Nevertheless, to understand how the system works, it is important to know how each element works and contributes to the system.

A. Define the Target Guest Entertainment Experience (TGEE)

Fundamental to the success of a TGEED System is an explicitly defined Target Guest Entertainment Experience. If the TGEE is left up to every employee's own definition of what it should be, the inevitable result will be inconsistency.

Using an analogy, if we asked thirty employees to purchase a gallon of green paint, undoubtedly they would return with thirty gallons of green paint. Equally likely, however, is that they will bring back thirty shades of green paint ranging from chartreuse to dark green. It is critically important to narrow this range into a spectrum that is defined by the casino. Left to chance, the spectrum will be far too broad.

The definition of the TGEE must also be as explicit as possible, using both objective and subjective descriptions. The definition should include both what the TGEE should and should not be.

For the system to work, it is critically important that a TGEE be created for each guest experience. In general terms, this means it needs to be identified for the casino experience, the beverage experience, the food experience, and the entertainment and recreation/relaxation experience.

These major categories need to be further broken down into more detailed components. For example, for the arrival phase of the service cycle, a TGEE should be drafted dealing with how arriving guests are directed to the hotel or parking entrance, the greeting given at valet parking, the handling of baggage at the front door, the script to be used at check-in, the explanation about the services offered by the hotel and finally, any initial familiarization issues with the room itself (e.g., how to use the telephone, television, honor-bar and the like). Each of these contact points should have a written TGEE narrative describing the target experience. In this case, the more TGEEs the better.

There are certain attributes that management may want to weave into every TGEE. For example, companies would be well advised to establish what they consider to be the fundamentals of service. For example, they might consist of customer recognition, speed, accuracy, professionalism and courtesy. Each TGEE would address these five fundamental elements of service for the particular service, product or amenity being described.

Only after describing the fundamentals of each service are the experiential elements which go beyond the fundamentals dealt with. Using the food department as an example, the gourmet restaurant definition of TGEE might include how to properly conduct table side cooking. The slot department might go beyond defining simply how to pay a slot winner and describe how to "celebrate" winners. The policies and procedures for a bartender could explain when and how to build showmanship into serving drinks.

It is important to create a detailed model of the elements which produce the customer experience. This should result in a rather extensive compendium of TGEEs that explicitly describe what we want to create for our customers. The acid test for each TGEE is whether there is sufficient detail to allow a multitude of employees to grasp and implement what is intended; by analogy, they all envision the same color of green paint.

B. Develop Standards and Expectations for Each TGEE

Each and every narrative-driven TGEE should be accompanied by performance standards and expectations. For example, a casino may seek customer recognition as one facet of a TGEE but what constitutes customer recognition? A standard and expectation might deal with this by stating:

1. Each employee will make eye contact with each customer they come in contact with, whether they are serving them directly or not. Employees will not look at the floor, the ceiling or walk through customer areas without making eye contact.
2. Employees will exhibit positive body language at all times. The essence of positive body language is to project an alert posture and an eagerness to serve. This preferably means having a smile on your face, but—if not that—at least having a "neutral" face. Employees will stand up straight, face the customer and not lean on anything nor cross their arms.
3. Each employee will greet the customer with an opening remark such as: "Good morning," "Welcome to ABC Casino," or "How may I be of service to you?" Employees will work their name into each greeting; for example, "My name is Chuck. How may I be of service to you?"

Standards should be objective as possible. For example, one might state: "It will not take longer than four minutes for a customer to receive change." Some TGEEs may require more subjective narrative descriptions in order to define the standard. Others may be clearer if suggested scripts are provided to the employees as bases for their own dialogues.

The test of whether a standard or expectation is valid is whether an experience outside of the TGEE can be identified and measured. If not, then the standards and expectations for that TGEE need to be further defined. There is no sense having a TGEE unless it can be measured. The system cannot self-correct if it cannot determine when the system or an element of the system is sub-performing.

C. Develop Written Policies and Procedures Which Implement and Deliver the TGEEs

This step is largely self-explanatory since almost all casinos have written policies and procedures. There may be a difference, however, in that a systemic approach means that these policies and procedures are not created in a void. Rather, they are driven by the defined TGEEs and the standards and expectations assigned to them.

The common practice of photo-copying the procedure manual from the last casino worked may not be appropriate because it does not embody the spirit, objectives and standards for the casino in question. Care must also be taken to ensure that procedure manuals are not just task and technically oriented. The manuals should also deal with the more subtle dimensions of service: courtesy, professionalism, entertainment and creating fun.

Securing the "buy-in" of the employees to a TGEED System is part of the challenge of implementing and maintaining the system. A helpful approach toward gaining employee support is to have the manuals not only indicate what and how to create the experience but to go further and explain why each aspect helps to create this experience. Perhaps each manual should have two columns. The first column would be the procedure itself, and the second column would explain the "why" and "how" of the procedure.

The field of industrial psychology long ago discovered that employees perform better when they know why they are doing a task. In fact, one very successful company has gone so far as to tell their line employees that if a supervisor or manager cannot explain why they want the employee to do something, they do not have to do it. A bit extreme, but this company views this commitment as a key element to their overall success.

If a TGEED Systems approach is taken, procedures should not be written to simply accomplish a task. They are drafted to create pre-defined experiences. The difference may appear subtle but the impact on what is created can be powerful.

D. Developing Hiring Criteria

It is often argued that in the service industry, who you hire is the primary determinant to the successful delivery of a company's TGEE. Like most service industries, it is not technically difficult to work in the casino business. Indeed, 90 percent of the jobs in a casino can probably be taught to 90 percent of adults. However, the mind-set it takes to deal with customers on a day-to-day basis and—more importantly—to actually enjoy and take satisfaction from the work of delivering TGEEs, is probably vested in only 10% of the adult population.

Historically, casinos have hired applicants based on technical or vocational abilities. The theory was that unsuitable employees would be identified during the probationary period or purged through a disciplinary process. By contrast, the objective in a TGEED System is to develop hiring criteria which are premised upon the TGEE's standards and expectations. The commitment must be to not hire anyone who does not fit the hiring criteria.

A hiring system must be an integrated subset of the overall system. It must range from proactively identifying target labor pools to developing applications, testing and interviewing processes that are able to identify employees who will fit into the TGEED System. Today, more companies are evaluating an applicant's basic personality, attitude toward life, natural courtesy and interpersonal skills as primary qualifying criteria along with the traditional evaluation of technical skills and background checks.

For example, if a casino deals to the premium player market, it may seek more professionalism in its casino hires: the ability to deal blackjack with precision, speed and following procedures with machine-like efficiency. A more low-end tourist oriented casino may seek more outgoing dealers where the premium will be not on game speed but on establishing contact and dialogue with customers. Service bartenders need to be quick. A bartender in the middle of the casino may need to be more a show person than a technician.

Just as engineers set specifications for machines, the more definitive a department head can be in establishing hiring criteria for an employee, the greater the chance the employee hired will deliver the TGEE. With the same philosophy, the Human Resources Department should be prepared to evaluate five or more employees for each position to find those who most closely fit the detailed hiring criteria. Otherwise, the hiring process becomes one of reactively hiring the best of what "walks in the door." The best chefs go to great length to draft detailed purchasing specifications for the food they use in their recipes. The most complicated machine can be made inoperative if the wrong part is purchased. Operational department heads should do no less for their basic "ingredients" and "parts"—the employee.

E. Developing Orientation, Training and Probationary Programs

The guest should not be the guinea pig for new and developing employees. Any new employee must be capable of delivering the TGEE from the first day on the job. The initial period of an employee with a company should be used to verify that this is the right person for the job. This is an evaluation period where employees are still earning their right to a job.

Preparing the employee to deliver the TGEEs is a multi-step process. The employee needs to be indoctrinated to the overall goals, values and culture of the company in order to become a "citizen" of the company. The employee also needs to learn the technical skills as well as the soft and fuzzy sides of the job. This period should also be used to educate the employee about all of the services offered at the facility and where they are located. The employee should learn the answers to questions likely to be asked by visitors. Employees' retention of what has been taught and the ability to execute to proscribed standards should be continually tested.

Employees should not merely attend orientation and take training classes. The company should test to ensure they have learned each step before preceding to the next.

This is also a good time to indicate to new employees what they should do when things go wrong. This deals with both the work environment of the employee (i.e., what to do if they feel they have been treated unfairly) and the service delivered to the customer (i.e., what to do if the hotel is sold out and they have a guest with a reservation in front of them). For companies who espouse empowerment of their employees, this is the time to explain fully what empowerment means, and when and how to use it. Furthermore, this is also the time to delineate when it is time to ask for help.

In all, this could also be viewed as a calibration process that fine tunes the employee's abilities to deliver the predetermined standards and expectations. Recognizing that not all employees will learn and adapt at the same pace, the calibration process should have built-in flexibility to deal with the learning curve of each individual. The standard should be that no new employee is allowed to get into a "live" customer contact or service delivery position until he or she is ready. It is a mistake to consider the training, preparation and calibration process as one mass block of employees moving through a training program together; such a perspective is far too simplistic.

Too much of a casino's human resource budget is spent on "after the fact" programs, retraining and retooling employees after they are hired and after they have completed their initial training. Perhaps if more were spent on hiring the right employees in the first place and preparing them thoroughly, the results would be more productive. The goal is not just to train the hands and feet, but to deal with the heart and the mind as well, to energize the employee to deliver the TGEEs.

F. Developing Monitoring and Evaluation Programs

Most casinos take a rather administrative and reactive view toward determining the effectiveness of their operations. When things go wrong many casinos resort to disciplinary measures as the corrective and ultimately purging device.

A systems approach takes a different philosophy. System architects realize that machines will deviate from their "factory" settings with use. Consequently, most machines which are purchased have instruments which continually measure their performance or undergo scheduled periodic maintenance that accomplishes the same thing. Why then is not the same approach applied to human resources?

Care must be taken to make sure the monitoring and evaluation process is not a thinly veiled "gotcha" program that leads to the termination of employees. The evaluation program should identify situations and employees who are not performing up to stated standards and expectations. Once identified, such employees should be sent for remedial training as a self-help and improvement program designed to aid the employee in surmounting the deficiencies.

Given the scope and sheer size of a typical American casino, resources need to be dedicated to the measurement and evaluation process. Realize too that the goal is to continually measure every TGEE. And monitoring must be thorough to be effective. It should take place 24 hours a day, seven days per week, across all departments. It should be done from the production side, with respect to employee performance, as well as from the consumption side of the experience, from the perspective of the customer.

This enormous task may require a department unto itself. At the very least, it will take a financial and management commitment to measurement. But to do otherwise relegates the casino to being reactive, waiting for individual circumstances or overall performance to deteriorate to the point where customers finally say something. Most customers do not complain when disappointed; they simply patronize another business offering the same service. This is all the more reason to develop a thorough, ongoing monitoring and evaluation program based on the TGEEs, standards and expectations.

G. Develop Remedial Programs

The goal of a monitoring and evaluating a program is to identify substandard performance in order to correct the problem. Oftentimes, the problem may be non-human—it may be equipment, system, procedure, or policy oriented. In other cases, the issue may be employee related, a problem that affects all or a large group of employees (e.g., a motivational problem in a department due to an overbearing manager, or the introduction of a new computer system that was not properly explained). However, most problems will be attributable to specific employees. Each problem needs to be addressed specifically to the situation at hand. The goal of the remedial program is to get the employee back to a state where he or she can once again produce the TGEEs.

This suggests that the company needs to identify resources that can spend the time to work with single, group, department or company wide performance issues. In smaller operations, this effort may have to be delegated to each department head, whereas in the mega-resort properties, a dedicated group of trainers could probably be devoted to this effort on a cost-effective basis. The employee needs to be tested prior to going back to contact with the customer. For the sake of the employee, the company and the customer, employees should not merely attend a remedial training program; they must demonstrate they are capable of delivering the levels of performance expected of them.

H. Develop Sanction Programs

The organization must be prepared to deal with employees who continually fail to perform up to standard. Since reducing price is not a practical solution to a substandard performance in the casino industry, the only choice is to remove a problematic employee until his or her performance returns to acceptable levels. The cost associated with this policy needs to be accepted and budgeted as another cost of doing business.

If the same employees keep needing remedial training, or are unable to pass the remedial training standards, then they need to be separated from the company. This should be viewed as separation rather than termination since the latter carries such a strong connotation of failure or the implication of wrong doing. In fact, the real issue is the "fit" between the company values and those of the employee. Blame is not the real issue, only performance. Nevertheless, whatever the label, anyone or anything that leads to substandard performance needs to be purged from the system, the part replaced, so to speak, only after significant effort has been expended to make things work.

I. Develop Award/Reward Programs

The reverse side of the sanction program is a reinforcement program. When an employee, work group, department or company is meeting or exceeding expectations, the culture needs to be reinforced with recognition, awards and rewards. In most cases, simple recognition and awards are helpful to culturalizing the achievement of TGEEs.

Many companies go beyond symbolic awards and monetary rewards and incentives for performance that meets or exceeds expectations. Meeting a standard may be as important as reinforcing performance that exceeds the standard. Thus, if the target average performance is established at the right level—and particularly if high standards are set from the beginning—then average performance should be recognized. The goal is to create a higher average, not just peak performance by a few.

Nevertheless, "heroes" can also be important to an organization because, by definition, heroes have the ability to affect a large number of people. Both average and superior performance can be rewarded with monetary incentive programs based on the measurable standards and expectations already established. Such incentive programs should be frequent, material and visible to all employees. The pay back for the company is that the award and incentive programs—properly structured and executed—can motivate the entire organization to better performance.

MAKING A TGEED SYSTEM WORK AND AVOIDING DETERIORATION AND FAILURE

Most casino companies practice one or more of the nine elements of the TGEED System. And there are a fair number of companies that practice all of the elements in one form or another. A commitment to a TGEED System requires, however, not only a commitment to each element of the system, but—more importantly—to the system itself. There are a number of forces and dynamics that can affect the success or failure of the system.

A. Commitment from the Top

A TGEED System needs support from top management in order to survive. It will require both time and resources, human and financial, to create and maintain the system. For most companies it will also mean change. As with any change, the detractors and skeptics will challenge the system and—at worst—attempt to discredit and eliminate it. A systems approach, by definition, will involve virtually every department of the casino and every casino of the company. In fact, a TGEED System is a means to implement a cultural philosophy, and creating or sustaining culture is very much the purview of senior management.

All of these concerns and issues require that the TGEED System be totally and unequivocally supported from the top. This support must exist during the development phase, the implementation phase and the maintenance phase. If this support diminishes, cracks or is inconsistent, the system will deteriorate and eventually fail.

B. The System should be an Element of a Customer-Driven Cultural Philosophy, Not Vice Versa

A TGEED System needs the motivational support of the organization, not because it is demanded but because the System is perceived as the best methodology to achieve a shared goal, customer service. Chronologically, a company culture which is committed to customer service must be adopted and established first, followed by implementation of the TGEED System, not the other way around.

C. Find a Hero

Even with the support from top management and a customer-driven culture, the TGEED System still needs a hero or heroes to fight for, implement and defend the system. This person may be the Chief Executive Officer or Chief Operating Officer but more often than not, they are too busy to "carry the flag" for the system.

More likely, the department head of Human Resources or Operations will be in charge of the program. It is possible, of course, to assign the responsibility to a lower rank. But the lower the rank of the person in charge, the greater the risk to the system since the decision time to correct a problem increases disproportionately with organizational distance between the manager and the problem.

Regardless, the most important factor is that the manager be a hero. He or she must be a zealot, focused on excellence and committed to ensuring that major threats as well as tiny cracks in the system are corrected quickly. The hero must fight for and receive the resources necessary to make the system function. And the hero must trumpet and promote the successes of the system in order to maintain and increase adherents to the system. The task of maintaining the system must be the hero's most important if not only responsibility. Otherwise, the risk will not be so much that the system fails outright as that the system will simply deteriorate and fade away.

D. Cost the System into the Pre-opening and Operating Budget

A TGEED System will be viewed as a soft development cost which always has to fight harder for limited development dollars than the "bricks and mortar" hard costs. If the project goes over budget, the soft costs are usually the first to be turned to as a likely place to save money. Similarly, when there are competing demands on operating expenses or when profit margins erode, the system will be harder to justify because it delivers benefits that are difficult to measure. Consequently, a philosophical commitment to the system by top management has to be backed up by a commitment of the financial resources necessary to support the system.

These additional costs include a commitment to hiring staff earlier than usual to draft the TGEEs and the standards and expectations for each TGEE. Likewise, hiring criteria are more detailed under a TGEED System, they need to be drafted early, and the number of candidates to be recruited for interviewing will have to be greater than typical approaches. The orientation and training programs will generally be more intensive as well. Finally, the monitoring and evaluation facet of the system may require an entirely new department, or—at the least—the creation of a new position and the hiring of additional staff.

The remedial training programs up to and including the cost of paying employees for the training at their normal wage, to keep them away from customer contact until they can perform to target levels, will also add an expense. The premise is that all of these expenses have a financial return through the creation of a competitive niche, the ability to create stronger loyalty and repeat visitation, and an increase in revenue in general. If management is unwilling to fully fund the system, the system will again deteriorate, fail or fade away.

E. Parochialism

Most gaming companies are vertically organized around departments. The TGEED System is a horizontal program involving virtually every department. It is possible to install a horizontal system while retaining strict departmental boundaries. The system has a better chance of succeeding, however, if a system manager is allowed to assist each department head with their portion. At the extreme, the system manager could dictate to the department head how to implement the system into their area of responsibility. The optimal situation, of course, is that the team of managers cooperate in achieving a shared goal, and titles and departmental boundaries become seamless. Anyone seeking to install a TGEED System approach will need to address the challenge of establishing such an all-inclusive system horizontally into the organization.

F. Commitment to the Task of Measuring

Many services are not measured because those responsible feel they cannot be measured. While it is certainly more difficult to measure service than production of hard goods, service can still be measured. Objective criteria such as the length of a check-in line or time to get a drink are easy to establish. Measuring body language is more difficult but still could be defined by watching a test sample of employees and defining a number of examples that constitutes positive body language. The evaluator, once calibrated, could then review operations and rank what he or she observes. Employee morale can be monitored with in-house surveys, peer group and focus group evaluations, in addition to the more standard measures of employee turnover, absenteeism and tardiness. Qualitative aspects of service such as courtesy could be the most difficult to measure, but surveys of customers could identify whether customer courtesy is perceived to be present or not. If not, then a team could be assigned to the potential trouble area to determine the sources or causes of the problem.

Simply put, the performance of the system fails if performance itself cannot be measured. Clearly, the area which will need the most new development in creating a TGEED System will be the identification of valid and accurate standards, expectations and measurements of each TGEE. The answers are there for companies willing to make the commitment, approach the challenge with an open mind, devote the resources and have the patience to put up with the inevitable setbacks that occur on the path to a solution.

CONCLUSIONS

Unquestionably, it takes greater commitment, effort and expenditures to sustain a TGEED System than a conventional approach. Not all companies are suited to the challenge and those which are not, may achieve greater—though not optimal—results by relying on traditional methods. For those companies who are willing to make the commitment, however, the reward should be material for the customer, the employee and the investors.

Some Potential Pitfalls of Casino Start Ups

Mary Ann Perkins

Much has been written about the equipment, the floor layouts, the marketing programs and the financial backing required for a successful casino opening. Less has been put forward, however, about how gaming companies develop their people and their organizations to deliver on the expectations created by a spacious new building or an authentic riverboat in a new or existing market.

With casinos opening in many new jurisdictions throughout the United States as well as in other countries, management theories are being developed which describe the organizational criteria that can lead to a successful casino opening. Whether looking at opening one of the largest hotel casino complexes in the world or a small riverboat casino operation, many of the characteristics are the same.

Starting a casino in a community new to gaming brings with it a learning curve for owners and operators as well as the pool of applicants seeking employment in this exciting new industry. It is interesting to note that many of the same management principles apply equally in new jurisdictions and in existing markets.

Research conducted by University of Michigan professor David Ulrich describes ways an organization can capture and sustain a competitive advantage (Ulrich 1989). He identifies four critical sources of competitive advantage: economic/financial capability, strategic/marketing capability, technological capability, and organizational capability. His work indicates most firms within a designated industry have very similar access to financing, marketing, and products. However, these same companies can set themselves apart by focusing on their people, their organizations, and their capacity to build a responsive people system that will capture a competitive advantage. It is easy to talk about responding organizationally, but it is not as easy to execute that strategy.

The focus of this article is to develop a framework against which Chief Executive Officers and senior management teams can check their organizational systems by reviewing ways to effectively manage people, strategies to develop an organization that will make a property competitive in a new market, and methods to introduce innovative people systems during a start-up.

To gather data for this article, the author's casino opening experience spanning the 1984–1994 time frame has been combined with information obtained in interviews with casino executives who have recent experience in opening all sizes and types of casinos. Some common organizational problem areas were noted:

- inexperienced leadership;
- neglecting basic employee needs;
- inaccurate staffing levels;
- failing to communicate clear and realistic expectations; and
- lack of attention to managing critical transitions.

The observations and suggestions about managing people contained in this analysis are offered to those responsible for planning, designing, and opening casino gaming operations of the future. Experiences from the casino industry—as well as the development of such an approach with one work group, the slot department of the MGM Grand Hotel, Casino and Theme Park in Las Vegas—are examined in an effort to identify, organizationally, successful strategies and potential pitfalls which can exist during start-ups.

INEXPERIENCED LEADERSHIP

Various characteristics of effective leaders are well documented: leaders are visionaries, strategic thinkers, skilled delegators, risk-takers, superb people managers, competent financial analysts, and they exhibit marketing acumen. Spencer and Spencer, in their book, *Competence at Work,* describe leadership characteristics of successful sales personnel which can also be applied to executives in the gaming industry:

- a high level of achievement motivation (someone who sets himself ambitious yet achievable goals and uses his time efficiently);
- an abundance of initiative (someone with lots of persistence who is able to respond competitively when challenged);
- strong interpersonal skills and the ability to decipher the attitudes and nonverbal behavior of others; and
- self-confidence (someone with no hesitation in taking on challenging assignments).

While not every effective casino executive needs to have worked his or her way up through the organization from a 21 dealer or a slot mechanic to a senior casino manager, an important additional quality is a thorough understanding of casino operations. Successful gaming industry executives also pride themselves on their ability to recruit and develop effective teams.

Ideally, it is probably best to hire managers and supervisors who have opened a casino before. Top decision-makers will recognize that the skills required to execute a successful opening may be different from those needed to operate in a day to day environment. Managers and supervisors should be comfortable conceptualizing the project and its components. Managers who are entrepreneurial and flexible in their management styles often do well in a start-up environment. Conversely, a person who relies on the rule book to guide decision making may be uncomfortable since the rule book is often being written as the property is being opened. One casino executive stated, "Some people with opening experience may not like living with a finished product, especially if they don't get everything they wanted." Thus, he expresses the belief that running a property is very different and much less exciting than opening one.

When senior management focuses its discussions in an interactive manner to develop the vision and market position for the property, it is usually very productive. It is important to have a strategic planner on the team early enough to write the plan, develop each functional budget and monitor requests from fellow executives for additional funds. The goal is to be clear about what attributes will make the property successful, to allocate proper resources to achieve that success, and to identify means to effectively communicate these attributes in a way that will generate excitement and confidence among employees.

Companies with multiple casino locations have an advantage when identifying managerial candidates. Often, they can move managers from one location to another. The transfer of culture is much easier since the manager already knows what the company wants to provide for its customers and what it expects from its employees. These companies can also access "opening teams"—employees who travel from a sister property to assist with the pre-opening training activities, or to work scheduled shifts during the first few weeks the property is open.

Eventually, employees at all levels need to receive the same message about the property. Dave Wirshing, former President and CEO of the Fitzgerald Gaming Corporation, noting the mix of cultures that can result when a new company is established or a new property opened, says, "Unless the leaders share the same values and culture and come together as a team soon enough in the development process to understand the big picture, you will have an assortment of operating styles which is sometimes difficult to untangle." Effective leaders are learning how to utilize the people in the organization to make these messages clear and create one set of core values from which to work.

On December 17, 1993, the MGM Grand, the world's largest hotel and casino, opened in Las Vegas. It opened below budget and three and one half months ahead of schedule. The slot department consisted of 500 employees and 3,506 machines, a high limit player area, and all aspects of slot marketing and player tracking. Andy Hommel, MGM's Vice President of Slots, had opened the Golden Nugget in Atlantic City and had definite ideas about how he wanted—and did not want—to operate. Hommel hired Perkins Corporation as the training consultant to the slot department to help prepare people and to develop training and communication programs for opening the world's largest slot operation.

Opening teams can learn by carefully studying previous openings to better understand what works or does not work. A mistake opening teams can make is to assume the problems which occurred during one opening will not be repeated. Thus, the MGM, Hommel and team learned as much they could about the openings of The Mirage in Las Vegas, the Grand Casinos on the Gulf Coast, the Taj Mahal in Atlantic City, and other American properties with recent opening or expansion experience. Much emphasis was placed on developing the MGM's slot operating philosophy, the operating procedures, the slot floor layout, the types of equipment to be used, and the demands the opening would place on the energy level of the entire team.

Hommel looked for start-up skills and opening experience in the candidates he considered for his team, but when it was not available, he focused on the skills which he felt made an equally important contribution to the team. These skills were customer relations, high limit player development experience, transition management (during ownership changes in a major Strip property), slot analysis, and slot security systems.

The slot team spent considerable time developing its own vision and mission statement and logo that would coincide with the property's statements. They wanted to articulate the aspects of the MGM's slot operation that would set it apart from others in the Las Vegas market. Considerable time was spent deciding how to communicate this information to all new employees.

The eight senior slot directors were hired at different intervals ranging from two years to four months prior to opening. An important staffing decision was made to bring the 30 shift managers onto the payroll thirty days prior to opening. They played a key role in developing procedures, designing and delivering training sessions, assisting with machine installation and various other duties, all of which allowed them to learn about the casino floor, the property and the philosophy of the department.

Hommel was a hands-on manager who continually challenged his team to verbalize the unique aspects of the operation. He conducted regular luncheon meetings ("Pizza with Andy") with the staff in a setting that reinforced the department's mission and encouraged two-way communication. He also challenged his management team to disagree with him. He placed a high value on managers who would bring new information and different points of view to any discussion.

The characteristics of effective leadership and the level of experience of the slot team played an important role in the development of the property's slot strategy. The interaction among slot management, the general manager and the president of the property also helped integrate the slot strategy into the overall property mission. Although technical problems with a coinless slot system and the player tracking system delayed the introduction of that technology beyond opening, overall the slot opening was considered to be highly successful.

Experienced leadership, particularly in the most senior level positions of the operation, is a critical component to a successful opening. Being able to recognize and recruit talented individuals—who might often have limited gaming experience—whose skills will intertwine with those of the rest of the team is also important. Individuals in leadership positions will have ample opportunity to use their administrative, communication and problem-solving skills during the months and weeks prior to opening a new casino.

NEGLECTING BASIC EMPLOYEE NEEDS

In the race to manage blueprints, floor layouts, major purchases, new systems, marketing campaigns, staffing levels, wage and salary items, and a myriad of other details involved in a start-up, sometimes the most basic of employee needs are overlooked.

This often happens even before the casino opens. During the start-up phase, the most important question prospective employees have for employers is, "Did I get the job?" With Human Resources departments accepting hundreds and thousands of employment applications for all available positions, some paperwork and even some people can get lost in the shuffle. Easy-to-administer applicant tracking systems should be established early in the planning process. At any given time, it should be possible for a department manager to know how many applications have been received, how many interviews have been conducted, how many job offers have been extended, how many offers have been accepted, how many security clearances have been obtained, how many drug test results have been returned, how many new hires have received gaming licenses, and so on. These are critical details which, if not properly administered, can delay the process and add unnecessary days and weeks to the time when a department manager has promised to let an applicant know if he or she gets the job.

Some thought should be given to the needs of employees after opening. New employees want to know about their schedule, their days off, where to park, where and when to pick up their uniforms, where and when to eat, how many hours of work to expect during the days immediately preceding and following the opening, how much overtime to expect, etc. They will want to know the procedure for changing shifts, the proper way to request an extra day off, the criteria used to assign or change work stations, the requirements for being considered for a promotion to the next higher level position in the department, the procedure for assigning vacation schedules, the procedure for determining lottery numbers, and how such numbers will be used by management. Procedures regarding handling of shortages and overages, or for documenting attendance and punctuality situations, are also important to a new employee. Some department managers unknowingly lose an opportunity to demonstrate their respect for employees' personal lives when they are unwilling or unable to clearly respond to employee questions about schedules and days off during the weeks prior to opening

Rick Cook, Director of Slot Operations for Gaming Corporation of America in Minneapolis, Minnesota noted:

> "Don't take the slightest thing for granted. In new jurisdictions where the basics aren't known, you are caught by surprise when an employee says 'where do I put my purse?' You haven't even thought about it. In established casinos in Nevada or New Jersey, we are used to having our supervisors handle these employee needs. Now we have supervisors who don't know the question or the answer."

In the casino business, the location of employee purses and coats in relation to the storage of currency is a consideration. And it is relatively easy to find the answer. But when you consider the number of easy questions that require an answer, management's time begins to mount up.

How can casinos insure that managers and supervisors are effective in anticipating the needs of employees? Obvious as it may seem, this is a logical place for employee involvement. Ask the front-line employees on the staff what their needs are. Visit other casino operations and ask front-line employees what their needs were at the time of opening. Listen to applicants from other casinos talk about the work environment in their current place of employment. Consider assigning the department training coordinator to serve as liaison between employees and management during the time immediately preceding and following the casino opening in matters dealing with employee comfort and services. In discussions about floor layout and design, management should always review its impact on employee travel time and the locations of employee services, the time clock, the employee cafeteria and wardrobe, as well as overtime guidelines, paycheck distribution, employee parking and rest rooms. Management should make a commitment to the basic needs of employees early in the development process of the new operation since this deserves as much time as the floor layout, restaurant offerings, and other product decisions.

The MGM slot management team took responsibility for identifying and responding to the needs of its employees at every step of the process. Identified steps included: the day an applicant made out an employment application at the MGM's Hiring Center, the initial interview, the official offer of employment (including shift, days off, and scheduled hours of work), invitations to tour the property during construction stage, class-room training, and rehearsal conducted for the final three days prior to opening. In each step, supervisory staffs were equipped to respond to every employee question. Hommel believed it was the job of his management team to take care of the employees.

For example, every new employee was told, "If you don't understand any part of the processing and training schedule, please call us back. If you have any questions about your work schedule or your days off, please call us back. If you are not sure where to park, call us back. Someone will always be here to help you." The phone rang off the hook in the Slot Office during the final 30 days prior to opening. After opening, employees widely indicated that they felt the Slot Office was responsive to them and their needs.

Certainly, the MGM had an impressive Human Resources recruiting, communication, and benefits package all designed to attract and retain the best talent available in the industry. But if an applicant was left waiting in the interview lobby for more than 30 minutes beyond his or her scheduled interview time with a slot director, Hommel wanted to know why. He wanted employees treated the way he would expect to be treated. He knew the best benefits package needed to be accompanied by fair and respectful treatment of prospective employees. Scheduling, shift assignment and days off were among of the first questions a new employee had for management. These answers were provided at the time the job offer was extended.

Considerable time and effort was spent helping employees learn their way around the property. In each slot carousel was placed a "you are here . . . " map showing casino restaurants, showrooms, restrooms, hotel lobby, elevators, etc. To help employees and supervisors get used to the work area, the MGM slot directors also made a conscious decision not to re-schedule or rotate people from one section of the casino to another during the first few weeks after opening.

How much does it cost to provide responsive human resource systems?

Unfortunately, the labor component of the gaming business is still considered an expense, not an asset. Dean Macomber of the Navegante Group observed:

> "I know what percentage of total revenue to spend on marketing during the pre-opening phase. It is usually two to six percent. But I would like to know the industry average for a human resources budget during the pre-opening phase. We know it is a critically important component to a successful opening, but we need to become more sophisticated in our tracking systems to know the amount of money to allocate for the human resources side of the business."

Management in a start-up environment needs to remember not to take the slightest thing for granted. They should remember back to the days when they were a front-line employee beginning their first job. Employees should be provided with as much information, as much support, and as many resources as needed to help them become comfortable with the new job, the new company, and the new supervisors. Doing so will result in self-assured, productive employees who treat customers better, and who are more likely to project a positive image to customers. The added benefit of higher retention rates may also translate to bottom line financial rewards as well.

INACCURATE STAFFING LEVELS

Casino companies spend considerable time, money, and energy introducing their new properties to their respective communities. The messages to prospective employees during the recruiting efforts include "we care about you," "we will train you," and "we will provide you with career opportunities." Over-staffing and the resulting lay-offs that typically follow casino openings can do considerable damage to the good citizen reputation the company is trying to establish. On the other hand, under-staffing may frustrate both employees and customers, causing them to look for a different place to work or a better place to play.

Inaccurate staffing levels also affect the recruitment of new employees. They are sometimes justifiably skeptical about joining a new venture since there may be a risk of being laid off. It is a common practice to over-hire by 10% in the expectation that there will be some employees who just won't like the work, won't be able to do the work, or won't realize what weekend or holiday work really is like until they experience it. Identifying the proper staffing level is always a challenge during an opening.

Staffing level decisions cannot be made in a vacuum. In a related discussion, Wirshing noted:

"It helps when the same manager who developed the staffing plan is the manager who opens and operates the property. Many assumptions are made about staffing levels that get lost in the shuffle when new people assume responsibility for managing an operation they did not develop."

Management should look at industry averages to help guide their recommendations, e.g. the ratio of slot supervisors or slot employees to the number of machines. Management should study recent openings to learn the impact of new technologies on staffing, such as the time and labor saved by computer systems that pinpoint employee access to machines. They must be realistic about the floor layout and customer expectations for service by recognizing that such things as a compact, well-defined area in a high traffic zone may require more staffing than average to properly service customers. Or since the high limit slot section always requires additional staffing, management should look for ways employees in other sections can cover the area when the regularly scheduled staff is on break. They should look at the floor coverage required by their procedures and consider travel time for the supervisor who has to approve all fills and jackpots over a certain dollar level.

Author Charles Handy presents a concept the gaming industry might consider (Handy 1989). It involves hiring a pool of core (permanent) staff members and a pool of flexible (temporary, part time, or "on call") staff members. Benefit packages could be designed which meet the needs of the flexible staffers, and also give them the freedom to work fewer hours during non-peak times, to take unpaid leaves of absence more often, or use their casino jobs as a part-time positions to supplement other employment. In addition, these flexible staff members could be provided enough status and privileges (i.e., paid holidays and sick leave entitlement) to make such positions attractive.

Another staffing problem in a pre-opening environment deals with staffing shortages. In some markets, especially those with more than one casino facility being opened in a short period of time, there might not be enough qualified applicants. Some people will accept more than one job offer and wait until the last minute to decide which job to take. Some are "just looking" and do not intend to accept a job offer made to them. Others are trying to improve their current job situation by considering employment at the new property.

Too often, the crush of management activities and decisions to be made during the two weeks prior to an opening does not leave time for a careful review of staffing levels. It is always prudent to have a back-up hiring plan for the 10% to 15% of front-line applicants who do not begin work as they had promised. It is conceivable that a department supervisor will have to spend the last 48 hours prior to opening and the 48 hours immediately following a casino opening interviewing candidates, extending job offers, and adjusting work schedules accordingly to allow for constantly changing staffing needs.

In anticipation of problems that would be caused by over-hiring, the MGM slot team tried to hire a more realistic number of employees and to tell them they would be working ten to twelve hour days with no days off during the first few weeks of opening. They also hired multi-experienced employees who could be moved to other assignments within the slots department if staffing levels required. Within 90 days of opening, approximately 60 slot employees had transferred to other slot department positions.

During the first few days of the operation, Hommel named a "swat team" which consisted of managers and key employees who would assist the slot operations directors on designated shifts with trouble-shooting as needed. These employees worked their regularly scheduled shifts, then remained at work for an additional four hours to work on the swat team. This also eliminated the need to over-hire in key supervisory positions. Because of this approach, no changes were made in the supervisory staffing level after opening.

Various forms of technology also affect staffing. One example at the MGM was the use of bill acceptors on every slot machine. It was not at all clear prior to opening how many change people would be needed in any given slot section, or how bill acceptors would affect the job duties of the floor person position. After opening, the number of employees actually needed to staff the slot department totaled 425, down from an original estimate of 500. Only 15 slot employees were transferred to the property-wide employment pool created to fill existing vacancies in other departments. (Of the original 500 employees 60 were laid off.)

Determining appropriate staffing levels is a dynamic process. It influences and is influenced by so many other aspects of the operation that it deserves considerable management attention. Because labor is such a costly item in a casino operation's budget, systematic reviews should be conducted throughout the planning process to insure that early estimates are still valid. Management should engage in discussions to research all possible solutions to staffing questions and be prepared to adjust numbers accordingly. Establishing an employment pool of employees who are placed on reassignment status is an effective way to maximize the investment already made in recruiting and training new employees. In many cases, a staffing overage for one department can be a resource to departments with staffing shortages.

FAILING TO COMMUNICATE CLEAR AND REALISTIC EXPECTATIONS

In a start-up environment, management's communication with new employees regarding job requirements and performance expectations is normally accomplished through training and communication programs and inter-department procedure review sessions.

A. Training and Communication

Frequent and effective communication and training during an opening cannot be over-emphasized. Even in an environment where many of the employees are familiar with the gaming industry, they are probably not familiar with the nuances of each particular casino. In addition, the communication priority is even more important when hiring managers in new jurisdictions with no casino experience. It is important to take the necessary time to explain what the casino expects of non-casino (i.e., food and beverage, security, hotel, marketing) managers. For managers and supervisors who have never worked in the gaming industry, management's message is the only way staffers can learn what is expected of them in such a new environment and in such a short period of time.

Managers and supervisors also need a clear understanding of the culture of the company, the operating procedures and guidelines, and the expectations senior management and owners have of them. Their involvement in team building activities, planning sessions, and logistical set-ups for the casino are critical. If management is able to repeatedly articulate the vision of the company and the competitive advantages of the property and its characteristics, it will help front-line employees to better understand the importance of their roles and to better understand the training they are receiving to help them perform satisfactorily.

Training occurs in a number of ways. Employees are exposed to training in formal training programs, in discussions and meetings with management, during work sessions which develop operating policies and procedures, during pre-opening tours and pep rallies, and during all activities which make up the last two to four weeks prior to opening.

The training curriculum should include the company's commitment to customers and service, and the property's unique product and service offerings which will provide a competitive advantage in the market. In addition, a description of how the department fits into the property organization is helpful. Finally, management's expectations of the job for which the employee was hired, and the presentation of opportunities to develop skills for responding to on-the-job situations which require the employee to use good judgment when dealing with customers or fellow workers are critical training objectives.

For the front-line employee in a start-up, training is not always a very interactive process, although it should be. Employees are new to each other and the company is new to all of them. Many times, employees are more anxious to know how management expects them to complete tasks than they are to practice scenarios that may evolve on the casino floor. Some employees are concerned they will give the "wrong" answer during training and this will adversely affect management's opinion of them. There can and should be discussion about the proper way to handle a disgruntled customer, but it should be within the context of company policy. To encourage discussion, trainers should ask new employees to relate experiences they have had as a customer or in customer service situations on a previous job. This gives employees a chance to share their experiences and to practice responses, but training discussions should conclude with a clear restatement of management's expectations.

Whose job is it to train new employees at every level of the organization? It is the responsibility of each operating manager. The human resource department usually coordinates this effort and provides direction and guidance to the management team regarding appropriate and effective training programs. They might access resources including training companies, training consultants, and the in-house training department staff to insure employees are provided with the necessary information to perform their jobs in a consistent and correct manner. Using department supervisors to conduct the training has the added advantage of insuring the supervisor understands department policies and procedures well enough to explain them and to respond to employee questions.

Providing effective supervisory training is especially important because, with the expansion of gaming into new jurisdictions, supervisors and managers are being hired who have responsibility for a gaming area, but have never worked in a casino before. Ann Reynolds, a casino shift manager at Ameristar Vicksburg, in Mississippi, noted: "I was one of the skeptical managers about hiring pit supervisors who had never dealt one hand to the public. Every single person we promoted directly from dealer school to supervisor has worked out well! We are all pleased with their progress."

B. Inter-Departmental Procedure Review

Clearly, there needs to be one set of procedures before training can be effective at the front-line. It is amazing how much valuable management time can be spent in discussions about procedures and the "proper" way to do a job or perform a task. In an organization where many of the supervisors came from different casinos with different procedures and different cultures, these discussions can last for hours and days. To keep these discussions from becoming unwieldy and unproductive, the leadership of the property must get involved, focus the discussions and clarify questions early so valuable time is not lost.

The operating managers and supervisors should prepare procedures early enough so that training materials can be prepared to describe and support them. At the same time, this is also an opportunity to review the company's commitment to customers and employees. Do the procedures make it easy for the staff to provide quality customer service? Or do the procedures tie the hands of the service providers and take time away from getting a customer back into action?

Procedure review sessions also become an important part of training and communication. Be sure internal controls are finalized well in advance of these discussions. Once the operating procedures have been finalized, it is critical to conduct a series of discussions among related department supervisors about the procedures. For example, cage, security, pit, slot, surveillance, and other operational supervisors should be brought together with the director of operations. They should systematically discuss each of the procedures which require inter-departmental action such as making table and slot fills, extending credit, making jackpot payoffs, closing and opening pit games, conducting the pit and slot drops, paying back markers, comping players to restaurants or shows, putting players into the tracking system, etc. The supervisors should be asked to describe for the group in detail how they and their appropriate employees would handle each situation. Observations should then be solicited from the other supervisors about the task being discussed.

Differences of opinion regarding operating procedures will be identified, and through discussion, the most effective method of accomplishing the task can be determined. Any conflicting issues that arise should be clarified right away; this should also reaffirm the importance of inter-department cooperation and teamwork. Since all departments are involved in resolving the potential problem, all parties affected by the procedure will understand the intent of management and the best way to execute the procedure. Not only will this approach guarantee a smoother opening; it will also help teach supervisors that senior management wants to provide hassle-free service to employees as well as customers. It may even form the basis for similar discussions in the future. Reviewing procedures on a regular basis breaks down barriers to effective communication and helps departments work better together.

At the MGM, Andy Hommel believed training was his responsibility and one he shared with every slot director, manager, and supervisor. Therefore, he reserved time and money to train each supervisor to be a trainer (22 of 30 actually conducted pre-opening classes). Team building activities were incorporated into the pre-opening management discussions about procedures, operating guidelines, and employee relations. Hommel continually encouraged the management team to discuss the "soft" side of the business, the people managing guidelines, which can quickly become inconsistent and confusing to employees once the doors are open. He knew these discussions would be referenced again after opening when it was noticed that one shift was enforcing a certain procedure in a different manner than the other two shifts. He wanted to avoid such problems from the outset.

Hommel opened every training class with the statement: "We are glad you chose us." He set the tone and the example for the supervisors (trainers) by telling the front-line employees how important they were to the success of the property. Since many of the slot supervisors were more experienced in slot operations than in public speaking, many of them were uncomfortable with conducting a training class. Every supervisor attended the "Train the Trainer" sessions provided by the MGM and The Perkins Corporation. Teams of supervisors were then assigned to conduct each class (24 eight-hour classes were scheduled during the ten days immediately prior to opening). At no time was a supervisor asked to conduct a class alone. In all cases, there was someone else in the room to assist as a co-facilitator.

After opening, several of the supervisors commented that the best part of the training for them was learning it was comfortable and appropriate to say, "I'm not sure, let me check." They found that front-line employees appreciated the correct response as compared to an overly confident supervisor who made up the answer in order to save face. The supervisors also carefully studied operating procedures prior to the training class so they could properly explain them to front-line team members. They spent considerable time discussing among themselves the exceptions to each procedure so they could be clear on all possible situations an employee might encounter.

At the MGM, we introduced a technique called "Andy's 20 Questions." Every employee was told that Andy Hommel had a special way of communicating with his team. He asked a lot of questions. Many times, they were questions with obvious answers. But he asked them nonetheless. In this manner, employees were prepared from early in the training to be comfortable with questions from Hommel or any other senior manager at the MGM. They learned it was the job of each employee to know the answer. Quiz sessions were built into the training sessions to reference the 20 Questions and rehearse the proper response. We also reminded the team that Hommel used this technique to be sure the front-line was receiving the most current and most correct information from the supervisors. Best of all, the customer received consistent responses from every slot employee.

After opening, the MGM slot management team recognized that the inter-department procedure review sessions represented an area where "we forgot to do training." Even though the slot operations staff knew about procedures, drop times, and various other services to be provided by the various departments in the organization, not enough time was spent in discussions among other department supervisors to uncover possible problems. "We thought they were telling their employees the same things we were telling our employees," Hommel said of the Cage function. "If I had it to do over, I would focus more time on the inter-department procedure review."

During the last few days prior to opening, every slot employee was scheduled to work their assigned shift, in their assigned location, with their assigned supervisor. This dress rehearsal—they wore red MGM logo tee shirts to help them identify fellow slot employees across the casino—was designed to give slot employees a chance to prepare their work stations, practice procedures, and familiarize themselves with the property and machines located near their work stations. A checklist of 50 procedures and specific job duties was provided for each employee to use as a guide during rehearsal. We believe it helped employees feel comfortable about their new job and their new work station. This also helped them have more time to devote to responding to customer questions and providing the level of service for which the MGM has become known.

In every casino operation, existing or start-up, better communication needs to be a management priority. Staff departments should not manage this process; rather, it should be an important part of every senior manager's job duties. It is also a continuing process. The advantages of strong focus on training and communication from the outset include building an expectation on the part of front-line employees and supervisors about management's commitment to keeping them informed.

Finally, it is critically important to let employees know what opening day will be like. Time should be spent acquainting employees with the stressful conditions that will exist once the property opens. Employees should be made aware of the crush of customers and the volume of money and transactions that will have to be handled accurately and efficiently during that busy time. Employees will need help understanding the priorities of the opening. They should also be reassured that the levels of intensity will diminish after the first few days or weeks.

LACK OF ATTENTION TO MANAGING TRANSITIONS

Management needs to be responsive to the various transitions which occur prior to, during, and immediately following the opening of a new property. A few of these transitions will be discussed here:

- the transition from construction to operation;
- the transition from installation to operation of new technology; and
- the transition from training in a mock casino environment to responding to real customers.

A. Transition from Construction to Operation.

In most companies, construction workers are hired locally and are part of a separate company that will not be present after the property has been opened. While construction management tasks are different from those of casino operations managers and supervisors, there are also similarities. Adhering to timelines is critical; approval processes must be known to all involved; changes in construction work orders require clarity and specific management attention.

There are also good reasons for both areas to be respectful of the other's responsibilities. The communication lines must be open and possible breakdowns in the schedule must be known to all parties in enough time to react properly. Every casino executive has stories to tell about the last few days prior to opening: "It won't be done on time." "There is no way we can make it." "The electrical outlets are nowhere near where they are supposed to be." "The casino guys didn't decide until the last minute they wanted that sign in that location." "It is a good thing I went to the design meeting when I did, or the surveillance cameras would have been blocked." The examples go on and on.

Dual Cooper, former Chief Operating Officer of Casino Magic, noted the most important "people consideration" in a start-up is the communication that must occur between the construction design team and the operations team. But, he said: "Too often, the designers don't bring the operators in to look at the blueprints and ask how it will work after it is built."

Simply communicating well can improve the transition considerably. Ideally, a construction project manager has been identified to manage this transition and knows where the potential problems are from an operating standpoint. This person usually remains on staff as the facilities director after the property is open. Another option is to designate a coordinator to represent the operations managers during the transition. For example, this person could check the actual work space and counter design after all the equipment has been installed. Somehow, the space on the casino floor always looks different than it did in the blueprint. Examples might include:

> There is not enough room between machines! There is no place to stack cups! The change banks block a customer's view of the machines or the section! These aisles are too wide! Those aisles are not wide enough!

It is important for the operating manager to make no assumptions. The manager should check and double check everything that is needed to ensure a smooth transition, a smooth opening, and an efficient operation.

B. Transition from Installation to Operation of New Technology

In start-ups, the dependence on the correct operation of computers, player tracking systems, point of sale cash registers, slot analysis programs, and various financial analysis programs is considerable. With every opening, there is new technology or a new twist on existing systems. Sufficient lead time must be allocated for the hardware and software to be installed, tested, and used prior to opening. It must be operable, not just ready to be used. Passwords should be distributed in time to allow employees to have an opportunity to become familiar with the equipment. In the cases where new technology is being introduced, the target date for installation must allow adequate time for training and testing. The transition from the vendor (or in-house MIS department) to the user will require management's attention and concentration to insure the systems function as described and to insure employees know how to handle the software and equipment.

Too often, discussions regarding new technology are strategic in nature and held between director or vice president level managers. The tactical problems are not heard in the boardroom. Assigning a supervisor to work closely with the vendor on new system installation will help insure that the tactical aspects of the installation are addressed, and should provide for a smooth transition.

C. Transition from Training in a Mock Casino Environment to Responding to Real Customers

Since most properties conduct the majority of the training during the last three to five days prior to opening, doing so on the casino floor has significant advantages. Ideally, some training and orientation will have been conducted earlier in the seven days immediately preceding opening which introduces employees to the company and its operating philosophies. Because management's attention during the last two or three days is often diverted to handling other pressing issues which arise at the last minute, employees may be seen standing around in small groups, reviewing training manuals, becoming familiar with the property, or otherwise unproductively attempting to train themselves. The precious few hours before actual opening can be utilized much more effectively by implementing the "Mock Casino" concept developed in Atlantic City to simulate employee-to-customer and employee-to-employee transactions on the casino floor.

The Mock Casino gives employees a chance to practice procedures just as they are to be executed when the casino opens its doors to the public. It is important to make these sessions as realistic as possible by conducting the Mock Casino during the employees' actual working hours: asking employees to wear uniforms for at least one of the days, asking employees to assume the role of the customer for periods of time during the shift, providing employees with customer scenarios to enact during the shift, serving mock cocktails to players, using the overhead pager and beeper systems.

Specifically, it is helpful to perform department functions which require interaction with employees from other areas. For example, managers should conduct several dry runs of the drop and the count and keep track of the time it takes to complete each. A Security Officer should be asked to accompany every supervisor making a fill. There should be enough play money and forms on the floor so that each employee can count down his or her bank and have it verified. This is an opportunity for them to practice counting and re-counting money. Mock customers can cash in chips and coin.

It is also an opportunity to practice procedures that involve employees from another department. Even though procedures have been written and approved by upper management, it may become obvious that they need modification in actual casino situations. Becoming fast and accurate in handling money during a training exercise is far different from handling huge volumes of cash on opening day. Employees cannot practice enough in the areas that involve the proper handling of money, the movement of money throughout the casino, and the documenting of money through the proper paper trail. Employees should be timed in opening and closing a game or counting down banks at the end of a shift. Progress should be evaluated from shift to shift.

Many gaming commissions provide summary memoranda which outline problems experienced in their jurisdictions during previous openings. This information should be shared with supervisors and used to guide debriefing sessions during the Mock Casino.

In most openings, much of the activity during the two to three days prior to opening is directed at finishing the property and making it ready to receive customers. Are there enough keys and locks? When will the keys be distributed to employees? Do the telephones, beepers, radios, and public address systems work? Money has to be placed on the floor, last minute construction tasks must be completed, missing supplies and equipment must be located. Is there enough money on the floor and in what denominations? Where can someone get more if an emergency fill is needed? How long will it take? Will the Cage be able to serve customers as well as employees from another department on a timely basis? Coordinating these operational priorities with the activities of the Mock Casino will help identify problem areas prior to opening day.

Andy Hommel became the designated transition project manager for the slot department during the last 30 days of construction. He spent considerable hours on the casino floor monitoring the progress of the various construction staffers. His priority was managing the slot technician component of the department efficiently and cost effectively so that every machine was tested and operable by opening day. They missed by ten percent; the coin free machines in the casino were not in operation until several days after opening.

The MGM opened with a variety of new products and concepts: 356 of its slot machines were coin free, bill acceptors were installed on every machine, and customers were promised "one stop shopping" which would reduce the number of times their calls for service would be transferred to another number. These new systems were a major part of the training effort, and each employee was introduced to the manual back-up system as well as the new technology. As it happened, the player tracking system was not on line at the time of opening, so it became increasingly important for each slot employee to become acquainted with frequent players and develop short-cuts for providing special services to those whose play warranted it. Also, the slot information system and related jackpot and fill triggers had to be accessed manually.

The MGM Grand opened three and a half months ahead of schedule and considerably under budget. Some of the problems created by that accelerated schedule were documented publicly. Six months after opening, announcements were made by the company stating first quarter revenues were considerably ahead of projections and continued efforts were being made to align expenses with industry operating standards.

Experienced start-up managers appreciate the importance of managing the transitions discussed above. The period of time immediately before and after the opening will challenge even the best of managers. All the discussions about what will happen when the doors open come to a halt on opening day. It is time to see whether the leadership is ready, whether employee needs have been met, whether the staffing levels are accurate, whether the opportunities for training and communication were effectively used, and whether the transition from planning to doing can be executed smoothly.

CONCLUSIONS

Successfully opening a new casino depends in large part on the ability of a company's leadership and staff to respond to a multitude of human resource challenges. Developing an organizational strategy can be as important as selecting the site or choosing an architect. This must become a major organizational focus. This article has concentrated on the importance of experienced leadership in providing for the basic needs of employees, communicating realistic expectations of management to employees, accurately projecting staffing levels, and managing the variety of transitions which occur during an opening.

Recruiting the right people to develop and execute a pre-opening strategy for a new casino property is probably the most important task a senior management team faces in ensuring a smooth transition from the planning stage through to a successful opening. The leadership must be knowledgeable about the customer, about the market, about the competition, about new technology, and about effective ways to utilize its human resources component. Where to locate, how to identify, and what compensation and benefits package to offer to successfully recruit these executives are questions which must be answered early in the start-up process. Then executive energy must be expended to properly motivate these individuals to sell their needs to upper management and to operate within the financial and margin parameters established for the property.

Once hired, the pre-opening team must be able to work together in developing a plan that will produce quality products and services provided by employees who are capable and enthused about their role in delivering the product. The company's human resource philosophy shapes this effort since it expresses the company's values regarding its employees. Paying attention to the basic needs of employees and providing clear and consistent expectations for employees are management responsibilities which are critical during pre-opening but also continue after opening. The focus may shift somewhat, and the operating managers will often assume greater responsibility for anticipating and responding to the needs of employees, but being attentive to employees should remain a priority. Developing systems to accurately track employment applications, interviews, reference checks, drug tests, and security clearances will form the foundation of communication with prospective employees about the status of their job requests. Training and communication programs during the pre-opening phase will focus on how and where employees fit into the company's service strategy and what is expected of employees on the job. These programs will usually expand considerably once the property is open to include a more in-depth discussion of the company's policies and procedures and additional skill training in the proper handling of customer situations.

Staffing levels are often dictated by pre-opening budgets which are usually prepared years in advance of the actual casino opening. Contingency funds are sometimes not sufficient to handle unforeseen expenses. There is always pressure to open under budget and some sacrifices are usually made. After opening, it becomes necessary to adjust and ensure that additional expenditures are still worthwhile. It may also become important to restate the property's vision and mission as it relates to the capital and staffing expenditures which are now required.

The ability of a senior executive to manage transitions receives little attention in the gaming industry. Yet considerable skill and experience are required to develop the proper organization structure to achieve the company's objectives and to see the big picture when managing all functions within the organization. Even though senior level executives have experience in openings or in managing operations of significant size, they often hire less experienced subordinates. It becomes critical for the senior executive to instinctively know the amount of direction required by a director or manager to complete an assigned task. It may be appropriate to allow subordinates the autonomy and authority to carry out their responsibilities, but the executive must stay close enough to the process to be able to intercept potential obstacles before they become major problems.

Senior managers must be able to see the property's future and continually communicate it to their management team. Companies that develop an organizational strategy, which emphasizes the human resources component, will have smoother openings and will also create a competitive advantage.

REFERENCES

Cook, Rick, Director of Slots, Gaming Corporation of America, Minneapolis, MN, personal interview, March 1994.

Cooper, Dual, Chief Operating Officer, Casino Magic Corporation, Bay St. Louis, Mississippi, personal interview, April 1994.

Falcon, Israel, Vice President of Gaming, Ameristar Corporation, Vicksburg, Mississippi, personal interviews, January–April 1994.

Fromm, Bill and Leonard A. Schlesinger (1994). *The Real Heroes of Business . . . and Not a CEO Among Them. World Class Frontline Service Workers: How do you find them? Train them? Manage them? Retain them?* New York: Currency/Doubleday.

Handy, Charles (1989), "The Shamrock Organization," *The Age of Unreason:* Cambridge: Harvard Business School Press.

Hommel, Andrew, Vice President of Slot Operations and Marketing, MGM Grand Hotel, Casino and Theme Park, Las Vegas, Nevada, personal interviews, July, 1993–April, 1994.

Hunter, David, Director of Slots, Binion's Horseshoe, Las Vegas, personal interview, April 1994.

Kenny, Michael, General Manager, The President Casino at Biloxi, Biloxi, Mississippi, personal interview, April, 1994.

Mitchell, James, Vice President of Human Resources, Biloxi Grand Casino, Biloxi, Mississippi, personal interview, April, 1994.

O'Donnell, Thomas, General Manager, Turning Stone Casino, Oneida, New York, personal interview, March 1994.

Reynolds, Ann, Shift Manager, Ameristar Casino Vicksburg, Vicksburg, Mississippi, personal interview, April 1994.

Spencer, Lyle and Spencer, Signe (1994). "Competence at Work."

Ulrich, David (1989), "Shared Mindset," *Personnel Administrator,* November.

Wirshing, David, President and COO, Fitzgerald Gaming Corporation, interview, March 1994.

Woolf, Larry, Chairman, President and CEO, MGM Grand Hotel, Casino and Theme Park, interviews, July, 1993–May, 1994.

Yeager, Charles, General Manager, Biloxi Grand Casino, Biloxi, Mississippi, interview, April 1994.

Why the U.S. Gaming Industry Needs a Coordinated Public Relations Strategy to Survive in the 21st Century*

Randolph Baker

If public relations is indeed the art of reputation management that its practitioners profess, it is arguable that there are two truisms with respect to the U.S. casino entertainment industry at the dawn of the 21st Century.

The first truism is that property-level casino executives have shown that they know how to use skillfully the myriad of communications techniques available to them. The second, upon which this short paper shall focus, is that the casino industry as an industry has failed to make its case convincingly to the American people.[1]

Five years ago conventional wisdom on Wall Street was that by the turn of the century legalized casino gambling would once again be commonplace in the United States. And, there was good reason to think that was true. The overwhelming majority of Americans approved of casino gambling in their state (although not in their town); localities wanted the jobs and economic development that casinos were bringing to other communities; and everyone wanted more tax revenues without raising taxes on themselves.

Today it's clear that the rush to legalize is largely over, and casino industry executives cite a myriad of reasons, including an improved economy and well-organized opposition from groups like the National Coalition Against Casino Gambling. None of these executives, however, list the failure by the industry itself to use proactive public relations to its advantage when it had the chance. Nor, is there more than token realization that the

---

* A version of this paper, based on lectures given at the University of Nevada, Reno in 1996, appeared in the Spring 1997 edition of *The Strategist,* a journal published by the Public Relations Society of America devoted to the study of public relations techniques in achieving marketing and public affairs objectives.

long-term future of the casino gaming industry itself may well depend upon the successful implementation of industry-wide public relations initiatives both now and in the years ahead.[2] This paper will argue that if the casino gaming industry as an industry does not aggressively create and maintain a positive image for itself, based on accurate and honest information, that the number of jurisdictions in which it is legal will decline over time.

In 1989, casino entertainment was legal in one state in the United States—Nevada—and in one city in a second state—Atlantic City, New Jersey. Today, it is legal in varying degrees in 25 states. Of the new gaming jurisdictions, about a third are riverboat gaming jurisdictions in the Mississippi River Valley, with the remainder for the most part being states in which Las Vegas-style gambling is permissible in varying degrees on Indian reservations due to a quirk in American constitutional law.

Rather than being in a continued expansive mode, the industry is in retreat;[3] a national gaming commission will soon begin a highly public debate on the role of gaming in American society that creators of the commission clearly hope will lead to heavy federal taxation and regulation;[4] and the public shares of most of the great casino companies are worth a fraction of what they were just three years ago. Meanwhile, casino gambling continues to attract more and more patrons, trailing only "going to the movies" as the most popular away-from-home entertainment option for the American people.[5]

To understand the premise that the industry's present problems are the result of poor public relations, one must understand something of the history of gambling in the United States of America and why the most recent explosion in legalized gambling took place.

THE THIRD WAVE

Gambling has been commonplace in American society on two previous occasions in our nation's history. These earlier periods were roughly from the mid-1700s to the early 1800s and from the mid-1800s until the early 1900s. The first wave is characterized in history by massive lotteries, including one used by the Continental Congress to help pay for the Revolutionary War; the second wave, by the mythic figures of the Mississippi riverboat gambler and the Western card shark. Both earlier eras ended in the wake of widespread corruption and a national turn-to-the-right religiously and politically.

I. Nelson Rose, the California legal scholar who first described the current era of gambling in America as the "third wave," has noted 70-year-cycles in legalization and jokes half-seriously that the current wave should end in about 2035, roughly 70 years after New Hampshire began the current period of gaming by legalizing a state lottery.

History may prove Professor Rose wrong for two reasons. Computer technology has eliminated the widespread corruption which precipitated the two previous cycles' coming to an end;[6] and, equally important, the industry itself has a chance through the tools of effective public relations to counter mistruths and partial truths being used by its opponents in their efforts "to turn back this evil tide even unto the very State of Nevada," as the Reverend Tom Grey, field director of the National Coalition Against Legalized Gambling punned before one group of West Virginia anti-gaming activists.[7]

REASONS FOR CASINO LEGALIZATION

Whether or not the "evil tide" is turned back, it is clear that there have been five causes for the explosion in casino legalization in this decade. They include:

- a dramatic shift in public opinion, from overwhelming opposition to the existence of legal gambling in the 1960s to clear majority support in the 1990s;
- a need in many states for substantive economic development, particularly in communities whose jobs-producing industries have constricted in size or physically disappeared;
- an almost universal need at both the state and local government levels for increased tax revenues that do not come in the form of increased personal or property taxes;
- the fact that the U.S. casino industry is owned for the most part by American or New York Stock Exchange-traded companies, thus eliminating the taint of Mafia control which clouded the gaming industry in its early years; and
- the consequence of the federal Indian Gaming Regulatory Act of 1988, which permits Las Vegas-style gambling on Indian reservations under certain circumstances.

Opponents of casino gaming believe the above factors were secondary at best to heavy lobbying by the gambling industry in those jurisdictions where privately owned (as opposed to Indian-owned) casinos have been legalized. In fact, *there has never been a single occurrence in American history where outside lobbying by casino interests played more than a minor role in a state's decision to legalize casino gambling.* And, the casino companies have done more to hurt their causes than to help them.

EXAMPLES OF POOR INDUSTRY PR

In several states—New York, Connecticut, Florida and Hawaii, for example—excessive lobbying by and casino companies publicly working at cross-purposes with each other eroded popular support into losing legislative positions. Even worse, in some states—notably Louisiana—casino industry actions in support of ethically questionable politicians and a seeming "public be damned" attitude by some major operators contributed to a genuine backlash (resulting in the November 1996 local votes in several parishes about whether or not to repeal all forms of legal gambling except the state lottery).

An excellent illustration of how companies work at cross-purposes occurred early in 1997 in New York State when Donald Trump, owner of several Atlantic City, New Jersey, gaming establishments, said the following of the aforementioned Reverend Grey: "This is the guy who you want in your camp." The occasion was after Reverend Grey teamed up with Trump's lobbyists to defeat a gambling bill for New York that would have threatened the Trump empire in New Jersey, "a stunning turnabout for a measure that, just a few weeks ago, had been widely expected to pass. The vote ended years of public debate and backroom intrigue, and dashed the aspirations of business owners and elected officials from the Catskills to Niagara Falls who had envisioned casinos as a golden remedy for their regions' ailing tourist economies. A state study had shown that casinos would have brought in $2.6 billion to the economy and created 38,000 new jobs."[8]

Although there are some excellent examples of good, often highly creative public relations in the new gaming jurisdictions in the 1990s, most having to do with property-level promotions, the gaming industry's real public relations bloopers are better known, as well as those which are causing the industry the greatest headaches today.

Here are four examples of "how not to do it," all of which fall within the highly visible political, community and media relations areas:

1. In Missouri, media allegations that the speaker of the state house of representatives had been hired by a major gaming company to assist with a matter under the legislator's possible control helped defeat the gaming industry's first attempt to pass a constitutional amendment permitting slot machines in the state's riverboat casinos. Subsequently, the gaming company was exonerated of all charges, although the now-former-speaker remains under scrutiny by federal authorities for alleged violations not related to gaming. While the issue remained under the media spotlight, however, a second statewide vote on the constitutional amendment was held, and the amendment passed—but only by the narrowest of margins.[9]

2. In Louisiana, the chairman of the company that won the license to build New Orleans' mega-land-based casino allegedly told reporters that the first thing he would do after opening the casino would be to get the state's law changed that prohibited the licensee from having a hotel or significant restaurant capacity—*despite the fact* that those were conditions precedent to New Orleans' political leadership agreeing to permit a land-based casino.

   A little over a year later, another executive of the same company publicly told gaming authorities that the company would not close its temporary facility. Within weeks, it closed the casino without notice, throwing approximately 2,500 New Orleanians into unemployment.

3. In California, one of the nation's largest gaming companies was found to be generously funding the efforts of opponents to gambling initiatives in that jurisdiction. Earlier variants of the same story occurred in Mississippi, Massachusetts and other jurisdictions as well. In one Mississippi local option election, for example, one gaming interest allegedly went so far as to anonymously digitally superimpose a photograph of prostitutes in front of the competitor's Las Vegas casino onto postcards bearing the composite picture sent to every registered voters in the county. The competitor had called for the election and was proposing to build a major facility on property closer to Memphis than that owned by the interest that allegedly mailed the postcards.

   The headline on the postcard read: "Casino gaming will bring new jobs to DeSoto County." (The same prostitutes later appeared in full-page ads in the Indiana suburbs of Louisville, Kentucky, before a gaming election under the headline of "Casino gaming will bring new jobs to Indiana." Instead of being in front of a well-known Las Vegas casino, however, they were standing on a darkly lit street corner.)[10]

4. In Florida, five separate casino groups coalesced behind a "Proposition for Limited Casinos" that would for all practical purposes permit the groups to have everything they wanted—a series of 47 small to mega-sized resort casinos across the state. Even though there was a high degree of support for gaming in the state and proponents spent more than $17 million pushing the referendum, it went down to resounding defeat, largely because no one asked "Does this specific proposal make sense for Florida?"

CURRENT INDUSTRY PR CHALLENGES

To keep the casino gaming industry legal beyond 2035, by which time Professor Rose's Wave Theory of Casino Gaming says the industry will be prohibited once again, the gaming industry needs collectively to develop and implement a long-range public relations strategy that will demonstrate it is a contributor to a community's economic success, that it does not cause crime, and that it does not contribute in a significant way to increases in rates of compulsive gambling. If the facts are not positive for the industry, as may be the case with respect to compulsive gambling, it should formulate a responsible position and act aggressively in a highly publicized manner.

The industry can begin in 1997 to do what it should have been doing throughout the decade by demonstrating before the current national gaming commission, as it did before the first federal gaming commission in 1976, that the industry is free of criminal taint and a positive contributor to—not a cannibalizer of—its host community's local economy. There is a great deal of anecdotal evidence and some empirical data by now to document positive economic impact of casinos in new jurisdictions,[11] despite several hypothetical economic models by academicians suggesting negative results.[12] The industry needs to communicate its positive message—and to keep communicating it, particularly in jurisdictions where legal gaming is now or imminently threatened to be under attack.[13]

When the last national gaming commission was created, its sponsors too were seeking the presidential nomination of their respective parties. But, the times were very different. Legal gaming existed only in Nevada and a few isolated jurisdictions overseas. Today, it is widespread throughout both the United States and Canada, and the Mexican federal congress is expected sometime in 1997 to consider a bill to legalize it in tourist areas there too. Meanwhile, gambling has been legalized or liberalized in at least a third of the world's countries.

AMERICAN GAMING ASSOCIATION

In 1995, the heads of several casino and gaming-equipment manufacturing companies organized the industry's first genuine national trade group, the American Gaming Association. The AGA, now composed of more than 80-member companies, was formed to combat the threat of a "sin" tax by the federal government and has succeeded thus far. If the national gaming commission ends up with a federal excise tax on the gaming industry as one of its primary recommendations—which remains clearly possible—the Association will face a real challenge: how to differentiate itself from the alcohol and tobacco industries for excise tax purposes.

Over the long-haul, the casino industry and its spokespersons need to focus attention on the issues of crime and compulsive gambling addiction. What little empirical research has been done to date on these issues suggests that the casino industry is in good shape on the crime issue but in trouble on the compulsive gambling issue. An argument which the industry used early on in conservative jurisdictions also merits repeat attention, i.e., as a Canadian columnist phrased it recently: ". . . any nation that dares to call itself a free society must allow people to make free choices on how they spend their own money. It doesn't matter if a minority, or even a majority, of the population disapprove of a product or an activity, the freedom to choose is fundamental."[14]

Thus far, the industry has created some localized, modestly funded anti-gambling efforts in a handful of cities that have casinos and, through the American Gaming Association, has announced a multi-year, multi-million dollar research project into the causes and prevention of compulsive gambling addiction.[15] No systematic attempts have been made, however, to inform the public-at-large of these efforts, despite two significant reports within the past couple of years that are unfavorable to the industry. (One, an empirical study in Iowa in 1995, suggests a cause and effect relationship between the coming of legalized casino gaming and significant increases in the prevalence of compulsive gambling addiction within the public-at-large. The other, prepared by a 'think tank' of experts from different disciplines, suggests that the rates of compulsive gambling behavior may be twice as high among teenagers as among the population as a whole, regardless of the status of legalized gaming in the teens' home states.)

The public relations challenge for the casino entertainment industry is to prove to the American people that its business is like any other—neither a miraculous cure for economic decline nor the embodiment-of-all-evil in a single entity. Neither wholly good, nor wholly bad. That will not happen, however, unless the industry "gets its act together." To do so means the industry must unite; must agree upon accurate, positive messages about itself; and must deliver those messages in a highly systematic fashion through each of the communications tools available, including institutional advertising.[16]

In short, it must be prepared as a unified body—subject, of course, to all relevant federal antitrust considerations—to spend a lot of money in a highly aggressive manner over a long period of time.

Part of being a unified body is for industry giants to agree not to undercut each other's efforts to win support for gaming in new jurisdictions. As the National Coalition Against Legalized Gambling's representative is reported to have written in a playful note to Donald Trump's lobbyist during the New York floor debate in early 1997: "The lion shall lie down with the lamb, but the lamb shall not get much sleep." To which the lobbyist wrote back: "But who is the lion?" The anti-gambling leader replied: "You'll know when we come after Trump."[17]

Rather than acting as a coherent whole, the industry to date has for the most part acted as a group of highly individualistic entrepreneurs whose only objective is getting what they want—preferably a *de facto* casino monopoly in a major urban area. If the companies which constitute this industry are not to see the "third wave" of gambling in the U.S. crash in upon them and sweep the remains into the abyss of history, they need to do a much better job—individually and collectively—of communicating with the public-at-large and with the legislators who set public policy for the 21st Century. The only way to do that is through sound public relations over a long enough period of time to make it work.

---

1. Public relations here is defined as the set of proactive, management-led, public-oriented communications activities that include issues management, institutional advertising, media relations, special events, lobbying, investor relations, community and industry relations, and employee relations designed to achieve a clearly defined, measurable objective.
2. In the February 1997 edition of *International Gaming & Wagering Business,* page 59, American Gaming Association President Frank J. Fahrenkopf, Jr., is quoted as saying that it is now time "to 'put a face' on the gaming industry and embark on a grassroots effort to show the industry's widespread economic benefits."
3. The November 1996 elections in many American jurisdictions provided *prima facie* evidence of gambling's continued plunge in popularity. In most of eleven states in which significant gambling issues were on the ballot, the gaming industry lost the vote. The exceptions, however, were of major significance, representing wins by the industry where it really wanted (and arguably needed) to win.

   In Arizona and Michigan, *statewide* referenda approved Las Vegas-style gambling in defined areas for the first time since New Jersey's voters legalized it for Atlantic City in the 1970s. Arizona's vote was to permit gambling on the reservations of five Indian tribes with whom compacts had not been negotiated and approved; Michigan's vote was to permit privately owned casinos in Detroit. (Other Michigan communities already have Indian gaming, so technically neither Arizona nor Michigan passed into the new gaming jurisdictions column.) Meanwhile, Louisiana voters decided to keep that state's riverboat gaming industry, to permit a single land-based mega-casino to go forward in New Orleans, and to rid itself of about half of the truck stock video poker parlors that has previously been legal.
4. Robert R. Detlefsen in *Anti-Gambling Politics—Time To Reshuffle The Deck,* The Competitive Enterprise Institute, October 1996, page 21, well summarizes one of the casino gaming industry's major concerns with the national gambling commission: "The real danger is that the commission will produce a report that scapegoats privately managed gambling even as it whitewashes government-managed gambling. Indeed, lotteries should be held to higher standards than casinos and other forms of privately managed gambling, because they are state-run monopolies. At the very least, state lotteries and casinos should be judged according to the same moral and economic criteria."

5. See the series of annual surveys of the casino entertainment industry commissioned each year by Harrah's Entertainment, Inc., 1023 Cherry Road, Memphis, TN 38117, (901-762-8600) which documents this phenomenon.

6. This view is one that the author has been espousing for some time but is one with which Professor Rose disagrees. For a related issue, however, consider the question of Internet gambling, which "is shaping up as the first substantial test of regulation of the Internet." See Terry Schwadron, "Postcard from Cyberspace: Gambling with our Freedom," *The Los Angeles Times,* November 18, 1996, section D, page 3.

7. This revealing pun was made by Reverend Tom Grey at one of several seminars for anti-gaming activists held in Charleston, West Virginia, in the late fall of 1994 just prior to a decision by the state legislature on whether or not to permit riverboat gaming in the state. The author, a genuine admirer of Reverend Grey's speaking and organizational abilities, was an uninvited guest in the audience.

8. James Dao, "Unlikely Allies: The Bill That Fell from Grace," *New York Times,* February 3, 1997, section B, page one, column 2.

9. One of the best series of articles ever written on the U.S. riverboat gaming industry looks at this issue and many others. The series, by Rick Alm and Keith Chrostowski, ran March 9–11, 1997, in the *Kansas City Star* and demonstrated that a newspaper that is admittedly anti-gambling can produce one of the most objective, professional in-depth analyses seen thus far, academic or journalistic.

10. The author had the misfortune of having been involved on the losing side in both the DeSoto County, Mississippi, and the Clark County, Indiana, elections in which those ads appeared.

11. As *The Economist* opined in a January 25, 1997, article entitled "A busted flush," ". . . it is far from clear that gambling benefits anyone except the casino operators." To counter this widespread notion, the American Gaming Association commissioned Arthur Andersen LLP to do an economic analysis of the consequences of gambling in the United States, which not unsurprisingly was very positive. The survey received some one-time play in newspapers serving cities in which gaming is present, but for the most part, the AGA failed to keep the story before the public and elected officials. Similar studies, such as one done by the University of New Orleans on the impact of gambling in the Crescent City and by Harrah's Entertainment, Inc. on the buying power of its employees in many states, have fared similarly, even when they were mostly positive.

12. See Robert Goodman, *The Luck Business: The Devastating Consequences and Broken Promises of America's Gambling Explosion* (New York: Maertin Kessler Books, 1995) and similar works heavily dependent upon his concept that for each dollar brought in by casinos to state and local government many more dollars go out in services than come in. At least one of Dr. Goodman's disciples has set the negative cash flow for casino entertainment as being as high as 50:1. Most say it's closer to 3:1.

13. In recent years, South Dakotans narrowly voted to retain VLTs, and Louisianans chose to throw VLTs out of half the state (while keeping riverboat gaming

and the land-based casino in Orleans Parish). Iowa, where the casino expansion began in 1984, and where more forms of gambling are legal than in any other U.S. state, votes on a county-by-county basis in 2002 on whether or not to keep any casino gaming legalized in the county to that date. At an average of $1.2 million an hour, 24-hours a day, the *Des Moines Register* reports that Iowans now spend three times as much on gaming as they do on groceries. ("Gambling in Iowa: Because It's There," March 23, 1997, section one, page one.)

14. Chris Sarlo, "Risky Business," *The Calgary Herald,* March 26, 1997, section A, page one.

15. *International Gaming & Wagering Business,* April 1997, page 17, reports that the National Center for Responsible Gaming has received firm commitments of $3.11 million to fund its activities over the next three years. ". . . the Center is the first nationwide, consolidated organization to promote research and collect information on problem and underage gambling," according to the article. "The main goal of the Center is to support unbiased research, fact gathering and data analysis for the purpose of better defining these problems and developing proactive, positive strategies to address them. It also creates prevention, intervention, and treatment strategies, acts as a national source of research findings and provides assistance to state and local governments to encourage responsible gaming practices."

Earlier the *Kansas City Star* in an article by Rick Alm reported that the center, under the leadership of Christine Reilly, "a Missouri social service activist," had been pledged $4.2 million over a 10-year period. (January 28, 1997, section B, page three).

16. A split in the United States Circuit Courts of Appeal is now wending its way to the United States Supreme Court over the issue of whether or not privately owned for-profit casinos may advertise on radio and television. If the High Court rules in favor of abolishing the prohibition, as it should in a rational society, television advertising would be the most effective medium available for such institutional messages. Otherwise, the ads would have to go into newspapers, which reach fewer than ten percent of the population, and into targeted direct mail efforts.

17. Dao, *op. cit.*

The Prevalence and Usefulness of Financial Stability Measurements in the U.S. Gaming Market

John R. Mills and Jannet M. Vreeland

The casino industry has experienced major changes in the past decade. The passage of the Indian Gaming Act in 1988 marked the beginning of major changes for this unique industry. In 1989 South Dakota legalized casino gambling in Deadwood, which marked the end of the two-state, Nevada and New Jersey, monopoly in the industry. As more states legalized gaming, the industry evolved and became more competitive. Even the last few years have brought major changes. The opening of new gaming in the Missouri and Louisiana jurisdictions has caused major shifts in a very competitive gaming market, while the impact of the legalization of casino gaming in Michigan has not yet been determined.

The proliferation of legalized casino gambling has forced state governments to examine their policies on the initial granting and renewal of gaming licenses. State governments have a vested interest, gaming tax revenues, in doing everything to ensure that the casinos they license are financially viable business entities. Over the past twenty years, starting with Nevada and New Jersey, the states with legalized casino gambling have developed criteria for assessing the financial viability of both new casino applicants and the renewal of existing licenses.

The newer jurisdictions use a Request for Proposal (RFP) process in determining who will receive a gaming license. While this RFP process is not perfect (as evidenced by the New Orleans fiasco), it has helped state and local governments in selecting applicants with a higher probability of opening and operating a successful casino. Once the casino is operational, it is in the government's best interest that it be a financial success, since government wants the consistent inflow of taxes from gaming revenues. While the government is concerned with many aspects of the casino industry, it places great emphasis on the financial stability of a casino and its ability to meet its financial obligations, particularly its gaming taxes and its liabilities for jackpots won. If a casino cannot meet its obligations, it creates negative press for the industry as a whole. If a casino's financial position is too weak, then the appropriate state gaming control board may take action, as happened in Mississippi.

"Jubilation forced to close doors"

The Mississippi Gaming Commission has closed down Jubilation Casino. The move marked the first time since gaming started in the state four years ago that the regulatory agency has shut down a casino without management's request. Commission officials took the initiative, saying the boat did not maintain the minimum required cash on hand and feared Jubilation might not have enough money to pay winners if jackpots were hit.

"They were having trouble," said Paul Harvey, executive director of the Mississippi Gaming Commission. "In essence they had very little money in their bank account. We felt it was in the public's best interest and welfare to shut them down"(*International Gaming & Wagering Business,* September 1996, vol. 17, No. 9, page 64).

The action undertaken by the Mississippi Gaming Commission raises two issues. First, from a public policy point of view, when is it appropriate for a regulatory agency to intervene in the running of a casino by shutting it down or imposing a new management team? Second, what criteria should these regulatory agencies be using to substantiate their intervention? This paper examines these issues in the following manner. First, the authors review public policy with regards to gambling by providing the history behind the regulatory agencies' role in controlling the operations of casinos. Then, the current regulations in gaming jurisdictions which give regulators the authority to affect a license are reviewed. In the third section, the authors will discuss the usefulness of financial stability evaluation. Finally, some positive benefits that can result from these regulations are discussed and recommendations made concerning financial stability.

PUBLIC POLICY OF GAMING JURISDICTIONS

Gambling has always had a negative connotation because many people believe that it is a socially unacceptable behavior. They believe that gambling focuses attention on luck rather than the more acceptable behavior of productive labor. Thus, while gambling is nearly as old as civilization itself (Rychlak, 1995, p.294), governments have also been regulating gambling practically since its inception (Rychlak, 1995, p. 295).

Within the United States, regulators have always suggested that all matters affecting public health and public morals should be subject to state regulation. With the exception of Iowa and Missouri, that did not enact explicit statutory policy statements, all of the states stress the need for public confidence and strict regulation of gaming (Franckiewicz, 1993, p. 1135). In addition, many states provide rules and regulations which address the statutory obligation of a casino licensee to establish and maintain its financial stability. Many of the newer states which have established gaming regulations have typically adopted regulations similar to those of Nevada and New Jersey. An analysis of the financial stability regulations of these two states provides a basis for evaluating the regulations adopted by other gaming jurisdictions.

PUBLIC POLICY OF NEVADA

In 1955, the Nevada Legislature created the Nevada Gaming Control Board which was to fall within the jurisdiction of the Nevada Tax Commission. The purpose of the Nevada Gaming Control Board, (NGCB) was to inaugurate a policy to eliminate the undesirable element in Nevada gaming and to provide regulations for the licensing and the operation of gaming. The Nevada Gaming Commission was created in 1959 with the passage of a complete Gaming Control Act (NRS 463). This act removed the Gaming Control Board from the Tax Commission and placed it under the newly formed Nevada Gaming Commission.

NRS 463.0129 articulates the public policy reasons for controlling entrance into Nevada's gaming industry and reviewing the performance and licenses of participants in the industry.

a) The gaming industry is vitally important to the economy of the state and the general welfare of the inhabitants.

b) The continued growth and success of the gaming industry is dependent upon public confidence and trust that licensed gaming is conducted honestly and competitively and that the gaming industry is free from criminal and corruptive elements.

c) Public confidence and trust can only be maintained by strict regulation of all persons, locations, practices, associations and activities related to the operation of licensed gaming establishments.

d) All establishments where gaming is conducted shall therefore be licensed, controlled and assisted to protect the public health, safety, morals, good order and general welfare of the inhabitants of the state, to foster the stability and success of the gaming industry and to preserve the competitive economy and policies of free competition of the state (NRS 463.0129).

The primary steps in maintaining this policy and protecting the integrity of gaming operations are through the initial licensing and subsequent control. Background investigations of prospective licensees (Frank, p. 1138,

1993) include assessing the integrity, honesty and good character of the applicant. An evaluation of the financing for the proposed casinos is also conducted during the licensing process. NRS 463.170 states that:

> A license to operate a gaming establishment must not be granted unless the applicant has satisfied the commission that:
> a) He has adequate business probity, competence and experience, in gaming or generally; and
> b) the proposed financing of the entire operation is:
> 1) Adequate for the nature of the proposed operation; and
> 2) From a suitable source.

Once a casino license has been granted, other regulations are in effect which are designed to provide a sense of the financial stability of the licensee. Nevada Gaming Commission Regulation 3.050 requires the applicant to show that adequate financing is available to pay all current obligations, and that working capital is adequate to finance the opening. The criteria for determining whether the financing is adequate are often subjective. The decision depends on several factors, including the size of the casino, the nature of past operations, the condition of the facilities, and the amount of debt service.

The regulatory effort to foster the stability and success of the gaming industry was further strengthened by including within NRS 463 a provision which allowed the Gaming Commission to suspend or revoke the licenses of individual licensees or a gaming establishment. NRS 463B (Supervision Chapter) provides for the appointment of a supervisor to manage and control a gaming establishment when the licensees are determined to be unsuitable or financially unstable.

While the regulatory environment in Nevada provides for unlimited licenses and allows the market to determine the success or failure of individual casinos, there was always a concern that Nevada could ruin its reputation if casinos were not able to meet their obligations to the gambling public or the employees of the casino. Legislators addressed this concern by implementing rules designed to protect the financial integrity of Nevada's casino industry and the State. These rules are incorporated into Nevada Regulation 6. Specifically, Nevada Regulation 6.150, also called the minimum bankroll requirement, is designed to provide assurances that cash is available for normal operating expenses and operating liabilities. It requires the following:

> Each nonrestricted licensee shall maintain, in such manner and amount as the chairman may approve or require, cash or cash equivalents in an amount sufficient to reasonably protect the licensee's patrons against defaults in gaming debts owed by the licensee. The

chairman shall distribute to the licensees and make available to all interested persons a formula approved by the commission by which licensees determine the minimum bankroll requirements of this section. If at any time the licensee's available cash or cash equivalents should be less than the amount required by this section, the licensee must immediately notify the board of this deficiency.

NRS 463.621 and NRS 463.623 were enacted to address the potential negative effects of corporate raiders and rapid expansions on the financial stability of the industry. NRS 463.621 states the following:

Some corporate acquisitions opposed by management, repurchases of securities and corporate defense tactics affecting corporate gaming licensees and publicly traded corporations that are affiliated companies can constitute business practices which may be injurious to stable and productive corporate gaming.

NRS 463.623 addresses this potential problem by requiring the NGCB to review and approve all corporate acquisitions opposed by management, repurchases of securities and defense tactics affecting corporate gaming licensees and publicly traded corporations that are affiliated companies. Given the major expansion plans of some of the gaming corporations both inside and outside Nevada, the corporate division of the NGCB is currently reviewing and approving or not approving all issues of debt and equity (per Regulation 16.110).

Nevada's gaming laws and regulations provide no guidance in terms of what is used when the NGCB reviews corporations' submittance for issuing debt or equity. A report by Christiansen (1991) provides evidence that four standard ratios plus "free cash" are applied on a case by case basis. Additional subjective factors are also used for influences that are not adequately captured by numerical analysis (Christiansen, 1991, p. A-31).

NEW JERSEY PUBLIC POLICY ON FINANCIAL STABILITY

New Jersey became the second state to legalize casino gambling, with the passage of the Casino Control Act on June 2, 1977. This law, which was codified as N.J.S.A. 5:12, required any applicant for a casino license to "establish by clear and convincing evidence the financial stability, integrity and responsibility of the applicant." What constituted clear and convincing evidence of financial stability was left to the New Jersey Gaming Commission.

New Jersey's gaming industry hit bottom from 1989 to 1991. Take-over attempts and a bad economy in 1989, 1990, and 1991 resulted in casinos with highly leveraged balance sheets and a wave of defaulted obligations and restructuring (Christiansen, 1991, p.3). In 1992, the New Jersey Gaming Control Commission proposed changes in the original regulations to provide for continuing assessment of the financial stability of its casinos. These regulations were adopted, and then amended. The most recent changes were placed into law in 1996 (N.J.A.C. 19:43-4.1-4.5).

19:43-4.2, Financial stability, now requires that:

a) Each casino licensee or applicant shall establish its financial stability by clear and convincing evidence in accordance with section 84(a) of the Act and this subchapter.

b) The Commission may consider any relevant evidence of financial stability provided, however, that a casino licensee or applicant shall be considered to be financially stable if it establishes by clear and convincing evidence that it meets each of the following standards:

1. The ability to assure the financial integrity of casino operations by the maintenance of a casino bankroll or equivalent provisions adequate to pay winning wagers to casino patrons when due. A casino licensee or applicant shall be found to have established this standard if it maintains, on a daily basis, a casino bankroll, or a casino bankroll and equivalent provisions, in an amount which is at least equal to the average daily minimum casino bankroll or equivalent provisions, calculated on a monthly basis, for the corresponding month in the previous year. For any casino licensee or applicant which has been in operation for less than a year, such amount shall be determined by the Commission based upon levels maintained by a comparable casino licensee;

2. The ability to meet ongoing operating expenses which are essential to the maintenance of continuous and stable casino operations. A casino licensee or applicant shall be found to have established this standard if it demonstrates the ability to achieve positive gross operating profit, measured on an annual basis;

3. The ability to pay, as and when due, all local, State and Federal taxes, including the tax on gross revenues imposed by subsection 144(a) of the Act, the investment alternative tax obligations imposed by subsection 144(b) and section 144.1 of the Act, and any fees imposed by the Act and Commission rules;

4. The ability to make necessary capital and maintenance expenditures in a timely manner which are adequate to ensure maintenance of a superior first class facility of exceptional quality pursuant to subsection 83(I) of the Act. A casino licensee or applicant shall be found to have established this standard if it demonstrates that its capital and maintenance expenditures, over the five-year period which includes the three most recent calendar years and

the upcoming two calendar years, average at least five percent of net revenue per annum, except that any casino licensee or applicant which has been in operation for less than three years shall be required to otherwise establish compliance with this standard; and

5. The ability to pay, exchange, refinance or extend debts, including long-term and short-term principal and interest and capital lease obligations, which will mature or otherwise come due and payable during the license term, or to otherwise manage such debts and any default with respect to such debts, the Commission also may require that a casino licensee or applicant advise the Commission and Division as to its ability to meet this standard with respect to any material debts coming due and payable within 12 months after the end of the license term.

PUBLIC POLICY ON FINANCIAL STABILITY IN OTHER GAMBLING JURISDICTIONS

The newer jurisdictions, starting with South Dakota, appear to think that financial integrity is an important characteristic of a casino licensee. Universally, these jurisdictions have incorporated some reference to financial responsibility or financial integrity in the various legislation that legalized casino and riverboat gambling. What they have not done, is codified the criteria that denote financial stability.

Table 1 was developed based on a phone survey of the various gaming control boards. New Jersey's criteria for financial stability was used as

TABLE 1
Summary of Financial Stability Measurements
Adopted in the New Jurisdictions

State	Bankroll	Operating Profit	Taxes	Capital Expenditures	Debt
Colorado	Yes	No	No	No	No
Illinois	No	No	No	No	No
Indiana	No	No	No	No	No
Iowa	No	No	No	No	No
Louisiana	N/R*	N/R	N/R	N/R	N/R
Mississippi	Yes	N/R	N/R	N/R	N/R
Missouri	N/R	N/R	N/R	N/R	N/R
South Dakota	Yes	No	No	No	No
*N/R = No response					

the benchmark against which the financial stability criteria of the new jurisdictions were compared. It appears that the majority of the new jurisdictions handle the financial stability criteria for licensing and renewals on a case by case basis. The most common criterion is a minimum bankroll requirement.

USEFULNESS OF FINANCIAL STABILITY EVALUATION

It appears that all the jurisdictions believe that evaluating financial stability at some level and at some point is important. The next question that needs to be addressed is when is an evaluation of financial stability most crucial. Talks with Nevada NGCB officers contributed a very useful observation: Where financial stability is concerned the must effective regulation is at the point of construction or the approval of indebtedness. Once the concrete is poured, or the debt is assumed, the regulator has lost much of his ability to prevent problems, including the problem of default. The time to apply regulatory pressure is before the fact: before ground is broken, or bonds are issued. Strict regulation after the fact is harder and much less productive (Christiansen, 1991, p. A-33).

Most of the new gaming jurisdictions which limited licenses issued RFPs and selected those operators who provided the best package to the city who issued the bid. However, the bidders typically minimized their risk and exposure by forming joint ventures. Many of these joint ventures were highly leveraged, with the partners contributing a minimum amount of equity financing. The end result is a highly leveraged company with a significant likelihood of running the operation into the ground, while draining off as much cash as possible. An initial assessment of the financial stability of such an operator is essential, but just as important is the on-going monitoring of the company's financial position.

Although it appears that the initial evaluation of financial stability of the licensee is crucial to a healthy gaming industry, the changing competition and environment within the gaming industry means that there will always be a need to monitor on-going casino operations. Regulators must be aware of different types of gaming competition, not only within each state but across state boarders. Some states, like Mississippi, have seen tremendous growth, but are currently experiencing casino failures because of an over saturation of the market. Other states which introduced limited casinos or riverboats are finding that the changing regulations in other jurisdictions, or the opening of additional properties have had a negative impact on their gaming operations. It is essential that regulators have the ability to evaluate and understand the financial position and stability of the gaming properties they oversee, as well as the industry as a whole.

Without this knowledge, how will they be able to understand the possible consequences of changes in regulations within their own jurisdictions, as well as other jurisdictions. For example, what impact will a change in the casino tax rate have on the casino properties? Or, what effect will the legalization of casino gambling in Michigan have on Illinois and Indiana gaming?

CONCLUSION

Regulators are very concerned with ensuring that they issue a gaming license to an operator who has integrity, honesty and good character. They also want the applicant to have the financing to build and operate the casino. They also need to be concerned that each property will continue to be maintained at a level which will continue to draw customers in the face of increasing competition. To do this, the operator must be continuously upgrading the property with capital maintenance projects. It also means generating enough cash flows and maintaining these funds in the corporation in order to fund these projects. The development of realistic financial stability measures will go a long way in providing relevant information to regulators for analyzing whether operators are in fact planning for the future. Regulators can also use the financial stability information to assess the strength of its gaming industry and the potential for its future.

REFERENCES

Christiansen/Cummings Associates, Inc. (1991). *Financial Stability: An Analysis Prepared for the New Jersey Casino Control Commission,* December 18.

Franckiewicz, Victor J. (1993). *The States Ante Up: An Analysis of Casino Gaming Statues,* Loyola Law Review, Vol.38, Winter, p. 1123–1157.

Goodwin, John R. (1985). *Gaming Control Law; The Nevada Model.* Columbus Ohio: Publishing Horizons, Inc.

Maron, David F. (1995). *The Mississippi Gaming Commission: An Analysis of the Structures, Duties and Regulatory Role of the Agency in Light of the Growing Mississippi Gaming Industry,* Mississippi Law Journal, Vol. 64, Winter, p. 635–657.

Nevada Gaming Control Act, Chapters 462–466, Incorporating amendments as of 1995.

N.J.A.C. 19:43-4.2 Financial Stability, As Amended, Effective 03/18/96.

Regulations of the Nevada Gaming Commission and State Gaming Control Board, Carson City, Nevada, as Adopted July 1, 1959 and current as of June 1, 1995.

Nevada Gaming Commission and State Gaming Control Board (1995). *Gaming Nevada Style.* Carson City, Nevada.

Rychlak, Ronald J. (1995). *The Introduction of Casino Gambling: Public Policy and the Law,* Mississippi Law Journal, Winter, vol. 64, p. 291–362.

Market Studies for New Gaming Jurisdictions

Lynn D. Constan

Urban Systems, Inc. has been involved in the 1990s with market feasibility studies for more than 25 gaming operators in Louisiana, Alabama, Mississippi, Missouri, Indiana, Iowa, Virginia, North Carolina, and Canada. These market studies provide estimates of the gaming market size in terms of both number of patrons annually and the total gaming revenue expected.

The company has also prepared statewide overviews of potential gaming markets in Texas, Florida, and Massachusetts. As part of the feasibility studies, Urban Systems, Inc. has conducted primary market research surveys in five states, both telephone and intercept surveys, collecting data on actual gaming behavior which we have used to develop assessments of other markets.

A variety of methodologies have been used for these analyses ranging from very simple to complex. The selection of the methodology depends mainly on the nature of the expected competition in the market area under study.

This analysis explores a number of methodologies that were utilized. It points out strengths and weaknesses inherent in each approach.

CONCENTRIC RING MODEL

The most simplistic model available for analyzing a gaming market is the concentric ring model. This method draws on the Atlantic City experience and is based on observed relationships between travel distance and gaming behavior. Basically, the model states that people who live closer to a casino venue are more likely to go and will visit more often than people with longer travel times. The two factors involved in developing such models are propensity and frequency where propensity is the percentage of the adult population which will visit the casino at least once a year and frequency is the average number of trips made by those who are casino visitors, or gamers. The number of gamer visits can then be estimated by multiplying the adult population in a given region by the estimated propensity to project the number of gamers, and then multiplying the number of gamers by the estimated frequency to project the number of gamer visits per year.

This suggests two further questions: How are the propensity and frequency factors estimated, and how does one determine the given area? The second question is addressed first.

The outer limit of the local market area is considered to be the maximum distance that would constitute a day trip. For our purposes, we consider a three hour drive as the outside limit of a day trip. This would allow for three hours travel to the casino, a four hour stay, and a three hour trip home for a round trip time of ten hours. In rural areas where traffic is generally light, a maximum distance of 200 miles is used to define the local market. In more developed areas with high density populations and congested traffic conditions which increase travel times, a maximum distance of 150 miles is used.

Since gaming behavior is known to vary with travel distance, the local market area is then subdivided into concentric rings of increasing radius. Generally, the inner ring has a radius of less than 50 miles, the middle ring a radius of between 50 and 100 miles, and the outer ring a radius of 100 to 200 miles. The adult population within each ring can be calculated from census data or other sources, and then by the application of the appropriate factors, the number of casino visits can be estimated.

This model, while simplistic, provides a good estimate for markets which have no significant competition within the local area and which offer only one primary gaming opportunity. It is not appropriate for new developing areas where there will be numerous gaming opportunities in various locations which produce considerable overlap among the market areas. As an example, drawing concentric rings of 50 mile radii around ten possible gaming locations in southern Indiana results in a situation which clearly shows the drawbacks to using this model, not only missing the competitive implications for any particular locale, but also double counting casino visits resulting in market overestimation. A method which addresses the effects of competition must be used in this type of situation.

MARKET AREA CARVE-OUT

In some areas, it is possible to conduct a closer inspection of the physical and social characteristics of the region to define discrete market areas and eliminate the overlap. This methodology was used in our analysis of potential Florida gaming markets. Our assessment was based on the 1994 "Limited Stakes" gaming referendum which would have provided for a 75,000 square foot casino at each of the thirty-one parimutuel facilities in the state, in addition to seven free standing casinos, including a mega-casino in Miami.

In this method, predefined areas serve as the basis for the market area definition. A number of types of predefined areas can be used. The Census Bureau defines Metropolitan Statistical Areas (MSAs) as free standing areas not closely associated with other MSAS. An MSA consists of a large population nucleus, a central city, and adjacent communities that have been determined to have a high degree of economic and social integration with that nucleus

Areas of Dominant Influence (ADIs) are another pre-existing geographical boundary that can be used to segregate market areas. ADIs are defined by the Arbitron rating services and identify areas which have the same media coverage. Designated Market Areas (DMAs) which are defined by the Nielsen rating service can also be used. Thus the same radio and television stations serve all the area within an ADI or DMA. Another option is to use Economic Analysis Areas (EAAs) which are defined by the Department of Commerce, Bureau of Economic Analysis. Similar to the MSA definition, these are areas that are economically related.

Each of these area definitions is useful in constructing gaming market regions. Although travel distance is important, it is also important to recognize with which metropolitan areas residents of outlying areas identify most closely. The reasons for this identification may be cultural, may be a result of historical development patterns, or may have to do with physical travel barriers such as limited river crossings.

In dividing Florida into market areas, Urban Systems evaluated all of these area definitions, along with interstate highway and other major access routes. Core areas were first identified as those counties common to each of the definitions. The fringe areas were then evaluated to assign the remaining counties to each of the gaming markets. This is a largely subjective process which we supplemented with interviews with local chambers of commerce and planning departments to confirm our assessment of the relationships between outlying areas and the central cities.

Once the market areas are satisfactorily defined, the analysis uses the concentric ring theory to assign propensity and frequency factors to the adult population living within the market area.

COMPETITIVE FACTORS

In other regions of the country, as gaming has become more prevalent, it is not feasible to carve out local market areas. The overlap between gaming market areas is such that a significant amount of cross-over activity can be expected. Although individual casino visitors may develop a preference for a single casino which they will visit exclusively, on average, patrons will sometimes visit one casino and at other times visit another. This behavior can be expressed in terms of percentages of gaming activity which will be captured by each location.

Many things will influence gamer behavior in this type of situation. Some of the factors can be quantified in terms of travel distance or relative availability, but much remains dependent of the relative preferences of potential visitors analysis. A county level map is prepared showing the primary travel routes and locations of competing casinos in the area. Areas are then delineated based on an assessment of similar characteristics in terms of competition and access.

Consider as an example an analysis of the competing casino venues in the Dubuque, Iowa market area. In 1994, there were nine casinos in the region, seven of which were riverboat casinos and two Indian casinos. There were also numerous Indian casinos in Minnesota and Wisconsin located just outside of the 200 mile area which could exert a competitive force on gamers in the outer ring.

For the Dubuque gaming market, the primary competition would be the riverboat casinos in the Quad Cities of Davenport/Bettendorf, Iowa, Rock Island, Illinois, and Clinton, Iowa. Moving outward, the riverboat casino in Peoria, Illinois and the Indian casino in Tama, Iowa were added to the list of competitors for the gaming dollar in the area. After each area was defined, based on distance and extent of competition, an attraction factor representing the percent of gaming trips generated in each area that will be drawn to the location under study was assigned.

As noted, this is primarily a subjective analysis based on relative travel times and the supply of gaming that is available in each location. Thus, for example, potential casino customers to Dubuque from the Joliet, Illinois area—where two casino riverboats boats were operating in 1994, and still other casino boats were closer to Joliet than Dubuque—are considered highly unlikely to travel the additional distance to Dubuque since a variety of gaming experiences are already available to them locally. By contrast, where there is only one other alternative, gamers are considered more likely to seek out other gaming venues. However, other considerations, such as the greater desirability of land based casino facilities versus dockside or mandated cruising riverboats, also need to be factored in.

After determining the total number of gamer visits generated in each county, the attraction factors are used to allocate the percentage of trips from the area to the market location under study.

GRAVITY MODEL

Sometimes the complexity of the market area is such that it is not possible to reliably develop attraction factors or to carve out individual market areas. As an example, Urban System's analysis of the relative potential of six Massachusetts casino markets began by drawing a 25 mile radius circle around each location. Because of close proximity of sites, even at 25 miles, there was considerable overlap between the markets. We then turned to the market carve out technique used in Florida. However, the MSAs and the ADIs area was so large that they did not offer any insights into market division.. The area was dominated by Boston with almost all of the proposed markets included in the Boston MSA and ADI. To evaluate this market, we then turned to a gravity model.

Gravity models are continuously used in location studies for commercial developments, public facilities, and residential developments. First developed in 1929 and later refined in the 1940s, the gravity model is an analytical tool which defines the behavior of a population based on travel distance and the availability of the goods or services under consideration at various locations. In the classic application to shopping behavior at retail centers, the gravity model states that—when confronted with shopping centers of equal size—an individual would tend to shop more often at the closer of the two centers. When considering shopping centers of unequal size, individuals would be drawn to the larger, more diverse center more frequently and from greater distances than to the smaller shopping center.

The general form of the equation is that attraction is directly related to a measure of availability such as square feet and inversely related to the square of the travel distance. This type of model can be applied in a similar fashion to casino venues.

Primary market research data collected by Urban Systems on the Mississippi Gulf Coast market confirms the applicability of the gravity model to casino developments. The number of casino visits made by location were analyzed by place of residence. In 1994, the Mississippi Gulf Coast gaming market consisted of ten casinos located in three cities along a 25 mile stretch of the state's coastline. As predicted by a gravity model, persons living to the east of the casino developments were more likely to visit the eastern-most casinos while people living to the west were more likely to visit the western-most casinos. There were two major exceptions. Two of the largest casinos were successful in drawing patrons from longer distances in spite of the increased travel times which is a finding fully consistent with the gravity model.

In developing a gaming model for the Gulf Coast, a constrained gravity model was used. Input from the concentric ring model was introduced to estimate the total number of gamer visits annually which would be produced by each geographic unit. Geographic units can be defined by any appropriate measure such as counties, zip code area, or even census tracts. The only requirement is that census data be available for each unit defined. The selection of the geographic unit depends on the characteristics of the study area. The county level is usually adequate except in the northeastern United States where the population is highly concentrated and there are only a few counties per state. The use of smaller divisions—such as five digit zip code areas—dramatically increases the amount of work required to develop the data needed to run the model.

Overall gaming behavior for each area is assumed to be driven by the closest casino location. For example, a gamer might live in an area where there are projected to be three gaming opportunities: one twenty miles away and two others seventy miles away. For each geographic unit considered in the analysis, propensity and frequency would be determined based on the travel distance to the nearest casino. Applying these factors to the adult population in each geographic unit then results in a total estimated number of gamer visits which will be generated from that area to all casino locations. The gravity model is then used as a probabilistic measure to distribute the gamer visits from each geographic unit to each gaming location.

Two factors are used to develop the attraction measures: distance and availability. Distance is simply the distance between the geographic unit and each casino location. Depending on the complexity of the study, distance can be calculated as actual road miles from the center of the area to the casino or measured as straight line distances.

Availability can be expressed in any appropriate unit of measure. The most accurate measures of availability for a casino study would be square feet of gaming area in each location, or more preferably, the number of gaming positions supplied. However, at early stages of analysis, detailed data on proposed casino developments is frequently not available. Availability can be expressed in terms of the number of casinos or number of licenses proposed for each location. Scaling factors can be used to reflect the relative attractiveness of cruising riverboat versus dockside or land based gaming if the area being modeled contains a mixture of types of casinos. The attraction measures are then converted to relative attractions or probabilities that an individual residing in a given geographic unit will visit each of the casino locations.

Competition from casinos external to the local market area under analysis can be included explicitly in the model by including the casino as one of the sites to be analyzed. As an example, in evaluating the gaming market for Norfolk, Virginia, we included Atlantic City as an external point in the model. Although we did not expressly calculate the Atlantic City market, we were able to evaluate the effect of such a large gaming center acting to siphon off visitors from the outer ring for the Norfolk market.

The gravity model method can be used on its own, as Urban Systems did in the Massachusetts analysis, or it can be combined with other techniques. In our analysis of Texas gaming markets, we were able to isolate seven gaming market areas. There were clear differences in the MSA and ADI areas between Texas and Massachusetts. In Texas the state is so vast that these areas are clearly defined. However, in Texas, the market area carve out did not provide a full definition of all markets under study. We were not able to isolate the Fort Worth market from the Dallas market, or to distinguish between the Houston, Galveston, and Freeport market areas. In this case, the gravity model was applied within these two market areas to distribute the total gaming market among the various locations.

The output from the gravity model is a matrix of percentages which are then applied to the total gamer visits generated by each geographic unit. In the Texas example, persons in Harris County (Houston) were projected to allocate 78% of their gaming visits to four casinos in Houston, 10% to a casino in Galveston, 4% to a casino in Freeport, and 8% to a Montgomery County location. This analysis was repeated for each county within the local market area. The number of gamer visits were then summed to yield market estimates for each of the proposed locations.

GAMER VISIT ESTIMATION

Each of these methodologies relies on evaluating gamer behavior in terms of propensity and frequency. All the work on propensity and frequency derives from the concentric ring model which relates gamer behavior to travel distance. Our primary market research, conducted through telephone surveys, has borne out the basic relationships-first that the percent of the population which will gamble decreases with increased travel distance, and second that the average number of annual visits made by gamblers also decreases with distance. Given those basic relationships, there are numerous other variables which affect gamer behavior and thus propensity and frequency values are unique for each region.

We have identified some qualitative relationships and general trends which impact propensity and frequency but we have not been able to construct strict quantitative relationships that are statistically significant. It is unclear whether the absence of a consistent mathematical relationship is because our studies have not yet yielded enough data points or whether we are not including some key element in the analysis, such as cultural or social values. Since Urban System's surveys have been conducted for private sector clients with specific objectives, we do not have the liberty to include social science questions which might answer questions of broader interest. However, every time a new survey is undertaken, we use an identical question structure whenever possible so that the data from the surveys can be combined to create a larger data set.

Some general relationships have been identified regarding propensity and frequency. There is a direct relationship between supply and participation. The greater the number of gaining opportunities in a region, the higher the participation rate. We have been able to develop regression equations for the periods of rapid growth in South Dakota, Colorado, and the Mississippi Gulf Coast which relate revenue to number of positions. These equations demonstrate that—up to a limit—increased supply results in increased demand.

This phenomenon is partly a function of supply and demand. When there is only a limited supply of gaming available in an area, it is not physically possible for all who might want to participate to go to a casino. It is also likely that as gaming becomes more available in an area, there is greater acceptance of it as a legitimate form of entertainment and thus it begins to appeal to a broader base of people.

However, in our analysis, each equation was location specific. Because of intervening variables, for example, the Colorado equation is not a good predictor of revenue generation in other areas. The type of gaming available in an area affects participation, with dockside or land based casinos generally attracting a higher proportion of people and with greater repeat visits than cruising riverboats. This relationship has been born out in our surveys where respondents overwhelmingly expressed a strong preference for a gaming experience which offered freedom of entry and exit. This observation was clearly reflected in a survey undertaken in the New Orleans area where respondents have been exposed to both cruising and dockside gaming thus lending validity to their expressed preference.

In looking at the effect of age on gamer behavior, we found that persons over 55 tended to have a lower propensity to gamble. A smaller percentage of this age group reported visiting casinos in the past year. However, among those who had been to a casino, they were the most frequent visitors. Lower income groups, those with household incomes under $15,000, also had lower propensities to gamble. Households in this category just do not have the disposable income available for entertainment expenditures that would allow them to be gamers.

In evaluating a new gaming venue, we recommend that basic primary market research be conducted on current gaming habits and public opinion to allow the estimation of future gaming behavior. We typically measure both prior casino experience and participation rates in other types of related behavior such as bingo, parimutuel wagering, lottery ticket purchases, and entertainment expenditures in general. We use these data to verify the respondents' predicted future behavior and correlate their responses with other areas for which we have similar data.

One cautionary note: We have found that in areas with little gaming experience, responses to the direct questions, such as: "If a casino were available in your area would you go and how often?" did not pass the test of reasonableness. This type of question asks for an uncommitted response. Since it asks people to predict future behavior with no requirement for following through on the responses, the answers can be unreliable especially in a situation where people are asked to predict how often they would engage in an activity with which they are unfamiliar such as gaming. As an example, in the areas where we have conducted research on actual gaming behavior, propensities for persons living within 50 miles of a casino typically range from the high 30 to high 40 percent range. Only on the Mississippi coast have we measured propensities over 50%. Frequencies for this ring range between 6 to 10 visits per year, although once again the Mississippi Gulf Coast values are extremely high.

In a survey of one prospective Missouri market, over 60% of the respondents indicated they would visit a casino if available, an extraordinarily high number, but with an average number of visits of only four per annum. We felt these responses were not representative of actual future behavior since they deviated so widely from the norm. Only 15% of respondents in the area had ever been to a casino, thus there was limited gaming experience on which to base a response. Because we had included surrogate measure questions, we were able to investigate the data in more detail, and were able to refine these numbers to better represent what in our opinion the expected market would be.

CONCLUSION

In summary, there are a number of different methodologies available to analyze a new gaming market. The determination of the most appropriate method depends largely on the market characteristics, particularly on the nature and location of the competing venues. One of the most important components in a market assessment is the collection of site specific data through market surveys. This is the component of the study most often neglected because of the time and or the expenses involved. However, it greatly adds to the accuracy of the analysis.

A Profile of Pro-Union Casino Workers in Northern Nevada*

Merwin C. Mitchell and Yvonne Stedham

Unions are a major concern to managers in many industries. The reasons for this are self evident in most cases. Most importantly, managers tend to feel that unions lower profits by increasing direct labor costs through wage and benefit gains and, by decreasing managerial effectiveness through the imposition of work rules, grievance procedures, seniority, and other constraints on the decision process[1]

For these reasons, understanding why some workers are pro-union and others are not is an important goal for personnel and human resource managers. This paper offers a profile of pro and anti-union workers in the gaming industry in Northern Nevada. Most of the results confirm intuition—but this by itself is a worthy goal of research. In addition, there are a few unusual results that the authors will address.

DATA COLLECTION

The authors surveyed workers in six Reno, Nevada casinos in the summer of 1991. A six page questionnaire was designed to measure intent to stay on the job, organizational commitment, and satisfaction with different job dimensions using established measurements of proven validity. Demographic, pay, and other related information was also solicited.

The number of observations for this particular study are reduced because two casinos in the sample refused to allow the authors to address any issue related directly to how workers feel about unions. The result was useful information on 237 non-supervisory casino and hotel workers.

---

* This article was previously published in *Gambling Research & Review Journal,* vol. 2, issue 2, 1995. Las Vegas, NV: UNLV International Gaming Institute, William F. Harrah College of Hotel Administration. Permission to reprint has been granted by the publisher and authors.

The sample was collected by simply asking everyone who came into the casino luncheon room to fill in the questionnaire. The sample is nonrandom because many workers do not use the cafeteria and includes a self selection bias because workers were not required to participate or tell the truth if they did participate. Of those asked to fill out the questionnaire about 70% said they would and of those about 55% actually finished. We feel that those who started the questionnaire and did not finish do not differ radically from the sample because the primary reason for failure to finish was the length of the questionnaire. The authors have no idea, however, of how the 30% who refused to fill out the questionnaire differs from the sample, or how those workers who do not use the cafeteria may differ from the sample.

DATA ANALYSIS AND RESULTS

None of the casinos had any workers covered under a collective bargaining agreement. Worker's attitudes towards unions were measured by asking them to respond to the statement **"A union would be very useful here."** Propensity to vote for organization was measured by the statement: **"I would vote for union representation if an election were held tomorrow."** Workers were asked to respond with the choices "strongly agree," "moderately agree," "neither agree or disagree," "moderately disagree," and "strongly disagree" with strongly agreeing yielding a value of "5" and strongly disagreeing equally a value of "1" for analysis. These are, of course, ordinal responses meaning, for example, that one cannot conclude that "strongly" is twice as large as "moderate" when it comes to a worker's intent or attitude. This limitation notwithstanding, this methodology is somewhat superior to the traditional yes/no choice that many studies have used. The approach used in this study results in a more sophisticated qualitative sorting. From the standpoint of survey results, this approach provides for the two extremes of strong anti and pro-union workers. Next, there are the more mild versions of union sentiment as well as the middle category of undecided that are, in other studies, forced to choose between yes and no but are likely, in an actual election, to simply abstain from voting. These groups differ in ways that illustrate the importance of allowing for degrees of sentiment over this issue. The analysis variables are listed and described in Table 1.

A CASUAL MODEL OF VOTING BEHAVIOR AND WORKER SENTIMENT

Whether you have a negative or positive view towards unions it is clear that unions act as an intermediary between management and the worker.

TABLE 1
Variable List and Description

Demographic and Background Variables	
1)	Age
2)	Female—1=female, 0=male
3)	Dependents
4)	Married—1=married, 0=not married
5)	High School dropout—1=HS dropout, 0=did not dropout
6)	High School graduate—1=High School graduate, 0=did not graduate
7)	Some college—1=worker has had some college but not 4yr degree
8)	4 year degree—1=worker has received a four year degree
Work and Market Characteristics	
9)	Tenure—number of months that this worker has been with this employer.
10)	Casinos—number of casinos this worker has worked at in the last 5 years.
11)	Years in Reno—number of years this worker has lived in Reno.
12)	Hours—average number of hours this employee works each week.
13)	Dollars gambled—average dollar amount this worker spends gaming each week.
Measures of Satisfaction and Work Attitudes	
14)	Commitment Index—an index derived from 14 questions that serves as a measure of how committed workers are to an employer or firm[2].
15)	Satisfaction Index—a composite derived from sub-indices reflecting attitudes about work, supervision, promotion, income, and coworkers[3].
16)	Stress—the worker rates the stress level of his or her job.
17)	(P) Being Fired—the worker rates his/her chance of being fired in the next month.
18)	Self esteem—the worker rates his/her chances of getting another job of equal value.
19)	Stay intent Index—an established measure made up of eight questions regarding a worker's future intentions to stay or quit—shown to be a good proxy for actual turnover[4].
20)	Benefits Index—an index composited from six questions regarding the provision of benefits[5].
21)	Work Index—separate subcategory for satisfaction index above that measures satisfaction with work specifically.
22)	Supervision Index—See (20)
23)	Promotion Index—See (20)
24)	Income Index—See (20)
25)	Coworker Index—See (20)

(continued)

TABLE 1

(continued)

	Measures 26–32 were obtained by asking workers to rate each statements with "strongly agree" = 5, "moderately agree" = 4, "neither agree or disagree" = 3, "moderately disagree" = 2, and "strongly disagree" = 1.
26)	Interest of Management—"My employer is interested in my well being."
27)	Supervisors—"My supervisor is good about following rules and procedures . . ."
28)	Control over hours—"I have a lot of control over the number of hours I work . . ."
29)	Control over schedule—"I have a lot of control over when I work during the week."
30)	Decisions—"In general, decisions regarding my job are made in an arbitrary fashion."
31)	Work effort—"I feel I work harder than my coworkers."
32)	Job helps home life—"This job contributes to a happy home and social life."
33)	Weekly earnings including tips on average over time.
34)	Number of dealers in sample—1=if dealer, 0=if not.

The greater degree of uncertainty that workers have concerning their jobs and the less their satisfaction with different aspects of their work, the higher their expected need or demand for union services. On this basis the authors predict that measures that are related to how workers feel about their job will be, in general, negatively correlated with their propensity to vote pro-union.

RESULTS

Table 2 presents means and their differences for workers who are likely to vote or not vote for unionization leaving out the group that responded "do not agree or disagree." Of the sample, 96 reported that they would be disposed to vote against union representation, 99 reported that they would be disposed to vote for representation, and 42 reported no inclination to vote either way. A one-tailed test for mean was employed which tests for measures that should reflect need for representation as described above (e.g., organization commitment). The data include a number of variables of interest for which the authors have no prior expectations (e.g., hours worked). Mean differences for these measures are subjected to a two tail test.

Table 3 presents correlation coefficients for the variables described in Table 1 for both union sentiment and voting propensity. Sentiment is a

TABLE 2
Sorting by Likelihood of Vote

Variables	Anti-Union	Pro-Union	Difference
Age (1)	38.086	36.132	1.954
Female (2)	0.479	0.555	.076
Dependents (3)	0.718	0.575	.143
Married (4)	0.406	0.353	.053
HS Dropout (5)	0.104	0.101	.003
High School Graduate (6)	0.260	0.303	.043
Some College (7)	0.458	0.373	.087
4-Year Degree (8)	0.072	0.171	.099**
Tenure in Months (9)	37.135	31.030	6.105
Casino Employers in last 5 years (10)	1.468	1.676	.208*
Years in Reno (11)	12.000	10.439	1.561
Hours worked per week (12)	37.979	34.121	3.858
Dollars gambled per week (13)	17.333	23.040	5.707
Commitment Index (14)	48.539	42.954	5.585***
Satisfaction Index (15)	118.483	107.754	10.729*
Stress (16)	3.225	3.587	.362**
(P) Being Fired (17)	2.083	2.252	.169
Self Esteem (18)	2.541	2.585	.044
Stay Intent Index (19)	42.950	39.753	3.197*
Benefits Index (20)	15.943	14.655	1.288*
Work Index (21)	22.261	17.658	4.603***
Supervision Index (22)	33.841	31.075	2.766*
Promotion Index (23)	11.638	10.593	1.045
Income Index (24)	11.883	8.750	3.133***
Coworkers Index (25)	30.915	31.131	.216
Manager Interest (26)	2.802	2.642	.16
Super follow rules (27)	3.531	3.653	.122
Control over number of hours (28)	2.927	2.848	.079
Control over work schedule (29)	2.568	2.808	.240
Decisions arbitrary (30)	2.869	3.000	.131
Work Effort (31)	3.281	3.212	.059
Job helps home life (32)	2.781	2.474	.307*
Weekly earnings with tips (33)	327.987	315.051	12.936
Percentage of respondents who are dealers (34)	0.322	0.363	.041

*Statistically significant at the .10 level; **statistically significant at the .05 level; ***statistically significant at the .01 level (one- or two-tail test as appropriate).

very good proxy for voting and the results for both sets of correlations are very close in most cases. Because the information in Tables 2 and 3 are so consistent the results will be described simultaneously[6].

Some important results illustrated by Tables 2 and 3 are:

- Demographic variables
- Education
- Job history
- Hours worked per week
- Intent to stay
- Organizational commitment
- General Satisfaction
- Benefits
- Stress

Demographic variables do not play a large role in determining a person's propensity to vote pro-union. Recent work by Fiorito (1992) and Silverblatt and Amann (1991) have found being female and younger in age are positively related to a worker's propensity to vote. While there is no significant support for this contention the qualitative direction of our data do not contradict these findings.

Those respondents with a four year degree are more likely to vote pro-union. Notice, however, that there is mildly significant negative correlation between having some college and union sentiment in Table 3.

With regards to job history, those who have worked at more casinos in the last five years are more likely to vote pro-union (this variable is marginally significant in mean differences and insignificant as a correlate).

Employees who work fewer hours are more likely to vote pro-union. Notice, however, that the fewer hours put in by pro-union employees is not reflected by a significant earnings difference. When earnings are viewed on an hourly basis pro-union workers' hourly earnings are, on average, 7% higher than their counterparts.

Pro-union workers report an increased propensity to quit. Along the same lines, workers who are less committed to the casino they work for are more likely to vote pro-union. Less satisfied workers are likely to vote for representation.

Pro-union workers are also less satisfied with benefits, work, and supervision as measured by our indices. Pro-union workers are less satisfied with income even though they earn more in hourly wages. Finally, pro-union workers report that their jobs are more stressful.

The results confirm the authors' intuition that pro-union workers will generally report less satisfaction with many job aspects as well as more stress. There are, however, some other important things this data illustrates besides those made obvious by the mean differences listed in Table 3.

TABLE 3

Correlates of Union Sentiment and Voting Propensity

Variables	Sentiment Mean	Voting Mean
Age (1)	−.035	−.056
Female (2)	.046	.072
Dependents (3)	−.068	−.047
Married (4)	−.067	−.041
HS Dropout (5)	−.046	−.004
High School Graduate (6)	.046	.035
Some College (7)	−.107*	−.096
4-Year Degree (8)	.151**	.154**
Tenure in Months (9)	−.032	.072
Casino Employers in last 5 years (10)	.060	.090
Years in Reno (11)	−.142	−.062
Hours worked per week (12)	−.088	−.129**
Dollars gambled per week (13)	−.006	.039
Commitment Index (14)	−.299***	−.222***
Satisfaction Index (15)	−.180**	−.132*
Stress (16)	.145**	.119*
(P) Being Fired (17)	.034	.041
Self Esteem (18)	.024	.015
Stay Intent Index (19)	−.144**	−.131*
Benefits Index (20)	−.106	−.090
Work Index (21)	−.191***	−.165**
Supervision Index (22)	−.156**	−.114*
Promotion Index (23)	−.121	−.067
Income Index (24)	−.235***	−.219***
Coworkers Index (25)	−.065	.002
Manager Interest (26)	−.068	−.048
Super follow rules (27)	.087	.046
Control over number of hours (28)	−.001	−.014
Control over work schedule (29)	.117*	.103
Decisions arbitrary (30)	.067	.056
Work Effort (31)	.010	−.014
Job helps home life (32)	−.101	−.098
Weekly earnings with tips (33)	−.021	−.035
Percentage of respondents who are dealers (34)	.041	.047

*Statistically significant at the .10 level; **statistically significant at the .05 level; ***statistically significant at the .01 level.

One of our most important results centers on the fact that pro-union workers report a small and insignificantly higher probability of getting a job of equal value (18). This finding contradicts other studies that finds that both union workers and workers that vote pro-union perceive their job marketability to be significantly lower than non-union workers and anti-union workers[7]. The significance of this is that pro-union workers in gaming cannot be typified as desiring representation because they are lower quality workers. Based on their perceptions of their abilities they are at least as qualified as their anti-union coworkers. There is also virtually no difference in their reported work effort relative to anti-union workers (31) and pro-union workers report getting along with co-workers as well as their anti-union counterparts (25).

There are also some conflicting signals being sent by the data. Notice that while pro-union workers are less satisfied with work, and supervision and are overall less committed to their organization, these attitudes are not well reflected in variables (26)-(30). In fact, pro-union workers tend to feel (insignificantly so) that supervisors follow rules better than their anti-union counterparts and that they have more control over when to work.

Another conflict arises with pro-union worker dissatisfaction with income and the fact that anti-union workers actually earn less on a per hour basis. This anomaly should be worrisome for managers who feel that they can stem pro-union activity by simply increasing wages. Other studies have shown that even if workers are satisfied with income and fringe benefits that this does not necessarily translate into satisfaction with other job attributes[8].

THE AMBIVALENT WORKER

Up to this point this analysis has ignored the ambivalent worker. There are some interesting features that arise with this group as well as some interesting differences between those with strong attitudes relative to those who exhibit moderate attitudes towards unions.

Age—Ambivalent workers (n = 44) are, on average, 30 years old—significantly younger than the rest of the sample.

Education—Ambivalent workers tend to be concentrated in the two categories of high school graduate and some college. Few are dropouts and few have four year degrees.

Attitude—Ambivalent workers tend to fit the profile of pro-union workers in measures that reflect attitude toward work. They are significantly less committed and satisfied than anti-union workers but not more committed or satisfied than pro-union workers.

Job Esteem—One interesting feature of job esteem (19) is that the avid pro-union and anti-union workers have considerably more job self-esteem than those who answered moderately. Ambivalent workers also have less esteem than those at the extremes though the difference is only marginally significant.

Dealers—As might be expected, dealers have attitudes. They are only found in the ambivalent group half as often as the rest of the sample.

CONCLUSION

Overall, this study confirms what most observers of workplace behavior would expect with some notable exceptions. Pro-union workers tend to feel that they are not paid enough and are less satisfied with non-pay dimensions of the job. On the other hand, when asked specific questions regarding supervision and job flexibility there is no evidence that they are less satisfied with specifics. This, we feel, indirectly points to the fact that many workers vote pro-union as a result of overall views regarding unions. If this is true, then management's ability to deal with pro-union sentiments maybe somewhat limited in the short run. In the long run, however, attitudes about the need for representation and a worker's overall political view of unions may be much more responsive to the work place experience.

Managers have considerable influence over the stress that workers experience. The robust relationship between pro-union attitudes and heightened stress clearly point to the need for managers to evaluate the full costs of imposing conditions that lead to tension and stress in the work place.

Finally, if one accepts workers' views of themselves as being free from systematic bias with relation to union attitudes, then there is evidence suggesting that pro-union workers are of average quality relative to the sample and that workers who are highly opinionated in either direction are likely to have the lowest regard of their own abilities. When sorted according to the degree of union sentiment, avidly anti-union workers have the lowest self-esteem. The temptation for personnel managers to try to hire strongly anti-union workers may cost the firm better employees if these results are generalizable. A more long run and sensible strategy would be to concentrate on decreasing stress and providing a workplace atmosphere that diminishes the workers' need for unionization so that both workers and management benefit.

---

1. Some economists do not feel that unions decrease productivity or substantially limit managerial flexibility. The "Harvard View" presents unions in a very positive light and is fully represented in Freeman and Medoff's *What do Unions do?*.

2. See Mowday et al. (1979).
3. See Smith et al. (1969).
4. See Prize and Bluedorn (1977).
5. See Heneman and Schwab (1985).
6. Multiple logistic regression simply confirm the results presented in Tables 1 and 2 for those variables exhibiting stronger significance and sheds no new light on the analysis.
7. See Kochan (1979), and see Odewahn and Petty (1980).
8. See, for example, Meng (1990), or Kochan and Helfman (1981).

REFERENCES

Bluedorn, A. C. (1982). "Theories of Turnover: Causes, Effects and Meanings," in S. Bacharach, *Research in the Sociology of Organization*, pp. 75–128. Greenwich, CT: JAI Press.

Fiorito, J. (1992). "Unionism and Altruism," *Labor Studies Journal*, Fall, pp 19–34.

Freeman, R. and Medoff, J. (1984). *What Do Unions Do?* New York: Basic Books.

Kochan, A. (1979). "How American Workers View Labor Unions," *Monthly Labor Review,* April.

Kochan, A. and Helfman, D. E. (1981). "The Effects of Collective Bargaining on Economic and Behavioral Job Outcomes." *Research in Labor Economics*, Vol. 4, pp 321–365.

Meng, R. (1990). "The Relationship Between Unions and Job Satisfaction." *Applied Economics*, Vol. 22, pp 1635–1648.

Mowday, R.T., Steers, R.M., and Porter, L. (1979). "Measurement of Organization Commitment." *Journal of Organizational Behavior*, Vol. 14, pp 224–247.

Odewahn, C. A., and Petty M. M. (1980). "A Comparison of Levels of Job Satisfaction, Role Stress, and Personal Competence Between Union Members and Nonmembers," *Academy of Management Journal,* Vol. 23, No.1.

Silverblatt, R. and Amann, R. J. (1991). "Race, Ethnicity, Union Attitudes, and Voting Predilections," *Industrial Relations,* Vol. 30, No. 2 (Spring), pp 271–285.

Smith, P., Kendel L.M., and Hulin C. (1969). *Measurement of Satisfaction in Retirement and Work: A Strategy for the Study of Attitudes.* Chicago IL: Rand McNally and Co.

Casino Operations Issues

Section 3

Player Loss: How to Deal with Actual Loss in the Casino Industry

Andrew MacDonald

The aim of this analysis is to place a mathematically sound base under the often haphazard process used by most casinos to calculate player complementaries or rebates. The goal is to create a process fair to both the players and the casino.

In most complementary and junket programs, casinos use either theoretical win or turnover upon which to calculate player complementaries or rebates. In some cases, particularly in the United States, junket programs simply rebate a percentage of loss to the junket organizer or to the player. Common rationales for giving a percentage of actual loss back to the player include: "so and so is a born loser" or "the money's in the bank" or "they do it in Vegas (or at Caesars or Hilton, etc.)."

Dealing with actual loss, however, is a difficult and often misunderstood issue. The problem is that the percentage rebated is often plucked from the air. It has no mathematical basis. The unfortunate result is that often no one knows what the theoretical or long-term cost of such a policy is to the casino company. This analysis suggests that good business procedure requires that a casino know precisely the cost of rebating percentages of loss, especially where it is a totally hard cost.

THEORETICAL VERSUS ACTUAL LOSS

The *theoretical loss* by a player is a combination of all winning and losing events experienced by a player in a game for a given number of results. Because most casino games are fundamentally biased against the player, the results are, from the player's perspective, negative. In simple terms, the loss may be calculated by multiplying the house advantage by the total amount wagered, or "handle," which is the number of decisions times the average bet. Factors such as average bet, time played, decisions per hour and house advantage are incorporated. Thus, rebating a percentage of theoretical loss takes into account both winning and losing situations and has a long-term validity as a policy.

However, when *actual loss* is being decided, most policies take into account only the amount of the loss. This is a risky policy because the percentage of actual loss rebated is not the same as the percentage of theoretical loss. For example, if a casino policy rebates a fixed percentage of loss greater than the house advantage, then the maximum theoretical cost to the company will be determined (approximately) by the rebate percentage divided by twice the house advantage, and it would *minimize* at the rebate percentage. In other words, if the rebate on loss percentage were 10% and the house advantage 1.25%, then the theoretical cost could range from roughly 400% at maximum, in an even chance game, and minimize at 10%. This maximum theoretical cost of course, would be realized if only one hand were played and the player then settled and was paid the rebate. (The minimum theoretical cost would occur if the player didn't settle until they had played a very large number of hands.)

Many would argue either that no one would play only one hand and then settle or that no rebate would be paid under such a scenario. The real problem is that, in normal situations, without play criteria it is the customer who may be in control of the net outcome. Criteria are essential to ensure that any rebate policy is valid. It is critical that other factors such as the number of decisions are incorporated. Much like the transition from paying complementaries as a percentage of drop or credit line to basing these on calculations of theoretical casino win, so too it is time that rebate on loss policies change to mathematically sound business decisions.

BASIC CRITERIA FOR CALCULATING REBATE ON LOSS

When rebating on loss, the conditional mean of all situations in which the player loses must be calculated. Because we are dealing with biased games, in all cases that value will exceed or equal the mean of all possible events, both winning and losing, which we refer to as the player's theoretical loss.

If a rebate on loss policy is to be sound, a percentage of the player's theoretical loss should be used to calculate an equivalent rebate-on-loss percentage for a given number of decisions. That can be accomplished by determining the percentage of theoretical loss relative to the conditional mean of only player losses.

METHOD OF CALCULATION FOR A SINGLE PLAYER

In a simple one-hand example in an even money game, if normally the casino were prepared to pay back 50% of theoretical loss, then for each

$1 wagered the player would receive 50% of the house advantage multiplied by the number of decisions. Regardless of whether the player won or lost, if the edge were 1.2%, then 0.6% of each dollar would be paid back to the player.

If only the player who lost was to be rewarded, then that player could be provided a rebate almost twice as large, as the net position would be compensated by the winning player receiving nothing. Why almost twice as large? Because the player would lose 50.6% of the time. Thus paying 1.186% of actual loss if settlement occurred after a single hand would be the equivalent of paying 50% of theoretical loss for the example cited.

As the number of hands increases so also does the percentage of actual loss which may be rebated until such time as the number of hands played is so large that in virtually every instance the player loses. At this point the rebate percentage on actual loss may equal the percentage of theoretical loss. In such a case the theoretical loss (mean) and the conditional mean are one and the same. If returning 50% of theoretical loss were the general policy, then the maximum rebate on actual loss would also be 50%.

How large a value for the number of hands would this take? In an even chance game with a 1.2% house advantage, the following can be calculated:

$$\text{One standard deviation} = \text{square root (N)}$$
where N is the number of hands.

99.7% of all results fall within three standard deviations of the mean, and 99.85% of all results would fall to the right of minus three standard deviations.

If we were to solve for the case when the break-even point is three standard deviations above the mean, we find:

$$3 * \text{ square root (N)} = \text{mean} = N * \text{house advantage}$$
$$\text{or } 3 \text{ square root (N)} = 0.012 * N$$
$$3/.012 = N/\text{square root (N)}$$
$$\text{Solving, } N = 62{,}500$$

Thus, if a player were to play approximately 62,500 hands and then settle, it would be appropriate to rebate 50% of whatever that player's actual loss was at the time.

We now know that for one hand it is appropriate to rebate 1.186% of actual player loss, whereas at 62,500 hands, 50% of actual loss may be repaid. Both scenarios maintain a 50% equivalency relative to theoretical loss in an even money game.

To determine points in between these extremes of number of hands, it is necessary to determine the conditional mean for each number of hands. The following crudely demonstrates the process of interpolation:

Number of hands N = 100
Edge = 1.2%
Even money game:
The mean = 1.2% × 100
= 1.2
1 standard deviation = square root (N)
= square root (100)
= 10

From basic statistics we know that—for normally distributed random variables—34.13% of results occur between the mean and one standard deviation, 13.64% of results occur between one and two standard deviations and 2.23% of results are greater than two standard deviations. From this we may roughly calculate the conditional mean for all player losses.

To do this we take the probability range and multiply this by the mid-point result

34.13% * {(1.2 + (1.2 + 10))/2}
13.64% * {((1.2 + 10) + (1.2 + (2 × 10)))/2}
2.23% * {((1.2 + (2 × 10)) + (1.2 + (3 × 10)))/2}

We can sum these to provide the conditional mean greater than the mean and then add the probability of results between 0 and the mean multiplied by that midpoint.

Without referring to normal distribution tables, this may be approximated by taking the mean divided by the standard deviation and multiplying this by 34.13%, then multiplying that by the midpoint of zero and the mean.

= 1.2/10 * 34.13% * 1.2/2
Thus the conditional mean = 2.116 + 2.210 + 0.584 + 0.025
= 4.935

This compares to the standard mean (theoretical loss) of 1.2. Thus if a 50% rebate on theoretical loss were desired, the rebate on actual loss based upon the above would be

Rebate on actual loss% = 50% * (1.2/4.935)
= 12.16%

As stated, this is a very crude example provided for demonstration purposes only.

MORE COMPLEX CALCULATIONS USING UNLLI

To more accurately calculate the percentage to be rebated it is merely necessary to utilize smaller sections when integrating and to refer to normal distribution tables for the probabilities or to utilize a lesser known statistical function referred to as the "*UNLLI*" or Unit Normal Linear Loss Integral. This is basically analogous to the sum of all possible values of a standard normal random variable's positive distance above the number "a," multiplied by their corresponding probabilities of occurrence.

To put this into practice the following steps may be followed:

1. Find expected loss for the player.
2. Find standard deviation of player result.
3. Calculate z = expected loss / standard deviation.
4. Look up UNLLI table corresponding to z (see Table 1).
5. Multiply UNLLI value by standard deviation.
6. Add number calculated from step 5 to number calculated from step 1.
7. Take whatever percentage of step 1 is to be returned and divide by the result of step 6.

Example:

$$
\begin{aligned}
\text{Hands} &= 750 \\
\text{Edge} &= 1.25\% \\
\text{Payouts} &= \text{even money} \\
\text{Theoretical loss equivalency} &= 50\%
\end{aligned}
$$

1. 750 * 1.25% = 9.375
2. square root (N = 750) = 27.386
3. (9.375 / 27.386) = 0.342
4. UNLLI = 0.2508
5. 27.386 * 0.2508 = 6.868
6. 9.375 + 6.868 = 16.243
7. 9.375 * (50% / 16.243) = 28.859%

EXAMPLE IN BACCARAT

Table 2 depicts the percentages of loss in baccarat which can be paid for various numbers of hands to maintain a 50% rebate on theoretical loss equivalence. From this it can be seen that quite attractive rebates may be paid.

A central question arises, however: what is the best or simplest manner by which to calculate the number of hands? While a simple method may be to take time played and employ standard decision rates, that is inappropriate due to potentially widely divergent bet levels. This is important be-

TABLE 1

Z	.00	.02	.04	.06	.08
	Unit Normal Linear Loss Integral				
0.00	.3989	.3890	.3793	.3697	.3602
0.10	.3509	.3418	.3329	.3240	.3154
0.20	.3069	.2986	.2904	.2824	.2745
0.30	.2668	.2592	.2518	.2445	.2374
0.40	.2304	.2236	.2170	.2104	.2040
0.50	.1978	.1917	.1857	.1799	.1742
0.60	.1687	.1633	.1580	.1528	.1478
0.70	.1429	.1381	.1335	.1289	.1245
0.80	.1202	.1160	.1120	.1080	.1042
0.90	.1004	.0968	.0933	.0899	.0866
1.00	.0833	.0802	.0772	.0742	.0714
1.10	.0686	.0660	.0634	.0609	.0585
1.20	.0561	.0539	.0517	.0496	.0475
1.30	.0456	.0437	.0418	.0401	.0383
1.40	.0367	.0351	.0336	.0321	.0307
1.50	.0293	.0280	.0268	.0256	.0244
1.60	.0233	.0222	.0212	.0202	.0192
1.70	.0183	.0174	.0166	.0158	.0150
1.80	.0143	.0136	.0129	.0122	.0116
1.90	.0110	.0104	.0099	.0094	.0089
2.00	.0084	.0080	.0075	.0071	.0067
2.10	.0063	.0060	.0056	.0053	.0050
2.20	.0047	.0044	.0042	.0039	.0037
2.30	.0036	.0034	.0032	.0030	.0028
2.40	.0027	.0026	.0024	.0023	.0022
2.50	.0021	.0018	.0017	.0016	.0016

cause when dealing with actual loss some bets may be statistically insignificant. To demonstrate by using extremes, if we had 1,000 hands with bets of $1000 and one hand with a bet of $1,000,000, clearly the player's final result will be primarily determined by whether they win or lose the $1,000,000 hand. It can be said therefore that the other 1,000 hands are insignificant.

A reasonable method of calculating the number of hands played for the purposes of determining a rebate on loss is to divide the total turnover ("handle") by the player's maximum bet. This criterion may be particularly

TABLE 2

Baccarat	
(Player/Bank 50% Equivalent)	
Hands	*Percentage Rebate on Actual Loss*
10	4.78
50	9.96
100	13.52
200	17.96
300	21.01
400	23.47
500	25.39
600	27.06
700	28.37
800	29.54
900	30.78
1000	31.75
1100	32.63
1200	33.29
1300	34.06
1400	34.79
1500	35.48
1600	35.96
1700	36.58
1800	37.01
1900	37.57
2000	37.95
2500	39.89
3000	41.34
3500	42.44
4000	43.48
4500	44.18
5000	44.88

useful when the casino uses a table differential which potentially allows an unlimited maximum bet to be placed.[1]

Determining the maximum bet placed is generally a simple proposition if dealing with an individual player. In a junket group situation, where members of the same group may for example bet against each other on baccarat, the bet could be considered to be the difference between the opposing bets, even though the turnover is the sum of the opposing bets.

For other non-even pay-off games such as roulette, the mathematics remains similar because the player wins more when he or she does win, but this occurs less often. Thus the percentage of actual loss which may be rebated is relatively less.

To incorporate this factor into the previously shown formula requires the calculation of the variance for a specific game for one result. In an even money game such as baccarat (when playing Bank or Player) the variance may be approximated as one and therefore the previously shown formula is valid.

In any game the calculation of variance is accomplished by summing the square of the player wins multiplied by the probability of the returns. The standard deviation then becomes the square root of the number of hands multiplied by the average squared result.

In a game with multiple betting options at the same game with varying payoffs but the same house advantage (e.g., roulette) the variance figure used when calculating a rebate on loss would necessarily be the maximum figure.

The appropriate numbers for the variance of single wagers at various games are:

- Baccarat = 1 (exact figures 1.00 player, .95 bank)
- Blackjack = 1.26
- Roulette = 34.1 (single number bets on single zero roulette)

EXAMPLE FROM ROULETTE

In games with multiple betting options at varying payoffs and house advantages, it would be appropriate to fully calculate the rebate payable on every option and utilize the variance from the result which returns the least to the player, as otherwise any requirements on data collection by staff may be prohibitive.

When performing this calculation the following formula may be used:

1. Calculate the variance for one play.
2. Find expected loss for the player.
3. Find standard deviation of player result as the square root of number of hands multiplied by the variance for one play
4. Calculate z = expected loss / standard deviation.
5. Look up UNLLI table corresponding to z.
6. Multiply UNLLI value by standard deviation.
7. Add number from step 5 to number from step 2.
8. Take whatever percentage of step 2 is to be returned and divide by the result of step 7.

TABLE 3
Roulette (Single Number Play on Single Zero Roulette)

Hands	Percentage Rebate on Actual Loss	Hands	Percentage Rebate on Actual Loss
10	1.79	1400	17.57
50	3.93	1500	17.97
100	5.44	1600	18.50
200	7.52	1700	19.01
300	9.10	1800	19.35
400	10.33	1900	19.83
500	11.39	2000	20.14
600	12.33	2500	22.00
700	13.19	3000	23.48
800	13.98	3500	24.79
900	14.58	4000	25.98
1000	15.27	4500	27.07
1100	15.93	5000	27.91
1200	16.55		
1300	17.00		

This then produces an example (Table 3) of rebate percentages applicable for the game of roulette (when playing single numbers on a single zero game) which maintains a 50% equivalence on theoretical loss.

CONCLUSIONS

Many would argue that all this information and calculation is too complicated to be of practical application in the casino industry. This analysis argues that the effort is worthwhile if a casino is to control its loss rebates in a businesslike manner. It is also less complicated than it seems.

First, the method provides a mechanism by which any existing rebate on loss policy can be analyzed to assess the long-term or theoretical cost to the business.

Second, in the high level junket segment, the method provides a means to structure variable percentage rebates on loss which can be both attractive and combined with rebates on turnover or the provision of other complementaries. Being criteria-based, any policies so developed would possess a long term validity.

Third, the method provides a challenge to incorporate a rebate on loss element into the standard calculation of premium player complementaries. A basic limitation of a complementary system based on theoretical loss is that, although the theory may be fine, players often complain that no consideration is given when they incur a substantial loss. To players, funds are a limiting factor which if depleted will limit the turnover they can provide. This may also mean that, adding insult to injury, they may have to pay for what they would normally be "comped." Some complementary policies address this in a superficial way but again these are not criteria-based.

Fourth, the method is not as complicated as it looks. To say that incorporating the above formula into a player-rating system would not be practical because it could not be calculated is incorrect. Most player-rating systems in large casinos are computerized, which enables any calculation to be undertaken.

Fifth, players will accept the method just as they accept other player-rating methods—largely on trust. In terms of what complementaries are provided, players already take most things on trust. For example, the decision rates per hour, house advantages, average bet levels and percentage of theoretical loss returned are generally unknown from the player's perspective. This method, however, can legitimately be praised as quantified, objective and equitable.

Of course, as in any player-rating system, success relies heavily on capturing good data initially. To do this it is imperative that the gaming staff performing this function realize its importance.

In summary, if the objective is to find the most equitable system upon which to base complementaries, some aspect of player loss should be incorporated, and from a business perspective that should equate to a standard theoretical cost.

An equitable system of this nature could be achieved by adding a rebate on theoretical loss to a percentage rebate on actual loss, and then providing the player either one, depending upon which is the greater of the two. Alternatively, a casino could provide solely one or the other.

Finally, if referring to UNLLI tables etc. is still considered too complex then the following approximation of a rebate on loss percent calculation may be of use:

$$ b = a * \left[\frac{Y * \sqrt{V * N}}{0.5Y * \sqrt{V * N} + 0.17Y^2 + 0.4V * N} \right] * \frac{100}{1} $$

where a = the percentage of theoretical loss equivalent
where b = the percentage of actual loss
where Y = theoretical loss to the player
where N = the number of hands played (turnover / maximum bet)
where V = the average squared result for one game

ACKNOWLEDGMENTS

The author wishes to acknowledge Peter Griffin, Professor of Mathematics, University of California, Sacramento; Jim Kilby, Sam and Mary Boyd Chair and Lecturer, UNLV; and Bill Eadington, Judy Cornelius, and the staff of the Institute for the Study of Gambling & Commercial Gaming, University of Nevada, Reno.

---

1. For a discussion of the differential concept, see Eadington, W. R. and Kent-Lemon, N. (1992). "Dealing to the premium player: Casino marketing and management strategies to cope with high risk situations," in W. R. Eadington and J. A. Cornelius (eds.), *Gambling and Commercial Gaming: Essays in Business, Economics, Philosophy and Science.* Reno, NV: Institute for the Study of Gambling & Commercial Gaming, University of Nevada, Reno.

DEDICATION

The author dedicates this paper to the memory of Peter Griffin.

Promoting to the Premium Player: An Evolutionary Process

John T. Bowen and James C. Makens

While casinos are filled with a generous cross-section of the population, premium players can account for a significant percentage of the revenue. Some casinos indicate that premium players can represent over half of their gaming revenue. Others, such as Caesars in Atlantic City indicate that players who can lose $5,000 or more per trip make up about 20% of their table revenue. Because of the increased competition in the gaming industry, casinos have made significant changes in their marketing approach to the premium player.

Justification of marketing promotions, increased pressure for a finite group of premium players, internalization of the distribution channels, globalization of the premium player, database marketing, and the emergence of the premium slot player have all been responsible for changing how casinos market to premium players. This analysis describes the manner in which these factors have influenced marketing to the premium player. The research for this work has included interviews with casino managers in Australia, Atlantic City, and Nevada.

JUSTIFICATION OF MARKETING PROMOTIONS

One of the first marketing tools for developing the premium player, the junket, was developed by accident. In 1961, a stockholder of the Flamingo Casino Hotel in Las Vegas flew a group of his friends to Las Vegas to show off his casino. The casino's management observed a significant increase in chip sales, or "drop," as the stockholder's wealthy friends tried their luck in the casino. This party proved the value of bringing premium players to the casino.

Because of this experience, the Flamingo identified premium players and started flying these players to the casino for a four-day, all expenses paid trip. In the early days of premium players, casinos did not make a detailed financial analysis of their promotions. In 1968, the Flamingo, questioning the value of their junkets, suspended junket operations. This move quickly provided evidence of their value as the casino drop fell by 50 percent. The Flamingo not only reinstated the program, but brought it back in an expanded version offering back-to-back junkets. The Flamingo knew its general junket program was effective because of this action, but it still was not able to evaluate the profitability of individual players.

Casinos quickly realized the importance of developing a method to determine the yield from premium players. The calculation of revenue from premium players involves several variables. The drop is the amount of chips purchased by a player. The amount a casino wins from the drop is known as the "hold." Casinos try to determine the hold a player will produce through knowledge of their average bet, time played, hands per hour, house statistical advantage, and theoretical win.

The house advantage varies by game and by player, some players being more skillful than others. To illustrate the concept, assume the house statistical advantage for a given blackjack player is 1.50%. The player has three gambling sessions of four hours each during a two-day visit to a casino. The player's average bet is $100 and the speed of play is 80 hands per hour. Thus:

Total Playing Time in Hours	12
Average Bet	$100
Total Hands (80 * 12)	960
Total Bet (Handle)	$96,000
Theoretical Win @ 1.5%	$1,440

The above example shows how misleading numbers can be. At first glance, one might think that a blackjack player betting $96,000 would provide the casino with a considerable win. A win of $1,440 is certainly a significant win, but not one that deserves unlimited comps. On the Strip in Las Vegas, the theoretical win for blackjack, when the player plays according to accepted "basic" strategy, is slightly over 0.5%. On average, players do not consistently play according to accepted strategy, raising the theoretical win to about 2%. However, good (hard) players often reduce the casino's theoretical win to less than 1%.

The theoretical win provides a guideline for justifying the cost of a promotion. In an interview, one vice-president of marketing of a major casino said that the promotion expense should be no more than 50% of the theoretical win. Items included in the promotion expense are airfare, lodging, food and beverage, limousine, and gifts. In the above example the player might receive a first class airline ticket at a cost of $600, a suite for two nights with a retail value of $200 per night, $300 of food and beverage, and the services of a limousine at a cost of $200. The player receives $1,500 worth of services to entice him into the casino. Clearly the expense of $1,500 is not justified on a win of $1,440. In addition to these expenses, bad debt risk is another expense casinos must factor into the costs of bringing in a premium player. The bad debt expense on lines of credit in Las Vegas runs about 4%.

Sometimes managers rationalize promotional expenses by claiming they are not all cash expenses. The variable cost of servicing a room might only be $20 per night and the preparation cost of the food might only be only 40%. However, one has to consider opportunity costs. In Las Vegas, where average occupancy is above 90% in the popular resorts and higher on weekends, the room would probably not go unsold. The food and beverage charges could be adjusted to reflect the actual cost of the product to the casino, but frequently this will not make a significant difference. In the example above the adjustment might reduce promotional expenses by $400. The truth is that many complementary goods and services, "comps," are real expenses to the resort, not soft money.

In the past, some casinos failed to evaluate individual players. They developed liberal comping for players and rebates to junket operators. These policies were responsible for the failure of a number of casinos. The changing global economy can also take a toll on the ability of some premium players to pay their debts. In the mid 1980s Caesars Palace had to write off $9.4 million in bad debts from its high rollers. Bad debt risk from international players can occur when their home countries experience such economic vagaries as the devaluation of the Mexican Peso (1982), the collapse of the Tokyo real estate market (early 1990s) and the fall in Middle East oil prices (early 1980s). Today, casinos know much better the value of each customer and develop comping formulas based on player worth.

When a casino uses outside agents, the agent's compensation must be paid out of the player's theoretical loss along with the comps provided for the players. The methods of paying the agents vary greatly. Atlantic City casinos compensate them at the rate of 8% to 30% of the player's theoretical loss. Agents in the upper end of this range are usually required to pay the player's expenses out of their commission.

Many Australian casinos use a technique based on the number of "turns." Turn refers to the number of times that the initial buy-in amount of chips is completely played. For instance, a player who purchased $25,000 worth of chips upon entering the casino would complete one turn when the entire $25,000 was bet. The common rate of commission in Australia is 2-2-2-1-1-1, with the numbers representing the commission paid (in percent) on the first turn, second turn and so forth. An agent would not receive commission until the player completed four turns. With this example, the casino does not stand to gain unless their theoretical win is over 1.5%.

Other methods commonly used are a flat fee per player, percentage of the player's front money, commission on nonnegotiable chips, commission on live chips, rebate on player's loss and a percentage of the casino's theoretical win. Although there are many different methods of compensating agents and players, they all come back to the theoretical win. In order to make sense for the casino, the package provided to attract players must not be greater than the theoretical win.

The variance in compensation packages for agents is due in part to how badly the casino wants the business of the agent's players and how well the casino knows the agent. Some casinos will on occasion even give away more than their theoretical win. They hope the player will play poorly and/or have bad luck. For example, some casinos in Australia have paid 1.4% of the turnover in baccarat as commission, when the theoretical win is about 1.1%. These casinos are prepared to cover any losses from their normal earnings. They have truly, and perhaps foolishly, entered the gambling business.

Most casinos have guidelines on the amount of the theoretical win they are willing to use for promotion purposes, generally in the area of 30% to 50%. Most casinos will negotiate individual deals and use the guideline as a target. However, some casinos have a standard compensation formula for all players and/or agents. For example, the Adelaide Casino would pay 1.2% of handle on nonnegotiable chips or 0.6% on live chips plus an additional 5% of the amount due for expenses. The second option is more popular with junket operators because the casino keeps track of the play and they get a percentage of each turn. Under this method if a junket turns one million dollars, the junket operator gets $6,000 plus $300 for expenses. The operator pays all expenses from this amount.

Peter Lawrence, of the Adelaide Casino, cautioned about giving special deals to get an agent's business. He claimed that once you give agents a particular deal, they will expect the same deal in the future. It becomes a regular operating procedure.

One of the biggest changes in the battle for the premium player has come in the area of compensation. Today casinos understand the theoretical win they can expect from a player and they base their commissions and comps on this amount. In the past this was not always the case.

INCREASED PRESSURE FOR A FINITE GROUP OF PREMIUM PLAYERS

The number of super premium players is small and certain casinos know and seek these players. In Las Vegas, Caesars Palace, the Desert Inn, and the Las Vegas Hilton have traditionally gone after this market. They have been joined in the 1990s by the Mirage, the MGM Grand, and a refurbished Bally's. Additionally, there is increasing pressure from hotels outside Las Vegas for this market. The pressure from new casinos entering the market has seen some casinos, such as The Golden Nugget, become less active in pursuing premium play. Even with some casinos exiting this market, the six resorts mentioned above have more than enough capacity to take care of the best players. Like most situations where supply exceeds demand, marketing wars have developed as each casino tries to protect and gain market share.

The use of credit as a marketing tool provides evidence of the battle. Credit, once a financial decision, is now being used as a marketing tool to attract players. Casinos compete for players by offering a larger line of credit than the competition, or by offering a player who has used up credit at one casino an additional line of credit at their casino. The line of credit for these players can run into several millions of dollars, creating the potential of significant losses if the player defaults. This level of player also has the ability of winning several million. Thus, the casino has a downside loss of several million dollars and upside potential of gaining a several million dollar note, a note that could be hard to collect.

This may not be a good business decision. The morality of the decision could also be questioned, since credit limits are usually set on one's ability to pay. But, decisions in war are not always rational.

Another strategy used to attract premium players is the creation of opulent accommodations. Casinos competing for the super premium players are spending millions of dollars renovating and building suites for top players. The Las Vegas Hilton in 1994 eliminated its top floor banquet space and built three guest suites at a cost in excess of $40 million. These suites feature their own tennis courts. In 1994, Caesar's Palace completed two $12 million suites, of 9,000 and 12,000 square feet respectively. Each suite includes a putting green and a lap pool. Besides these, Caesar's has ten 4,500 square foot fantasy suites. With this level of investment, one sure bet is the competition for the top premium players will continue to be fierce.

INTERNALIZATION OF THE DISTRIBUTION SYSTEM

Another trend is the internalization of the distribution system. Most of the large resorts in Las Vegas have internalized the role of the junket operator for domestic players. These casinos employ "hosts" to develop and promote the play of premium players. The hosts identify premium players and develop a package to attract them to the casino. Hosts negotiate directly with the player and work out transportation, accommodation, food and beverage and other services that fit the needs of the player.

One of the main benefits of using hosts is the casino can develop a relationship with the player. The host can add the player's activities and their likes and dislikes to the casino's database. This information enables the host to provide a high level of service during the player's visits and to know what marketing offers are likely to attract the player back. Through the host, the casino can develop a relationship with the player.

When a casino uses external agents there is always a question of whose customer the players are, the agent's or the casino's. Conflicts can and do occur between junket representatives and the casino over the issue of client list proprietorship. Since the livelihood of independent junket depends upon quality client lists, they often fear sharing premium player information with others.

Hosts can also increase their value through the development of player lists. Smart casino managers make sure key members of their staff have contact with and become known to the premium players. They want to create an environment in which the player will feel welcome even if the host leaves. If all the contact with the player is only through one host, there is little to be gained by using hosts instead of junket representatives. The true advantage of internalizing the distribution process comes from developing a relationship with the player.

There are other reasons, beside customer loyalty, for internalizing the development of premium players. For example, when casinos use a compensation system based on turns, agents have been known to try to change the negotiated deal after play is started. They will threaten to take their players to another casino after the fourth turn unless 2 % is extended to all turns. If the casino calls the agent's bluff and loses the junket, the players often become very upset because they have to move, particularly if they are winning. Commonly, players blame the casino for the inconvenience of having to move. If the casino gives in to the demands of the agent, however, the cost of doing business increases. By integrating the distribution channel into their own operation casinos can eliminate the possibility of power plays by external agents.

Another problem with outside agents is they extend credit to their players after they have used their line of credit at the casino. This problem is especially critical with international agents because they have access to the player in his home country. They can exert pressure on the player to pay their obligation, causing the player to put a priority on paying the agent's loan over the casino's. The agent's pressure to collect the loan can also create negative memories of the trip, removing any desire the player may have of returning to the casino that was the source of his problem. Two additional disadvantages of working with junket operators are the casinos have additional bookwork and the casinos might not need the junket operator's business in peak seasons and on weekends.

Casinos are also internalizing the overseas distribution system. They are reducing the need for international representatives by opening branch offices in regions that are major sources of players. The Australian casinos, in part because of their heavy dependence on international business, use junket operators to a greater extent than those in Las Vegas. The Australian casinos need exposure in many international markets and junket representatives offer them a way to gain this exposure.

While Australia relies heavily on junket operators and Las Vegas has turned to hosts and branch offices, Atlantic City is caught in the middle. Many casinos have exhibited a start and stop attitude toward junkets. Patt Medchill, Senior Vice President of The Grand in Atlantic City, feels some casino marketing and executive departments are often in philosophical conflict concerning the values of junkets. Medchill feels that the primary fear of junket representatives is that casinos will decide to suspend all business.

The trend toward internalization is likely to continue as casinos realize the advantages of developing a relationship with their players. However, junket operators still provide a valuable service to casinos. They allow casinos efficient access to markets, particularly markets that are not large enough to justify a branch office. Junket operators will always have a place in the distribution system.

GLOBALIZATION OF MARKETS

Like most other businesses, gaming is no longer a domestic business. Players come from all points on the globe. Thus, a casino marketer must understand the world marketplace. When one country's economy is faltering, another may be thriving. Casinos must be on the lookout for emerging markets and market opportunities.

For example, Trump Castle hired Guisseppe Antonelli in 1994 to expand its marketing presence in Europe. He staged his first project to attract Italian holiday clientele. The event, named "Natale All'Italiana" (Christmas Italian Style), attracted 3,000 players to two shows. Bally's in Las Vegas hired the vice-president of Far East marketing from Trump's Taj Mahal for his knowledge of the Asian markets. Bally's and Trump Castle, like other casinos, hire marketing managers who understand the culture, the economy, the banking system, and the language of the countries they are targeting. Like all businesses involved in international trade, casinos must understand the environments of foreign markets.

One advantage of being strong in several international markets is that different cultures celebrate different holidays. Casinos can look for opportunities to attract international players during holidays that coincide with the casino's need periods. This is one way of managing demand. However, problems can be created when important dates for different markets overlap. For example, one vice-president of marketing said, "What the hell do you do when Super Bowl Sunday and Chinese New Years fall on the same weekend."

The increase in Asian visitors to Las Vegas from 121,000 in 1985 to 346,000 in 1992 illustrates the importance of the Asian market. Kevin Malley, former president of the Desert Inn, said that 90% of the Desert Inn's top 100 gamblers were from Asia and that close to half the casino's revenue came from Asian gamblers. He added this was typical of other casinos at the time, such as The Mirage and Caesars Palace.

Australian casinos report that most of their premium players originate in Hong Kong, Manila, Singapore, and Taipei. These players are typically self-employed males in their late thirties to early sixties who stay for three to five days. In addition to these markets, American casinos receive players from Vancouver, Mexico City, and cities in South America. Some casinos have also started to develop the European market.

DATABASE MARKETING

The development of inexpensive, yet powerful computers and user friendly software is responsible for the growing importance of database marketing. A properly designed slot club database can provide useful information about the player's interests, allowing the casino to develop marketing offers based on these interests. The casino can upgrade information on the player during each visit to the casino. The player's preference in restaurants, menu choices, and entertainment other than gaming can be tracked. Through information provided by hosts and floor supervisors, casinos can develop databases for players who are not members of the casino's club.

One of the major breakthroughs in database marketing is the development of software systems that allow the integration of information from the casino's different databases. One previous problem with databases is that they could not communicate with each other. There was a database for the slot club, one for the hotel operations and one for the pit. New systems have been developed which allow the integration of these databases. Thus, it is now possible to develop a comprehensive record for each player.

The databases allow the casino to niche market and develop special promotions for specific segments. For example some casinos have identified slot players that like to play golf and have sponsored golf tournaments for players who qualify. One casino, for example, has a free tournament for its top players, using its database to generate the names of those players who have a sufficiently high level of play to justify an invitation. When a new entertainer starts at the casino, the casino can use the database to find all of the premium players who enjoy that specific entertainer, and then use the appearance of the entertainer as a hook to draw the player to the casino. The trend in databases is toward niche and micro-marketing. The database allows the casino not only to track the play of a customer, but also to develop a relationship with that player by developing a marketing offer tailored to their wants.

EMERGENCE OF THE PREMIUM SLOT PLAYER

Slot machines now account for the majority of revenue in most casinos. The growth of slot play has led to the emergence of the premium slot player. The following factors contribute to the importance of slot machines:

1. Sixty-eight percent of all casino players play slot machines more than table games.
2. The increased level of play is on machines above $1. In Las Vegas casinos, the $5 machines experienced a 30 percent increase in play between 1992 and 1993. This is the fastest growing denomination of slot machines.
3. The theoretical win on slot machines is higher compared to table games. In Las Vegas the house win on a $1 machine averages between 4 percent and 5 percent, while in Atlantic City the win averages between 8 percent and 10 percent. This compares with table games where the average theoretical win is between 1.5 percent and 4 percent.
4. The labor cost of slot machines is lower than table games.
5. The theoretical loss of the player can be controlled. Even in video poker the payout can be set assuming optimum play by the players. Thus, the casino makes an additional return from those players who do not play according to optimal strategy. In the end the casino can gain a consistent return.
6. Because of the value of slot payouts, casinos are not subject to extreme losses. A baccarat player betting $50,000 a hand can walk away after a win streak and create a loss that will be noticed on the daily report. A consistent level of earning is becoming more important as casino companies are increasingly being traded publicly and corporate controllers are having more influence over operations. Some casinos have moved away from premium table game players because they want consistent returns without the fluctuations such players can bring.

While the minimum expected play of the premium table player is usually $30,000 and can be as high as $100,000, programs for premium slot players start at $2,000. Programs to market to premium slot players emulate those for premium table players. For example, one Las Vegas casino gave players back 10% of their loss after they spent $1,667. Some casinos are giving their players additional bonuses of one to two percent of the handle in the form of complementaries or presents. This is similar to the rebates casinos offer representatives who bring in premium table players.

Database marketing and the growth of the premium slot player market are linked. The Golden Nugget in Atlantic City is credited with the development of the first slot club in 1982. Featuring a slot club is no longer a competitive advantage—it is something the player expects. Originally, it was common for casinos to base the points on the number of coins played, with point bonuses given on certain jackpots. Today, casinos are using point systems to encourage players to play the games that are most beneficial to the house. For example, players receive fewer points on video poker than reel type slot machines where the house advantage is greater. Additionally, as the denomination of play increases the relative number of points earned per dollars played increases. The value of the points allocated typically averages from five to ten percent of the theoretical win.

The key to successful marketing to slot players is a good database system. The database allows casinos to identify and market to premium players. Smart casino managers use their slot club to generate a database that provides useful marketing information, not just names of players. Casinos can use the different characteristics of slot club members for segmentation purposes. Through proper use of its database a casino can create effective promotions for specific segments of its slot club players.

CONCLUSION

The marketing to premium players has been influenced by a number of factors: justification of marketing promotions, increased competition for a finite group of premium players, internalization of the distribution channels, globalization of the premium player, database marketing, and the emergence of the premium slot player. Today's marketing programs aimed at the premium player have become very sophisticated. The expense for every player should be justified by the return it will bring.

On a strategic level casinos are faced with developing an international portfolio of players. Those casinos wishing to reduce risk will develop their portfolio from different regions of the world and avoid reliance on one area's economic viability.

The development of sophisticated databases will lead to more niche marketing and micro marketing in the future, particularly with the premium slot player. Casinos will use their marketing programs to develop relationships with their players. As this relationship marketing matures, the distribution systems will become internalized.

REFERENCES

Baratta, Amy, (1993). "Sheraton plans major expansion at Desert Inn," *Travel Weekly,* October 14, p. 47.

Franklin, Stephen, (1994). "Spreading the ante; Casinos make bigger wagers on smaller betting," *The Chicago Tribune,* January 10, p. 1C.

Freedman, Bill, (1982). *Casino Management.* Secaucus, New Jersey: Lyle Stuart, Inc., p. 149.

Gros, Roger, (1994). "Going Global," *New Jersey Casino Journal,* February, pp. 20–21.

Harrah's Casino Hotels, (1993). "The Harrah's Survey of U.S. Casino Gaming Entertainment," *Harrah's Casino Hotels,* February, p. 18.

Heller, Matthew, (1985). "Caesar's new world," *Forbes,* November 4, p. 218.

Kilby, Jim, (1994). Lecturer in Gaming, personal interview. Las Vegas: UNLV.

Pledger, Marcia and Dunn Ashely, (1991). "Asians Give Vegas Full House," *Los Angeles Times,* January 11, p. 1.

Pledger, Marcia, (1994). "Local resorts cater to Far Eastern high rollers," *Las Vegas Review-Journal,* March 20, p. 15E+.

Pro-Active Measures to Guarantee a Safer and More Secure Casino

Fredric E. Gushin and William J. Callnin

Casino gaming has historically been one of the most intensely regulated industries in the world. Strict licensing of those companies and individuals that participate in the industry is one of the basic principles of casino regulation. Government's review of casino operations is also a critical component of casino regulation. Over the last several years a new pattern has been emerging. Jurisdictions are now competing among themselves to attract casino development. Relaxing what has traditionally been tight government regulation of the industry is an increasing trend. Therefore, casino companies must take an active role in regulating themselves. Government regulation can be limited and nonintrusive if casinos take the "bull by the horns" and adopt structures, procedures and policies to regulate themselves. This paper will focus on those things a casino operator can and should do, not only to avoid excessive regulation, but also because it makes good corporate and business sense to do so.

RULES, REGULATIONS AND INTERNAL POLICIES

All casino licensees have an obligation to conduct operations fairly, to assure that all monies are accounted for and that the games are fairly played. Their obligation to do so and to comply with whatever regulatory structure is in place is separate and independent from government's role to monitor compliance. The regulatory framework in which a casino operates is important because it could have significant influence on the parameters of a casino's marketing program, the way in which the games are played and the company's corporate structure. For example in Australia, casino credit is generally not permitted as a matter of law and therefore an important aspect of a typical casino operation is precluded. Other jurisdictions limit hours, betting limits and/or casino advertising.

Casinos can unilaterally adopt certain internal procedures and rules which minimize cheating or which contribute to a safer and more secure casino. In the jurisdictions where exclusive licenses are issued casinos do not necessarily compete with other casinos in the same jurisdiction, it might be easier for a licensee to adopt some of these internal measures. In the United States, casinos fiercely compete against each other and it may not make economic sense for one casino to adopt internal rules that while important from an integrity perspective, might result in impacting its marketing and thus its bottom line. Unless all casinos in the same jurisdiction adopt the same rules, it is very difficult for a single casino to do so.

Here are a couple of examples of how internal procedures can have a positive influence on securing casino assets. In New Jersey there is a regulation which states that at the game of blackjack, the player cannot touch the cards. That rule has eliminated one entire aspect of cheating at blackjack, namely the marking of the cards by a player. Historically, in the game of blackjack player tampering with cards has been a problem. New Jersey adopted that rule by statute but there is nothing to prevent any casino in any jurisdiction from adopting a similar rule as an internal procedure. Second, many casinos which cater to the high limit baccarat player change cards after every hand. This has likewise removed marking of cards by a player as a threat to the game. While such an internal procedure will cost the casino more cards in the short term, just one scam may cost the casino hundreds of thousands of dollars. As casino operators know, pai gow and pai gow poker are difficult games to control. Should these games be run as banking games or merely as games in which a vigorish is paid and the players play against each other? These types of decisions are important from the business perspective and will also have an impact on the integrity of overall operations.

CORPORATE COMPLIANCE PROGRAMS

The corporate culture of a casino licensee can have an impact on making a safer and more secure casino. Corporate investigations and compliance programs are important aspects of corporate behavior. Self-governance and corporate compliance make sense for a variety of reasons including the corporation's responsibility to its shareholders as well as the genuine and ongoing need to cooperate with regulatory agencies and law enforcement. It may, in fact, improve the bottom line.

Corporate compliance is not unique to the casino industry. The last several years have seen a constant barrage of indictments and trials against major businesses and some of their key personnel. In the U.S. the ongoing bank investigations have resulted in corporate executives going to jail for fraud and in multi-million dollar fines being levied against some of the largest brokerage and law firms. Indictments and trials relating to the worldwide BCCI scandal continue and in past years we have seen widespread insider trading scandals and various prosecutions for fraud involving overbilling of the U.S. Defense Department.[1] All of this highlights the point that in the first analysis it is the responsibility of the casino operator to take charge and take responsibility for its own actions and those of its employees.

Casino licensees must maintain a corporate norm consistent with the highest standards of honesty and integrity in the conduct of their business-standards generally higher than those applied anywhere else outside the gaming field.

How then do gaming companies meet their responsibilities? The place to start would be what have become by now standard features of most casino legislation requiring internal security systems and controls; separation of functions; and effective training and education programs. But separate and apart from government requirements, it would appear that gaming licensees must take actions on their own to prevent problems from recurring and which, in the long term, will improve their companies.

All too often the corporate response is defensive—a reaction after the fact and usually in response to some sort of regulatory confrontation. Unfortunately, by that time, the damage has already been done, and the company's reputation and character may be badly tainted. If, on the other hand, proactive procedures such as compliance programs and investigative audits were initiated by the company, and if ethics committees, ombudsmen or judiciary boards were in place to handle enforcement issues, then breakdowns or signs of developing trouble could be detected early so as to permit corrective measures in advance of government intervention. Having identified the particular problem, taken steps to remedy the situation, and made the requisite disclosures all on its own, the company stands in much better stead, having blunted the force of a regulator's initiative.

The biggest incentive for corporate sponsored "self-investigations" came in the early 1970's in the United States with the inception of the Securities Exchange Commission's "voluntary disclosure program." Realizing that it lacked the resources to investigate each case carefully, the SEC in 1974 sought and obtained consent decrees in which corporate defendants, accused of wrongdoing, agreed to appoint special committees of their boards—composed entirely of directors unaffiliated with management—to carry out independent "business ethic reviews" of their internal operations. As the benefits of this method of investigation became apparent, the SEC began to encourage corporations to come forward voluntarily and perform the same type of independent investigation that consent decrees had required. This effort to induce corporate self-investigation became known as the "voluntary disclosure program" which promises more lenient treatment and the chance to avoid formal investigation and litigation in return for thorough self-investigation and complete disclosure of the results to the SEC.

The desirability of corporate voluntary investigations should be obvious, especially to gaming companies. With procedures in place to promote compliance on a sustained and systematic basis by all levels of management and subsidiary operations, entry into a highly regulated field like casino gaming need not present the kinds of problems which might otherwise exist.

But to be truly effective, companies must strive to ensure both the credibility and the accountability of the corporate investigation. When dealing with regulators and convincing them that a thorough job has been done, the key is credibility of the investigator and of the internal investigative process.

Of course, who should conduct the internal review will vary with the nature of the inquiry. Both in-house and outside counsel have assumed increasing responsibility for the conduct of special internal investigations. In some cases, the aim of these inquiries is to identify and weed out dishonest employees and it seems that the general counsel, compliance officer or outside counsel who regularly work for the corporation and who know it and its personnel can probably do as good a job, if not a better job, than any special independent counsel.

But when the corporation itself is under a cloud, it may be better advised to hire new or independent counsel who have no past or ongoing relationship with the company because there's a greater likelihood that the perception of the effort will be to do what's right, uninfluenced by past associations. Although the company may prefer consulting with their regular outside counsel, the best remedy where there's been a "pervasive breakdown of business ethics" is to retain tough, scrupulously honest outsiders with reputations for integrity and fearlessness, who can come in and conduct a thorough probe.

Finally, what information should be disclosed to regulatory agencies? As much as it takes to convince regulators that the company is capable of detecting problems and effecting remedies short of official intervention. As with the SEC's voluntary disclosure program, the goal is to encourage cooperation between the corporation and the governmental agency. This goal is defeated by interjecting claims of corporate confidentiality, attorney-client privilege or work product which only serves to shield valuable information from regulatory authorities. Rather, the presumption should be complete disclosure. The company's internal investigative report and its underlying documentation should offer the governmental agency a roadmap of the transactions or policies under review and help it determine whether the company's self-policing measures are effective and whether the reform devices it implements satisfy all governmental concerns. A well-documented record of internally scrutinized activities and the corporation's control systems also aids in the ability to show in the course of an outside investigation that a breakdown was an isolated lapse and not a widespread corporate practice.

CORPORATE STRUCTURE

Beyond the corporate compliance issues already discussed, the licensee's structure and organization are important components in protecting assets. The casino's surveillance department and internal audit functions must be independent from operating management in order to be effective and credible. In most gaming jurisdictions, the surveillance department operates independently of all other departments. As a practical matter, the supervisors of the surveillance and internal audit departments generally report to the Chief Executive Officer of the casino company regarding administrative and daily operations; for matters of policy, purpose, authority and hiring/firing these supervisors report either to an independent audit committee or to the holding company's senior surveillance or internal audit executive who, in turn, reports to the independent audit committee of the Board of Directors of the holding company.

Why have these separate reporting lines for surveillance and internal audit? Functions performed by these departments are critical to maintaining the checks and balances underpinning the integrity of casino operations. It is these departments which monitor routine corporate compliance. Without the independence of these departments, it is not possible that the surveillance department, for example, may monitor the activities of senior executives for wrongdoing or questionable behavior. If surveillance reported to those officials, they might attempt to cover up their activities, divert surveillance or otherwise impede review of their activities. Under this example, it is clear to see how the independence and objectivity of the surveillance department might be compromised.

Another important aspect of corporate structure which can impact on making a safer and more secure casino is the composition of the Board of Directors. There should be a number of independent board members with no ties to operating management. Generally, the independent members of the board serve on the audit committee and executive committee providing necessary perspective, objectivity and independence.

COORDINATION OF VARIOUS LAW ENFORCEMENT AGENCIES

Law enforcement agencies have jurisdiction over various aspects of casino operations. For example, in the United States, the FBI, Drug Enforcement Agency, Immigration and Naturalization Service, and the Secret Service all have jurisdiction over various aspects of a casino operation. In addition, the casino regulatory agency and state police have primary regulatory and law enforcement jurisdiction within the casinos. All of this can create confusion, conflicting demands and a series of ongoing investigations for the casino operator. Police agencies can be extremely competitive and it is no secret that they guard their jurisdictional responsibilities fervently.

Without being perceived as interfering with criminal or regulatory investigations, it serves the casino licensee well to try to coordinate these activities. In that regard, the relationships between law enforcement agencies and surveillance departments are among the most critical interrelationships of the regulatory process. In addition to properly notifying a designated regulatory or law enforcement agency of all questionable, suspected or illegal activities which may be observed or come to the attention of the surveillance department, this procedure, which has the effect of communicating vital law enforcement information to the authorities, is critical in combating casino crime. Under most regulatory processes, casino licensees do not independently conduct their own investigations and report the results to law enforcement. Rather, at the time a fraud or other cheating activity is taking place, it is generally the obligation of the casino licensee to promptly notify either the regulatory agency or a law enforcement agency.

One of these agencies will in most cases assume responsibility for the investigation and will likely coordinate activities with the surveillance department. In most instances the surveillance department provides the best evidence used in prosecuting casino crime, namely a quality videotape of the incident which will convict the perpetrators.

Stepping back a bit, it is important for all agencies involved in regulating and law enforcement activities to coordinate their activities. As noted, this is often a lot easier said than done. Nevertheless, one way to accomplish this is for various law enforcement agencies to enter into "Memos of Understanding" regarding such issues as which agency will have primary jurisdiction over activities which may occur within the casino, sharing of investigative information and sharing of intelligence information. For example, in Atlantic City, the New Jersey State Police and Division of Gaming Enforcement have primary jurisdiction over criminal activities occurring within casinos. Local police and county prosecutors rely upon the investigations conducted by these agencies and do not generally conduct their own parallel investigations. A decision is made to either prosecute individuals on a state level or refer the matter to the county prosecutor based on standards and agreements. Minor matters are referred to municipal courts.

Coordinating federal law enforcement in the States is more difficult and oftentimes comes down to a matter of personalities, but it is nevertheless crucial to have written procedures and memos in place. There is not much a casino licensee can do except to encourage coordinated law enforcement and always cooperate with reasonable requests of law enforcement agencies. The relationship between law enforcement officials and the surveillance director and how that person is perceived by law enforcement will have an impact on these issues as well.

MODERN SURVEILLANCE TECHNIQUES

There are four basic elements to effective surveillance control. First, the casino has to have in place a viable system of internal controls and enforce those controls. In that way the surveillance department will be able to detect deviations from the approved procedures. Not every deviation will be a criminal conspiracy but deviation from controls are usually a tip off that something may be wrong or will indicate that better supervision is needed.

Secondly, surveillance officers must be constantly trained. Surveillance officers must have thorough knowledge of how all games in the casino are played and also be technologically proficient in the operation of the equipment. Frequent training for every officer is critical.

Third, communication from the casino floor to surveillance is of primary importance. Remember that floorpersons and pit bosses are field supervisors and they should normally be the first ones to detect suspicious betting patterns, improper procedures, suspicious body language and other questionable activity. Communication to the surveillance room is a one-way street in that floor supervisors must notify surveillance; in most instances surveillance will not notify the floor of the results of the surveillance. Some casinos will automatically tape high limit play, keep a dedicated camera on progressive slot machines and film the entire count. Oftentimes, regulatory requirements will require the filming of the count and the retention of tapes for a designated period of time. On its own, the casino should develop retention procedures and, as indicated earlier, promptly notify regulators of illegal or suspected illegal activity.

Fourth, it is important that standards utilized in observing casino action be uniform. General surveillance standards typically used in the industry are listed in Appendix A. Having uniform standards essentially levels the playing field among all casinos and makes it certain that the surveillance department can operate effectively.

ELECTRONIC GAMING

Technology has dramatically altered what used to be called slot machines and what today are called electronic games. The popularity of these types of games is enormous and constitutes up to 70% of casino revenues in some jurisdictions. One really does not have to have a high degree of skill to play these games, there is not the same type of pressure on the player as may be the case in table games, and it is simply the player against the mathematical odds.

As technology has changed, new and creative ways to cheat electronic games have become evident. There is a real danger of a new breed of slot cheat emerging and understanding new computer based slot machines as well, if not better, than the manufacturers and regulators.

However, there are a number of relatively simple measures which casinos can take on their own or in conjunction with regulatory agencies to minimize this type of cheating. First, testing of gaming related computer chips (EPROMS) by government or independent testing laboratories provides an effective way to determine whether chips may have been tampered with. Once these chips have been determined to be in compliance with any regulations that may exist in the jurisdiction relating to randomness and/ or payouts, the casino should seal these gaming EPROMS into place and periodically inspect each device, thus assuring that they have not been subject to tampering. Finally, before any large jackpot is paid out to a winning patron, the device should be inspected to determine if the seal is in place and whether there is any evidence of tampering. It should also be noted that slot data systems offer a variety of controls relating to the integrity of slot play.

GAMING SYSTEMS STRATEGIES TO PREVENT CRIME

The reality of casino crime is that all too often casinos are the victims of such crimes. During the early years of legalized gaming in Atlantic City, the industry was hit with scams and frauds so easily detectable that many of the thieves had not even spent the money or left the casino hotel before they were arrested. However, as time went on, crimes became more elaborate.

There is no doubt that casino crime has become increasingly more sophisticated and complex over the years and thus much harder to solve than in the early days of casino gaming. Take the case of counterfeiting— the use of bogus chips, slot tokens and fake currency—has risen dramatically in recent years. For example, in the summer of 1986, thousands of dollars of high quality counterfeit chips were found at several casinos in Atlantic City. While that had been the largest counterfeit chip scam uncovered in New Jersey to date, it was also one of the most difficult to detect. The fake chips were the best counterfeits ever seen in Atlantic City, the quality being so good that they had initially escaped detection and it was only the extreme alertness of a casino teller that accounted for this discovery. It is also significant to note that the fake chips were manufactured in Taipei, Republic of China, and that similar counterfeits found their way into other casinos in other jurisdictions as well.

No one knows for sure how much marked cards, shaved dice and other cheating at gaming tables cost the industry. Despite controls, those scams, which are detected and prosecuted, suggest that losses could run in the tens of millions of dollars.

One of the largest cheating scams uncovered in Atlantic City involved a well-planned and well-executed international baccarat conspiracy which bilked several casinos out of $2.7 million over a five month period in 1984. So subtle was the scam that it took investigators two years to completely unravel and as the scam was unraveled, it was learned that its success depended on one of the co-conspirators controlling the baccarat shoe and dealing cards to other players colluding in the scheme. Because of the inherent weakness of the dealing shoe, which has since been corrected by the promulgation of regulations, the dealer was able to peak at the first card and determine its value. Aware of its value, the dealer would then decide to deal the card or hold it and deal a second card. The mastermind of the plot would instruct the other players at the table to bet with the bank or player when a certain co-conspirator controlled the shoe and at other times instructed the players to offset each others' wagers. Several individuals who participated in this scheme were subsequently extradited to New Jersey from Hong Kong for prosecution.

Many of these cases highlighted what is now obvious and confirm some of our early suspicions that criminal groups throughout the world organize to rip off casinos. Many of the most significant criminal cases were conspiracies, which were professionally organized and international in scope. Criminal conspiracies of this sort require sophisticated investigative techniques by both the casino and regulators, the development of confidential informants and good police work. In addition, comprehensive internal control procedures provide accountability at all levels of a casino's operation. Fortunately for us, we know that these groups will gravitate toward the path of least resistance and will simply move on to other jurisdictions where controls are not as pervasive. That is why seminars and conventions are valuable forums for all jurisdictions to exchange information.

The best strategy to protect table games is for the floorpersons and pit bosses to adequately supervise the games. Protection of the games and gaming integrity should be the primary aspect of these jobs. Other functions relating to player ratings, issuance of complimentaries and player relationships are important but should take a back seat to games protection.

Coordination between the pit and the surveillance department, as already noted, is also important to the protection of table games. Moreover, when accounting identifies areas of concern, these matters should be communicated to surveillance so enhanced monitoring can commence.

Having internal controls in place relating to gaming equipment such as cards, dice, dealing shoes and other equipment also comprise an effective strategy. For example, accounting for all cards and dice at the end of a gaming shift will reduce the possibility of individuals trying to insert or remove equipment from the games and will establish accountability over the equipment.

It is the authors' belief that casinos should promulgate fairly specific rules under which all games are played. These uniform rules are important for a variety of reasons, most important of which is that deviations from established procedures may reveal improper activities or even collusion between dealers and players.

Replacing playing cards after use in high stakes baccarat games will reduce the possibility of using marked cards. Inspecting and using a micrometer on dice at craps and pai gow poker will minimize possibilities of using tampered dice at these games. Playing pai gow poker as a non-banking game is also used by some casinos because pai gow poker is so susceptible to cheating.

Finally, we generally recommend that casinos implement a drug treatment policy. It is obvious that drug use by casinos workers contributes to games being ripped off. For example, a casino worker seeking extra money to purchase drugs is far more likely to participate with others in an effort to cheat at table games. Having an aggressive drug treatment program acts to identify workers with such a problem before law enforcement gets involved.

LAUNDERING MONEY

In all cash intensive businesses there is a heightened proclivity for criminals to use the business as a conduit to launder illicit profits. The catchall phrase "money laundering" is a popular term used to describe the process of legitimizing proceeds of illegal activities. It is the method by which unlawfully obtained funds are converted or substituted into new money or other assets in order to mask the criminal source of these funds.

As it relates to casinos in the United States, there were a series of criminal cases in the mid-1980's which highlighted the use of casinos as a vehicle to launder money usually from the illegal drug trade. In 1985, the Bank Secrecy Act was amended to include casinos within the definition of "financial institutions." That meant that casinos, like all other businesses, were required to file currency transactions reports with the Internal Revenue Service for all cash transactions of $10,000 or more.

In 1993 the regulations governing casino currency transaction reports were modified after several years of discussions between law enforcement, casino regulators and the casino industry. Casinos are now responsible for gathering information and filing currency transaction reports. One of the more controversial aspects of these regulations requires casinos to verify and record the identity of certain customer information on transactions of $3,000 or more. The actual filing of the CTA takes place at the $10,000 level but casinos are responsible for aggregating transactions of customers at the $3,000 threshold. The vehicle most casinos utilize to gather this information is out of the player rating systems which have become increasingly sophisticated over the last several years.

Casino currency transaction procedures cover the receipt of $3,000 or more in currency for bets and purchase of chips, when a casino knows or reasonably should know, were from one person in one gaming day. Internal procedures usually also cover slot token purchases and redemptions and all other purchases involving cash or cashouts of more than $3,000. If a patron refuses to provide the required information, the casino is required to maintain a list of those customers for whom the casino was unable to verify information.

Moreover, the regulations require each casino to establish and maintain a Bank Secrecy Act compliance program comprising a system of internal controls, independent testing, training, and an individual to assure compliance.

Obviously, casino management should not encourage money laundering activities and should work closely with law enforcement. When the Bank Secrecy Act was first amended, the casino industry expressed concern about how this would hurt business and be resisted by customers. Because all casinos were required to abide by the same rules, after some initial resistance, compliance today is the norm and patrons find that rules are the same throughout the United States. The Bank Secrecy Act has been extended to Indian gaming in 1996 and will be extended to cardrooms effective August 1, 1998.

There are measures casinos can take even in the absence of regulations to reduce incidents of money laundering. For example, when a patron places a large amount of cash into safekeeping or as front money and then only after minimal play wants to secure a check for that cash, the casino could refuse and return the same cash to the patron. Patrons who buy-in with large amounts of cash and then quickly cash out are immediate suspects of money laundering. All of these things should be tip offs and casinos should not knowingly allow themselves to be used for this purpose. To do so harms the image of the entire industry.

CONCLUSION

Overall, separate and apart from government regulation there are many things casinos can do to guarantee a safer and more secure casino. In the final analysis, these proactive measures function to the benefit of casino companies and improve their bottom lines.

APPENDIX A

GRAPH 1
Surveillance/Internal Audit Reporting Lines

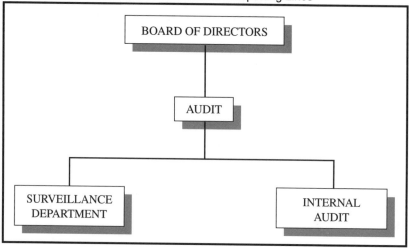

APPENDIX B
STANDARDS FOR CCTV OVER THE CASINO AND RELATED AREAS

TABLE GAMES
Dealers—hands, face, upper body
Patron—face, hands
Spectators around the table
Chip tray
Chips on the table
Table number
Location number
Roulette Wheel
Big Six Wheel

NOTE: One camera shall be used for the entire games of blackjack and roulette; one camera shall be used for each half of the table at craps, baccarat and Big Six.

SLOT MACHINES
Patron's face
Slot Machine handle
Reels
Slot machine glass and facing
Coin acceptor
Slot machine location
Jackpot light

CASINO FLOOR
All exits/entrances
Ability to track person on the casino floor
Cage
All cash drawers
Teller's face, hands, body
All banks located within the cage
All offices within the cage
Patron's face and hands
No hidden areas within the cage
Mantrap

COIN REDEMPTION AREA
All cash drawers
Teller's face, hands, body
Patron's face and hands
All equipment within the coin redemption area
No hidden areas

COUNT ROOMS
All counting equipment and scales
Soft count tables
No hidden areas
Faces, hands and bodies of all count room employees

MISCELLANEOUS
Armored car area
Slot repair room
Secondary coin route
Coin holding areas
Signage obstruction
Change machines
Bill changers

VISIBILITY
Dealer at table
Gaming table inclusive of chip tray
Patron at table
Gaming activity taking place at table

---

1. The BCCI scandals related to improper banking practices of an international bank.

Voluntary Turnover Among Non-supervisory Casino Employees©

Yvonne Stedham and Merwin C. Mitchell

As gaming is expanding nationally and internationally, existing gaming operations are facing increased competition for employees with gaming experience. This study investigates the factors related to employee turnover in the gaming industry. Workers of six casinos in Reno, Nevada were surveyed concerning their work attitudes and turnover intentions, resulting in a sample of 492 observations. The sample represents all non-supervisory job types typically found in casinos. Pearson correlations and multivariate regression analysis were employed to investigate the relationships among turnover intentions and job satisfaction, specific satisfaction dimensions, organizational commitment, worker perceptions, pay, and labor market conditions. The results show that job satisfaction and organizational commitment are most strongly related to turnover. In contrast to previous findings, labor market conditions and pay play only a minor role in an employee's decision to quit. Instead, perceived lack of job security, satisfaction with supervision, and perceived employer concern with employee well-being emerge among the most important factors. The results imply that employers in the gaming industry can manage employee turnover by providing effective supervision that is based on employee participation and fair treatment of employees. Training of supervisors, therefore, may be a relatively inexpensive method of controlling employee turnover in casinos.

Compared to European countries and Japan, the U.S. workforce is extremely mobile (Adler, 1991; Dowling, Schuler, & Welch, 1993). Even though workforce mobility may have a positive effect on an organization's

©1996 Human Sciences Press, Inc. This article was previously published as: Stedham, Y. and M. Mitchell (1996). Voluntary Turnover Among Non-supervisory Casino Employees, *Journal of Gambling Studies,* Vol. 12(3), Fall. Permission to reprint has been granted by the authors and publisher.

flexibility and thus may be to the employer's advantage, voluntary turnover or "quits" can be quite costly. Surveys of employee turnover report turnover cost between $500 and $7,000 per occurrence (Milkovich & Boudreau, 1991; Stedham, 1989). Employees who leave an organization voluntarily have to be replaced and replacements have to be trained. It takes time until the new employee performs at the level of the previous job holder. Turnover in the service industries, such as gaming, has additional costs because employees develop relationships with specific customers. The service that a customer receives becomes associated with the employee rather than with the particular business and such "goodwill" is lost if the employee resigns.

Extent of employee turnover varies across industries. Table 1 summarizes turnover rates for a variety of industries and the data show that industries characterized by jobs that require extensive interaction of employees with the public report the highest turnover rates. Turnover is excessively high in non-manufacturing industries: for example, turnover in gaming in Nevada far exceeds turnover in any other industry. Employers in the gaming industry attribute high levels of turnover primarily to the "transient" character of their workforce; this is viewed as a consequence of movement of workers who have a high degree of geographic mobility.

Traditionally, casino management has not considered turnover a major problem because employees easily could be replaced. Most casino jobs require only basic skills; this contributes to management's perception of an unlimited labor supply. Until recently, employers have generally opted to keep replacing employees rather than attempting to manage turnover rates.

For some time, scholars in a variety of fields have been concerned with understanding employee turnover. Much research along these lines has been generated by scholars in sociology, economics, management, and industrial psychology. Numerous studies have illustrated how organizational, individual, and labor market factors contribute to explaining voluntary employee turnover. The concept of organizational support and of perceptions of the employer as caring and their relationship to turnover have recently been discussed (Eisenberger, Cotterell, and Marvel, 1987; Stedham, 1989). Comprehensive studies that focus on understanding employee turnover in the gaming industry in particular, however, have not been previously conducted. The extremely high levels of turnover, its implied costs, and the increase in demand for workers with gaming experience make worker turnover analysis in gaming a worthy topic. This paper addresses this topic by focusing on understanding the relevance of job satisfaction and organizational commitment to the turnover decision of gaming employees. Organizational and individual factors related to these two attitudes are identified. The relevance of perceiving the employer as

TABLE 1

Annual Turnover Rates[1] by Industry and by Region (1993)

By Industry	
Manufacturing	6.4%
Non-Manufacturing	10.4
Finance	10.4
Hotel-Gaming[2]	60.3
Non-Business	11.2
Health Care	13.2
By Region	
Northeast	8.4%
South	10.0
North Central	7.6
West	8.8

Source: Bureau of National Affairs, Bulletin to Management, BNA Police and Practices Series March 10, 1994

[2]State of Nevada, Employment Security Research. The casinos that participated in this study reported turnover rates of between 35 and 100% for non-supervisory employees.

Note: [1]Rates are computed as

$$\frac{\text{Number of separations during month}}{\text{Average \# of employees on payroll during the month}} * 100 \text{ and then annualized}$$

concerned with employee well-being as well as factors related to such perception are investigated.

VOLUNTARY EMPLOYEE TURNOVER

Early research on turnover identified "perceived desirability" and "perceived ease of movement" as the primary determinants of employee turnover (March & Simon, 1958). Since this early approach, numerous turnover models have been developed. In general, the perceived desirability of movement has been equated with job satisfaction alone (Jackofsky & Peters, 1983), and the perceived ease of movement has been equated essentially with the number of perceived job alternatives. Hulin, Roznowski, and Hachiya (1985) conclude that these two constructs, satisfaction and alternatives, serve as the major conceptual underpinning for much of the literature on employee turnover. In fact, most studies on turnover focus on the relationship between job satisfaction and turnover. Causes and correlates of satisfaction as their effect is manifested in turnover have been identified (Price, 1977). Cotton and Tuttle (1986) and Lee and Mitchell (1994) comprehensively summarize the results of studies based on this approach. Bateman and Strasser (1984) summarize recent research focusing on organizational commitment as a predictor of employee turnover.

The results of previous research on employee turnover are summarized in Table 2. They show turnover to be related to individual characteristics (demographics and attitudes), particularly satisfaction with pay, work itself, supervision, co-workers and promotional opportunities, organizational commitment, perceptions of job security, employee age, tenure, education, number of dependents, and to turnover intentions. Turnover has also been shown to be related to organizational and job characteristics such as pay, employee benefits, organization size, union presence, and to labor market characteristics.

VOLUNTARY TURNOVER IN CASINOS

Recently the concept of organizational commitment has been studied in the context of "exchange ideology" (Eisenberger, Fasolo, & Davis-LaMastro, 1990; Witt, 1991), which describes the exchange between worker and organization as a mixture of economic and social exchanges (Organ & Konovsky, 1989). While social exchange consists of obligations that are broad and based on trust, economic exchange is comprised of fairly explicit obligations to take place at a specific time and is enforced by a formal contract. Based on this proposition, Eisenberger et al. (1990) conceptualize commitment as a trade of loyalty and effort for social rewards and material benefits. Eisenberger, Cotterell, and Marvel (1987) suggest that any kind of helping behaviors incurs obligations and repayments which strengthen a mutually beneficial exchange. That is, employees who perceive their employer as caring about their needs and well-being feel an obligation towards the employer that will manifest itself in positive attitudes and behaviors (Salancik, 1977). Eisenberger et al. (1987) find that such "perceived organizational support" yields better attendance, formal performance, and affective attachment to the organization. In particular, organizational support is significantly related to organizational commitment and job satisfaction.

To date, there have been no empirical studies of the gaming industry that comprehensively investigate the determinants of perceived organizational or employer support. We argue that, in the organizational context, helping behaviors include providing employee benefits, systems for employee involvement, and employer demonstrations of fairness. We expect variables reflecting perceived employer concern with an employee's work and family welfare to be positively related to the worker's commitment to

TABLE 2
Research on Voluntary Turnover—Summary of Results

Variable Studied	Results
Demographics[1]	
Age	Negatively related to turnover
Tenure	Negatively related to turnover
Education	Inconclusive
Number of dependents	Negatively related to turnover
Turnover Intentions	
Intention to stay or quit	A strong predictor of actual turnover behavior. (Mobley, 1977)
Attitudes	
Job satisfaction	Negatively related to turnover and positively related to organizational commitment. (Locke, 1976) All aspects of job satisfaction have been negatively related to turnover. (Price, 1977)
Organizational commitment	Negatively related to turnover. (Mowday, Porter, & Steers, 1982)
Organizational and Job Characteristics[2]	
Pay level	Negatively related to turnover
Employee Benefits	Level of benefits, variety, flexibility, and vesting requirements are related to turnover. (Stedham, 1989)
Voice mechanisms	To what extent employees can voice their opinion is negatively related to turnover (Spencer, 1986)
Organization size	Inconclusive
Presence of union	Negatively related to turnover. (Becker, 1978)
Labor Market Characteristics[2]	
Alternative job opportunities (Actual or perceived)	Negatively related to turnover. Generally, the strongest predictor. (Hartman & Perlman, 1986; Terborg & Lee, 1984)

Sources: [1]Cotton and Tuttle (1986) provide an extensive review of turnover research. Their review is based on a meta-analytic approach including 120 sets of data. They summarize the relationship of 26 variables with turnover. The studies that investigated the relationship of demographics, turnover intentions, attitudes, and presence of union with turnover can be reviewed in the Cotton and Tuttle (1989) summary.
[2]The relationship of pay level and benefits program characteristics is summarized in Stedham (1989). Spencer (1986) investigated the relationship of voice mechanisms with turnover. Among others, Terborg and Lee (1984) report results concerning the relationship of organization size and alternative job opportunities with turnover.

the employer, job satisfaction, and propensity to stay on the job. Hence, variables reflecting workers' feelings of job security should be negatively related to intent to quit and positively related to commitment and satisfaction measures. We also expect pay and benefit levels to be negatively related to a worker's propensity to quit. Measures of satisfaction (general and specific), organizational commitment, and worker control over job attributes are expected, of course, to be negatively related to quitting behavior. We expect the worker's job self-esteem or view of market alternatives to be positively related to intent to quit but we have no prior expectations of how it should be related to commitment and satisfaction measures. We also examine the view that turnover in gaming is a result of a transient workforce.

Note that worker alienation plays an important role in how workers view their work. Feelings of powerlessness have long been documented as a major contributor to worker alienation and are endemic to the casino industry (Pavalko, 1988; Frey, 1986). Alienation and job satisfaction are similar and related concepts (Pavalko, 1988). In this study, we included some of the indicators that have been used to measure alienation such as perceived lack of control and perceived meaninglessness of work, but we did not comprehensively measure "alienation." We expect the relationship of these variables with satisfaction, organizational commitment, and intent to quit to be consistent with the sociological literature on alienation.

METHOD

Sample

Individuals from the Institute for the Study of Gambling and Commercial Gaming at the University of Nevada, Reno assisted the authors in gaining the cooperation of six large Reno casinos. Questionnaires were distributed to employees on-site. Casino management included fliers about the project with each paycheck the week prior to the survey, explaining that the university was conducting research and that responses were to be anonymous and confidential. One of the two researchers involved in the study was on-site and handed an explanatory flier to each individual who came in the lunch room, and asked him/her to fill out the questionnaire. Of those asked, about 7 out of 10 workers agreed to participate and, of these, about 65% actually filled out and returned the survey, resulting in an overall response rate of 45.5%.

Even though we were not able, given our data, to systematically compare respondents and non-respondents, we can say with confidence that the questionnaire's length was the primary deterrent for those who started

TABLE 3
Demographic Characteristics of the Sample
N=492

Sex	Male 52%	Female 48%			
Marital Status	Single 32%	Married 36%	Living Together 9.4%	Divorced 19.1%	Widowed 2.3%
Race	Caucasian 71%	Asian 8.6%	Hispanic 12.4%	Black 3%	American Indian 1%	Other 4%
Education	Less than H.S. 13%	High School 27%	Some College 38%	Bachelor Degree 12%	Graduate Work 4%	Other 6%
Job Type	Dealers 26%	Casino Floor 24%	Bar/ Cocktail Jobs 10%	Hotel Jobs 9%	Kitchen 8%	Other Customer Contact 21%

Note: Numbers may not add up to 100% because of rounding errors.

but did not finish the survey. Most of the respondents who did not finish indicated to the researcher who was present that it would take too much of their break time to complete the 63 items of the survey.

Note also that because university representatives officially conducted the survey and gave repeated assurance of confidentiality, we feel that answers were generally quite honest and forthcoming. Workers were asked to be honest or *not* fill in the questionnaire and supervisors were expressly alerted against any attempt to influence participating subordinates.

A total of 541 usable responses were generated. Of the survey participants, 7% were supervisors. Their responses were not included in the analysis. Twenty-six percent of the respondents were dealers and 24% of the respondents held jobs on the casino floor (cashier, change person, Keno, and slots). The remaining participants were distributed across bar/cocktail jobs (bartender, cocktail waitress/waiter), kitchen jobs (cooks and other kitchen jobs), hotel jobs (custodians, maids, maintenance jobs, and porters), and other customer contact jobs (clerks, bellman/bellhop, security, valet parking jobs). About 12% of the respondents were Hispanic, 8.6% Asian, and 3% Black (see Table 3). The authors had anticipated language problems and provided a Spanish version of the questionnaire that was used by twenty-two of the respondents.

Measures

Voluntary Turnover. Voluntary turnover was measured as intent to stay. Intent to stay or leave is the immediate precursor of staying or leaving behavior. Price and Bluedorn (1977) recommend using "intent to leave" or "intent to stay" as an approximation for turnover. Evidence supports the link between intent to stay or leave and actual attrition (Mobley, Horner, and Hollingsworth, 1978). In this study, the Staying or Leaving Index (SLI) was the measure for turnover (Bluedorn, 1982). On a 7-point Likert scale, respondents were asked to rate their chances of still working with the current employer in three months, six months, one year, and two years. Respondents were also asked to rate their chances of quitting their current employer within the next three months, six months, next year, and the next two years. The responses were scored in such a way that the higher the score, the lower the likelihood of quitting and the greater the likelihood of staying.

Job Satisfaction and Satisfaction with Employee Benefits. Job satisfaction was measured using the Job Descriptive Index (JDI) which measures satisfaction with work itself, pay, promotion, supervision, and co-workers (Smith, Kendall, and Hulin, 1969). Scores on these satisfaction dimensions were combined to provide an overall satisfaction score. Satisfaction with employee benefits was measured based on the benefits satisfaction subscale of the Pay Satisfaction Questionnaire (PSQ) (Heneman and Schwab, 1985).

Organizational Commitment. The definition of commitment (Mowday, Steers, and Porter, 1979) implies more than mere loyalty to an organization. It involves an active relationship with the organization such that individuals are willing to give something of themselves in order to contribute to the organization's well-being. Mowday, Steers, and Porter (1979) developed and validated a measure of organizational commitment, consisting of 15 items to which respondents express their level of agreement on a 7-point Likert scale.

Employee Perceptions and Individual Characteristics. Respondents were asked to indicate on a 5-point scale (1=very unlikely; 5=very likely) how likely they were to be fired or laid off. The higher the score on this question, the lower the level of perceived job security. A single item was used to measure perceptions of the employer's concern with employee well-being. Respondents indicated their level of agreement with the statement, "My employer is interested in my well-being" on a 5-point scale (1=strongly disagree; 5=strongly agree). Several indicators were used to measure workers' perceptions of the work context. Respondents were asked a series of questions concerning the extent of input they have into scheduling their work hours (number of hours to be worked during a week and when to work during the week). They were also asked to indicate to what extent they agreed that "My supervisor is good about following rules and procedures established by my employer" and that "In general, decisions regarding my job are made in an arbitrary fashion." These questions were answered based on a 5-point scale (5=strongly agree; 1=strongly disagree). Respondents also indicated their level of agreement with the statement, "This job contributes to a happy home and social life" on a 5-point Likert scale. Workers' perceptions of alternative job opportunities were measured by their response to the following question: "Given your age and education, and the current economic condition, how difficult do you think it would be for you to find another job of comparable pay in the Reno area?" Respondents answered based on a 5-point scale (1=very easy; 5= very difficult).

Finally, respondents indicated their weekly rate of pay (including tips) with their current employer, and their age, sex, marital status, race, level of education, and number of children under 18 living at home. They also indicated for how long they have been working for their current employer (tenure), for how many casinos they have worked during the past five years, and for how long they have lived in Reno.

Statistical Methods

Frequencies, means, and standard deviations provide a general description of the sample. The relationships between variables were evaluated based on Pearson correlations. The correlations between the relevant variables were evaluated with respect to magnitude and significance. A multivariate regression analysis was conducted to provide further insight into the relationship between intent to stay and the study variables, and between organizational commitment and the study variables.

RESULTS

Table 3 summarizes the demographics. Almost as many women as men participated in the survey, most of the respondents were single; those who were married had an average of 0.6 children, and 54% of the respondents had some college education including 12% who had a bachelors degree and 4% who had done some graduate work. Only 13% of the respondents had not completed high school. The results with respect to education are surprising. More than half of non-supervisory employees in gaming have education above high school. Stereotypically, the gaming workforce is seen as unskilled and uneducated. These results do not support that perception.

TABLE 4
Means and Standard Deviations for Study Variables
N=492

	Mean	S.D.	Min	Max
Age (years)	37.0	11.0	19.0	73.0
Number of dependents	0.6	1.0	0	5.0
Tenure (months)	35.0	41.0	0	352.0
Number of casinos worked at	1.7	1.2	0	9
Time lived in Reno (years)	11.0	9.2	1.0	55.0
Job contributes to happy home and social life (1=strongly disagree; 5=strongly agree)	2.8	1.3	1.0	5.0
Perceived employment opportunities— Perceived difficulty in finding a new job (1=very easy; 5=very difficult)	2.6	1.3	1.0	5.0
Lack of job security—Perceived likelihood of being fired or laid off (1=very unlikely; 5=very likely)	2.3	1.1	1.0	5.0
Pay—per month including tips (U.S. $)	303.1	126.0	100.0	828.0
Control over number of work hours	3.1	1.4	1.0	5.0
Control over when to work	2.8	1.4	1.0	5.0
Superior is perceived as following rules	3.7	1.7	1.0	5.0
Decisions are made in an arbitrary fashion	3.0	1.2	1.0	5.0
Perceptions of employer concern with employee well-being	2.9	1.2	1.0	5.0
Job satisfaction	114.4	37.7	31.0	207.0
Satisfaction with supervision	33.2	14.2	3.0	54.0
Satisfaction with coworkers	31.2	14.6	1.0	54.0
Satisfaction with employee benefits	15.9	6.3	6.0	39.0
Organizational commitment	46.3	11.8	15.0	75.0
Turnover—Intent to stay	40.4	11.6	8.0	56.0

Given higher levels of education, it needs to be investigated what job expectations these gaming employees have and to what extent these expectations are met.

Table 4 represents the means and standard deviations for the remaining variables in this study. With an average age of 37 years, respondents were somewhat older than expected. On average, respondents had been with the current employer for almost 3 years, had lived in Reno for 11 years, and had worked for 1.7 casinos during the past five years. These results do not support the transient character of the gaming workforce. On average, the respondents were neutral concerning their job's contribution to a happy home and social life. Respondents felt that it was neither easy nor difficult to find a new job of comparable pay in the Reno area. On average, respondents thought that it was fairly unlikely that they would be fired or laid off. Though the level of pay, including tips, was moderately low, the range of pay was very large due to the great variety of job types included in this study.

Although many of the remaining values in Table 4 seem to fall in the middle or neutral regions, for most variables in this study, a small minority of workers gave neutral responses ("3" for questions measured on a 5-point Likert scale), while strong majorities lined up on either side of the issues, leading to a number of mid-range averages and large standard deviations.

Pearson correlations for the relevant variables in this study are summarized in Table 5. Since not all respondents answered all the questions, the sample size, on which particular correlations are based, varies.

The correlational analysis provides insights concerning the relationships among variables most strongly related to turnover. With respect to interpreting the signs of the correlations, recall that turnover was measured as intent to stay. As expected, perceptions of lack of job security are related to a decrease in the intent to stay. The correlation between lack of job security and intent to stay is high, negative, and highly significant. The only variables that are more strongly related to intent to stay than lack of job security are job satisfaction and organizational commitment. Note that lack of job security is correlated with satisfaction overall and with satisfaction with supervision and co-workers. The highly significant negative correlation between lack of job security and perceptions of employer concern supports our expectations. A similar result is found for the relationship between lack of job security and perceptions that one's job contributes to a happy home and social life. The negative, highly significant correlation between lack of job security and organizational commitment supports our expectations.

The strong significant positive correlations between satisfaction with supervision and control over the number of hours worked and, over when to work, are as we expected. These variables also have an independent effect on turnover as indicated by the significant positive correlations with intent to stay. The positive and highly significant correlation between satisfaction with supervision and perceptions of the employer as caring is unusually high. Satisfaction with supervision is one of the variables most strongly related to organizational commitment. Satisfaction with supervision is more important to organizational commitment than satisfaction with co-workers. Both satisfaction with supervision and satisfaction with co-workers are significantly related to intent to stay.

The relevance of perceptions of fair processes and decisions to satisfac-

TABLE 5

Pearson Correlations Between Study Variables

237≤N≤492

Variable	1	2	3	4	5	6	7	8	9	10	11	12	13	14	15	16	17	18
1. Number of dependents																		
2. Tenure	.05																	
3. Number of casinos worked at	.04	-.24***																
4. Time lived in Reno	-.02	.31***	.01															
5. Job contributes to happy home and social life	0	-.11***	0	0														
6. Perceived employment opportunities	-.01	-.23***	-.02	-.05	.05													
7. Lack of job security	0	-.02	.06	-.07	-.20***	-.09*												
8. Pay	-.02	.29***	.07	.16**	-.02	-.22***	-.13**											
9. Control over # of hours worked	.01*	.08	.05	.07	.25***	-.03	-.12*	.07										
10. Control over when to work	.06	.12**	.02	.07	.28***	-.04	-.11*	.08	.72***									

11. Superior is perceived as following rules	.05	−.06	−.01	.06	.28***	0	−.10*	−.01	.26***	.22***								
12. Decisions are made in an arbitrary fashion	−.13**	.05	.03	.11*	.18***	.01	−.05	.03	.13**	.19***	.13**							
13. Perceptions of employer concern with employee well-being	−.03	.04	−.05	.07	.45***	.02	−.19***	−.02	−.31***	.25***	.41***	.18***						
14. Job satisfaction	.05	0	−.12*	.07	.47***	−.04	−.12*	.13*	.15*	.15*	.40***	.03	.41***					
15. Satisfaction with supervision	.03	−.05	−.05	.06	.43***	−.01	−.17***	0	.20***	.20***	.57***	.08	.43***	.75***				
16. Satisfaction with coworkers	0	0	−.08	.09	.24***	−.01	−.18***	.05	.12*	.12*	.26***	.07	.28***	.75***	.47***			
17. Satisfaction with benefits	−.06	−.06	−.06	−.05	.40***	.06	−.16***	−.05	.26***	.26***	.23***	.16***	.48***	.33***	.30***	.17***		
18. Organizational commitment	.01	0	−.04	−.02	.44***	−.01	−.16***	−.03	.28***	.29***	.39***	.08	.56***	.53***	.50***	.26***	.43***	
19. Turnover	.05	.18***	−.05	.13*	.28***	−.20***	−.32***	.23***	.15**	.15*	.14	−.02	.26***	.40***	.27***	.22***	.21***	.48***

Note: ***p<.001 **p<.01 *p<.05

267

tion with supervision is supported by the extremely high significant positive correlation between satisfaction with supervision and "superior is perceived as following rules" (r=.57***). The correlation between perceptions of the superior following rules and perceptions of the employer as caring is very high, positive, and significant. Similarly, the correlation between "decisions are made in an arbitrary fashion" (reverse scoring) and perceptions of employer concern is significant. Perceptions of fair practices are related to organizational commitment and to intent to stay.

The extremely high positive significant correlation between satisfaction with employee benefits and perceptions of employer concern supports our expectations. Satisfaction with benefits is very strongly related to organizational commitment and to intent to stay.

The extent to which the job is perceived as contributing to a happy home and social life is consistently very highly correlated with several variables in the study, including the control over work schedule variables and the supervision variables. The correlations between the job's contribution to happy home and social life and perceiving the employer as caring is particularly high. The job's contribution to happy home and social life is also very highly correlated with job satisfaction and moderately correlated with intent to stay.

The significant positive correlations between satisfaction and intent to stay and between organizational commitment and intent to stay are much higher than the correlations between any of the other relevant variables and intent to stay.

Table 6 provides regression results for an ordinary least squares (OLS) estimation with intent to stay as the dependent variable. Table 7 provides OLS estimates for how the study variables are related to the organizational commitment index—the strongest predictor of intent to stay. The adjusted R-squares are .427 (p<.0001) and .535 (p<.0001), respectively, implying that the variables we have chosen explain a reasonable amount of variation on both dependent variables.

Notice that, while the regression results support the correlational results, there are a few variables, for instance, pay, that lose power in the multivariate analysis. This occurs because there are very strong collinearities among the independent variables in both of the regression specifications. In this case, the primary value of the multivariate analysis is to evaluate the overall explanatory power of the dependent variables as measured by the adjusted R-squares.

DISCUSSION

The results of this study have important implications for managerial behavior—in essence, some very good news that the problems presented by

TABLE 6

Results of Regression Analysis of Study Variables on Intent to Stay
(N=146)

Independent Variables	Parameter Estimate b		Partial t
Number of dependents	.04		.06
Tenure	.05		1.99*
Number of casinos worked at	.52		.86
Time lived in Reno	.14		1.78
Job contributes to happy home and social life	.59		.75
Perceived employment opportunities	−1.85		−2.95**
Lack of job security	−2.03		−2.67**
Pay	.01		1.07
Control over # of hours worked	−.14		−.18
Control over when to work	−.84		−1.10
Superior is perceived as following the rules	−.35		−.37
Decisions are made in an arbitrary fashion	−1.32		−1.81
Perceptions of employer concern with employee well-being	−2.10		−2.38*
Job satisfaction	.02		.37
Satisfaction with supervision	.06		.49
Satisfaction with co-workers	.05		.50
Satisfaction with benefits	.23		1.43
Organizational commitment	.54		5.19***
Constant		11.51	
R		.71***	
R²		.50***	
Adjusted R²		.43***	

***p<.001
**p<.01
*p<.05

poor employee attitude and high turnover rates can indeed be "managed" to a better degree. The reader should note that our analysis draws conclusions about causality, which is risky to some extent since our data are cross-sectional and, therefore, cannot by themselves imply causal relationships. However, we suggest that causality can be inferred from correlative

TABLE 7
Results of Regression Analysis of Study Variables on
Organizational Commitment
(N=146)

Independent Variables	Parameter Estimate b		Partial t
Number of dependents	−.28		.48
Tenure	.02		1.14
Number of casinos worked at	.50		.98
Time lived in Reno	−.06		−.92
Job contributes to happy home and social life	1.74		2.69**
Perceived employment opportunities	−.53		1.01
Lack of job security	.69		1.09
Pay	0		−.49
Control over # of hours worked	.03		−.04
Control over when to work	.47		.73
Superior is perceived as following the rules	1.23		1.60
Decisions are made in an arbitrary fashion	−.08		−1.14
Perceptions of employer concern with employee well-being	3.50		5.17***
Job satisfaction	.19		4.34***
Satisfaction with supervision	−.16		−1.69
Satisfaction with co-workers	−.25		−3.14**
Satisfaction with benefits	−.11		−.86
Constant		17.05	
R		.76***	
R^2		.59***	
Adjusted R^2		.54***	

***$p < .001$
**$p < .01$
*$p < .05$

relationships when managerial intuition and parallel evidence says it makes sense to do so.

Perceptions of lack of job security have a very strong negative impact on a worker's intent to stay and increase the likelihood of leaving. The only variables that are more strongly related to intent to stay than lack of job security are job satisfaction and organizational commitment. The fact that lack of job security is negatively related to satisfaction overall and to satisfaction with supervision and co-workers implies that in addition to an independent effect of lack of job security on intent to stay, lack of job security has an impact on turnover through an impact on job satisfaction. Furthermore, employees who feel that they might be fired or laid off are less likely to think of their employer as being concerned with their well-being, and they are less likely to think of their job as contributing to a happy home and social life. Overall, perceptions of lack of job security have a very strong negative impact on employee attitudes and behaviors. Any attempt to manage employee turnover must address this variable. Using lack of job security as a management tool involves major risks with respect to employee turnover.

Our results clearly show that workers prefer to be involved in decisions that concern their job and working conditions, and, in particular, decisions with respect to work schedules. Allowing employees some control over work and scheduling decisions generates important positive effects on employee attitudes. Workers who perceive that they have more control perceive their employer as more caring, are more satisfied with supervision and nearly every facet of the job, and are more committed, thus less likely to quit.

If workers are satisfied with supervision, they are also more likely to see their employer as caring, which implies that they seem to credit the employer with effective supervision. Rather than attributing problems with supervisors to the individual supervisor, employees see it as the employer's responsibility to ensure effective supervision. This is of great importance since satisfaction with supervision is one of the variables most strongly related to organizational commitment. Satisfaction with supervision is more important to organizational commitment than satisfaction with co-workers.

The next question to ask is, what contributes to satisfaction with supervision? Workers who believe that their supervisors follow the rules and make fair decisions are more likely to be satisfied with supervision. This clearly implies that an employer can affect employee attitudes and behaviors by ensuring that supervisors implement and follow fair rules and processes. It is not sufficient to have processes in place. Supervisors must be trained and reinforced in using these processes. Perceptions of fair practices also have a direct impact on organizational commitment and intent to stay. The fact that the correlation between fair supervision and intent to stay is lower than the correlation between fair supervision and satisfaction with supervision, and the fact that the correlation between satisfaction with supervision and intent to stay is high, imply that perceptions of fairness affect turnover primarily through an impact on satisfaction with supervision. Notice also the deleterious effect when workers feel "decisions are made in an arbitrary fashion." This variable is significantly related to all measures related to perception of the job as well as intent to stay.

The importance of employee benefits to employee attitudes and behaviors has only recently been recognized. The results of this study show that satisfaction with benefits has a strong positive impact on organizational commitment and intent to stay. These relationships are truly remarkable in contrasting with the negligible effects that pay has on the same variables. This divergence is likely, in part, due to the effect of tips on workers' overall pay, but there is no denying that the importance of employer-provided benefits not be overlooked when it comes to these important characteristics. Hence, providing benefits that actually satisfy workers' needs and preferences may be worth the increased labor cost as they may reduce costs resulting from turnover.

Finally, several of the study variables are related to perceptions of the job contributing to a happy home and family life. Positive experiences on the job seem to contribute to perceiving the job as having a positive impact on non-work life, resulting in an overall more positive attitude towards the job.

IMPLICATIONS FOR MANAGEMENT

Historically, casino management has been characterized by "management toughness" (Macomber, 1984) and a climate of distrust, dependence on luck, reliance on personal loyalty, utilization of job patronage via "juice" or personal connections, and autocratic decision-making (Frey, 1986). Macomber (1984) maintains that the focus of managing casino employees has been on game control, and the result has been a strict management style. Frey (1986) concludes that control has been maintained by a lack of job security, and by other measures such as restriction of communication between dealer and customers, close supervision, and the routinization of tasks. Smith, Preston, and Humphries (1976) investigated the working conditions of casino card dealers and found that dealers experience relatively high levels of alienation. The primary causes of this experience include over-control and close surveillance of dealers by bosses, as well as the dictatorial attitude and unfair practices of bosses. The evidence presented here indicates that those practices most strongly contribute to the high turnover rates in gaming.

Specifically, job security emerges as one of the most important variables. In interviewing workers the most qualitative complaint we heard was: "You are constantly reminded that there are 10 people waiting for your job." Managers who engage in such behavior should remember that there may also be more than 10 other casinos at any given time taking applications for new employees. Managers concerned with employee turnover and attitude must recognize the fact that using job security as a management tool involves real cost that many managers in other industries find unacceptable. Employee participation, even simply with respect to work scheduling and being treated fairly and by the rules, is associated with effective supervision. Workers who operate under such conditions are more satisfied with every aspect of their job, are more committed to the firm they work for, and in turn are less likely to quit. This is good news for managers, since promoting job and schedule flexibility and getting supervisors and managers to be fair is not an especially expensive proposition.

As discussed above, employees credit the employer with effective supervision. Overall, these results indicate employers should provide training which focuses on supervisory skills in contrast to job security considerations. Emphasizing participatory techniques, rules and regulations, as well as treating employees fairly can have a salutary effect on employee turnover. Important also were the results that indicate that employees expect much more from their jobs than income. Employers should recognize the positive social effects that truly caring about workers will have in the long run. The data furthermore suggest that if an employer provides desired benefits and effective and fair supervision, the employer is perceived as caring, which in turn increases an employer's commitment to the employer and decreases the employee's likelihood to quit.

Casinos are facing a more competitive environment in many jurisdictions in the U.S. In order to remain effective in that new context, operational changes are required. Casino management must realize that labor markets for experienced gaming employees are tightening and employee turnover is becoming more costly. The results of this study provide important insights into possible reasons for the heretofore extremely high turnover rates as well as guidelines for managing turnover among non-supervisory gaming employees. From an employer's perspective, turnover can be controlled by ensuring that supervisors are trained, that they treat employees fairly through following the rules set forth by the employer, and by involving employees in decisions that directly affect their working conditions. These are fairly inexpensive interventions relative to the cost of turnover and negative worker attitudes. We encourage managers to explore the possibilities.

REFERENCES

Adler, N. J. (1991). *International dimensions of organizational behavior.* Belmont, CA: Wadsworth.

Bateman, T. S. & Strasser, S. (1984). A longitudinal analysis of the antecedents of organizational commitment. *Academy of Management Journal, 27,* 95–112.

Becker, B. (1978). Hospital unionism and employment stability. *Industrial Relations, 17,* No. 1.

Bluedorn, A. C. (1982). The theories of turnover: Causes, effects, and meaning. In S. Bacharach (Ed.), *Research in the Sociology of Organizations, 1* (pp. 75–128). Greenwich, Conn.: JAI Press.

Bureau of National Affairs (1994). *Bulletin to Management—BNA's quarterly report on job absence and turnover,* 4th Quarter 1993.

Cotton, J. L. & Tuttle, J. M. (1986). Employee turnover: A meta-analysis and review with implications for research. *Academy of Management Review, 11,* 55–70.

Dowling, P. J., Schuler, R. S., & Welch, D. E. (1993). *International dimensions of human resource management.* Belmont, CA: Wadsworth.

Eisenberger, R., Cotterel, N., & Marvel, J. (1987). Reciprocation ideology. *Journal of Personality and Social Psychology, 53,* 743–750.

Eisenberger, R., Fasolo, P., & Davis-LaMastro, V. (1990). Perceived organizational support and employee diligence, commitment, and innovation. *Journal of Applied Psychology, 75,* 51–59.

Employment Security Research, April 1994, Carson City, Nevada.

Frey, J. (1986). Labor issues in the gaming industry. *Nevada Public Affairs Review, 2,* 32–38.

Hartman, E. A., & Perlman, B. (1986). *Prediction of individual turnover vs. organizational turnover rates.* Paper presented at the annual Academy of Management meeting, Chicago, IL.

Heneman, H. G. III, & Schwab, D. P. (1985). Pay satisfaction: Its multidimensional nature and measurement. *International Journal of Psychology, 20,* 129–141.

Hulin, C. L., Roznowski, M., & Hachiya, D. (1985). Alternative opportunities and withdrawal decisions: Empirical and theoretical discrepancies and an integration. *Psychological Bulletin, 97,* 233–250.

Jackofsky, E. F. & Peters, L. H. (1983). Job turnover: Reassessment of the March and Simon participation hypothesis. *Journal of Applied Psychology, 68,* 490–495.

Lee, T. W. & Mitchell, T. R. (1994). An alternative approach: The unfolding model of voluntary employee turnover. *Academy of Management Review, 19,* 51–89.

Locke, E. (1976). The nature and causes of job satisfaction. In Dunnette, M. (ed.) *Handbook of Industrial and Organizational Psychology.* Chicago, IL: Rand McNally.

Macomber, D. (1984). Management policy and practices in modern casino operations. *The Annals of the American Academy of Political and Social Science, 474,* 80–90.

March, J. & Simon, H. (1958). *Organizations.* New York: Wiley.

Milkovich, G. T. & Boudreau, J. W. (1991). *Human Resource Management.* Homewood, IL: Irwin.

Mobley, W. H. (1977). Intermediate linkages in the relationship between job satisfaction and employee turnover. *Journal of Applied Psychology, 62,* 237–240.

Mobley, W. H., Horner, S., & Hollingsworth, A. T. (1978). An evaluation of precursors of hospital employee turnover. *Journal of Applied Psychology, 63,* 408–414.

Mowday, R. T., Steers, R. M., & Porter, L. (1979). The measurement of organizational commitment. *The Journal of Vocational Behavior, 14,* 224–247.

Mowday, R. T., Porter, L., & Steers, R. M. (19820. *Employee-Organization Linkages.* New York: Academic Press.

Organ, D. W. & Konovsky, M. (1989). Cognitive versus affective determinants of organizational citizenship behavior. *Journal of Applied Psychology, 74,* 157–164.

Pavalko, R. M. (1988). *Sociology of occupations and professions.* Second edition. Itasca, Illinois: F. E. Peacock.

Price, J. L. (1977). *The study of turnover.* Ames, Iowa: The Iowa State University Press.

Price, J. & Bluedorn, A. C. (1977, August). *Intent to leave as a measure of turnover.* Paper presented at the 37th Annual Meeting of the Academy of Management, Orlando, FL.

Salancik, G. R. (1977). Commitment and the control of organizational behavior and belief. In Staw, B. M. and Salancik, G. R. (eds.), *New directions in organizational behavior.* Chicago, IL: St. Clair Press.

Smith, P. C., Kendall, L. M., & Hulin, C. L. (1969). *The measurement of satisfaction in work and retirement: A strategy for the study of attitudes.* Chicago, IL: Rand McNally & Company.

Smith, W. R., Preston, F., & Humphries, H. L. (1976). Alienation from work: A study of casino card dealers. In W. Eadington (Ed.), *Gambling and Society* (pp. 229–246). Springfield, IL: Thomas.

Spencer, D. G. (1986). Employee voice and employee retention. *Academy of Management Journal, 26,* 488–502.

The Use and Cost of Promotional Chips and Tokens

Andrew MacDonald

Casinos regularly issue promotional chips and tokens to attract players. The objective is obviously to increase profits by inducing the public to gamble at that particular facility. The promotional chips are also used effectively to discount the standard retail price of items offered by the facility, such as room, food and beverage services where, depending upon occupancy or utilization levels, the retail cost differs from the marginal cost to the company.

The practice has been used successfully for many years. The purpose of this analysis is to suggest that it is profitable, but only when used with caution. For an obvious example, if occupancy is low during a particular period, then the cost of providing a room to a customer is effectively the cost of cleaning and servicing that room. If occupancy is high, however, the cost is that of the potentially displaced revenue from a normal sale. Thus, it is particularly sensible to use the practice during non-peak periods where packaging an attractive offer brings players who would not otherwise be present.

One highly marketable method by which this can be achieved is to provide package customers with a room at standard retail and include promotional chips to add value. However, caution is needed. If the chips are merely cash chips, customers can easily cash them out; there is no incentive for them to play in the casino. Thus the provision of cash chips to discount the room rate may attract only those customers interested in a cheap room. The promotion would be of little value to the overall operation.

A more effective technique would be to provide *match play tokens* or non-negotiable chips. Match play tokens require a player to match the value of the token played with an equal or greater value of cash chips. This practice marginally reduces the cost to the company of providing match play tokens, but of more value is the fact that people attracted by

277

the package have a propensity to gamble as they are also willing to place at risk their own money.

These tokens are often used on a "with exchange" basis. This increases the amount in match play tokens which may be provided to each customer and thus enhances the market perception of added value. In such circumstances each token can be used once only; that is, if the bet wins the token is removed. On an even chance game, if the player bets a $5 cash chip and a $5 match play and the bet wins, then the player is paid $10 and the match play token removed. Since bet and payout provide a total return to the player of $15, the match play could therefore be described as having a $2.50 betting value. If this is the case and we wish to discount a room by $50 we could provide the customer with $100 in match play tokens as part of the room package.

Under this system, if a purchaser of the package doesn't gamble, then they would pay full price, as match play tokens have no value except in play. Only by gambling the full amount does the customer receive the discounting value. An added advantage of this system is that there is no need to rate (record) play for this player. All calculations on discount have been made prior to the sale and no requirement exists to monitor how much and how long the player gambles.

Such a simplistic analysis is, however, fraught with danger. More detailed calculations are required to determine the potential cost to the company of the unrestricted use of match play tokens.

In any game the cost of providing a chip to a player is the probability of the player winning multiplied by the total return to the player (bet plus payout). In the case of match play tokens (with exchange), the cost is the probability of the player winning multiplied by the payout only (i.e., the bet component is not returned). In an even chance game with a 1.5% house advantage, the cost of a token is 49.25% of its face value. As the token must at least be matched with an equivalent cash chip bet, the cost of the token may then be reduced by the mathematical expected loss from this required bet. In this example that reduces the 49.25% by 1.5% to 47.75%. At the Adelaide Casino in South Australia, all tokens at their face dollar value are treated as drop. A tax implication also exists, which in Adelaide is 20% of net win. This increases the cost to 58.2% of the value of the tokens provided.

What if, however, the tokens could be used on non-even payoff games such as roulette? In this example, if the player bets only on straight ups the initial cost of the token is 94.59% of its value. The benefit derived from matching the token is 2.7%, thus reducing the cost to 91.89%. After tax, the cost is increased to 93.51%.

In such a case the implied cost of the token can rise from 58.2% of the dollar value of the token to 93.5% of the value if played on single numbers on roulette.

Details of the above calculations are shown below.

MATCH PLAY TOKENS
(with exchange)

Cost assessment:

Terms = p(w) = probability of player winning
r = standard returns (payout + bet)
V = value of match play token
Match Play Cost = V * p(w) * (r − 1)

Example One:

For even chance game:
where p(w) = 0.4925
Cost = V * 0.4925 * (2 − 1)
     = V * 0.4925

Example Two:

For single zero roulette:
where p(w) = 1/ 37 playing straight ups
Cost = V * 0.027 * (36 − 1)
     = V * 0.945945

The incremental benefit in this example is due to the requirement to match the value of the token with an equal or greater value of cash chip.

Benefit = V − V * p(w) * r
       = V * (1 − p(w) * r)

Therefore

sub total cost = V * p(w) * (r − 1) − v * (1 − p(w) * r)
               = V * (2p(w) * r − p(w) − 1)
               or V * {{p(w) * (2r − 1)} − 1}

Example One expanded

     = V * 0.4925 − V0.015
     = V * 0.4775

Example Two extended

     = V * 0.945945 − V0.027027
     = V * 0.918918

A tax implication exists due to the fact that all tokens (at their face value) will be treated as drop. Tax in South Australia at 20% of net win.

$$\text{Tax} = 20\% \, (1 - \text{Sub Total Cost})$$

Therefore

$$\text{Grand Total Cost} = \text{Sub Total Cost} + \text{Tax}$$
$$= V * \{0.8 * (2p(w) * r - p(w) - 1) + 0.2\}$$

Example One Continued

$$\text{Grand Total Cost} = V * 0.582$$

Example Two Continued

$$\text{Grand Total Cost} = V * 0.9351344$$

Thus areas of concern exist if the tokens are used on non-even payoff games. As this may potentially cause problems in that the discounting value of the match play when associated with a retail purchase is then not constant, which limits the marketability of the product if the upper value is used.

To overcome these concerns it is possible to implement one of the following:

- Restrict usage to even money bets only;
- Restrict usage to blackjack and baccarat;
- Accept varying percentage cost as commercial risk and assume a weighted 75% cost element;
- Pay only even money for the match play component of a bet even if placed on higher payout bet; or
- State on the token that it pays at 50% of the marked value.

The simplest alternative and the one generally adopted is to restrict usage to even money bets only.

Once this is done, it is possible to structure an off-peak package which includes match play tokens using a 60% cost element on the value of the tokens provided. A multitude of options exist to package not only room, food and beverage items but also a travel component.

It must be remembered, however, that the primary objective is to increase profits, not just revenue or headcount. Therefore, any package should be structured to attain at minimum play levels a break-even result after all costs are considered, or preferably a level of profit which does not impinge upon the marketability of the service given that is already impeded by off-peak restrictions, etc.

An example of a break-even package is the following:

One night's accommodation (mid-week only), including $300 in match play tokens plus dinner for one in the buffet restaurant. Assume a normal rack rate of $270, but excess room availability during mid-week.

```
Assumed Revenue = $300
          Costs = $180 Match play costs (at 60%)
              + $60 room marginal cost
              + $10 marginal meal cost
              + $20 advertising and marketing overhead
              + $20 labor and administration overhead
              + $10 sales commission
            Net = 0
```

COST ASSESSMENT

The difficulty here is that the advertising and labor allocations are volume-based. This means that if the package is unsuccessful, the advertising allocation will increase dramatically, whereas the labor allocation may reduce only to zero. It is therefore important to structure the package so that it is appealing to the potential market. To accomplish this it may be necessary to conduct market research prior to advertising the package.

In conclusion, therefore, when structuring any promotional package the following should be considered essential elements:

- The objective is to increase profits; therefore, set that objective.
- Conduct detailed analyses and identify all cost elements prior to staging.
- Adopt a break-even structure.
- Conduct market research and follow-up to identify appeal and/or success.
- Analyze results and consider whether this is the best way to achieve the result.

If the business cannot be operated in this businesslike manner, then the casino may be gambling itself on such promotions, and often it might be better not to do the promotion at all. A responsible guideline to follow is:

"We are in the gambling business, not in the business of gambling."

Casino Design and Ambience

Section 4

The Spell of the Sensuous: Casino Atmosphere and the Gambler

Felicia F. Campbell

The shaman in the jungle and the gambler in the casino have more in common than might appear on the surface. Both momentarily lose their identities in their environments; the shaman merges and submerges in the naturally chaotic world of nature, while the gambler enters the altered state of "the action" in the artificially chaotic, virtual world of the casino.

This paper will discuss those parallels described, using as a basis a philosophical work, David Abram's *The Spell of the Sensuous: Perception and Language in a More-Than-Human World,* from which the title of this paper is taken; a novel, Edward Allen's *Mustang Sally,* and comments from Las Vegas gamblers. As this is not a statistical study, the author makes no claims regarding the number of gamblers that the paradigm may fit.

David Abram would be more than a little surprised and probably somewhat appalled at the use to which I have put his work. *The Spell of the Sensuous* draws on personal interviews with shamans around the world, as well as Edmund Husserl's phenomenology and Maurice Merleau-Ponty's radicalization of phenomenology. This is simpler than it sounds.

Phenomenology is the study of direct experience, and perception is, of course, the way we sense or perceive things. Abram defines perception as "an open activity . . . a dynamic blend of receptivity and creativity by which every animate organism necessarily orients itself to the world (and orients the world around itself)" (50).

As we are all aware, our physical perceptions are limited to our five senses; thus we can never fully comprehend an object. For example, we can see only the part of a slot machine immediately before our eyes, and cannot view the back, sides, top and bottom at the same time as we see the front. Neither can we see the mechanics of the machine without opening it, nor can we discover the molecular structure without destroying the object as a whole. Perception of those parts of the machine that we do see changes with each gaze because of shifts in light, dust or age. Each object presents facets, which catch the eye, as well as hiding others. When the body responds to this presentation, the thing that it is responding to answers in kind by in a sense inviting us to focus our senses on it. Perception then, as Merleau-Ponty points out is "this reciprocity, the ongoing interchange between my body and the entities that surround it . . . a sort of silent conversation that I carry on with things, a continuous dialogue that unfolds far below my verbal awareness—and often . . . *independent* of my verbal awareness . . . an improvised duet between my animal body and the fluid, breathing landscape that it inhabits" (52–53).

Consider the gambler, sniffing the air of the Strip, first deciding which casino calls to him, then after selecting and entering it, looking for the table or machine that calls him. Something will draw him to his "lucky" table or machine and he will insist that there is a kind of communication between himself and the object.

Pack Schmidt, anti-hero of Edward Allen's comic novel, *Mustang Sally,* is a third rate professor at a third rate university in the Midwest, where he feels life is being leached out of him. A devoted but low-roller gambler, he finds a kind of rebirth in Las Vegas and expresses his reaction to the Vegas scene this way:

> But it's not just the games; it's the whole town, something I can feel in the back of my jaw every time I see a picture of the Strip on television, the way the town bathes itself in light, the way you can just walk into it and get lost and nobody will come chasing you with papers to grade . . . after one of these trips, when I go home again to my office, and the house . . . everything goes better for a few weeks. I stride from office to parking lot, my briefcase swinging briskly at my side and I feel perked up and cleaned out, like a man who has just had a session on a kidney dialysis machine (14–15).

Clearly there is a reciprocity, a give and take, between the Schmidt and his overarching environment. Perhaps as Abram believes "the human intellect (is) in, and secretly borne by our forgotten contact with the multiple non human shapes that surround us" (49). Again referencing Merleau-Ponty, Abram suggests that the world of perception involves "attunement or synchronization" between one's own rhythms and the rhythm of the thing perceived. The way we dress, the way we walk, the way we wear our collars, all are ways of synchronizing ourselves with our environments (54).

Pack Schmidt, a small time gambler who refers to himself as "The Hero with a Thousand Dollars," sniffs Las Vegas and remarks, "Everything sits out in front of me, unspoiled like a new deck of cards, like fresh pins in a bowling alley, though I don't bowl anymore" (12), and sees the night laid out in front of him like "a big toy" which reactivates all of his favorite superstitions, which include wearing for luck a herring bone jacket, missing a decorative button on one cuff (17). Clearly, he is preparing himself for engagement with the gods of chance, as a shaman will ritually prepare himself for engagement with the spirits. The rituals or superstitions that are so well known among gamblers fit this pattern of preparation or synchronization. As a gambler in her mid-sixties said to me,

> "When I come to Vegas, it's as though the whole city were putting on a huge party and it's just for me. I blend with it and while I'm walking through deciding where to play and during all the time I'm playing, I'm not my usual self but someone entirely different who is part of the whole wonderful whole."

What happens for both her and the fictional Schmidt is what Abram describes in terms of the natural world when he explains that "In contact with the native forms of the earth, one's senses are slowly energized and awakened, combining and recombining in ever-shifting patterns" (63).

Those of us who have spent any length of time in the natural world as compared to the technological world are aware of the soothing nature of chaotic landscapes in which the patterns exist, yet are never repeated in exactly the same fashion. Turbulent streams, jagged mountain peaks, desert dunes, irregular forests, all soothe us in a way that the harsh linear geometries of the contemporary cities, factories and offices in which most of us are imprisoned cannot. Our economy is based on convincing us that fulfillment lies in our interactions with newer model houses or cars or pairs of athletic shoes, but, as Abram points out, manufactured items from milk cartons to washing machines have a certain life, but are *constrained* (italics added) by the specific functions for which they were designed, thus are limited in what they can teach us, and reiterate without variation, requiring us to "continually acquire *new* built technologies, the latest model of this or that if we wish to stimulate ourselves" (64).

Casinos, while manufactured, are built to speak to us, to lure us, to stimulate us into merging with them, and to convince us that they are ever-changing, drawing us into a fantasy world, illuminated by countless, flashing multicolored lights. In some strange way, the constantly changing faces of the gaming casinos are the other end of the spectrum of the chaotic landscapes of nature in which patterns constantly iterate, or repeat, yet are never exactly the same, and, perhaps, this leads to the altered state of consciousness which I am paralleling with the shamanic state.

Our fictional Schmidt uses the imagery of nature to describe the Strip. "From the darkness of the valley floor," he says, "hotels rise in a soft light, like tropical shells. . . ." As he gazes at the massive shapes of huge hotels, he "can almost hear the casino sound, an ocean of bells and of buzzers. I can't wait to let that sound wash all over me. To let it rinse away the musty smell that collects in my office when it's too cold to open the window" (20). In another spot, he refers to "the casino sound, like a thousand cash registers and a thousand video games all jumbled together in a kind of musical surf of bells and wheels and coins dropping into metal pans" (24). We get the strong feeling that he reacts far more strongly to the casino environment than he would to the sea to which he compares it.

A sense of smell is, of course, a large part of our sensory experience, and the odor of casinos is distinctive. While some casinos have found that spraying aromas, such as apple scent, increases wagers; for Schmidt, the normal casino smell is enough to transport him. Neither clean nor dirty, mixed with substances from tobacco to sweat, perfume and halitosis, he says casino air "is blended and softened to produce something warm and round and lived-in" (24). This is for him an essential part of the experience, and so important to him that he gambles only at tables where people are smoking. Even though he is a non-smoker, he feels that non-smoking tables are unlucky, the smoke somehow part of the ambiance. Thus as Merleau-Ponty explains, at the heart of even our most abstract thoughts is "the sensuous and sentient life of the body itself" (45). The body in this sense is not the mechanized body of sinews and bones, but the body as it actually experiences things. This eliminates the dichotomy between body and soul in terms of sensate experiences. As Abram puts it, "the body is my very means of entering into relation with all things" (47).

Recognizing a tenet of chaos theory that everything is connected to everything else, the gambler, like the shaman or magician, may draw heavily on superstition or magic. Schmidt never uses the word win and believes it is good luck to be polite even to machines (29). He can "feel the presence of luck, like a ghost hanging over the huge signs, over the excited flowery torch of the Flamingo," over everything. Even the wind joins in as it blows down the Strip, a sign of good luck. Like the shaman or sorcerer, Schmidt has entered into the altered state by shedding the accepted perceptual logic of his culture. Like the shaman, Schmidt has "the ability to readily slip out of the perceptual boundaries that demarcate his particular culture— boundaries reinforced by social customs, taboos, and most importantly, common speech or language, in order to make contact with, and learn from, the other powers in the land" (10).

When he is in Las Vegas, Schmidt recognizes his place in the scheme of things. Chaos theorists know that everything affects everything else, and so does Schmidt, who realizes that timing is everything.

" . . . See a penny, pick it up, change the world—walk in the front door of the Riviera one second later, one second earlier, and the world is transformed" (17), later, "every time I turn my head I cause myself to step up to the crap table a second later, every step I take changes the world. What a responsibility" (71).

Like the shaman, Schmidt alters the common organization of his senses to enter into rapport with the non-human sensibilities that animate the local landscape (Abram, 9).

Here in a neon jungle, Schmidt seeks a kind of vitality and rootedness that he cannot find in his normal environment and is unlikely to search for in nature. He has isolated himself from nature and animals, but not from a need for sensate experience, an experience that for good or ill moves ever closer to virtual reality.

Everything about casinos is designed to assist gamblers in slipping the perceptual boundaries of their worlds. Even linear time and space are smashed. While the casinos are famous for not having clocks in view, the Strip itself with its dazzling variety of themed casinos representing diverse historical eras and geographical settings destroys the concept of an orderly, linear timeline and traditional geography, mixing everything from ancient Egypt to medieval Europe to New York in a dizzying equality of time and space.

Schmidt sums up his experience, saying, "Oh, my town, Vegas, my new plaything, merciless and soft. Sometime when I get drunk I am going to bend over, with my ass toward Mecca, and kiss the shampooed carpeting of my motel room, because this has been a difficult year" (27).

Much the shaman, Schmidt is on a journey and the journey aspect of the experience is important. As one informant who moved here because she loved gambling told me, "For the first three years, it was magic. Then I began to realize that it wasn't going to go away, that I didn't need to rush out to a casino every time I had some extra money. Gradually I'm finding myself irritated by the other players, by the noise in general. Where I used to find the loudspeakers announcing another winner exciting, now I think 'Oh, Shut up.'"

Perhaps this is why the *Wizard of Oz* theme failed at the MGM. The shamanic gambler may neither want to identify with Dorothy, nor discover the man behind the curtain manipulating everything.

REFERENCES

Abram, D. (1996). *The Spell of the Sensuous: Perception and Language in a More-Than-Human World.* New York: Pantheon Press.

Allen, E. (1992). *Mustang Sally.* New York: W.W. Norton.

Story Spaces: Any Casino's Romance & How It's Told

David Kranes

A man wants to escape.
His job holds him prisoner twelve hours a day. The thermometer's at 20—no sun for a week. He's tense, restless; the work-a-day is draining. If he could just. . . . ! He has a couple of days, not time, really, to fly somewhere. Still, there are these two books—"tropical thrillers" he's been saving—and so he gives them a try.

The cover of the first tries too hard for attention, still the writer's name has a certain marketplace ring: *Harrah's*. The man opens and reads, but not a lot is happening. The prose seems flat. Who's who isn't clear and *where* in the tropics is vague—some place with a palm tree and an alligator. He starts with the first paragraph again and—he can't tell—the story's either boring or confusing. So he closes the book, sets it aside, picks up the other.

Again, the cover doesn't really grab him. Still, the colors have depth, a certain verve, and the image has more focus. This book's by a new writer—*Rio*—which is, at least, a ***place*** he's heard about. Our man opens and starts in. And he can't tell how many hours later it is when he finishes—because the time dissolves—but, when he closes the cover, puts the book down, he's gratified. He's *been* somewhere—*away* from his cold, sunless, routine everyday. He feels satisfied. He wants to read the book again. He wants to recommend its enchanting, even mysterious, journey to friends.

Commanding stories capture us. Inspired storytellers bear the aura of magic.

"No matter what form the dragon may take, it is of this mysterious passage past him, or into his jaws, that stories of any depth will always be concerned to tell, and this being the case, it requires considerable courage at any time, in any country, not to turn away from the storyteller." Flannery O'Connor

Casinos are story spaces. The best ones compel. We linger in hopes of some mysterious passage, the fire of the dragon. A good story **transports;** it takes you for a "ride," and the *ride* quickens your pulse. In a good story, the reader identifies with the hero, *is* the hero—moving through stimulation, risk, encountering strangers, finding heightened pleasure. A good story makes us hungry for more: we *want* something; we want *more* and we get it. In a good story, we're always asking, "what happens next?" We chase mystery, hunger for surprise. In a good story, we always give ourselves over, *trust* the writer. Any good story wraps itself, like atmosphere, around us—puts us in an exotic place and gives us all the heady ambiance of that place. And when the story ends, all the hunger that it's provoked, during submission, is satisfied. You want to hear the story again; you want to remember it; you want to tell it to others.

The best casinos—those returned to and made "legendary" to others—have gone beyond *theming*. A theme is never the whole song; it's only a line that helps us recognize the music. A theme is not a story; it's just one point the story makes. A theme is never the whole exciting experience; it's just a couple of measures of the experience. If you can hum or state the theme, most times you don't have to hear the music or read the story. The best Las Vegas architects and design teams have begun, now, to go *beyond theme* and become artful storytellers. And there are some absorbing stories in the wings waiting still to be told—but that's another story.

Two casino resorts in Las Vegas currently tell a similar story: *The Rio* and *Harrah's*. The first is telling its Carnival story with style and imagination. The second is telling a Carnival story that is a yawner.

CASINO TALES: TWO CARNIVAL STORIES— THE RIO & HARRAH'S

Browsing for Adventure and Romance: The Bookjacket

A casino's architectural form and facade is its *bookcover.* When the new MGM opened, it had a great Emerald City bookcover but was a confused-at-best read. The cover to the story *The Rio* tells may not make you want to snap the book off the table and begin reading, but it's lucid. The towers cut the sky without competition—a sculptural advantage very few Las Vegas casinos have. The rich reds and purples and greens suggest depth of color, richness of story, and if stories are said to have "local color," that color has to begin outside. If the color had reflection below from Guanabara Bay, we could be in the actual Rio de Janeiro. Sugarloaf or Corcovado Mountains could be rising just in the background. There's engaging clarity, style, singularity, individuality.

The new *Harrah's* is a different story. And it's short. If you can tell a book by its cover, this book *is* its cover: vaguely vivid, lit, glitzy, contoured, ultimately confusing about what's inside. There are colored balloon-or-champagne-sparkle globes, some masked motley figures which could be carnival masquers or Elizabethan jesters. What is it suggesting? What is it promising? It's more like jots and notes, paint samples and fabric swatches toward a cover of a book hoping to tell a story about Carnival. It's promoting its brand name—*HARRAH'S!*—not, like *THE RIO,* invoking a romantic place.

Harrah's inherited the old Holiday Casino riverboat: a rather narrow frontage space paralleling Las Vegas Boulevard with a paddle-wheeler cover, behind which were add-on, tacked-on spaces moving progressively back from the boulevard. The inherited space was a patchwork and, in no way, comprised any overall *World.* Once you entered the doors, it was a *Casino*—generic, cramped—and not much else. It told no particular story beyond that of sawdust-joint gaming. So, now there's a new cover—with bubbles or balloons and jesters, a cover which is "celebratory" or "bubbly" at best.

AWAKENING APPETITE

Critic/theorist Kenneth Burke writes: "[story] form is the creation of an appetite." Novelists speak of "hooks." Gamblers speak of "sharks" and "fish."

The creation of an appetite in the mind. We are led by our noses. "Is that ahi tuna that I . . . ?" "Is that pesto. . . . ?" "Is that veal picatta . . . ?" And, as Dr. Pavlov, proved: we are all creatures with salivary glands. Bells ring; lights flash; coins drop; hunger rises—with it, adrenalin. "Is this a hot machine?. . . . a back-line dice game?. . . . a six-deck shoe rich with tens and aces?" Look at the chips stacked! Hear the coins and bells! Look at all the green chips lined up in the rack! *I smell . . . ! I taste. . . . ! The creation of an appetite.*

We read the world in a cross-over of senses—the whole comes to us (as storytellers would say) as "synaesthetic." We *taste* winning by seeing chips or hearing coins. When we "take the ride," we send our senses out as scouts. They report back. "Out there, there is a craps table, where the assembled are cheering, clapping." Is there a casino-message in this? Should dealers not only be shills but cheerleaders? Should change people more actively lead players to "hot" machines? What is the difference between a casino where dealers inhibit enthusiastic noise and a casino where the same dealers almost *songlead* it? Are there restaurants where waiters *discourage* appetite? Where they say things like, "the Chilean sea bass tastes like soap?"

Why are more and more restaurants of the open-grille style? We enter.

We send our senses on a scouting mission. They come back and they say, "Fabulous Rib-eye!" And so we move forward, grow excited, ask to be seated, order, wait. And it's all a function of well-targeted appetite. Of course, if the rib-eye arrives and looks like the charred rafter of a smoking house. . . . When our appetite's whetted, we want at least the *sense* of a fine meal.

There are, of course, other appetites. Another critic compares good stories to good strip-tease. Stories and casinos both have their erotics: tantalization, hunger, a certain withholding, a being teased close, a wait, the lure of even greater pleasure. For many, the rhythm and dance and foreplay *is* the play, *is* the game and meal.

The Rio's *appetite for carnival* and its attendant tropical story begins with the artful sculpted brass parrots on the entry doors. And it's the artful and whimsical iteration of parrot figures, nautilus shells, bleeding tropical colors [reds, purples, oranges, greens], water which extend and re-extend the flavor of carnival throughout The Rio. Of course all the traditional Pavlovian gaming *salivary* cues are there: bells, falling coins, dealers in tasteful tropical shirts. There are some new twists. The dice tables are smaller—more conducive of communal enthusiasm. The dealers, like good waiters, *know the menu,* know the history and facilities and plans of The Rio: they are *hosts* as well as dealers.

Then there's *The Rio food.* No other casino in Las Vegas has so many good restaurants, such highly reviewed good food, fine wine. The new Wine Cellar is a vintner's delight. The Seafood Buffet makes the Top 10 list of Vegas's Best Deals. The Carnival World Buffet satisfies both gastro-nomic and visual appetites. Whimsical baskets of food entice—rotating in the air above the buffet area. On my last visit to The Rio, I entered with an appetite for both play and food. I had such an exceptional seafood dinner at Buzio's that—even after a losing dice session—I felt satisfied. As with the "ride" of any good story, the loss was just one of the dips. And I won't mention, for fear of being inappropriate, other sensual appe-tites and their connection to the cocktail waitress uniforms.

If good stories *stir appetites,* only Harrah's new Carnival Court en-trance awakens taste or yearning. The Carnival Court comes closer than any other area of the resort to relating a Harrah's Carnival story. Yet the other entrances assault rather than awaken the senses. Beyond The Car-nival Court's stimulus and with the possible exception of Claudine's, Harrah's is where you *don't* go to pursue appetite. This is cramp-and-gas stuff—too heavy; too much and without taste. Or there's the notion that *taste* is garlic, or taste is black pepper. Harrah's inhibits appetite. Or it equates appetite with an airport food-court. Little is palatable or subtle. In story terms, the appetite-creation level at Harrah's is akin to a rerun of

The Simpsons: not much taste; not much nourishment. The food tends to sink through the digestive system. When appetite is pursued on most levels in this vague carnival story, the "reader" of the story only feels logy, tired. Appetite and excitement meet at Harrah's carnival and the reader wants to take a nap.

Consider two *Breakfast Scenes.* The Rio's breakfast scene would take place at its Beach Cafe, and the scene has subtlety. Though both "scenes" use the fruit colors of carnival, Rio bleeds, mutes and modulates its colors to give them more richness and subtlety. The painted hillside, the overlook; scenes on the available wall space of the Beach Cafe have depth, some artistry; they are evocative, atmospheric, even mysterious. And the Beach Cafe "opens" to the Rio's larger story. It's space literally interpenetrates with the casino and the outside beach. It says "Copacabana." It says "Roderigo Lagoon." In this breakfast scene the carnival's fuller, richer story is always being suggested.

Harrah's breakfast scene, at its Garden Cafe is comic book. All illustration is flat, broad and cartoonish. It mixes metaphors. There are large wooden children's-theatre-set flowers—to go, I suppose, with a wooden completely untropical picket fence. There's no blending of colors; they're broad, flat, almost assaultive. All the greenery is painted on. And this breakfast scene doesn't "open" to the larger story. It opens to the lobby, to banks of slots. And the food itself. . . . ! Suffice to say: the Beach Cafe has a bakery on premises; the Garden Cafe probably has The Pillsbury Dough Boy.

TAKING THE RIDE

We want any story-experience to be active, thrilling, breathtaking. Note how many new casinos have connecting roller-coasters. A roller-coaster is an amusement-park *three-minute story.* You move mysteriously into it. It promises thrills. It inches forward briefly, then, suddenly, "grabs" you. It takes your breath away; there are sudden turns, drops, ascents. You are in a kind of uncommon *transport.*

Writers talking to other writers discuss building the "ride" of their story, their novel. Readers-in-the-know will talk of "taking the ride" of a given narrative, not knowing where, precisely it was going to take them, but giving themselves over to it. In the best roller-coaster, in the best story, you step into the front seat of the front car, strap yourself in, throw your hands into the air and trust the ride. Let the word hit the street, though, that the coaster at The Stratosphere has lost a wheel, and, the next day, more than half the seats will go begging. *If you don't trust the ride, you don't take the ride*—and all the marketing in the world isn't going to matter.

If you let go—leave the gravity of the work-a-day world behind (and we all *want* to)—you have to trust.

Casinos, like stories, hope to be thrilling *rides*. "I rode The Thunderbolt seventeen times!" the proud teenager says. "This is my twentieth time staying at Treasure Island," the woman from Iowa, standing behind me in the check-in line, says. We ride for thrills; we ride for pleasure; we ride because we trust the ride.

The ride of The Rio is exceptional. A ride is motion. It sweeps you up, along. You give yourself over and trust it as it rises, falls, turns corners. Rides clatter and whir and drive with pulse-racing sounds—always with the sense of sweeping forward. And, from first entrance, The Rio sweeps. Wisely: enough is legible; enough is clear, so that, as it fans out and sweeps left and right, you somehow *trust* the sweep, the sense of ride and motion. It invites you aboard rather than making you feel cautious or hesitant.

Tropically driven music creates ride and motion. Curvilinear paths create ride and motion. A strong sweep of vertical space creates ride and motion. And the ride grows most exciting in the new Carnival Village addition. Staircases sweep up and down. Crowds move along the upper, circling street. Water moves. There are aerial floats—animated boats, masks—which ride the air on tracks. There are carnival parades that descend and march and bring us with them, parading through their carnival world. They scatter unexpected surprise-rewards in the forms of coupons. There's *Rio Rita* who moves among us, speaks to us, enhances the ride of her own story. And though the ride of The Rio can engage surprisingly, suddenly, it feels always to be delight and never intimidation. It is the kind of ride patrons return to again and again to re-experience—not a ride one is bored with or exits from white-faced and queasy.

So The Rio transports. It is motion, simulates motion. But you are never lost anxiously in the crowds.

Harrah's ride lacks transport. It's a balloon ride—or the here-then-gone buzz of sparkling wine: hot-air, froth, champagne bubbles transporting the player just about as far as flat champagne and about as visible. The bubbles or globes or balloons or "worlds" or whatever they are get picked up in the design thematizing inside. But, because their story lacks any clear suggestion or direction, we don't *travel*, we don't move, we aren't moved. We never ride a roller-coaster we can't track. All that's encountered seems more like unclear advance promotion for adventure than adventure itself. There's no browsable adventure or romance. There's no enlivened story to take any ride on. Oh, there's decent New Orleans jazz being played, and you ride the trumpet and trombone and banjo for a while, but toward . . . ?

Despite its cover changes, the book remains very similar to the tired, sawdusted Holiday riverboat—without the water.

ENVELOPING THE LISTENER: SETTING

Especially in oral cultures like The Apache, the *place* where the story occurs is critical. If someone hears a good story, *"the place will keep stalking him."* Without compelling place, for story listeners, events will seem to "happen nowhere." Story events, to have lasting effect, must be spatially anchored, spatially rooted. "A story envelops," someone else has said. If the place of any story, then, compels and envelops us, the story will. The stronger the place, the more actively we become participants in the activities of that place.

If, then, casinos tell stories—the story of Treasure Island, the story of King Arthur's Court—the more vivid the place details, the more eager the player-hero's active entry into the tale. It's the broken crockery in the blue lagoon, the pearls dangling from the bar spars, that makes the weekend pirate all the more active a swashbuckler. Writers call it *verisimilitude,* and they work hard to achieve it. Half-hearted gestures at place, too-easy clichés of place, make a casino-story's hero skeptical of the tale. A story-casino without carefully detailed and believable *place* is a book to be set aside after a few pages.

The more rich and layered the sense of place, the more participation in its adventure. Our dreams thrive on dense verisimilitude. The richer a place's layering, the more effortless our living there. One observer—David Abram—writes, "The number and complexity of the [details] associated with any Dreaming site varied in direct proportion to the abundance of food, water and/or shelter to be found at that place." Hoteliers take note.

In The Rio's story, *the place keeps stalking you.* It's endlessly atmospheric and evocative. The always-close details of its *place* are careful, rich, imaginative. Place has density, depth, detail. Parrots. Shells. Water. Color. These place elements are layered and relayered. Place is never just a passing gesture—some plastic tropical plant to make a thematic point. It's real; it's lush; it's dense. It stalks. *The story of The Rio is always spatially anchored.*

There is no atmosphere in the new Harrah's—only redecoration. One speaks of "local color" in a story or novel, but any *local color* must be painted with, not simply chosen. As already noted, both The Rio and Harrah's have chosen tropical, fruit-rich colors. The Rio has painted scene after scene with those colors, created atmosphere, ambiance, place. Harrah's has slapped the colors on without subtlety; its local color looks like a tourist in a bad beach-boy shirt.

Harrah's is without verisimilitude. This is not a place that will stalk its guests; it's not a "happening" place. It doesn't invite dreams, beckon the imagination, suggest the explorable. The new Harrah's is without spatial anchoring.

BEING THE MASKED MAN, THE HERO

In any good story, there's a hero. Could be a man; could be a woman—still, there's this *person* we're following—the most important rider on the roller-coaster. In the casino's story—the hero is *you, is me.* We're the masked man, riding into town; we're the mysterious stranger; we're the one who can overcome odds, fend off fate, turn the situation around, exhibit grace under pressure, make a difference. As long as the writing is good, as long as the details are specific and close and right, we can pull it off. The more specifically detailed the *World* OF *The Story,* the more chance the Hero has of success.

For American gamers in particular: being the "stranger" riding into town has power. One writer writing about stories and their hero says, "[the hero] is either deliberately concealing his identity or. . . . doesn't know it himself or. . . . can change his shape at will. In other words: he is wearing a mask; he appears in disguise, he carries a secret." Players read these books; they gather systems, lore. They sail their ship into the lagoon at Treasure island, disembark, arrive as their own pirate, masked, carrying the special map, the secret. And a casino like Treasure Island does everything to support and encourage such a story.

By surrounding players with floating/marching carnival revelers, Rio designers encourage patrons to feel themselves *heroes* in its carnival story. It's a casino-story in which we *want to play,* act out, celebrate, be extravagant, let go. We want to be the *real* sports bettor among the character mannequins and helmets in the Sports Bar. Treasure Island sells quality *Cirque de Soleil* masks. It would be an interesting "narrative" experiment for The Rio to provide carnival masks for any guests with the whim to try them. Or, at the entrance, a kiosk might sell (inexpensively) artful carnival masks. With this, might the sense of *being the masked man, the hero,* the sense of active player be expanded? Would more inhibitions be dropped?

Regardless: The Rio encourages its patrons to *play hero* at carnival time. The "story" is both clearly and invitingly shaped. The elevated street and shops and vantage overlooks enhance a *hero sense of superiority.* In fact, that same sense of extended "height" and size is promoted throughout the resort by the well-articulated and animated use of vertical space. We feel constantly "heightened" either by looking down on others or by being drawn up to wonderful and whimsical images above. The "stretching" of ourselves in this carnival world is always rewarding. We look up above the blackjack pit, for instance, and are drawn into the sculpted nautilus chambers on the ceiling. Chambers! (Chapters!) Chambers within chambers! And if we feel larger-than-life-enough, we can cross the brief space from the Ipanima Bar and visit the beautifully appointed, richly wood-grained high-stakes pit—it's own nautilus chamber: a tropical "Havana" world all by itself.

Again, in notable contrast, since Harrah's has no manifest story taking gamers on a ride, no trackable narrative, a player/guest can't really be the resort's hero. There's no extension of the masked figure on the facade/cover outside and a resort story inside. There's no identifiable dragon or mystery or passage. We're told *"Harrah's World"*—but what that *"World"* is isn't specified, defined. Unlike The Rio, Harrah's gives us no details to build on. So no guest can confidently *enter:* take the lead, play the hero's part. Any player has to make up his own story, improvise. The plot's not designed; the setting lacks verisimilitude; the scenes aren't clear.

The Rio constantly "frames" scenes for the hero/player to step into. And if dealers and service employees are seen as the supporting cast against which the hero enacts adventures, most of these supporting characters at Harrah's act like they're tired of being in this particular book. Imagine the pirates at Treasure Island hating Robert Louis Stevenson for placing them there.

PLAYING DETECTIVE: WHAT HAPPENS NEXT? MYSTERY

No one wants to read a thriller that's over before it begins. We may hunger to know how it all turns out—but we find the not-knowing delicious along the way. Any story rich with "what happens next?" excites us. We like playing detective. We like solving. We like crossing the bridge from the certain into the uncertain and back again. We like finding what's missing and identifying it. There is a kind of *artfully-designed surprise* which never confuses us, which will only delight us. Mystery is a temporary break in the usual universe, a momentary hole in the rules.

Any casino which continues to unfold surprises is a page-turner. "What's over in that corner?" "What's down these stairs? Up these stairs?" We love following leads. "I've heard there's an Asian restaurant on the second floor that's wonderful!" Writers plant leads, hint, suggest, foreshadow. Writers lead the readers into and then through the surprise-thrills of their mystery.

Only The Mirage unfolds its story as well as The Rio. To stroll The Rio's floor and story is to encounter repeated and artfully designed surprise.

There are no cliches, no stock scenes. The Buffet isn't just another buffet. It's different. It unfolds. You can't take it in all at once. The Sports Book isn't just another sports-book-scene. You read it with interest. Parades arise with sudden energy. Floats sail the air above. You walk a "side street" and discover art on the wall. But it's not just hotel-art-on-the-wall, not generic cliches. It's museum quality. It's the *Rio Collection*—part of which also graces the walls of the acclaimed restaurant, *Napa*. Yes: all the art has a tropical imagery, use of color, texture, feel. But it's individual and exciting. It bears close reading.

And the beauty of this—as with a good novel—is: one never feels lost in The Rio. Every time one comes back—*re-reads* The Rio—there's more. But the richness of the story is never confusing. There's tropical allure, tropical mystery. The cues are always: read closer, explore, search out. Perhaps the clarity of being set against the actual sky excites this. On a recent visit, my wife and I watch a stunning moon eclipse as we ate our dinner at Buzio's.

At the new Harrah's, no alluring story *unfolds*. It never overcomes its Center-Strip squeezed location. It creates on long winding lanes, no sense of the more distant, explorable and hidden away. There's a difference be-tween engaging mystery and confusion. Mystery is an enticing gap in the larger world. Confusion is the world not adding up, its gaps not filling in. How do the outside and inside of the "new" Harrah's fit together? What is the significance of the "globe" motif? Why has the single Louisiana [New Orleans / Carnival] restaurant, *Joe's Bayou,* been eliminated in favor of a non-carnival *Asia*? How is one to read the textured, swirling "starry night" ceilings: night skies over carnivals? festive fireworks above play? new galaxies to explore? In Harrah's "inviting" space always seems some bad illustration of space. And what is the image relationship between the black confetti-flecked carpet and the other carpeting choices? In The Gar-den Cafe, how does one "read" the gap between French Provincial chairs and formica tables? When the new *Carnival Harrah's* was in process, in the late Spring of 1997, I overheard a hard-hat worker and a casino execu-tive—the floor around the elevators near the lobby already torn up—dis-cussing which color of replacement tile might be best. Who is the designer here? Talk about *confusion* rather than *mystery!*

Harrah's has no pursuable narrative line; there are only scattershot im-ages vaguely around the target-notion of carnival. The new *Carnival-Harrah's* is concept-driven, logo-driven. Designers seemed to be thinking about ad campaigns before they considered what story the resort might tell.

SATISFYING OUR APPETITE: THE CLOSING PAGES

Good stories promise, suspend, surprise and, ultimately, fulfill. They cre-ate a heady appetite, then satisfy it. There is something *perfect* about a good story, a good "read." The palate seems enriched, delighted. Writers talk about "paying off" the elaborate tales they construct, all the turns and sudden dips and lifts of their "ride." Because, finally, any story is over;

you arrive. You close the book; the ride stops; you go home from the vacation. But the desire, always, is that you do so *satisfied*—glad you've taken the ride, ready for your next romantic adventure.

How does the *unsatisfied* in a story get voiced? "It didn't really *end;* it just *stopped*" is one voicing. "It just left everything up in the air; I didn't like it." Satisfaction is bound to implicit promises and expectations at the start. Satisfaction is never random or chance; it's highly engineered, determined. At the end of a good story, there is a very determined something that is "paid off." If a pint of Treasure Island Rum, for instance, were to be delivered to guests' rooms on check-out morning, that would be a right and satisfying conclusion.

The Rio satisfies. I have never left the "book" of The Rio without being glad that I "picked it up again." The Rio is a *complete experience.* A good story meets readers halfway. It's a text that brings itself to the reader at least as much as readers bring themselves to the story. And The Rio constantly brings itself to the visitor with offerings of satisfaction: this shop, this restaurant, this pool, this suite, this pit of tables by this particular bar, this bank of slots. The casino wraps itself around the pool, radiates from the pool—so that the eclipse comes to *Ipanima.* Most areas make use of open walls, open "windows," so that, as in a good novel the "character" and imagery of one "chapter" articulates with the character and imagery of another. If one looks up at the ceiling in the new Carnival Village area, one sees circles radiating out. And this is emblematic of The Rio's story and energy, radiating its mystery and ambiance and atmosphere and excitement out and out. Not overwhelming. Not assaulting. Radiating and satisfying.

There can't, unfortunately, be closing pages to a story which hasn't been told. There can't be an instilled experience-appetite which has been satisfied. And that's the story at Harrah's: *no* story; no wind up; no climactic scene. They've shot a two-hundred-million dollar epic and not told a story.

TELLING MY OWN STORY: A FINAL PERSONAL ANECDOTE

On July 4th of 1997, I called both The Rio and Harrah's. I had business in Las Vegas later in the month and was curious how I would be engaged by the room reservation departments at both hotels. I have player cards at both hotels which qualify me for casino rates.

The reservation staff at The Rio were always warm, informed, gracious. The rooms were described in inviting detail. "You'll have a great time!" the clerk said. With any questions they were unable to answer, they connected me with the concierge's desk. Their summer rates were very attractive.

Harrah's was a more confused and off-putting experience. The first reservations clerk quoted a summer casino rate for a suite. When I talked with a second clerk, I was told they *had* no suites and that the price which had been quoted to me was for standard rooms. I got transferred to VIP Services where I was treated very unlike a VIP. I was told I "failed to qualify" for casino rates on suites and was quoted a price which was four times the price of the suite originally quoted, four times the price of a suite at The Rio.

Do I need to say which of these two Carnival Stories has my continuing attention?

A Qualitative Investigation into the Characteristics and Synergistic Relationships of Non-Gaming Recreation/ Entertainment Facilities in Casino Environments

Jack B. Samuels

This exploration has its origins in the author's earlier writings which were presented at a variety of forums in the1980s including the International Conference on Gaming and Risk Taking, held in Atlantic City (Samuels, 1985), and *The Economist: Travel and Tourism Analysis* (Samuels, 1986). These earlier works were the first published studies to discuss the importance of non-gaming recreations to the success of casino gaming.

Specifically, studies were conducted to see what would happen if casino gaming became legal in venues competing with Atlantic City including the Poconos (Pennsylvania), the Catskills (New York) and a number of other areas. The findings suggested that non-gaming activities made these areas more attractive than Atlantic City prior to the infusion of casino gambling, and that non-gaming attractions would also make these areas more attractive gaming destinations than Atlantic City if casino gaming were introduced to these areas. Further, it was concluded that unless Atlantic City radically changed its non-gaming attractions, it would be highly vulnerable to market failure if the competing areas legalized gambling.

Although it cannot be said with certainty that this early analysis instigated the move by Las Vegas into family entertainment, it can be said that the work was published before this phenomenon began to occur in Las Vegas. Furthermore, a number of gaming interests may have been influenced by the study including the Tropicana Hotel and Casino in Atlantic City which utilized it somewhat to justify the development of an indoor amusement park. It is clear that this work was pioneering in setting forth the idea that casino gaming all by itself might not be attractive enough to sustain tourism or economic activity and that the synergistic relationship between non-gaming casino attractions and the overall tourism environment were of paramount importance in perpetuating gaming activity, particularly in competitive environments.

As a result of the previously completed research and observational analysis of the current market this analysis sets forth some observations, recommendations and conclusions regarding the synergistic marketing relationships between casino and non-casino recreations.

METHODOLOGY

The researcher has used a simple case study approach to completing this research. A number of categorizations of various characteristics of non-gaming facilities—characteristics measurable on a one to ten point scale—were used to judge overall success of the facilities.

The basis for the development of these scales is the author's years of experience with studying the amusement and entertainment industry as well as a review of the available but limited literature on the popularity of amusements, attractions, and entertainment. It is important to note that all of the work done refers to such facilities not attached to gaming attractions. Therefore the author's own intuitive ideas have modified any existing thinking on this subject to make the conclusions stated herein.

In one study (McClung, 1991) a relative importance of different types of attractions was established as well as a relative importance of different themes. An index scoring showed the importance of attractions and themes systems based on relative importance. For example, it could be inferred that the most highly rated type of attraction, "Exhibits/attractions promoting learning," was approximately 50% more attractive to the group of 3039 persons surveyed than "gift or souvenir shops." The list of attractions in the order of importance with their index scores were as follows: exhibits/attractions promoting learning 1.191; variety/quality of restaurants 1.177; animals in their natural habitats 1.140; general shows and entertainment 1.106; animal shows 1.035; water rides 1.026; thrill rides .970; big name entertainment .965; rides for small children .947; roller coaster .929; cartoon characters .919; movie based rides entertainment .818; gifts or souvenir shops; .776. For the types of themes the ratings where as follows: educational exhibits 1.170; exotic animals 1.090; technology 1.058; botanical gardens 1.043; wilderness 1.028; history 1.025; river trips 1.018; foreign cultures .984; live entertainment .969; water rides .963; animal shows .952; flower displays .949; fantasy .937; and nightclub .813.

In the other most relevant study (Thatch and Axinn, 1994) overall attributes of parks were rated by 358 non-randomly selected respondents. The researchers were able to list the most important attributes for parks that the respondents liked. This researcher has converted the researchers' raw findings into a relative scale similar to the one utilized by McClung, but since they had to be calculated differently, the two scales do not have direct numerical relevance to one another. The most important attributes relative to one another in the order of most to least important are: cleanliness 3.5; rides 3.0; nice scenery 2.0; shows and family atmosphere (tie) 1.85; roller coaster 1.75; overall prices 1.39; line control 1.34; proximity (closeness to home) 1.29; and food 1.00.

Both of these studies give some insight into various factors which make attractions, entertainment, recreational facilities attractive to the public. They are, however, inconclusive and simply provide some intuitive insight into what the public really likes.

THE EFFECT OF CASINO GAMING ON THE OVERALL RECREATION/ENTERTAINMENT/TOURISM MARKETPLACE

Before we examine the success of non-casino recreational facilities within various casino facilities it is worthwhile to briefly explore the overall relationship of gaming facilities to the entire recreational, entertainment, tourism marketplace. This provides a basis to say something about the appropriateness of casino gambling in a given marketplace that already exists due to its non-casino aspects.

Our previous research illustrates the fact that casino gambling all by itself is inadequate in the long run to guarantee success. This becomes increasing true as gambling competition increases. There is no reason to assume that casino gambling is in fact any more attractive than any other recreational activity in attracting the consumer's dollar. Casino gambling can survive as a leisure or entertainment attraction by itself and be a driving force in tourism only if there is limited access to casino gambling in the given marketplace. Many Indian reservation gambling locations are successful because of the limited competition provided them. The highly successful Foxwood's and Mohegan Sun casinos in Connecticut are an excellent example of this. Casino gambling is wildly successful there because they are the most accessible gaming facilities available to a large New England marketplace.

Casino gaming, however, may not succeed in areas where tourism or leisure lifestyles are strongly ingrained with other features. The failure to date of the casinos in New Orleans provides an excellent example of this phenomenon. Dining and partying are just too prevalent to the environment in New Orleans to make casino gambling a priority activity for most people. Furthermore, there are other more desirable casino locations in the nearby marketplace.

Using this framework, in the author's opinion, casino gambling would be a bad idea in the Orlando, Florida area. There, non-gaming recreation and entertainment abound to a limitless extent. Although casinos might by themselves be successful in this environment based on utilization by the local population, they probably would not be a high priority item for tourists. Furthermore, in the unlikely event that they did become a high priority item for tourists, they might greatly damage the economy for the existing recreation/entertainment enterprises. A recent example of casino development in conjunction with the tourism environment available was the decision to legalize gaming in St. Croix rather than in St. Thomas or St. John in the U.S. Virgin Islands. The healthy and robust tourism environment on St. Thomas and St. John might be damaged by the establishment of casino gaming. However, St. Croix could greatly benefit from gaming. St. Croix has land available for casino development and does not have the strong retail oriented economy of St. Thomas. St. John is mostly National Park with limited development and is oriented to eco-tourism oriented.

The bottom line is that jurisdictions considering casino gaming must more carefully consider the impacts of this activity on the entire leisure, entertainment, and tourism environment. Casino gambling is not a cure-all for tourism development problems and it can in fact cause considerable damage to the environment if not properly executed.

RECREATION/ENTERTAINMENT IN THE CASINO ENVIRONMENT

A categorization scheme for types of facilities and characteristics of types of facilities within the casino environment has been developed. These are presented in Table A and Table B, respectively. Table C presents ratings of twelve different facilities utilizing the factors presented in Table B.

Table A clearly illustrates that the number and types of non-gaming recreation/entertainment options being offered in casinos has proliferated in recent years. Each type of attraction has different characteristics that appear to contribute to varying levels of success. These characteristics are listed in Table B.

Each factor named in Table B has a description of the factor as well as an "overall power rating." The overall power rating represents the relative importance in contributing to the success of the synergistic relationship between gaming and non-gaming recreation/entertainment facilities. This synergistic relationship is subjective and is defined as "how successful the non-gaming attraction is in enhancing casino based revenues from the author's observations."

In Table C the author uses his subjective judgment to rate twelve casino entertainment/recreation facilities using the above factors in the rating. Note that the numbers shown for each factor are not related to the relative importance factors in Table B, but rather illustrate the strength of the facility shown in the emulation of each particular factor on a scale of 1 to 10

TABLE A

Types of Non-Casino Entertainment/Recreation

Type	Description
Health Clubs/Athletic	One of the more common types of facilities, sometimes featuring upscale spa services.
Non-Health Club/Athletic	Active recreations and sports as golf, tennis, roller skating, ice rinks, etc.
Showrooms/Production	Extravaganzas that usually run for extended performance runs
Showrooms/Headliner	These change frequently.
Movie Theaters	Movie theaters located inside of casino complexes.
Game Arcades with Redemption or Midway/Joint Games	Larger game arcades that feature coin-operated video, pinball, and amusement devices and also offer redemption games (games that tickets are earned which can be redeemed for prizes) or midway/joint games that have prizes awarded directly at the game.
Game Arcades without Redemption or Midway/Joint Games	Smaller game arcades that offer no redemption or midway/joint type games.
Child Play Facilities	Child care, and child play facilities which incorporate imaginative soft play elements into their facilities that can occupy and entertain children for hours.
Themed Shopping and Dining with Entertainment Element	A themed entertainment complex that incorporates shopping and dining with some themed entertainment.
Themed Shopping and Dining with Entertainment Element and Integrated Casino	A themed entertainment complex that incorporates the elements of the prior category with a fully integrated casino operation.

(continued)

TABLE A
(continued)

Type	Description
Themed Casino Environment with Automated Entertainment	A themed casino environment that offers automated entertainment.
Themed Amusement area with rides, shows, shopping and non-casino games	A themed amusement park.
Traditional Recreations (separate from the casino)	Traditional recreations that are offered within the hotel but not within or in close proximity to the casino (i.e. bowling, pool tables, darts, shuffle alleys, miniature golf, etc.)
Integrated Traditional Recreations	Traditional recreations integrated within the casino environment.
Prize Alterations	Extensive use of merchandise prizes especially those of a recreational, leisure, sports, or travel nature.
Interactive Casino Games	Casino game areas that include an interactive element of some sort.
Themed Dinner Entertainment Attraction	A themed dinner entertainment attraction.
Multi-facility Accessible Attraction	An attraction which is shared by a number of different operators.
Architectural Attractions Entertainment	Ranging from spectacular building design to shows that are integrated into the façade of a structure.

TABLE B

Characteristics of Non-Casino Recreation/Entertainment

Name	Power Rating	Description
Internal Proximity to Casino	9	Closeness of attraction/entertainment to gaming areas.
External Attraction	8	Ability to draw people to overall facility.
Uniqueness of Facility	10	Uniqueness of the attraction within the overall realm of entertainment/ recreation.
Ability to Change	8	It is important for longevity for the facility to be able to change.
Immediate Integration	5+	Integration of unique entertainment factors into traditional gaming scenarios. The "+" may increase due to the overall concept of the facility.
Overall Experience Support	4	Recreation/Entertainments that are viewed more as hotel amenities than attractions. As such, they probably have more effect in encouraging people to stay in the hotel than to visit the casino.
Parental Support	6	Facilities that directly assist the visits of parents traveling children.
Length of Experience	8	The overall length of the experience is important and appears to be optimal at one half-hour or less when free and about two hours when a fee is paid.
Ancillary Enterprises	7	Food service and merchandising.
Monetary Factor	8	The relationship of cost to the casino experience. A higher cost is not necessarily negative if one can draw regular paying (noncomplementary) patrons.

points. A comment and rating for overall effectiveness are given for each facility. The overall rating takes into account the type of facility, rating it within that type.

Pirate Show—Treasure Island Hotel & Casino   Overall rating: 8
This show is an absolute crowd stopper and is effective in drawing people to the hotel/casino complex that is well themed throughout.

Masquerade Village—Rio Suites Hotel & Casino   Overall rating: 10
This attraction is top of the line in execution and concept. The shows take

TABLE C
Ratings of Selected Casino Entertainment/Recreation Facilities

Attraction & Site	Proximity to Casino	External Attraction	Uniqueness of Facility	Ability to Change	Immediate Integration	Overall Experience Support	Parental Support	Length of Experience	Ancillary Enterprises	Cost of Experience
Pirate Show Treasure Island Hotel & Casino	5	10	10	5	0	0	3	8	0	9
Masquerade Village Rio Suites Hotel & Casino	10	0	10	10	10	0	3	9	10	9
Kids Quest Boulder Station Hotel & Casino	7	0	4	4	0	9	9	N/A	1	8
The Circus Act Circus Circus Hotel & Casino	10	3	7	8	0	0	10	9	7	8
Grand Slam Canyon Circus Circus Hotel & Casino	3	6	4	5	0	0	7	7	5	6

Attraction										
Inter-Active Slots Circus Circus Hotel & Casino	9	0	3	8	9	0	0	3	0	7
Star Trek Experience Las Vegas Hilton	10	4	10	7	4	2	7	8	9	9
Swimming Pool Complex Rio Suites Hotel & Casino	7	3	5	4	10	7	6	7	3	9
MGM Grand Adventures MGM Grand Hotel & Casino	2	3	5	5	0	0	7	7	6	6
Exterior Structure Luxor Hotel & Casino	3	10	9	2	0	6	2	2	2	7
Entertainment Luxor Hotel & Casino	8	3	5	5	0	3	6	6	3	6
Cub Experience MGM Grand Hotel & Casino	2	0	10	5	0	0	2	8	10	9

place above the casino floor. They are different almost every time you see them and they are free. In the author's opinion, this is close to the ultimate in casino entertainment attractions.

Kids Quest—Boulder Station Hotel & Casino　　　Overall Rating: 7
This attraction provides reasonably priced childcare for children and can keep them happy for hours. Although adequate, casinos may eventually compete to see who can have the flashier childcare facilities. Since this casino serves a good number of locals, such a facility is even more important.

The Circus Act—Circus Circus Hotel & Casino　　　Overall Rating: 8
This is the original family entertainment attraction in casinos. The attraction is still a great one as the entertainment takes place directly above the casino floor and is also great for entertaining children as there are family games and entertainment virtually all in the same area.

Grand Slam Canyon—Circus Circus Hotel & Casino　　Overall Rating: 5.5
Hard to believe that the company that first developed family entertainment attractions in casinos could make such a big mistake. A completely uninteresting facility that provides nothing that is unique. Furthermore, it is some distance from the main casino action, although the new shopping and dining arcade helps to decrease the "spatial distance" from the main casino. They could have made it unique by making an indoor water park with a partially retractable roof. However, length of stay may have been a little too long.

Inter-Active Slots—Circus Circus Hotel & Casino　　　Overall rating: 5
The Hurricane Zone slot areas provide periodic value added entertainment experiences for slot players and also periodically increases their chances for winning. An early generation of this sort of thing has potential for attempts on a greater scale.

Star Trek Experience—Las Vegas Hilton Hotel & Casino
　　　　　　　　　　　　　　　　　　　　　　Overall Rating: 9+
The author predicts that this facility will be a huge success by integrating a heavily themed casino directly into the entertainment areas. Unique ancillary experiences also greatly enhance the operation. Time and cost factors will be flexible which will enable a wide variety of different types of complimentaries and different types of customers to partake in the facility.

Swimming Pool Complex—Rio Suites Hotel & Casino　　Overall Rating: 9
Like everything else at this hotel the swimming complex is done with class. The complex greatly adds to the total ambiance of the hotel and unlike other hotel pools, it carries through the theme and experience that is "The

Rio." The hotel frequently does promotions around the pool areas that draw additional people to the facility. Fancy water slides would make it a ten.

MGM Grand Adventures—MGM Grand Hotel & Casino
Overall Rating: 6.5

This has been the other major disaster of Las Vegas, comparable to Circus Circus' Grand Slam Adventure Canyon in terms of being poorly conceived. It contains no rides or attractions that are a "must experience." In fact, the attraction that gets the most attention is the Sky Coaster, a "bungee jumping" attraction. This attraction was added after the park had been open for some time and tends to have far more spectators than participants. It is also too far away from casino. In 1998, MGM announced it would cut the size of its theme park by over 50% and build a Marriott Hotel on the vacated land.

Exterior Structure—Luxor Hotel & Casino
Overall Rating: 9

The structure of the Luxor on the outside is probably the most eye catching of all of the Las Vegas facilities. It provides a good photographic venue and certainly draws people to the facility.

Luxor Entertainment—Luxor Hotel & Casino
Overall Rating: 7

This opened as a mediocre entertainment facility that soon experienced difficulties. The Nile River Ride—which was not very interesting—was removed in a major renovation in 1996. A mediocre show called *Luxor Live* was also replaced. There is a standard motion simulator ride that is a somewhat above average experience and can be changed like all such rides by replacing the film footage. There are also extensive IMAX movies that can also be changed, and a state of the art game room sponsored by SEGA.

Cub Experience—MGM Grand Hotel & Casino
Overall Rating: 7

This is an excellent attraction in a small but eye-catching facility. Research shows that animal attractions are greatly successful, which explains why Disney is building an animal based theme park. This researcher had not seen this type of animal encounter attraction anywhere before and it fits the MGM Lion symbol perfectly. It provides a lot of visibility and return for little investment. In retrospect, MGM should have used animals with their theme park instead of the mediocre rides and attractions that were expensive but ineffective.

SUMMARY AND RECOMMENDATIONS

The author offers the following summary points and recommendations resulting from this investigation:

- The levels of success of various entertainment and recreation activities are quite varied. Success does not necessarily flow from large investments. The opportunities for creative ideas that enhance casino revenues are enormous.
- Areas that remain relatively untouched are those that involve the integration of casino games directly into an entertainment, recreation environment and the utilization of more traditional recreations in and around the casino including sports bar concepts that include pool tables, darts, shuffle boards, etc. There is, however, enormous opportunity still in all of the concepts that have been discussed herein.
- Things that seem to work the best include:
  - Limiting rides and attractions to several major ones like themed and extremely large roller coasters, motion simulators, or large flume rides rather than a whole bunch of mediocre attractions. This enables a short stay rather than a long stay for customers and seems be effective in drawing people in to partake of the one spectacular activity.
  - Unique dinner theater attractions and shows are staple items. The development of unique dinner theater attractions that rely heavily on special effects and have flexibility in terms of operational levels will undoubtedly be a continuing trend.
  - Carrying the theme throughout the operation with several different attractions seems to have a good synergistic effect. This approach is well executed at the Mirage and Treasure Island Hotel Casinos.

RECOMMENDATIONS FOR FUTURE RESEARCH

This work is exploratory in nature. The work presented in this analysis, however, can provide the foundation for more scientific quantitative investigations that will try to better define which concepts in entertainment and recreation best enhance casino revenues and the overall casino hotel experience. Until such quantitative research is completed, this work should provide the basis for an insightful exploration of the synergistic relationship between gaming and non-gaming recreations and entertainment.

REFERENCES

Axinn, C. and Thach S. V. (1994). Patron Assessments of Amusement Park Attributes. *Journal of Travel Research,* Winter, 51–60.

McClung, Gordon (1991). Theme Park Selection: Factors Influencing Attendance. *Tourism Management,* June, 132–9.

Samuels, J. (1985). Atlantic City in a Competitive Environment: Can It Survive? In W. R. Eadington (ed.), *The Gambling Studies: Proceedings of the Sixth National Conference on Gambling and Risk Taking,* vol. 2, pp. 33–39. Reno, NV: Bureau of Business and Economic Research, College of Business Administration, University of Nevada, Reno.

Samuels, J. (1986). Gambling in the U.S.A. *The Economist: Travel and Tourism Analyst,* June. London: Economist Publications.

The Necessity and Process of Mass-Customisation within the Conventions of Clubland: Cultural Identity and Invention for Gamblers and Tourists

Laurens Tan

Gamblers and tourists are surrounded by a symphony of images and merchandise in a staged fantasy environment. As distinct consumer-groups, their environments are designed to attract them, keep them there or keep them coming back for more.

In their multitudes, they respond and choose with their buying power. Their choice of goods, services and destinations is often seen as popularist, stereotypical and conventional, and is in turn marketed and promoted by campaigns that predict, effect and control their buying behaviours. The globalised economy further generates this stereotyping across cultural borders. There is no need to reinvent what is already proven a success elsewhere.

Design can be seen to be a collusive tool in this context. Like other forms of collusion, design can be the determining factor in how value is to be added, and will directly contribute to marginal profit. It may be the single operational influence to optimizing turnover opportunity within the marketplace. It may also simply be seen as the value-added *voice* of pragmatism. If consumers can be seen to "buyer-behave" similarly over borders, the "safe bet" design will be the convincing and risk-free option all investors dream about: Planet Hollywood, Warner's Stores, Hooters, KFC, Virgin, the successful "themes."

Risk-taking prevails in all walks of life and business. Decisions are made on likely outcomes. Some decisions involve bigger stakes than others. Few manage to not gamble at all. In business and in design, risk is a vital ingredient for progress. The action of not seizing an opportunity ends up equating to a loss, i.e., one takes a risk by not taking a risk.

The loss in the case of global stereotyping is the loss of cultural identity. Franchised theme establishments are beginning to fail as the global formula falters. Take the Australian Casino Centre, for example. Unlike the model of Las Vegas, the mecca of gambling and entertainment, where everything happens in one place, Australian casinos are dispersed to every city. Gone is the attraction to visit a location specifically to gamble. It's no wonder some casinos are struggling to survive as their uniqueness is eroded by competing duplicative concerns. The local is snared by the clubs and pubs closer to home, and the tourist has had her gambling fill back home. If you can't distinguish one place of interest from another, what's the point of travel? This of course doesn't only apply to casinos.

This paper looks at two multimedia projects as research prototypes and design solutions that deal with the effects of globalisation and mass-design:

The first project, *To Remember Buy,* is a survey and design approach to souvenirs. The project is relevant in the context of mass-customisation and shares a common ground with design solutions for slot machines. The projects are linked by the notion that there is a necessity for mass-customisation as a realistic solution to the current trend of everything looking the same, the global side effect that comes with the economies of scale.

The second project, *Octomat ESM* Series [established as "Vegas of Death," April, 1996], considers the gamblers' interface with the gaming machine: ergonomic, aesthetic, intellectual and entertainment "comfort." The series is a multimedia and sculptural design project consisting, in its first stage, of eight experimental slot machines to be exhibited at Conrad Jupiters Casino in Surfer's Paradise, Queensland, Australia, and is planned to tour to other casino and entertainment centres. *Octomat ESM* Series relates directly to the gambling and risk taking theme and considers the ubiquitous influence of Las Vegas and its "enterpreneurial" aesthetics.

The two projects each use as basis for design analysis and as centre-piece, the most iconic emblem of tourism and gaming respectively—the snowglobe and the slot machine. The project has since become the core of the writer's doctoral thesis and current production schedule. Based on the principle of mass-customisation, the projects' objectives are to engage the entrepreneurial world rather than confining itself to being a theoretical model.

A RELATIONSHIP BETWEEN ART AND INDUSTRIAL DESIGN

The most common path of development within Industrial Design is that of stream-lining. The existing object is given an "upgrade facelift." At best, new technological development or information will benefit the size, look or function of the object. It'll be faster or look faster, be more compact, more efficient, more contemporary in context, and cheaper to make. The benefits of good design deserve to be shared and exploited. A clever invention should be good news globally, which won't be restricted in origin or nationality. A new fish sauce may well be a blend of New Mexican and Hainanese origins, for example. It's only now that the two are able to be entertained after decades of tuning our respective cultural palates.

THE SOUVENIR

Let's now turn to the most ubiquitous example of global distribution— the souvenir. Souvenirs are prime images of popular culture, often seen as representing bad or bland taste and gratuitous merchandising. I'm re- fering to low-price mass-merchandised novelty items found in designated souvenir shops in any tourist port. These shops are almost identical across the world—from the shops on Cavill Mall, Surfer's Paradise in Australia, to those on 42nd Street in New York City, or near the Notre Dame in Paris. Apart from few locally made and designed items, most souvenirs are made in Hong Kong, China or Poland. Consumers hunt through the souvenir shelves looking for the "authentic" and novel, and from recent surveys most have not found their objects of desire.

Global mass production of the souvenir is not new. The Wai Choy Company in Hong Kong has probably been the largest manufacturer and supplier of the snowdome worldwide for several decades.

Recently it appears that the world souvenir has had its touristic particu- larity eroded. The very elements which define the souvenir—its aesthetic uniqueness and its ability to voice national/cultural identity, has been lost in a haze of rampant stereotyping.

The souvenir is an interesting example. Becoming extinct is the chintzy, kitsch object—the hula bikini dancer on a stick variety, the old-fashioned snowdome (snowglobe) with the 3D frieze, the glow in the dark Statue of Liberty. Once identified as Kitsch or bad design, the local souvenir at least showed an honest interpretation; an honesty which allowed for humour and theatricality. The romantic or nostalgic attraction associated with the souvenir is still central to marketing touristic experiences as examplified by the Hard Rock Cafes, Ripley's Believe-It-Or-Nots and Madame Tus- seaud's Wax Museums.

TO REMEMBER BUY

To Remember Buy [TRB: established in August 1994] is a multifaceted and transdisciplinary research project directed towards the souvenir, engaging with its design, theory and consumption. TRB's first survey will be at the Museum of Sydney in 1998/99. Visions of Sydney are expressed through touristic merchandising: innovation in souvenir design is through the process of re-evaluating the cities' other qualities, and through developing alternative relationships between representation and representational object (see Appendix).

The project is simultaneously an empirical and practical undertaking which tests maker/designer and audience/consumer responses to the speculative productive future of this poorly understood commodity. The disciplines and theories of Anthropology, Cultural Geography, Tourism Studies and Design, Fine Arts and Crafts will inform the project and provide a comprehensive analysis to determine where the vital areas of research may be. Research will consist of philosophical criticism, data analysis and ultimately initiatives for a new design methodology through visual means.

To Remember Buy will consist of a modular display of up to 200 souvenir objects. Accompanying these objects will be eight multimedia units which will be interactive to allow the audience to gain cultural understanding and background to the development of the objects. The modular electronic displays will include floor logos and neon signage which will place the viewer contextually within tourist culture and cement the visual experience of a heightened consumer culture.

The Museum of Sydney will be the opening venue for TRB which has been proposed to continue through other Australian touristic centres. TRB will also be interpreted in a variety of ways when the project is staged in the Pacific centres of San Francisco, Honolulu, Hong Kong, Auckland and Kyoto. This network is purposeful in that it forces out issues that promote the re-invention of authenticity, and how this is locally defined.

THE 'CLASSICISM' OF POPULAR CULTURE

"To follow one's taste means to sight the goods that are objectively allocated to one's own social position and which harmonise with one another because they are approximately of equal rank." [Bourdieu]

Collectors of memorabilia range considerably in their commitment to and understanding of their collections. Their motivation may be profit, fun, status or simply a way to add meaning to daily consumptive routines. For some it is a way to organise their leisure-time materialism into a manageable and objective-based thematic focus.

Clubs and zines are formed to optimise and heighten collectors' scope to be better informed about the status of collector objects. For instance, the change in design of Bibendum, better known as Michelin Man, (the French tyre company's logo) in the seventies, or the recent change in design of the common snowglobe, or best market values for Coca Cola bottles from different production periods.

Collectibles are not necessarily desired for their *good* design. Often

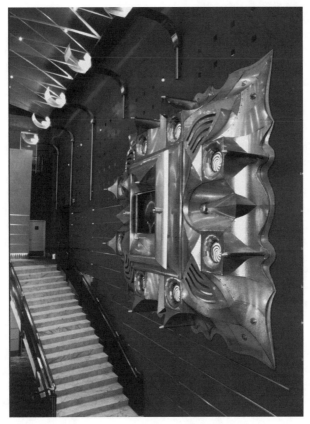

©Laurens Tan 1995.

"bloopers" or short-runs are sought after for their rarity or their place within a historical context.

In a discussion about good and bad design, it isn't always clear that what we refer to as kitsch is necessarily bad design. Refer to Gert Selle's observation of what design means: "realization of a dream of luxury, beauty, belongingness, shelter, adventure, individuality and cultural identity."[1] Selle refers to a "lived" culture rather than an "as-if" culture in determining useful criteria for design, and that a normative and pedagogical traditional "official" design theory cannot claim social supremacy in its judgements of good taste or good design. He also postulates that the kitsch concept is obsolete, that anonymously designed "real product culture of the mass-everyday" is founded on true experience and need and desire.

The collector offers us a micro-encyclopaedic tour of visual culture history in the face of changes and counter-changes in image and identity within popular culture merchandising. "Classicism" in Popular Culture are the memorable moments in design. Often anonymous, design for the mass-everyday is adjudged by the collectors; an effective critical voice, and astute, esteemed in their astuteness and knowledgeability by cultural writers and museum curators.

CONVENTION & THE CLUB: CAN'T SHAKE THAT HABIT

Within the Australian context, "Club" describes the generic social gathering place prevalent in mid-suburbia. In Australia, the Club is a traditional members' non-profit organisation linked by central cultural union-like interest: Returned Services Leagues [RSL], Australian Football League [AFL], Australian Rugby League [ARL], Surf Life Saving Club [SLSC], Cricket, Bowling. Steel Workers' and Trade Union Clubs. The Club is an integrated centre for social drinking (mostly beer), gaming (pokies or slots, horse racing, Keno and Bingo), cheap buffets, movies, Gym, Cabaret and Member-nights.

Within the context of this paper, I wish to propose that "Clubland" refers to the whole genre of entertainment centres. Clubland conventions are those habits and expectations that give places of gambling and entertainment the expected familiarity: a certain smell, standard lighting and colours, rest rooms in the right place and the jangling songs of the slots.

Comforting rituals, such as familiar tunes on the radio, weekly fast-food, repetitious TV soaps and the nightly news, evolve as creature-needs and panacea for the work or home-stressed. It's a home-away-from-home.

THE SLOT MACHINE

The slot machine is visibly the most identifiable icon of all gaming images. Throughout the world there are versions of these unmistakable colourful backlit boxes, in Pachinko parlours in Japan, the American Indian reservations, to the pokie clubs in Australia and their extraordinary monopolistic presence on the Las Vegas Strip.

The "humble" slot machine was developed by Charles August Fey in 1894, after earlier similar "chance" machines by fellow engineer-migrant Gustav Schultze. Pioneer slot machines were first made and played in the San Francisco area. Mass-production followed as the machines became lucrative. Even in its Mills Bros. days, decoration was soon regarded as gimmick, and the look of the slot underwent sequential simplification. From a retro-point of view, the early mechanical slots until the 1950s are much more beautiful in appearance and in operation: a direct contrast to the technology-oriented contemporary counterpart.

Variations between machine designs were more prevalent in the early machines, from mini walk-in theatres to automatic trade clocks to gambling guns. Some models were camouflaged from violating prohibition laws. The styling of slots changed in appearance when its operation changed from the mechanical to electric in the 1930s and to electronic/microprocessor units in the 1970s. Cabinet design, like the jukebox and the softdrink vending machine, became more typical and recognizable.

Over recent years, however, the machines became more generic, even among different competing brands. The Lowboy/Mid/Highboy cabinet is about as much variety as you're going to get since electronic units were introduced. They are user-friendly in size and scale. There is nothing imaginative, dynamic or beautiful about these fridge-like boxes: stereotypic, modular, designed to sit in rows, and to carry standard-sized back-lit graphic displays. There are only minor variations in cabinet and hardware design. The machines only have to fulfil the essential and expected functions—access to controls and ease of reading slot images. Cabinet dimensions, ease of maintenance and interchangeability became important.

The bye-word for the slot machine industry is evolution, which is driven by the typical consumer: the 54-year old female player. To this median group familiarity means comfort. New designs are introduced via an educative or familiarisation program, a slow trickle of change. Look at the new machines, for example. Variants are in the form of design additives: dual games, not new games, extensions on existing cabinet designs, rather than complete new forms. Let's not distract the player at our whim.

THE 'CLASSICISM' OF LAS VEGAS

One of the saddest moments was a recent visit to Young Electric Sign Company (Yesco), in Las Vegas to find that the *boneyard* (elephant graveyard of old discarded casino signs on the backlot of Yesco) had been cleared. Perhaps the only semblance of a museum, the lot is now only represented by the Neon Museum at the mouth of the Fremont Street Experience. Although Venturi's analysis of the Vegas Urban layout still holds, new development shows an inevitable sophistication. My two favourite Strip casino signs are examples of the Venturi model: the Frontier and the Stardust. Like many other properties, the signage often bears little relation to its interior. The Frontier, according to the "Best of Las Vegas" website has been voted as the hotelsite second most deserving to be imploded (after the defunct El Rancho Hotel and Casino). If there is to be an update for the Stardust, then perhaps the theme should be in the manner of the hotel's marvellous sign, designed in the 1950s by Ad-Art's Paul Miller. As retro regains a momentum, Las Vegas, of all places on earth, as the originator of sign-as-architecture needs to only reflect upon itself to be the source of inspiration it once clearly was.

THE CASINO IN AUSTRALIA

There are now fourteen casinos across Australia from Hobart, to Surfer's Paradise to the new Crown Casino in Melbourne. Their style, practical appearance and cultural identity is relatively difficult to fathom. As most international resorts and theme-parks go, their plan and design is based on the successful parent American prototype. In a bid to not copy the Vegas blueprint, many Australian casinos stumble for identity. The classicism of the Vegas model leaves only two choices for casino designers/ architects: to adapt or abandon.

OCTOMAT

The Octomat ESM Series (to be exhibited publicly in 1999) will appear to be innovative in its cabinet and game/multimedia design. Each ESM prototype (ESM 97-01 to 99-02) will offer design alternatives in both external appearance in the way the game looks and plays and how the player interacts with the machine and engages with the game. The exhibition will be a complete environment for players. The response will give feedback to the industry as to how much the consumer can take.

MASS CUSTOMISATION

It has become obvious that to compete, theme-establishments can no longer sit on their generic laurels: across franchise branches, city-to-city, and between competitors across the strip. Customers—gamblers and tourists—don't want to be bored by re-runs. Their hard-earned dollars will go to the first property that takes an interest in furthering their gambling adventures.

The emergence of every new casino must affect the turn-over of existent casinos. In Las Vegas, where one wonders when the market will be saturated, the constant and annual addition of new theme-casinos, will keep current casino-themes in check for their ability to maintain their market share. In Australia, this problem would be exacerbated by market size.

The exponentiality of the information age gave birth to globalisation, and a resulting cultural stereotyping is beginning to show the law of diminishing returns. The necessity to mass-customise is evident. The economies of scale can continue to serve the global marketplace. Like the special edition automobile release [country tourer, ski-fx, sport ranger], with minor but distinct value-additions, each release would refresh the clients' attention. The task appears to be simple enough. Let's check back in a year's time.

1. "There is No Kitsch, There is Only Design!" in *Design Discourse,* ed. Victor Margolin, University of Chicago Press, 1989.

REFERENCES

Anderton, F., Chase, J. and Collie, K. (1997). *Las Vegas.* London: Ellipsis.

Baudrillard, J. (1989). *America.* London; NewYork, NY: Verso.

Coward, R. (1977). *Language and Materialism Developments in Semiology and the Theory of the Subject.* Routledge.

Crick, Malcolm (1994). *Resplendent Sites, Discordant Voices.* Poststrasse, Switzerland: Harwood Academic Publishers.

Docker, J. (1994). *Postmodernism and Popular Culture: A Cultural History.* Cambridge and New York: Cambridge University Press.

Elsner, J. and Cardinal, R. (1994). *The Cultures of Collecting.* Melbourne: Melbourne University Press.

Fey, M. (1994). *Slot Machines: The First 100 Years.* Reno, NV: Liberty Belle Books.

Faine, S. (1996). *Traditions and Tourism: The Good, the Bad and the Ugly.* Monash.

Graburn, N. (1979). *Ethnic and Tourist Arts.* Berkeley: University of California Press.

Gunew, S. and Rizvi, F. (1994). *Culture Difference and the Arts.* Sydney: Allen & Unwin.

Hirsch, E. D. (1987). *Cultural Literacy: What Every American Needs to Know.* Boston: Houghton Mifflin Company.

MacCannell, Dean (1992). *Empty Meeting Grounds: The Tourist Papers.* London: Routledge.

Margolin, V. (1989). *Design Discourse: History, Theory, Criticism.* Chicago: University of Chicago Press.

MacCannell, D. (1989). *The Tourist: A New Theory of the Leisure Class.* New York: Schoken.

Michaelis, A. (1994). *DDR Souvenirs.* Taschen Cologne.

O'Rourke, P. J. (1997). Russian Roullette, *Rolling Stone,* February.

Ross, Andrew (1989). *No Respect.* New York: Routledge.

Said, E. W. (1995). *Orientalism, Western Conceptions of the Orient.* Penguin.

Shields, R. (1992). *Lifestyle Shopping.* London: Routledge.

Smith, V. L. (1994). *Hosts and Guests.* Cambridge.

Stern, J. and Stern, M. (1991). *The Encyclopedia of Bad Taste.* New York: Harper Collins.

Stewart, S. (1993). *On Longing: Narratives on the Miniature, the Gigantic, the Souvenir, the Collection.* London: Duke.

Tronnes, M. (1995). *Literary Las Vegas: Portraits of America's Most Fabulous City.* Mainstream.

Tuchmaan, M. (1994). *Magnificent Obsessions.* San Francisco: *The San Francisco Chronicle.*

Venturi, R, Scott Brown, D. and Izenour, S. (1996). *Learning from Las Vegas.* Cambridge, MA: MIT.

APPENDIX

To Remember Buy
Events and Publications

Three Survey Exhibitions were initiated and wholly produced and marketed by the project team, involving over 250 participants (not necessarily art practitioners) from the local areas who responded to the project's design brief:

"Just a Memento" Wollongong: inaugural exhibition at Project Contemporary Artspace, Wollongong, July, 1995. [Opened by the Lord Mayor of Wollongong]

"Just a Memento" Western Sydney: Casula Powerhouse, September 1995.

"Just a Memento"/The Art of Tourism: NSW Tourism Conference, chaired by Phillip Adams/Parramatta City Council, November 1995.

Publication of a substantial "memento" exhibition catalogue [Illustrated in Colour with essays by Craig Bremner, Keith Clancy, Laurens Tan, Gillian Thomas] "Just a Memento" Wollongong [20 pp., first print]; "Just a Memento" Wollongong & Western Sydney [28 pp., second print].

Adams Paul, Tan, Laurens and Thomas, Gillian: "Memories are Made of This," *Smarts,* March 1996, Issue #5, p. 24.

Publication by the Department of Communication and the Arts, *Arts Today with David Marr,* ABC Radio National Interviewed by Martin Portus, April 2, 1996. Ivana Jirasec, Curator, Contemporary Crafts Centre. Julian Leatherdale, Director of Film, Laurens Tan, School of Design, University of Western Sydney Nepean.

Zjilko, Helen, Thomas, Gillian, and Tan, Laurens: "Just a Memento," *Object,* Nos. 3 & 4, Sydney, February 1996 [Publication of the Contemporary Centre for Craft].

McMillan, Richard: Artnotes, pp 35–36, *Art Monthly,* #85, November 1995.

Richardson, Juliet [Ed.], "Alumni Grants," *The Outlook University Alumni Magazine,* University of Wollongong, Spring/Summer 1995.

"To Remember Buy" Consumers' Questionnnaire, research trip to Alice Springs, Uluru, Australia to conduct survey of tourist perception of souvenirs. The survey was administered at airports, tourism and retail centres. A seven page questionnaire was completed by 260 respondents.

OCTOMAT ESM SERIES
EXHIBITIONS

Game Play
Exhibition of installations linking games and multimedia. Curated by Shiralee Saul, in conjunction with "Being Connected," Austalian Film Corporation Conference on Multimedia, Royal Melbourne Institute of Technology, July 1998. National Tour until 1999.

Altered States/Cracking the Binary Code
A symposium that was part of the *Interact Asia Pacific Multimedia Festival,* Melbourne Exhibition Centre and Chauvel Cinema, Sydney. November 1997 to January 1998.

Pan Pacifica Festival
Featured a screening of "Altered States," Croningen, The Netherlands. Curated by Helen Stuckey, Shiralee Saul, including Alyson Bell, Alan Dorin, Troy Innocent, and John Tonkin. January 1998.

Lawyers Guns & Money III
Experimental Art Foundation, Adelaide. Curated by Richard Grayson, Linda Marie Walker with artists Rebecca Cummins, Mike Stephenson, Patricia Picininni, and Laurens Tan. August to September 1997.

Vegas of Death: Death: An Insight of Life
Australian Exhibition Tour, commissioned by Rookwood Necropolis, 1996–1998; Laurens Tan, Tom Arthur, Fiona Hall, Leah King Smith, Anne McDonald, Robyn Stacey, Ken Unsworth. Wagga Wagga City Gallery, Campbelltown City Gallery, Bunbury Regional Gallery WA, and UWA Gallery. 1997 and 1998.

Toward More Adventurous Playgrounds: Casino Lost; Casino Regained

David Kranes

"How many daydreams we have. . . . of Doors! The door is an entire cosmos of the Half-open. It is one of the primal images; [a door] accumulates desires and temptations: the temptation to open up. At times it is closed, bolted, padlocked. At others, it is open, that is to say, wide open."

Gaston Bachelard, The Poetics of Space

"The *other* side of a doorway differs radically from the *inside* of a doorway."

David Kranes

Let's start with stories. "Stories transport," I've read. And in the casino game—*transportation*—drawing all those people from 'there' to 'here', *their spaces* to *ours,* is critical. And "stories transport," to finish the quote, ". . . to worlds beyond troubled ones."

So: when we cross from everyday lives into casino-space, we cross from the sometimes 'troubled' *real* into the *imagined. Work* to *Play. Practical* into *Possible. Mundane* into *Extraordinary. Conditional* into *Unconditional.* In short, we cross: from the daily reminders and realities of "loss" in our lives into the fantasies of "gain." "The imagination gives rise to the idea of possibility and the *what-might-be* beyond" (Herbert Kohl, *Should We Burn Babar?,* p. 62). Create a casino; make people imagine! The space of any thriving casino needs to be *extraordinary;* it must feel *unconditional;* it feels to be a place in which what one's life has lost might—even temporarily—be regained. A casino space has much more to do with *how-we-dream-ourselves* than with *how-we-live-ourselves.*

Story time! Once upon a time, long-ago, far away in America. . . . only a single state—imagine that!—had casinos. I've heard *Ne-vada* wrongly translated as: *Don't go there—"Ne-vada."* But everyone did. And does—

still. But if you wanted to play—long ago, far away—Nevada was the *lone* place to transport yourself. Male. Wild. A bit forbidden.

And if you were a palace-*maker* for this only-game-in-town, it was arithmetic. Pure; simple. Buy land. Put up walls—at the edges—leaving what you could spare for parking. Compute: how many tables, machines, how many basic-accommodation rooms the cubic footage would bear. And—gaming license in hand: contract . . . subcontract: *do* it. Simple arithmetic.

"Once upon a Time." It was a seller's market. And players strode through the door, scanned for *Action,* didn't look left, right, headed for the tables, took their money out and played. Men—players my architect friend calls "the Johnny Lunchpail crowd." And, when they were tapped out, they left.

So that's *Story #1:* "How it Was." Long ago. Far away. Remember: stories transport. They take us to worlds that are not our own.

Story #2—my own: "The First Time I Gambled." I was—but am no longer—an Eastern Boy. I grew up in the möbius strip that includes Harvard University and MIT—a world in which brilliant people defeated major diseases between breakfast and lunch. Nobel Prize winners sipped sherry in my living room. What was Gaming? Gambling? My closest touchstones were *chess . . . math* puzzlers. I knew Nevada was a *state*—but of *what*?

So I was an "innocent;" a "virgin"—ready to be "transported" and teaching at the University of Utah, when a law professor friend said, "Hey: We're going over to Elko; come along?" And I said sure. I thought: *Fine; we'll go there; see a new part of the West, be with friends. But I won't play; I won't gamble.* Clearly I was not what a casino executive would deem a "target group."

Then, on a given night—before the trip—our friends visited. With cards. Chips. A craps layout. John Scarne's book on casino gambling. "Just in case," they said; "just in case you *do* play—some things to think about. So we spent an hour. And following the Don't Pass strategy laying full odds—I turned $40 into over a hundred. *I won't play,* I thought. *But it's good to know—if—what works.* Unbeknownst, you see, I was moving *into* the "target group" category: "virgin," yes, but with a slightly whetted appetite.

But the truth is: it wasn't dipping my toes on my own living room carpet that most primed me. It was the journey. To Nevada. Stories transport. *Images* transport. So it was transport *into* an *imagined* Nevada that hooked me: crossing over—one state to another. State-of-mind gliding to state-of-mind.

You see: the more a casino recalls details of our daily lives, the *less* we want to *go* there, let alone *stay.* So it can't bear down. Like Every Day. It can't regulate. It can't put us under the clock. It can't bore. It can't feel unspontaneous. Unstimulating.

Did you know—fact—that if no stimuli impinge from the immediate environment, an animal will seek stimuli (why not in a casino) or *invent* them? An animal will always *leave* the dull everyday and—scent of fantasy in the wind—stalk the imaginable. Teased by suggestion—I was more the "target audience" casino builders eye *now*. I was the *Unlikely Gambler*.

And what happened in The Crossing—from state to state was: The rising of Expectation, increase of Appetite. It started in dusk. Leaving Salt Lake, after work: . . . four-thirty. And by the time we'd reached the Salt Flats, it was dark. Amazing! I was going to Nevada! To *maybe* gamble! And I had already crossed from everyday street and office lights into the mysterious desert, into uninhabited space. It was a ride! it was a trip! a journey! And then! . . . *ohmyGod,* then! . . . it began to snow. I mean: could this be more exciting?! To leave work? leave obligation? pierce the dark? cross an Ancient Sea? battle snow?! I mean, I know my Homer; I know my Odyssey—and I was there; I was *it,* Baby. It doesn't—as they say—*get* any better than that. It was thrilling!

We stopped first in Wendover; fueled; got new wiper blades; went for a look-see—into the old State Line Casino: Johnny Lunchpail from top to bottom, what seemed an airplane hanger totally congested—using all the square footage it could use—tables, machines. So I wandered around. And I can't tell you anything—today—about the *casino;* it didn't register. But I stood behind a winning blackjack player who thought I brought him luck and kept handing silver dollars over his shoulder to keep me in my place, from not walking away with whatever luck I embodied. I mean: I was hooked now, and I'd never played.

Story #3: again personal. The title of this story is: "The Magic Casino." Or it could be titled: "The casino I Went Back to Again and Again." It goes like this: Back in the early days—when I *drove* to play, "transported" myself via roads—the place I always chose was Cactus Pete's in Jackpot, Nevada. It was a bit farther than Elko—and a good two hours past Wendover. But it became a "magic" casino, and it was the first casino I ever wrote a story about. What had caught my eye was a standard promotion: second night free, Fun Book, $2.00 in nickles—*that* stuff. And like Wendover, it required a crossing over—state to state—*Idaho* to Nevada. If you can "cross over," you can change. If you can assume another "state," you can assume another life: reimagine yourself.

And why I went back and back was: clearly, the crossing *gave* me something; didn't disappoint me. Again—brought to feel *more than myself*—I drove through volcanic lava, crested a final hill, and arrived into the music of my childhood: The Sons of The Pioneers (I'd seen every Roy Rogers movie at the University theatre) were playing for the weekend at Cactus

Pete's. So: here was a casino that was at-the-same-*time myth, dream, fantasy, memory.* I was hooked. Swayed. "Transported." And my crossing had involved enough time to let it enter—enter *me:* it wasn't just hokey sidewalk-to-lights-and-slot-bells. There was passage. Transition time and space which let excitement stir, the "new world" to take hold.

At Cactus Pete's I felt "released" and "secured"—both at once. "Released" in that I was bound by no previous structures of my life. I was in "Wild West" space. I was in "casino" space. "Secured" because Cactus Pete's wrapped itself around me like a friend. It anchored me in the music of my childhood. The *empressario* of Jackpot, a man by the name of Al Huber, always extended himself. I'd get wrangled onto his jeep and up into the hills, where he'd show me the wild horses, disclose the trout streams, point out where the thermal springs bubbled into the Wheeler Ranch. And there were dealers who'd heard I was "a writer" and who offered me stories on their breaks—across the street at The Horshu—for a drink. And there was "Hayden"—Carl Hayden—Pete's and Jackpot's chief publicist—who'd once been Hemingway's friend, and he'd slide himself into my booth at breakfast and pick up the bill—all, probably six dollars of it.

What I'm saying is: I went back and back, played almost *only* at Cactus Pete's, because *it was Wonderland and Home at the same time.* I had all the comforts of Kansas, all the adventures of The Emerald City—in the same place. Why go anywhere else?

Gambling is a curious activity. We want to relax—and we want our blood to boil. . . . all at once. Want to be both fully *in* and *out* of control—without contradiction. "*Managed Wildness.*"

And here's a notion to think about. Gamblers gamble, players play: so that they might recover their losses. *Obviously,* you say; but I say, *wait a minute: I'm not talking about people lined up at the ATMs because they've gone through their initial stake.* I'll say it again: *Gamblers gamble so that they might recover their losses.* The more, then, a casino can create the sense-through-space of a World Passed, a World Lost, the more it seems to "redeem" those losses to the gambler.

Last story! one told me by a former compulsive (a man of considerable power) as to *why he started and, for years, couldn't stop.* The World Lost here, you'll see, is Camelot. Our man—back in November of 1963—was a police detective in NYC. When the news broke that President John F. Kennedy had been shot in Dallas, *all* New York police were required to report to their precincts. Who knew what foreign invasion the assassination foretold? Who knew in what ways every trained police officer might be needed? The back rooms of precincts, then, were full. Of idle and waiting officers, detectives. And in that "waiting time," *"Games"* grew up. And though he'd never played, Our Man, joined into a dice game. "I'd lost my

President," he said; "I'd lost his Dream of Camelot. And I wanted to Win him back. *I wanted to bring John Kennedy back to life.*" He didn't. He lost $165. And then he tried—for years—to win *that* loss back. Nearly $200,000 later, he stopped trying to recover what had been lost.

What have we Lost in our World? Sunlight. Water. Green space and flowers. The Past—especially certain nostalgized and charming eras. Childhood. For Americans: The Old World, Europe. The railroads were almost lost. The Frontier is vanishing. As much, then, as those shaping the spaces and image of a casino can appear to be giving us *back* our Lost Worlds—*returning* us to them and them to us—they will, at the same time, be all-the-more freeing us to "play."

Look at what Steve Wynn has done: he has given us back the animal kingdom, water, green space, the power of fire. Sure: it's all a Mirage. But . . . we get transported. We "enter" the Mirage hopeful, expectant, willing to "play"—in water, among flowers, at the tables.

So—story time over—keep in mind the two lessons presumed: First, that players want to be "transported" to their play; they seek destination to enter fantasy (and this may be why New Orleans is a precarious gaming destination: namely "travelers" travel to New Orleans, *first,* for *another* fantasy than gambling; they gamble *after*). And second, we want what feels "lost." Give players a Lost World and they will be playing in a space which seems, in part, *immune* to loss.

How does one create and what are the most essential elements in such a space?

THE ARGUMENT

" . . . by changing space, by leaving the space of one's usual sensibilities, one enters into communication with a space that is psychically innovating."

Gaston Bachelard, *Intimate Immensity*

Casino expansion is everywhere. Still, there are "Lost Worlds" with locked doors. Or which have declared bankruptcy or are on the verge of doing so.

How to survive? Who will grow? Who will fold?

Today's Lost Worlds offer white tigers! Moving ancient statues in a fountain. They attempt (badly) to recreate Oz! Or Treasure Island. Places of story! They build a pyramid, rebuild Paris, rebuild New York, New York! But we *have* Paris: we have the original! And we have New York New York. . . . such as it is! Should the planners stop? reimagine? If it's not Lost—don't Find it!

The point is: what are the best ways to "construct" a "place" when the activity central to that place is *play*? How does one best design a space—its "stuff," its "skin" such that the wandering pilgrim, entering, feels a rush, feels at once empowered by adventure—yet feels: "I'm home!"?

GOING HOME: APPROACH AND ANTICIPATION

One sets out toward a lover, for the mountains to ski, toward the Mall of America to shop, or across the desert to Elko: and a stirring occurs; an internal drama of what's-to-come; an anticipation.

Because the closing of distance, the becoming proximate—"Nearer to Thee"—*has force, near* can be emotionally powerful. The senses grow more keen, more acute. The promise of the "arrival" moment surges. . . . it recedes. In that sense, the *approach* is very tidal, very rhythmic. It's dramatic. It's a strip-tease. It's foreplay. *Approach is critical.* If one wants the "pilgrim," the "entrant," to feel a sense of "flow," a good deal of that can be designed and engineered. A badly paved, a bumpy or unposted approach can create disappointment. Over-anticipation can lead to a loss of spirit and exhaustion. Players won't play if they are dispirited or lost.

Space's relationship to spirit and vitality is no new notion. It has been central to city planners and theologians, playwrights and psychologists, architects and biologists. A biologist describing the viability of a cell may use language not unlike that used to describe the power of a gothic cathedral. (Or the drawing power of a casino.) All might speak about centers and thresholds, about *exchange* between the inside and the outside. And it wouldn't be outrageous to hear the designer of a new hotel casino use the neurologist's term, *receptor sites.* One reads discussions of *amiable places,* of *enriched* and *impoverished environments.* Susan Toch, an environmental planner has studied and described what she terms "*enabling environments.*"

There are spaces which, upon our entry, make us feel empowered and emotionally expansive. There are other spaces which can make us feel disempowered and contracted. In other words: certain spaces flood us with energy and make us feel we are winners; other spaces bleed energy and make us feel that we are losers. Some spaces, when we enter them, feel to be *play grounds* literally—where the urge to play feels spontaneous. There are spaces which, when we enter them, discourage play—where the elements deaden play impulses in the human emotions.

People "read" place on an unconscious level. Any place we enter has its "legibility." Surviving casino hotels will be those which are pleasurably legible. For those casinos that perish, the writing has for years been writ large, and there is little a new owner or a new management team can do. Such operations have been "legible" as tombs—in the way their patrons have "read" them—for some time now.

Many casino spaces have been shaped and arranged to optimize profits.

And that is fine—if it doesn't discourage the *spirit* of play, the *urge* to play. Many casino spaces have been shaped and arranged on the basis of imitation: *this is what a casino looks like.* And that is fine as well—as long as these don't discourage the player. Many casinos seem to have arranged their spaces on the basis of some jaded assumption: "players will play; give 'em a little fake opulence and opportunities for action, and they'll spend their money." As a long-term survival tactic—grounded as it is in the compulsive player only—such an assumption begs disaster.

I can walk into any hotel-casino and almost immediately know its survival potential. I have done it repeatedly: turned to a friend and said: "This place draws people," or "the life of this place is limited." When Atlantic City was first announced as a destination gaming site, I felt the notion—on the basis of all I know about place and space—to be novel but as inherently doomed as Las Vegas is inherently inspired. In his landmark book, *Homo Ludens* (Man, The Player), Johan Huizinga notes that *play is not ordinary or real life. It is a stepping out of "real" life into a temporary sphere of activity with a disposition all its own.* However ingeniously smoked and mirrored, Atlantic City can never feel to be such a "step" into unreality. It can never be a true Oasis, a true Mirage. The lie is too patent, the illusion too clear.

The "problem," in most cases, is that a casino management's need for *space utilization* conflicts with the casino patron's need to *experience space.* Builders tend to *measure* space, to think quantitatively, in Euclidean terms: "How many slots can I fit into *x* square feet?" Players tend to think of space in qualitative, topological terms: "How does this space make me *feel* when I cross the threshold from *real* life into it?" These conflicting needs come head to head with the casino the loser. A casino may have managed to get ten more slot machines, eight more tables into a given area than seemed mathematically possible. A patron approaches and emotionally "reads" the *chaos* of the space and walks away.

What are some of the elements necessary to a casino-hotel's ongoing vitality? What is it that the human organism seeks out in any space? What are the elements that make a given space "legible" in the most inviting and energizing of ways?

THE VOCABULARY OF THE EYE: REDISCOVERING "HOME"

" . . . People have within them various brain-body mechanisms that react to different aspects of their surroundings."
Tony Hiss, *A Sense Of Place*

Despite all the selling of "getaway" packages, *Home* is what, at heart, we always hope, ironically, to get away to. We are all seeking to inhabit that space which most empowers us, which feels most rewarding, most secure, most natural, most intimate.

How, then, does *Home* feel? It feels *centered* certainly—as though there were a strong and clear vertical axis ascending its core and around which all "home life" revolves. Mary Richards says, in her book, *Centering:* "When on center, the self *feels* different: one feels warm, in touch, the power of life a substance. . . . drinking it in and giving it off at the same time quiet and at rest within." Again: "The world is always bigger than one's own focus. And as we bring ourselves into center wherever we are, the more of that world we can bring into service, the larger will be the capacity of our *action* and our understanding."

Of particular interest to the world of *casino space,* is Richards' notion that, "the way to center is by abandonment." Among Richards' other gifts, she's a potter. She speaks about the relationship between center and abandonment in another way: ". . . What is freedom? First of all, freedom seems to mean the absence of external restraint." One can let go of outside restraint—one can abandon one's own restraints, enter the *flow* of a place—if there is a *felt* or *perceived center.*

HOME'S FRONT DOOR: "THRESHOLDS"

"The door is an entire cosmos of the Half-open. In fact it is one of its primal images, the very origin of a daydream that accumulates desires and temptations: the temptation to open up the ultimate depths of being."

—Gaston Bachelard, *The Poetics Of Space*

The *thresholds* of the space are of enormous importance. The entries. Crossing *into* any power-filled space will feel magical, vital, mysterious. The pulse quickens. The lungs fill. One feels a particular charge in the "crossing over." "We are priests—always knocking on the door of mystery," Johann Huizinga says. The adrenalin surges; yet it is a focused surge, not the surge of fear or anxiety. It is the lift one feels upon returning home, to a charged and familiar space. Also: once *in* the space, one wants a clear knowledge of the threshold *out.* We want to feel the choice and freedom of passage. We want to feel we can take the empowerment of any "special" place with us, at any time, back out and into the world. We cross in as pilgrims; we cross out as priests.

FEELING AT HOME: "FLOW"

"Go with the flow," we are told. And—yes; right—it's a buzzword. Still, the buzzword has received some instructive comment. People "in the flow" are happy; they're connected. They're energized, naturally "high," feeling vital. They're *players*. A critical objective of an architectural space is that those people who hoped to be active in it feel its "flow."

Those examining spaces address *flow*. One psychologist, Mihaly Caikszentmihalyi. "Mr. C." (as a chummy pit boss might call him) has monitored *flow* and its absence with some 25,000 subjects, beeping them eight times a day for an "experience sampling." Writer Winifred Gallagher, in her *The Power Of Place,* takes up "Mr. C" and his findings. Ms. Gallagher addresses *flow* by first noting places *without* "flow." She finds them "inhospitable"—unlike "home." They are places which configure to make people feel *outside* the pleasures of optimum experience. "Access to the right settings," she says, "is so important to attaining our peak experiences."

What, then, characterizes such experiences? "When we're in *flow,*" Ms. Gallagher says, "whether while playing the violin or climbing a mountain, our actions merge with our awareness. *We stop being spectators of our own experience.*" Addressing this dissolution of self-consciousness another way, she says: " . . . *our activity dictates our experience* of time rather than the clock. This intense focus also means we forget our daily problems."

What characterizes the places? Ms. Gallagher gives us Mr. C's conclusion: "People are usually happiest in settings in which they're relieved of others' demands and in control of their own actions." He has found a decided preference for wide-open spaces and that, " . . . we're generally happiest *in public settings with other people around.*"

Could be the right casino!

To optimize "flow," then, is a major objective in the creation of a casino space. And if a player feels "in the flow," what are some of *flow's* elements?

WHAT'S THE BEST PLACE FOR THE SOFA?: "ORDER"

"Play creates order, *is* order."

Johan Huizinga, *Man The Player*

Home's *center* provides a second necessity: that *home* feel *ordered.* Studies of sacred spaces show that such "shrines" create space which feels particularly ordered and secured from the chaos of the outside world. Thus, whatever might feel like chaos or *disorientation* within a casino will only serve to drive players away.

My wife and I once looked at a house in Salt Lake which I spontaneously fell in love with. Why? Though I could list qualities, they didn't equal my response. And then I realized: *the "order"—the "shape" or configuration of the house—felt very much like the house I had grown up in.* We didn't buy the house. I think I wasn't ready to settle, and I knew: if we bought that house. . . . I would never leave it.

Order though—as any biologist and dreamer-of-houses knows—isn't simple geometry or symmetry. In fact, sheer geometry and symmetry feel cold and dehumanizing. Systems order themselves in richly various ways. As long as a given system doesn't *contradict* itself, it can seem ordered. Someone entering a space need only pick up initial clues which allow him to *trust* that there are "rules" of design in operation. It would seem, in fact, that the ideal *experience of order* is two-fold: First, one senses that the space has inherent design; and second, one "reads" that the space contains the unseen, is explorable, has mystery. "Mystery," Mary Richards says, "sucks at our breath like a wind tunnel. Invites us into it."

In his book, *A Sense Of Place,* author Tony Hiss calls this double-edged sense of order, "simultaneous perception." Of it, he says, "I feel relaxed and alert at the same time." Of a favorite park, Prospect Park (" . . . a place that seems to welcome experiencing"), he captures order's double edge this way: "welcome [and] safety, wonder [and] exhilaration."

Hiss then tells an instructive anecdote about being in Grand Central Station, a space which he'd known well but one which had undergone some spatial reconfiguring. With the addition of arcade shops and food counters, its familiar spatial envelope had shrunk. "I felt hurried along," he says; "my breathing was shallow and constricted. He says he felt brushed and touched by others, even though he wasn't. " . . . nearby foot-falls and normal tones of voice registered as loud but blurred." Thus he describes a kind of spatial chaos, of panic. What to do? His response would seem to underscore the necessity of "escape alcoves," doorway "grottos" or "islands" (what, in Gothic cathedrals, might be "chapels") in large and busy spaces of hubbub. "The only alternative to hurrying forward seemed to be to swerve right at random and come to rest in front of a shop."

Hiss's stepping out of tumult, the rushing water, calms him. It gives him a moment to "re-fit" himself to the space, to reread it and find its rhythm, to turn its "noise" into a kind of music. With this, he feels, " . . . a slight lightening in my shoulders," and " . . . saw in front of me a differ-ent light: grayer, clearer, brighter, less intense." When he reenters the termi-nal and its human traffic, he speaks of there being only a *single sound:* "Vast and quiet, it seemed evenly distributed throughout the great room. This sound, pleasant in all its parts, regular in all its rhythms, and humor-ous and good-natured, seemed also to have buttoned me into some small, silent bubble of space."

HOME-LINES: "THE STRAIGHT AND THE NOT-SO-STRAIGHT"

" . . . The curve welcomes us and the oversharp angle rejects us . . . the angle is masculine and the curve feminine. . . . the beloved curve has nest-like powers; it incites us to possession, it is a curved 'corner,' inhabited geometry."

Gaston Bachelard, The Poetics Of Space

Sheer geometry is often the most expedient and economic way to solve a given problem of space—the definition of space, the partition of space. *A straight line, after all, is the shortest distance. . . . etc.* But casinos aren't office buildings; they aren't warehouses. *Expedience destroys experience. Casino space and the grid design are enemies.* Most often, casinos are spaces in which players are trying to *escape* expediency and practical economics. As such, casinos might best employ the more organic, feminine, natural and sexual use of the curve. Bachelard also speaks of " . . . [seeking] warmth and quiet life in the arms of a curve."

The most enticing and alluring and stimulating casino spaces are those which make principal use of the curvilinear rather than the straight. In brief evidence, a Michigan husband-and-wife research team, Stephen and Rachel Kaplan, believe that we have a hardwired and innate preference for winding paths. Such paths, they feel, provide "mystery" for the wanderer. In their thinking: landscapes provide 'mystery' when they " . . . give the impression that one could acquire new information if one were to travel deeper into the scene." Such a truth is demonstrated elegantly by all the winding paths at The Mirage. So many people, without realizing it, look up consciously for the first time to find themselves dead center in the casino.

Architect Christopher Alexander's *A Pattern Language* articulates the results of an eight-year study examining why certain places "make people feel alive and human." Alexander ranks certain of the 253 aspects or *patterns* with special priority. For example: we humans, it seems, are made to feel particularly vital in an *identifiable environment.* Like much of the organic world, we thrive on *sunlight* and shrink from darkness. In a similar "light," we respond positively to *warm colors.* We like the shoulder-to-shoulder people-energy of *pedestrian traffic* but shun, wherever possible, motorized traffic. The pervasive presence of *the elderly,* interestingly, gives us comfort and joy. And we take energy out of *the presence of an accessible greenspace.* Less primary in Alexander's study but central in the studies of other is *the presence and sound of moving water.*

HOME'S GARDEN: "GREENSPACE"

"Tranquil foliage that really *is* lived in, a tranquil gaze discovered in the humblest of eyes, are the artisans of immensity. These images make the world grow."

Gaston Bachelard, Intimate Immensity

Human connection to greenspace, evidence reveals, is crucial. It's an almost-Lost World. We evolve from "savannahs," and research shows that memory of and nostalgia for the natural may be hardwired in us. Recovering patients in hospitals recover faster where windows look out on a natural setting. Students in schools learn more directly if their school interfaces with green landscape and trees. *Accessible green.* Its *real* presence—not its *silk* or *plastic* presence—appears to trigger those senses of "center" and "order" which orient us pleasurably within a space, which make us feel "at home."

A related issue is *sunlight.* Sunlight suppresses the production of melatonin in the pineal gland. Melatonin production enhances sleep. In overabundance, melatonin enhances depression. The use of lamps which simulate first sunlight in the workplaces of geographic locales seasonally scant of sun, have helped shape a more energized workforce. There are phototherapists working in similar ways who are discovering that chronic depression in patients dissolves for weeks at a time after infusions of sunlight. One such researcher, Michael Terman, uses what he calls a "tropical dawn machine." Is it outrageous to suggest that casinos, in sunlight-deprived places, equip themselves with "tropical dawn machines?"

Especially in locales and climates which otherwise *deny greenspace and natural sun,* interiors which can offer these, as mood "supplements," act toward optimizing a "vital" space. Las Vegas is naturally abundant with palm trees, sun; Atlantic City isn't. To offer opulent glass and steel, chandeliers and carpet merely repeats the better office-space gestures of Manhattan or Philadelphia.

"PLANTING" HOME'S GARDEN

What does one do with an empty, bleak, sere and rectangular ten-acre piece of land? *Plant it!*

Filled with contours and colors and shapes and textures, a dismal space becomes inviting; it takes on a life. One goes to Monet's Giverny in Normandy or to Villa Lante in Viterbo, Italy, to experience just how excitingly a lifeless plot of land might be *planted.*

Villa Lante and Giverny represent two classic ways of planting. Villa Lante presents the formal Italian garden. Giverny offers the natural or English garden. Both are highly calculated. The Italian garden flaunts its calculation in impressive manicured shapes and geometry. The English garden hides its calculation by creating the illusion that all has been spontaneous; everything flows into everything else. The Italian garden's dramatic presence is style, wit, elegance; it's superior and intellectual. The English garden's dramatic presence is more emotional and earthy. Someone within an English garden feels a part of the landscape. Someone in an Italian garden feels a spectator.

Needless to say, architectural interiors are similarly planted. And it's important that players moving through, experiencing such spaces, not feel themselves in scapes untended or overgrown, spaces being used for a landfill. My comments will draw, often, upon this notion of *planting the space.*

THE MUSIC OF HOME: "ACOUSTICAL SPACE"

"Music creates order out of chaos."

Anthony Storr, *Music And The Mind*

The above is a given. Musicologists rephrase Storr's line variously. "Music structures time," they say. And: " . . . music has a power akin to that of the orator." And: " . . . there is a closer relation between *hearing* and emotional arousal than between *seeing* and emotional arousal." And " . . . music connects the otherwise unconnected and random."

The corollary of this is, of course: *noise creates chaos out of order.* Any given space takes a shape from its sounds. Are those sounds "music" or "noise?" If a prime spatial objective of a casino is to make a play feel "flow" and "at home:" how is the *sound* contributing. A given *play-space* might visually arrange itself in the most comforting and liberating ways. If that same space, at the same time, allows sound to be a din, to be cacophonous, it might undo most of what it has—through architecture and design—created. A final quote: "Rhythm imposes unanimity upon the divergent; melody imposes continuity [flow] upon the disjointed, and harmony imposes compatibility upon the incongruous" (Yehudi Menuhin, *Theme & Variations*).

One recall's Tony Hiss's disorienting experience in Grand Central Station, mentioned in the section on *Order.* Builders and shapers of casinos have a powerful tool—would they use it: the shaping of sounds within— the optimizing of *music* rather than *noise.* It is crucial that a "place of play" be (in its sounds) beautifully legible and not a scribble.

READING HOME: "LEGIBILITY"

What is the heart of any place's "legibility?" (A term coined by Drs. Stephen and Rachael Kaplan, Michigan psychologists.) Architect and writer, William Lam, argues that people are constantly vigilant for information relating to five crucial elements in their livelihood: *orientation, defense, sustenance, stimulation and survival.* First: it is vitally important that a place give us a *legible* "read" on these points of information. Second: it is important that the "read" we get be positive. If we feel *oriented,* if we feel *safe,* if we find *sustenance* and *stimulation,* then a joyous and liberated *survival* will appear guaranteed.

The delicate balance of place-*legibility,* in the terms of the Michigan psychologist team who coined it, is: " . . . an environment that looks as if one could explore it extensively *without* getting lost." It would seem, then, that we like mystery. We like surprise. But we need assurance that—though a given place has hidden nooks and crannies—we will not get lost. *Above all,* we need *orientation:* vantage, prospect, centeredness. The trick, then, of any large casino, is to provide "explorable space" which never makes the customer feel disoriented.

A final story. When my children were children, our family took a trip to Washington State's Olympic Peninsula. A lodge we stayed at had two adjacent playgrounds, equidistant from the lodge. One had been assembled by the Park Services; the other, created by the Quinault Tribe. Equidistant as they were, one was always full and active—the other, empty. Because one was just a space with some play "stuff" in it. The other was a playground. I'll let you guess which was which.

Today's casino world is one which hopes to convert the "unlikely" player into a player. In that world, it is not enough, simply, to provide games and play. One has to understand as deeply as possible, what "play" *is*—and then build play *grounds.*

Studies of Casinos
and Competition

Section 5

An Economic Analysis of the Effects of Casino Gambling on the Kentucky Race Horse Industry

Robert G. Lawrence and Richard Thalheimer

The focus of this study is the potential impact of the introduction of casino gaming into the Kentucky race horse market. In particular, the study estimates potential loss of jobs and associated spending determined under the assumption that Kentucky racetracks, horsemen at those racetracks, and Kentucky breeders would experience a loss of pari-mutuel wagering (handle) and purse revenues as a result of competition from casino gaming. A plan to mitigate the potential damage from casino gaming is investigated in this paper.

A comprehensive survey and analysis was conducted to determine expenditures and employment of Kentucky racehorse owners, trainers, and breeders. The first part of the analysis estimates employment and expenditures, while the second part approximates the potential impact of casino gaming when introduced onto the market.

A literature search for econometric analyses of the impact of gaming on pari-mutuel wagering was conducted, along with a survey of states in which casino gaming had been introduced into an existing horse race wagering market. The results were analyzed to give a possible range of the anticipated impact of the introduction of casino gaming on Kentucky pari-mutuel wagering.

The final configuration of casino gaming that will exist in the Kentucky region—location (state, county) and type (riverboat, land based)—was not apparent when this study was performed in 1994. At the time, an Illinois riverboat existed in direct competition with Bluegrass Downs racetrack in Kentucky. Riverboats were to be soon introduced along Indiana's Ohio River, competing directly with many of Kentucky's racetracks. This report developed a number of scenarios that present a wide range of possible outcomes, under different assumptions, as to the final configuration of casino gaming.

The most extreme case scenario presented in this analysis is the closure of all Kentucky racetracks facing direct competition from off-site land-based casino gaming located in the state. A mid-range scenario is presented in which Kentucky does not have casino gaming but faces competition from casino gaming on the Ohio River. Those racetracks located on the river where a riverboat is also located are assumed, for the sake of illustration, to cease operations. A third scenario is presented in which each Kentucky racetrack has a land-based casino on-site and suffers an initial loss in handle and purses, as is the case in the first scenario. Unlike the first scenario, however, purses are supplemented from casino "win" to pre-casino competition levels at each racetrack. In addition, breeders' awards are allocated from casino "win" to Kentucky breeders. This is a variant of the proposal by *Kentucky To The Front,* a group of Kentucky racetracks, which has advocated purse supplements to levels greater than those existing prior to casino competition (*Lexington Herald-Leader,* 1993). Under the assumptions of the third scenario, the impact on jobs and expenditures of the Kentucky race horse industry is the lowest of the three possible scenarios.

An additional consideration is evaluated as a supplement to the last scenario. Under this consideration, as proposed by *Kentucky To The Front,* purses are supplemented to levels greater than those existing prior to casino competition. The resulting direct impacts on employment and expenditures per $1 million increment are computed. Finally, consideration is given to the feasibility of the proposed purse supplement program in terms of return on the racetrack-casino investment.

EXPENDITURES AND EMPLOYMENT

To conduct this analysis, the industry was first divided into its Thoroughbred and Standardbred components. Each of these groups was further divided into three distinct sectors:

* racetrack operations;
* owner/trainer operations; and
* breeding operations.

A. Expenditures

1. Racetrack Operations In 1992, there were eight pari-mutuel racetrack facilities in Kentucky that conducted live racing. The racetracks, the days they raced, and their average daily handles are given in Table 1.

Direct expenditures by these racetracks were computed using information from their 1992 financial statements. Certain adjustments were made to avoid double counting.[1] Total expenditures include operating expenses

TABLE 1
Kentucky Racetracks
1992 Days & Average Handle

	Days	Average Daily Handle
Thoroughbred		
Churchill Downs	79	$2,243,289
Keeneland	32	$1,960,996
Turfway Park	103	$1,641,778
Ellis Park	61	$1,263,225
Standardbred		
Red Mile	48	$160,725
Riverside Downs	73	$24,279
Quarter Horse		
Bluegrass Downs	14	$36,790
Steeplechase		
Dueling Grounds	1	$149,505

TABLE 2
Expenditures by Kentucky Racetracks—1992

Racetrack	Expenditures (Nearest $100,000)
Total Thoroughbred	$84,100,000
Total Standardbred	$6,200,000
Total Quarter Horse	$1,400,000
Total Training Centers	$1,800,000
Total	$93,500,000
Source: Track Financial Statements.	

for racing and other expenses such as interest. Table 2 gives the total estimated expenditures by the Kentucky racetracks in 1992.

Over $93 million was spent by these racetracks for salaries and purchases from other industries. Not included in the racetrack impact are pari-mutuel tax payments. Pari-mutuel tax payments to state government are made out of handle wagered at each racetrack and are given in Table 3.[2]

2. Owner/Trainer Operations Thoroughbred, Standardbred, and Quarter Horse owners (the racing stables) and trainers were included in the owner/trainer sector of the Kentucky racehorse industry. A primary source of income to owners and trainers are purses collected and disbursed by

TABLE 3
Pari-Mutuel Tax

Racetrack	Total
Total Thoroughbred	$13,659,451
Total Standardbred	$155,200
Bluegrass Downs	$9,014
Total pari-mutuel (including KTDF)	$13,823,665
Sources: Kentucky State Racing Commission and Kentucky Harness Racing Commission.	

the racing associations. To avoid double counting of the expenditures and employment made from purse revenues, owners and trainers were treated as a single entity. Expenditures from purse revenues are a major source of the economic impact of owner/trainer operations. Purse money is also a source of revenues to owners for the purchase of yearlings from breeders.

Random samples of Thoroughbred and Standardbred owners were obtained from complete lists of licensed owners (racing stables) provided by the Kentucky State Racing Commission and the Kentucky Harness Racing Commission. These lists provided the basis for a combination mail-telephone survey. The owner surveys were the basis for determining the daily costs of owning a racehorse. Due to the itinerant nature of their work, the much smaller trainer population was surveyed by conducting personal interviews of random samples of trainers located at five Kentucky racetracks. These surveys provided the basis for estimating the employment associated with owning and training racehorses.[3]

Thoroughbred: Owners of racehorses make a wide variety of expenditures that have an impact on the state economy. The distribution of total expenses paid by owners, including training fee expenses, was determined. Expenses include items such as: jockey fees, veterinarian and farrier expenses, vanning, nominations and trainer commissions, depreciation on horses, interest, travel, and other business expenses such as telephone or office supplies. As a single category, daily training fees make up the largest owner expense. Daily training fees represented an estimated 40.9% of total Thoroughbred owner expenditures, and 50.0% of total Standardbred owner expenditures. Training fees averaged $41.77 per day for Thoroughbred trainers. Other Thoroughbred owner expenses were $59.30 per day for a total owner cost of $101.07 per day. Training fees for Standardbreds averaged $25.07 per day. Other Standardbred owner costs were an additional $25.07 per day for an estimated total owner cost of $50.13 per day.

Knowing the distribution of racing days and daily owner costs, it is

TABLE 4

Total Kentucky Thoroughbred Racing Stable Expenses

Track	Training Fee Expense Per Day	Other Owner Expense Per Day	Horse-Days	Training Fee Expense Per Year	Other Expense Per Year	Total Expense Per Year
Ellis	$38.67	$55.85	101,650	$3,930,806	$5,677,617	$9,608,422
Turfway	$39.45	$56.98	235,053	$9,272,841	$13,393,600	$22,666,441
Churchill	$44.70	$64.56	367,920	$16,446,024	$23,754,475	$40,200,499
Keeneland	$45.62	$65.89	203,670	$9,291,425	$13,420,443	$22,711,868
Bluegrass	$29.60	$42.75	31,346	$927,842	$1,340,165	$2,268,007
Training Centers	$20.83	$14.58	337,650	$7,033,250	4,922,937	$11,956,187
Total			1,277,289	46,902,187	62,509,236	$109,411,423

possible to estimate total racing stable expenses. For example, if the daily owner's cost is $94.52, as it was at Ellis Park, and data are available on the number of horse-days at Ellis Park, then total expenditures can be estimated. Horse-days are calculated based on the monthly stall occupancy at a given track. For example, if a track has 1,000 stalls that are fully occupied for two 30-day months, then that track would have 60,000 horse days. The number of horse-days, when multiplied by the daily owner costs (trainer's fee plus other owner expenditures), result in an estimate of total owner expenditures. The daily training fee, "other" owner expenses, horse-days, total estimated annual owner expenses, and the ratio of purses (owner revenues) to expenditures are given in Table 4.

Data in Table 5 indicate that Thoroughbred-racing stables earned about $48 million in purses in 1992, but their total expenses exceeded $109 million. The ratio of purse revenues to expenses was about 45%. Thus, in general, owners of racehorses are not expected to cover their costs through purse earnings.

Standardbred: Information from the distribution of the total expenses paid by owners, including daily training fees, revealed that Standardbred owner daily training fees were slightly more than 50% of total training costs. Table 6 gives the daily training fee, other owner costs, and total expenses per year for the two Standardbred tracks.

The ratio of purses (owner revenues) to total expenditures is shown in Table 7. Data in Table 7 show that Standardbred racing stables earned about $4 million in purses in 1992, but their total expenses exceeded $13.5 million. The ratio of purse revenues to expenses was about 30%.

TABLE 5
Thoroughbred Racing Stable Revenue and Expense

Track	Total Purses (000)	Total Expense (000)	% Purse to Expense
Ellis	$6,731	$9,608	70.1%
Turfway	$14,660	$22,666	64.7%
Churchill	$17,932	$40,200	44.6%
Keeneland	$8,285	$22,712	36.5%
Dueling	$665	*	*
Training Centers	$0	$11,956	NA
Subtotal-Thoroughbred	$48,273	$107,142	45.1%
Bluegrass	$349	$2,268	15.4%
Total	$48,622	$109,410	44.4%
*Dueling Grounds had only 1 day of racing in 1992.			

3. Breeder Operations The survey procedure for Kentucky breeders generally followed that described in the owner (racing stable) section above.[4] In this case, however, the emphasis was on computation of expenditures and employment per FTE horse. The concern here is with the relationship between foal production and increases or decreases in purses and the resulting impact on breeder expenditures and employment. Expenditures or employees per horse were needed in order to determine the impact of changes in purse structure due to competition from casino gaming. If a $1 million reduction in purses results in a given reduction in horses at the breeding farm or at the track, then the reduction in expenditures and employment can be determined.

Thoroughbred: There were approximately 561 Thoroughbred farms in Kentucky in 1993. The typical inventory of horses at those farms includes stallions, mares, weanlings (horses less than one year old), yearlings, and for part of the year at least, yearlings in for sale preparation, to be broken, or to be trained, and older horses on the farm as "turn-outs" or "lay-ups." For this analysis, weanlings are assumed, on average, to be weaned four months prior to their January 1 yearling birth date. Yearlings are assumed to be kept an average of nine months beyond January 1. The length of time horses were on the farm for sale prep, breaking, training, as lay-ups or turn-outs was determined from the returned questionnaires. On average, the Kentucky farm FTE horse population was 50.8 horses.

Farms with training facilities were analyzed separately. A major difference between farms without commercial training facilities and those with such facilities is in the size of the operations. The mean expenditure of farms with major training facilities was $2,741,457 versus $660,946 for the

TABLE 6
Total Kentucky Standardbred Racing Stable Expenses

Track	Training Fee Expense Per Day	Other Expense Per Day	Horse-Days	Training Fee Expense Per Year	Other Expense Per Year	Total Expense Per Year
Red Mile	$28.73	$28.73	195,050	$5,603,787	$5,603,787	$11,207,574
Riverside	$21.40	$21.40	54,800	$1,172,720	$1,172,720	$2,345,330

TABLE 7

Standardbred Racing Stable Revenue and Expense

	Total Purses (000)	Total Expense (000)	% Purse to Expense
Red Mile	$3,434	$11,208	30.6%
Riverside	$ 565	$ 2,345	24.1%
Total	$3,999	$13,553	29.5%

typical breeder. On a per horse basis, that meant an average expenditure of $21,770 versus $13,008. In terms of inventory, commercial training farms were also much larger, boarding more than 43 mares on average versus about 21 on the smaller operations. Physically, commercial training facilities are much larger farms as well, averaging almost 1,500 acres versus fewer than 400 for the less diversified farms.

Standardbred: Standardbred breeders are more diversified than Thoroughbred breeders. Typical of many Standardbred breeding operations (Downs and Lawrence, 1978), the Kentucky data suggest that breeders often keep and race their produce. This may occur for several reasons. For example, given virtuallu no weight constraints (a driver is mounted on a sulky or jog cart and not up on the horse), and fewer requirements for a training track, it is much more economical to get a horse to the races. Many breeders can break, condition and train at home or at a county fair track and ship in to race with much less investment than can their Thoroughbred counterparts.

No distinct group of farms with training centers was identified because this diversification is common. For example the number of horses in for sale prep, breaking, training, lay-up or turn-out averaged more than eight (versus 2.27 for the typical Thoroughbred farm).

The distribution of Kentucky Standardbred breeders' expenses is shown in Table 6. Major costs include wages and salaries (23.96%), and their associated expenses such as employee benefits, stud fees (2.75%), feed and bedding (4.78%), and expenses such as interest and repairs in the 3% range. Depreciation of bloodstock was about 13%. The average annual total expenditure per farm was $465,024.

B. Employment

1. Racetrack Operations The racetracks employ full-time year-round personnel, part-time year-round personnel, and seasonal personnel. The seasonal personnel include pari-mutuel clerks, with the largest number being employed during the live race meet. A smaller number are employed

TABLE 8
Racetrack Employment

Racetrack	Employment (FTE)
Churchill Downs	732
Keeneland	455
Turfway Park	339
Ellis Park	313
Dueling Grounds	104
Total Thoroughbred	1,942
Riverside Downs	37
The Red Mile	125
Total Standardbred	162
Bluegrass Downs*	63
Training Centers	56
Total	2,223

*Bluegrass Downs conducted Quarter Horse racing in 1992 and so was not included with the Thoroughbred racetracks.
Source: Racetrack Survey

when the racetrack is not conducting live races, but is receiving the simulcast signal from other racetracks in the state. A survey of each of the racetracks was conducted to obtain monthly employment data in 1992 for both the track and concessionaires. Employment can vary greatly by month. For example, at Churchill Downs, the lowest figure for employment by the track and its concessionaire was 330 while the highest was 1,812. Employment in 1992 was computed on a full time equivalent (FTE) basis as the average over the twelve-month period for that year. Table 8 gives employment by racetrack.

2. Owner-Trainer Operations Training horses is a labor intensive activity and trainers employ a wide variety of people such as assistants, stable foremen, hot walkers, exercise riders, grooms, security, and other personnel. Most often in Kentucky, these are permanent employees, but exercise riders, hot walkers, and others work under contract, generally at a fixed fee per horse.

Thoroughbred: Table 9 shows the number of individuals employed per horse by the trainers randomly selected and interviewed at the four Kentucky Thoroughbred tracks. Employees fall into the following categories: trainer, assistant trainer, stable foreman, hot walker, exercise rider, groom, security, other paid, and unpaid. It should be noted that the average employee per horse is largest at Churchill Downs and at Keeneland. As might

TABLE 9
Employees Per Horse—Ellis, Turfway, Churchill Downs and Keeneland

	FTE Employees Per Horse
Ellis	0.662
Turfway	0.694
Churchill	0.823
Keeneland	0.716

TABLE 10
Thoroughbred Trainer Employment Summary

Track	Employees Per Horse	Horse-Days	FTE Employment
Ellis	0.66	101,650	256
Turfway	0.69	235,053	627
Churchill	0.82	367,920	1,165
Keeneland	0.72	203,670	561
Bluegrass	0.44	31,346	53
Training Centers	0.44	337,650	611
Total FTE Employees			3,273

be expected, at the tracks with the highest purses and thus the highest earnings of owners and trainers, the trainers would be able to afford marginally more labor per horse.

The total number of FTE jobs in the backstretch is based on the number of horse-days at each track. Once the number of days are determined for each track, and the number of employees per horse has been calculated, then the FTE employment can be estimated. As shown in Table 10, the number of full time, year-round jobs was 3,273 FTE employees in 1992.

Standardbred: Standardbred racing is less labor intensive than Thoroughbred racing but is still a labor-intensive industry. Based on responses to a random sample of trainers at the Kentucky Standardbred racetracks, there were an estimated 0.44 FTE employees per horse compared to a weighted average of about 0.74 per horse for Thoroughbred trainers. Total employment is estimated at 423, as shown in Table 11. It is again based on employee per horse and horse days.

3. Breeder Operations
Thoroughbred: The number of FTE employees per horse was computed for farms without commercial training centers. A significant number of employees are hired for seasonal work such as for the breeding season

TABLE 11
Total Standardbred Trainer Employment Summary

Track	Employees Per Horse	Horse Days	FTE Employment
Red Mile	0.44	195,050	330
Riverside	0.44	54,800	93
Total FTE Employment			423

or preparing horses for auction sales. In addition, unpaid labor is not uncommon on the smaller farms although much less a factor in Kentucky. Part-time employees were treated as working half time year round. Seasonal employees were considered to work full-time for an average of four months per year. In 1992 there were an estimated 14.2 FTE employees per farm or 0.28 employees per horse.

Farms with commercial training activities are much larger and consequently employ three times as many FTE's (41.8 vs. 14.2). Their employee per horse ratio was 0.31 or about 3.2 horses per employee vs. the 3.6 horses per employee on the traditional breeding farm. Given the more labor-intensive activity of breaking, training, conditioning, and otherwise handling horses, this is not surprising.

Standardbred: Unlike their Thoroughbred counterparts, many Standardbred breeders own, train, and maintain their own horses. In terms of horse care, the operations tend to have more family member participants than Thoroughbred operations.

On average, the Kentucky Standardbred farm FTE horse population was 48.34 horses. The average number of employees per farm was 8.32, about 60% that of a Thoroughbred farm. FTE employment was 0.17 per horse, or almost six horses per employee.

THE IMPACT OF CASINO GAMING ON PARI-MUTUEL HORSE RACE WAGERING

Because casino gaming is a substitute for pari-mutuel wagering, the introduction of casino gaming into an existing pari-mutuel wagering market is expected to result in reduced wagering as patrons substitute a portion of the new product for the existing product. The introduction of casino gaming in these markets, with the exception of Las Vegas, Nevada, and Atlantic City, New Jersey, is a relatively new phenomenon. As a consequence, there has been little empirical work conducted which investigates the impact of casino gaming on pari-mutuel wagering because of data limitations in these newer markets. A study published by the University of Louisville, Department of Equine Administration (Thalheimer and Ali, 1992),

TABLE 12

Summary Effects of Competition

Evidence Of Effect Of Competition On Pari-mutuel Wagering	Estimated Impact
Econometric Studies—Casino Gaming	
New Jersey (Thalheimer and Ali, 1992)	−34%
Recent Non-Econometric Evidence—Casinos Near Racetracks	
Illinois: Fairmount Park Thoroughbred	−31% to −39%
Illinois: Fairmount Park Standardbred	−34%
Illinois: Quad City Downs	−37%
Iowa: Prairie Meadows*	−34%
Connecticut: Teletheatre*	−74%
Minnesota: Canterbury Downs*	−74%
Survey Results—Gambling	
U.S. (Kallick, Suits, et. al., 1976)	Found that casinos are strong substitutes for horse race wagering.
Econometric Studies—Lottery Gaming	
New Jersey (Thalheimer and Ali, 1992): Thoroughbred and Standardbred	−17%
Ohio/Kentucky (Thalheimer and Ali, 1990): Thoroughbred and Standardbred	−22%
Kentucky (Thalheimer and Ali, 1991b): Thoroughbred Standardbred	−15% −22%
U.S. (Simmons and Sharp, 1987): Thoroughbred	−36%

*Excluded from final analysis due to factors, in addition to casino gaming, occurring over the same time period. The impact of the introduction of casino gaming in the Bluegrass Downs (KY) market was eliminated since that racetrack switched from Quarter Horse to Thoroughbred racing the same year.

contained an econometric analysis of the determinants of wagering, including casino gaming, on pari-mutuel horse race wagering in New Jersey. The results of this study are given in Table 12. Changes in handle at racetracks where casinos have been introduced into existing pari-mutuel horse race wagering markets are also investigated in this report and results are summarized in Table 12.[5] Finally, results of several empirical studies on the impact of state lotteries, a weaker substitute for pari-mutuel wagering than casino gaming, are also summarized in Table 12.

A. *Estimated Impact of Casino Gaming On Pari-mutuel Horse Race Wagering In Kentucky*

When this study was undertaken, the configuration of casino gaming, as it will affect Kentucky pari-mutuel racetracks, was not certain. In June of 1993, Indiana passed legislation allowing 11 riverboat licenses to be granted. Subsequently, riverboats opened in East Chicago, Hammond, Gary, and Michigan City in northern Indiana, as well as in Evansville, directly across the Ohio River from Henderson, Kentucky. Also, riverboats opened in the communities of Lawrenceberg and Rising Sun, in the region bordering Kentucky and Ohio, near the Cincinnati metropolitan area, and in 1998, another riverboat was scheduled to open just across the river from Louisville. These developments resulted in riverboat gaming approximately 25 miles from Turfway Park in Florence and about 10 miles from Churchill Downs in Louisville.

The currently existing racetracks farthest from the proposed riverboat gaming opportunities are Keeneland and The Red Mile in Lexington, and Dueling Grounds in Simpson County. Keeneland and The Red Mile in Lexington will be about 70 miles from the nearest possible riverboat gaming location near Carrolton, Kentucky or about 95 miles from riverboat gaming in Cincinnati. Driving time to either location, however, is about the same at about 90 minutes each. Dueling Grounds is hours away from the nearest possible riverboat location but will likely suffer a loss in handle from population centers such as Bowling Green in their market area which are closer to the riverboat sites.

In addition to new competition from riverboat gaming in Indiana, racing in Kentucky has already faced competition from riverboat gaming in Illinois across the river from Bluegrass Downs in Paducah. This apparently was a large contributing factor to that racetrack's sale in 1994 to casino gaming interests. Since competition from casino gaming is a certainty due to its recent introduction or legalization in surrounding states, we make use of the evidence, both econometric and from observation of changes in handle at racetracks where casinos have been introduced.

The impact of a state lottery on Kentucky racetracks was found to vary from -15% to -22%. Results of studies for New Jersey racetracks and racetracks nationally range from -17% to -36%. Since, from national survey results, the lottery was found to be a potentially weaker substitute for pari-mutuel wagering than casino gaming (Kallick, et. al., 1976), we rely more heavily on the econometric study of New Jersey wagering and observation of changes in handle at racetracks where casino gaming has been recently introduced. The econometric evidence produces an estimated impact of -34%. The evidence from changes in handle in markets where casinos have recently been introduced, and for which the casino impact can possibly be separated from other factors, produces estimates of -31% to -39%. The impact is expected to vary depending on the location of the casino relative to population centers in the racetrack market, and to the price and quality of the product being offered at the casino relative to the racetrack. The estimated impact of -34% from the econometric study of wagering in New Jersey (Thalheimer and Ali, 1992) is an average over all Thoroughbred and Standardbred racetracks. Thus, it is possible under some casino configuration scenarios (e.g., riverboats in Indiana and Illinois, no casinos in Kentucky) that a racetrack such as Dueling Grounds may be impacted less than -31%. Others, such as Ellis Park, may be at the upper bound of -39% or possibly even greater should they be closed due to insufficient profits. The casino impacts are estimated under current market conditions.

It is possible that the impact of casino gaming will differ among locales due to differences in consumer preferences. However, results of the studies examining the impact of the introduction of the lottery in New Jersey (New Jersey Lottery), northern Kentucky/southern Ohio (Ohio Lottery), and Kentucky (Kentucky Lottery) indicate that racetrack patrons in each of these locales reacted similarly in their pari-mutuel betting behavior. This might suggest that racetrack patrons would react similarly to the introduction of casinos in different locales.

CASINO IMPACT SCENARIOS

The base year for this analysis is 1992, the last year for which complete data were available when the study was undertaken. The scenarios presented in this study represent only a few of many possible outcomes. Scenarios were developed using empirical evidence, supplemented with judgment by the research team where no empirical evidence exists. For example, it was assumed that the impact of casino gaming opportunities on a racetrack declines as the distance of the racetrack from the casino increases. Several scenarios with detailed assumptions were provided so that an order of magnitude of the impact of the introduction of competition from casino gaming could be determined. Since the future configuration of casinos was not known, the framework for analysis of possible impacts under various casino configurations is provided in this study. Each of the scenarios assumes an impact from casino gaming after a possible initial phase-in period.

A. Overview

Three scenarios are presented below, based on the 1992 configuration of racetracks in Kentucky. They were selected to present a maximum, intermediate, and minimum impact of casino gaming on the Kentucky race-horse industry. Each scenario summarizes the estimated impact of the introduction of casino gaming on racetrack industry employment and expenditures.

B. Scenario 1

Under this scenario, every Kentucky racetrack faces direct competition from casino gaming. This would be the case, for example, if land-based casino gambling were permitted in Kentucky but not at Kentucky racetrack sites, so that every racetrack, including the land-locked tracks Keeneland, The Red Mile, and Dueling Grounds would face direct competition from casino gaming. Under the worst-case circumstance, the 39% loss of handle and attendance revenues would lower profitability to such an extent that each of the racetracks would close. This may not be the actual case since racetracks will cease operations only if they are unable to earn a sufficient return on their capital relative to the next best alternative. Under this scenario some of the racetracks may have positive income but the income generated from operations would not be sufficient to yield an acceptable return on the capital investment commensurate with the risk of that investment. It was beyond the scope of this study to determine the current market value of each of the racetracks and then compute the required return on these assets. Instead, this scenario was merely presented as one possible outcome based on conversations with track operators in Kentucky and based on the evidence of the size of the impact on horse race wagering resulting from the introduction of casino gambling into the market area.

The loss to the breeding industry of a total elimination of racing in Kentucky would not be 100%. Since Kentucky's breeding industry is international in scope, it is not solely dependent on Kentucky racing. The impact of the introduction of casino gaming on the Kentucky breeding industry is an indirect one to the extent that loss in purse revenues at the racetracks result in reduced owner incomes available for purchase of Kentucky bloodstock. Since horses bred in Kentucky are sold internationally, the loss of Kentucky racing *ceteris paribus* would not result in a substantial loss of the Kentucky breeding industry. The number of foals produced and sold, however, would fall as the demand for those horses decreases due to a loss of racing opportunities and due to a loss in purse money needed for bloodstock purchases.

It is expected that a reduction in purses and thus a reduction in the expected price of racing stock will lead to a reduction in the demand for weanlings (foals), yearlings, broodmares, and stallions. A simple statistical model was developed relating the value of national purses to the number of registered Thoroughbred foals over the time period 1929 through 1991. Knowing the change in registered foals (weanlings), the associated change in the number of yearlings, broodmares, and stallions can also be computed. Given the change in the total number of horses, and the associated FTE jobs per horse at breeding farms, the change in total employment can be computed.

C. Scenario 2

Under this "mid-range" scenario there is riverboat gaming in surrounding states but no casino gaming in Kentucky. Each racetrack facing direct competition (less than a 30 minute drive) from riverboat gambling is assumed to be unprofitable with a 35% reduction in revenues and ceases to operate as a live race facility. It is assumed that the remaining racetracks maintain their existing number of racing days and simulcast to off-track-betting facilities in the locations where the racetracks have folded. In those areas, the impact of competition from casino gaming on inter-track wagering (ITW) handle is assumed to be -35%. Churchill Downs, with riverboat gambling in the market area but assumed to be more than 30 minutes away, is assumed to sustain a -25% impact on its live racing. Keeneland and The Red Mile, slightly more insulated from the riverboat gaming competition, are assumed to sustain a -20% impact on their live racing. Finally, Dueling Grounds and the Eastern Kentucky Racing market areas are assumed to be the least impacted by casino gaming at -15% each.

The assumptions for the casino impact by track location on both live and ITW handle were estimated. It is important to note that even though riverboat gaming is assumed to have a -20% impact on live race handle at an inland track, like Keeneland, the impact on total handle is different because of the impact on its ITW signal at other locations in the state, most of which will be near riverboat gaming venues.

D. Scenario 3

This scenario assumes that there is land-based casino gaming in Kentucky, and furthermore, that the casinos are located at each racetrack site. Pari-mutuel wagering at each of the racetracks would likely suffer the maximum decrease possible.[6] Unlike Scenario 1, however, the casinos would be owned by the racetrack associations, and under the proposed plan by *Kentucky To The Front,* the racetracks would continue to provide the live racing product and would not cease operations. Under the proposal of *Kentucky To The Front,* the estimated reduction in purses caused by the direct competition from casino gaming at the racetracks would be offset.

Purses would be increased to the same or greater levels than before the introduction of this new competition. Because purses would not decrease under this proposed plan, revenues to owners and trainers would not decrease and so their employment and expenditures should remain unchanged.

Finally, under the proposed plan of *Kentucky To The Front,* there is a breeder award supplement to Kentucky breeders from racetrack-casino "win." This direct infusion of funds into the Kentucky breeding sector would result in increased employment and expenditures.

Handle and thus employment and expenditures associated with pari-mutuel wagering at the racetracks are expected to decrease as current pari-mutuel wagering patrons divide their fixed incomes between the existing pari-mutuel wagering opportunities and the newly introduced casino gaming opportunities. The impact on handle and the proportional impact on related racing jobs and expenditures is expected to be at the maximum of the range of estimates provided earlier in this report. If purses are supplemented to levels above pre-casino competition levels there is likely to be an increase in handle and related jobs and expenditures due to the "quality" effect.

Although handle and associated employment and expenditures by the racetrack sector of the racetrack-casino are expected to decrease, total employment and expenditures may not decrease if the employment and expenditures by the casino sector of the same racetrack-casino more than offset the declines in the pari-mutuel wagering sector. Estimation of the increase in employment and expenditures attributable to the casino sector of the racetrack-casino is not within the scope of this report.

Finally, it should be mentioned that the live racing product at the racetrack-casinos would exist in the future if that sector of the total portfolio were profitable. Because of the purse supplements, Kentucky racetracks should enjoy a relative national advantage over other racetracks around the country which are also facing competition from casino gaming but which will not receive external funding for purses as is proposed under the *Kentucky To The Front* plan. If purses are supplemented to levels above current levels, the quality effect will be even greater. The provision of live racing signals to out-of-state locations is a highly competitive and potentially lucrative new source of funds for the beleaguered racetrack industry. Those racetracks that provide the highest quality and best-priced products to national and international outlets are likely to be the ones that will retain live racing in the future. Many racetracks with lower quality and higher price of wagering will likely become simulcast outlet sites and cease to provide the unprofitable live racing product. As with the estimate of employment and expenditures of the casino division of the racetrack-

TABLE 13
Direct Economic Impact—Employment

	Tracks	Horsemen	Breeders	Total
Scenario 1: Reduction In Handle=100.0% Reduction In Purses=100.0%	−2,223	−3,961	−473	−6,657
Scenario 2: Reduction In Handle=62.1% Reduction In Purses=62.1%	−1,116	−2,056	−294	−3,466
Scenario 3: Reduction In Handle=38% Reduction In Purses=0% Breeder Awards=$10 million	−850	0	208	−642

casino, an estimate of the increase in out-of-state wagering on Kentucky racing attributable to the relative (and possibly absolute) increase in quality racing is beyond the scope of this project.

E. Summary of Direct Economic Impact

A summary of the direct impact on employment and expenditures of the introduction of casino gaming into the Kentucky pari-mutuel wagering market under scenarios 1 through 3 is summarized in Tables 13 and 14.

The impact of casino gaming on race horse industry employment varies from −642 under Scenario 3 (Kentucky racetrack-casino assumption) to −6,657 (casinos in Kentucky but not at racetrack assumption). Under the assumptions of Scenario 3, there is a negative impact on racetrack employment from the estimated decrease in handle due to location of land based casinos at racetrack sites. However, the net impact on overall employment is likely to be positive since the casino division of the racetrack-casino complex will create additional jobs.

The impact of casino gaming on race horse industry expenditures varies from −$31 million under Scenario 3 (Kentucky racetrack-casino assumption) to −$260 million under Scenario 1 (casinos in Kentucky but not at racetrack assumption). The negative impact of casino gaming on expenditures under Scenario 3 is attributable to the loss in handle and thus spending by the racetrack sector of the race horse industry. Since purses are supplemented to pre-casino levels, no loss in jobs is expected for the horsemen with horses-in-training. A positive impact on breeders is expected due to the direct injection of breeder award money into that sector of the race horse industry.

TABLE 14

Direct Economic Impact—Expenditures

	Tracks	Horsemen	Breeders	Total
Scenario 1: Reduction In Handle=100.0% Reduction In Purses=100.0%	−$107,300,000	−$130,800,000	−$22,000,000	−$260,100,000
Scenario 2: Reduction In Handle=62.1% Reduction In Purses=62.1%	−$55,900,000	−$66,600,000	−$13,600,000	−$136,100,000
Scenario 3: Reduction In Handle=38% Reduction In Purses=0% Breeder Awards=$10 million	−$40,900,000	$0	$10,000,000	−$30,900,000

F. Total (Direct Plus Indirect) Economic Impact

In addition to the direct economic impact of the race horse industry in terms of employment and expenditures, there may be an additional indirect impact created by the introduction of direct employment and expenditures into the economy. For example, total direct spending by race horse owners and trainers for labor, for services from veterinarians, farriers, jockeys, and for inputs such as feed and bedding, create employment and income for businesses in those sectors. A portion of the income to labor that other industries and government created by the initial round of expenditures is diverted to savings and the remainder is spent on other goods and services such as food, clothing, shelter, wholesale, and retail goods, services, and so forth.[7]

G. Economic Impact of Purse Supplements above Existing Levels on Direct Employment and Expenditures

Not included in the economic impact estimates for Scenario 3 are estimates of the effect of purse supplements from casino "win" above pre-casino levels. Econometric demand models for Kentucky Thoroughbred (Thalheimer and Ali, 1991-b) showed an estimated increase in handle for an additional stakes race. An additional $50,000 stakes race on a given day, is expected to result in a 15.4% increase in handle. An additional $100,000 stakes race is expected to result in a 22.1% increase. The addition to handle was found to increase at a decreasing rate as the value of the stakes purse increased. Also, the addition to handle was estimated to decrease with an increase in the number of quality stakes races offered on a given day. For Standardbred racing, an additional quality race of $23,000 was estimated to result in a 7.4% increase in handle on that day, while an additional $46,000 race would add 9.9% to handle. For Standardbred racing, as for Thoroughbred racing, the increase in handle from an additional quality race was seen to decline with an increase in value and/or number of quality races offered on a given day.

In order to evaluate the effect of additional purse supplements, the impact on handle per $1 million in purse supplement above current levels was computed. In order to make this computation, an assumption about the distribution of purse money must be made. In Table 15 it is assumed that the $1 million purse increment for Thoroughbred racing will fund ten $100,000 stakes races to be distributed among all of the Thoroughbred racetracks.[8] For the Standardbred racetracks, it is assumed that $1 million in purse supplements will fund twenty-two $46,000 stakes-quality races.[9] The quality purse configuration that is used in the following example

TABLE 15
Handle Impact of $1 Million Increase in Purses
Above Pre-Casino (1992) Levels

	Thoroughbred	Standardbred/ Quarter
Average Daily Handle-Post Casino Competition	$1,089,533	$45,195
Days	276	135
% Change In Daily Handle Per Additional Quality Race*	22.1%	9.9%
$ Change In Daily Handle Per Additional Quality Race*	$240,787	$4,474
Number Of Quality Races Per $1 Million Purse Increase	10	22
Change In Post-Casino Handle From Additional Quality Races	$2,407,870	$98,428
Post-Casino Handle Before Purse Supplement	$300,711,243	$6,101,352
% Change In Total Handle From Additional Quality Races	0.8%	1.6%

*A quality Thoroughbred race is defined at $100,000 and a quality Standardbred race is defined as $46,000.

should not be taken as a recommendation by the research team for that particular configuration but rather for illustration only.

The additional handle generated by patrons wagering more on races with higher quality is compared to total handle to compute the percent increase in handle and purses above the pre-casino competition level. The computations for the additional $1 million in purse money for both Thoroughbred and Standardbred racetracks are given in the table below. It should be noted again that the configuration (purse value and number of stakes) used is one of many possibilities. The data presented here allow the interested reader to compute the purse impact based on alternative assumptions.

From Table 15 it can be seen that each additional $1 million in purses to fund quality races of $100,000 and $46,000 for Thoroughbred and Standardbred racing, respectively, is estimated to result in respective total handle (and purse) increases of 0.8% and 1.6%.

For horsemen, there is a direct and indirect impact of the change in purses on expenditures and employment. For expenditures, the direct impact of an increase in purses is assumed to go directly to horsemen's revenues and corresponding expenditures. The indirect effect of the increase

TABLE 16

Direct Employment Impact Per $1 Million Additional Purse: Thoroughbred

	Tracks (1)	Horsemen (2)	Breeders (3)	Total
Direct Purse Expenditures ($1 Million=2.1% Increase)		83	9	92
Increase From Additional Handle From Quality Races (4)				
Handle Increase (0.8%)	10			10
Purses (0.8% of $43.3 Million= $386,400)		28	4	32
Total Direct Impact Per $1 Million Increase In Quality Rates	10	111	13	134

(1) Total Post-Casino Employment: 1,236
(2) Total Post-Casino Employment: 3,485
(3) See Computation Procedure In Scenario 2.
(4) Quality Thoroughbred race defined as $100,000 stakes for this example.

in purses from additional wagering and thus purses as a result of offering more quality races is also expected to go directly into horsemen's revenues and thus expenditures. The indirect relationship between purses, foal registrations, horse count, and expenditures per horse or employment per horse for breeding operations as given in Scenarios 2 and 3 is also used in the computations given in the tables below.

H. Employment and Expenditure Impacts of a $1 Million Increase in Purses Above Current Levels

Tables 16 and 17 give the impact on direct employment and expenditures of increasing purse funding from casino revenues to levels above those existing prior to casino competition. The tables show the impact for an additional $1 million in quality races at Kentucky Thoroughbred racetracks.

As shown in Tables 16 and 17, an additional $1 million in quality purses results in an increase of 134 direct jobs and $2.5 million in direct spending in the Thoroughbred race horse industry. One million dollars of the spending increase is due to the direct injection of purse money from casino win while the remaining $1.5 million is due to the induced impact of the ten additional $100,000 stakes races on handle and through handle on racetracks, horsemen with horses-in-training, and breeder expenditures.

Tables 18 and 19 give the impact on direct employment and expenditures of increasing purse funding from casino revenues to levels above

TABLE 17

Direct Expenditure Impact Per $1 Million Additional Purse: Thoroughbred

	Tracks	Horsemen	Breeders (1)	Total
Direct Purse Expenditures		$1,000,000	$439,153	$1,439,153
Increase From Additional Handle From Quality Races (2)				
Expenditure Increase (0.8% × $61.7 million post-casino)	$493,600			
Purses (0.8% × $48.3 million post-casino)		$386,400	$169,289	$555,689
Total Direct Impact Per $1 Million Increase In Quality Races	$493,600	$1,386,400	$608,442	$2,488,442

Note: 0.8% increase in handle assumed to result in 0.8% increase in expenditures and purses.
(1) See Computation Procedure In Scenario 2.
(2) Quality Thoroughbred race defined as $100,000 stakes for this example.

TABLE 18

Direct Employment Impact Per $1 Million Additional Purse: Standardbred

	Tracks (1)	Horsemen (2)	Breeders (3)	Total
Direct Purse Expenditures ($1 Million = 23% Increase)	0	109	2	111
Increase From Additional Handle From Quality Races (4)				
Handle Increase (1.6%)	2			2
Purses (1.6% of $4.3 million = $68,800)		8	0	8
Total Direct Impact Per $1 Million Increase In Quality Races	2	117	2	121

(1) Total Post-Casino Employment: 137
(2) Total Post-Casino Employment: 476
(3) See computation procedure in Scenario 2.
(4) Quality Standardbred race defined as $46,000 purse for this example.

TABLE 19

Direct Expenditure Impact Per $1 Million Additional Purse: Standardbred

	Tracks (1)	Horsemen (2)	Breeders (3)	Total
Direct Purse Expenditures	$0	$1,000,000	$96,180	$1,096,180
Increase From Additional Handle From Quality Races (2)				
Expenditure Increase (1.6% × $4.7 million post-casino)	$75,200			$75,200
Purses (1.6% × $4.3 million post-casino)		$68,800	$0	$68,800
Total Direct Impact Per $1 Million Increase In Quality Races	$75,200	$1,068,800	$96,180	$1,240,180

Note: 1.6% increase in handle assumed to result in 1.6% increase in expenditures and purses. Standardbred includes Bluegrass Downs Quarter Horse for this example.
(1) See computation procedure in Scenario 2.
(2) Quality Standardbred race defined as $46,000 purse for this example.

369

those existing prior to casino competition for the Kentucky Standard-bred racetracks.

As shown in Tables 18 and 19, an additional $1 million in quality purses results in an increase of 121 direct jobs and $1.2 million in direct spending in the Standardbred race horse industry. One million dollars of the spending increase is due to the direct injection of purse money from casino win while the remaining $0.2 million is due to the induced impact of the 22 additional $46,000 stakes races on handle and through handle on racetracks, horsemen with horses-in-training, and breeder expenditures.

I. Additional Considerations

In order for the purse supplement program to be feasible in the long run, the additional handle generated by the supplement should produce revenues that compensate for the additional cost, including an adequate return on investment. For example, as shown in Table 15, handle is expected to increase $2,407,870 for each additional $1 million in quality purses at Thoroughbred racetracks above pre-casino competition levels. The effective takeout rate for Thoroughbred racetracks in 1992 was 19.5%.[10] At this rate, the additional $1 million in purses generates about $470,000 in additional revenues. For Standardbred racetracks, an additional $1 million in quality purses is expected to result in $98,428 in additional handle. At an effective takeout rate of 22.6%, revenues would increase $22,245.

Not included in the total revenue increases at Thoroughbred and Standardbred racetracks are additional attendance-related revenues such as those from admissions, concessions, parking, and programs generated by the expected increase in patron participation. Most importantly, the impact on handle generated from simulcasting the additional quality races to out-of-state locations is not included in the additional revenues. This is an unknown and relatively new factor which enters into the consideration of the profitability of the improved purse program.[11] If purses are supplemented from casino win, the Kentucky racetracks will be better able to compete with other major racetracks on a national level for interstate simulcast revenues. In today's national wagering market, it is reasonable to expect that those racetracks which are able to provide the best quality racing at the lowest price will be those most likely to survive and maintain live racing with its associated jobs and expenditures. Other racetracks, less able to compete, will likely become primarily receiving sites with reduced or even elimination of the live racing product. If the additional intrastate plus interstate handle generated from the investment in better purses more than compensates for the added investment, the undertaking will be profitable and the racetracks will continue to fund added purses and maintain live racing in the long run.

1. For example, purse expenses are excluded since they are covered in the owner/trainer operations impact.
2. Source: Kentucky State Racing Commission, preliminary reports for 1992.
3. For a detailed discussion of sample design see the "full report."
4. For a description of sample design see the "full report."
5. For a detailed description of circumstances surrounding the introduction of casinos in this report see the "full report."
6. It is possible that there would be some alleviation of the maximum impact if new patrons who come to the racetrack to engage in casino gaming also wager on the Kentucky racing product. The size of this impact is not known and is assumed to be small.
7. Estimates of the indirect and total impacts are given in the "full report."
8. See Thalheimer and Ali, 1991b.
9. See Thalheimer and Ali, 1991b.
10. Source: Kentucky Racing Commission.
11. There was no appreciable interstate simulcasting from Kentucky racetracks at the time the study was performed relating changes in handle to changes in quality races (Thalheimer and Ali, 1991b).

REFERENCES

Association of Racing Commissioners International, Inc., *Pari-Mutuel Racing 1990,* A Statistical Summary.

Connecticut Gaming Policy Board, Division of Special Revenue, *Annual Report.*

Doocey, Paul, (1993). "Operators Vie For Gaming Licenses In Indiana," *Gaming and Wagering Business,* December 15, 1993.

Horseman and Fair World, Horseman Publishing Company, Lexington, Kentucky, various issues.

Illinois Gaming Board, *Annual Report and Wagering Study,* 1991.

Illinois Racing Board, *Annual Report.*

Iowa Racing and Gaming Commission, Annual Report.

Kallick, M., D. Suits, T. Dielman, and J. Hybels (1976). *Survey of American Gambling Attitudes and Behavior,* prepared for the Commission on the Review of the National Policy Toward Gambling, by the University of Michigan Survey Research Center, Institute for Social Research, Appendix 2, *Gambling In America.*

Kentucky Racing Commission, Lexington, KY.

Kentucky Thoroughbred Association, Lexington, KY.

Kentucky Thoroughbred Farm Managers Club, Lexington, KY, *Kentucky Thoroughbred Farm Directory 1993.*

Kentucky To The Front, an organization of all Kentucky racetrack associations except Keeneland and Riverside Downs (at the time this report was written).

Lawrence, R. G. and J. Downs (1978). "Costs and Returns of Maryland's Standardbred and Breeders," University of Maryland, Agricultural Experiment Station, AREIS A-11, College Park, 1978.

Lawrence, R. G. (1972). Maryland's Racing Industry: Its Participants, Organization and Economic Impact, University of Maryland, Agricultural Extension Service, MEP 298, December, 1972.

Lawrence, R. G. (1988). "An Economic Look At Kentucky's Equine Industry," Bureau of Economic Research, University Of Louisville, 1988.

Lawrence, R. G., W.R. Jones, and F. E. Bender (1978). "Market Analysis of Maryland's Horse Industry," University of Maryland, Agricultural Experiment Station, MP 927, October, 1978.

Lexington Herald-Leader, "Kentucky Tracks Aren't ruling Out Adding Casinos," June 27, 1993.

Minnesota Gambling Control Commission. Minnesota Racing Commission, *Annual Report,* Bloomington, MN.

Simmons, S. and R. Sharp (1987). "State Lotteries' Effects on Thoroughbred Horse Racing," *Journal Of Policy And Management,* April, 1987, pp. 446–448.

The Blood Horse, Lexington, KY, "Statistics For The 1991 Breeding Season Live Foal Percentages," September 11, 1993.

Thalheimer, R. (1989). "An Analysis of Intra-State Intertrack Wagering, New Jersey—A Case Study," Department of Equine Administration, School of Business, University of Louisville. Published in abbreviated form as "The Impact of Intrastate Intertrack Wagering, Casinos, and a State Lottery on the Demand for Pari-mutuel Horse Racing, New Jersey—A Case Study," in *Gambling and Commercial Gaming: Essays in Business, Economics, Philosophy and Science,* Eadington, W. R., and J. A. Cornelius, eds., University of Nevada, Reno, 1992, 285–294.

Thalheimer, R. and M. M. Ali (1991b). "The Effect of Intra-State ITW and other Key Factors on the Demand for Pari-mutuel Horse Race Wagering in Kentucky," Department of Equine Administration, College of Business and Public Administration, University of Louisville.

Published in journal form as "Demand For Pari-mutuel Horse Race Wagering With Special Reference To Telephone Betting," *Applied Economics,* 24, 1992, 137–42.

Thalheimer, R. and M. M. Ali (1992). "An Analysis of the Impact of Intra-State Intertrack Wagering, A State Lottery and Casino Gambling on Pari-mutuel Horse Race Wagering, New Jersey—An Expanded Analysis," Department of Equine Administration, College of Business and Public Administration, University of Louisville.

Thalheimer, R. and M. M. Ali (1995). "The Demand for Parimutuel Horse Racing and Attendance," *Management Science,* 41, pp. 129–143.

Thalheimer Research Associates (1986). *The Impact of Kentucky's Thoroughbred Racetracks on the Kentucky Economy,* Lexington, KY.

Thalheimer Research Associates (1987). *The Economic Impact of The Thoroughbred and Quarter Horse Racetrack Industry and The Race Horse Breeding Industry on the State of Florida,* Lexington, KY.

The American Racing Manual 1993, Daily Racing Form, Inc., Hightstown, NJ.

The Jockey Club Fact Book 1993, The Jockey Club, New York, New York.

Thoroughbred Times, "Pari-Mutuel Summary for 1992," Lexington, KY, July 30, 1993.

U.S. Department of Commerce, Bureau of Economic Analysis, *Regional Multipliers: A User Handbook For The Regional Input-Output Modeling System (RIMS II),* May, 1992.

U.S. Department of Commerce, Bureau of the Census, *Statistical Abstract of the United States,* 1992.

U.S. Trotting Association, *The Trotting and Pacing Guide,* 1993 Edition, Columbus, Ohio.

Interregional Demand for Casino Gaming: An Analysis of the Impact of New Casino Gaming in Pennsylvania on Atlantic City Casino Revenues

Jeffrey A. Lowenhar, Brian Repsher and Lawrence X. Taylor

During the last several years casino gaming has expanded into numerous jurisdictions across the United States. Rapid growth took the form of land based and riverboat gambling. By the late 1990s, over 25 states had some form of casino-type wagering, and it is anticipated that additional states will pass some form of casino legislation over the next few years

One of the more interesting dimensions of this rapid change in legal status is the effect on demand for gambling in the aggregate, as well as demand within specific markets. This analysis constructs a financial model to forecast revenues and the potential impact of new gaming jurisdictions.

The following is a partial list of variables used in the financial model:

- Casino square footage and mix of dedicated gaming space—tables games versus slots
- Annual market growth—in nominal and real terms
- Gaming statistics
- Projected gaming revenues
- Total population within primary market and tourist market
- Percentage of adult population who approve of recreational gaming
- Estimated market penetration capture rate
- Market share of total visitations
- Estimated per visitation player worth

Along with the financial model, this analysis includes a case study of proposed riverboat gaming in Philadelphia. In 1993 and 1994, there was serious consideration of riverboat casinos along the riverfront in Philadelphia, which would have had significant competitive impacts on Atlantic City's casino industry. The case study analysis assimilates currently available information and historical data to construct a model quantifying the impact that gaming in Southeastern Pennsylvania and Philadelphia would have on Atlantic City, within a reasonable order of magnitude. This includes financial projections based on the estimated number of licenses, revenues from operations and the percentage of revenues derived from the core Atlantic City market. With this case study analysis, we raise questions and provide insight on the negative effects that casino gambling in Southeastern Pennsylvania and Philadelphia would have on the mature gaming industry in Atlantic City.

It should be noted that similar competitive impacts are likely to become more common among casino jurisdictions throughout the United States, and among foreign countries competing for similar player bases. Competition between Iowa and Illinois, between Illinois and Indiana, between Michigan and Ontario, and between Nevada and Indian casinos in California, Arizona and Oregon, all could be analyzed with the methodological tools presented in this analysis.

BACKGROUND

Atlantic City, New Jersey, the world's second largest casino gaming destination, had experienced tremendous growth in terms of revenues and visitor popularity throughout the late 1970's and 1980's with peak visitation of 33 million in 1988. However, from the late 1980s onward, the growth in Atlantic City revenues declined from the previous stellar performance and slowed to a crawl. The decline in casino revenue growth can be attributed to a number of reasons; however, the foremost cause of this recent slowdown was the expansion and legalization of casino gaming across America. Prior to 1991, Atlantic City had an absolute monopoly of legal casino gaming on the East Coast with the only domestic competition coming from the gaming capital of the world, Las Vegas, Nevada.

The expansion of casino gaming has its roots in the changing mores and norms of society. Recreational casino wagering has become a socially acceptable form of entertainment. As society has modified its stance on casino gaming, the legalization of the gaming product has spread.

State and local governments, looking for ways to supplant their budgetary coffers, have realized the enormous revenue generating and economic development potential associated with casino gaming. With the approval of their constituents, states and local municipalities enacted legislation legalizing casino gaming in its various forms. This extensive growth in the availability of casino gaming took the form of riverboat gaming operations, floating dockside facilities, Indian casino gaming, casinos at racetracks, or outright casino development.

THE POSSIBILITY OF GAMING IN SOUTHEASTERN PENNSYLVANIA AND PHILADELPHIA AND ITS EFFECT ON ATLANTIC CITY

In the early 1990s, the issue of casino gaming within the State of Pennsylvania and City of Philadelphia was actively discussed. This issue gained additional urgency as a result of the ongoing expansion of casino gaming throughout the country. If such casinos were authorized in Pennsylvania, it would provide many opportunities for savvy casino operators to develop and expand into the newly created Pennsylvania gaming market. However, for Atlantic City, the introduction of casino gaming within Pennsylvania—and particularly within the Southeastern Pennsylvania and Philadelphia areas—would have a dramatic negative impact on its casino industry.

It is the position of the authors that riverboat gaming in the Keystone state and particularly in Southeastern Pennsylvania and Philadelphia, given the state's population and familiarity with casino gaming, would be popular and successful with rational enabling legislation permits. The population distribution and the available river frontage would allow for development of full-scale riverboat casino complexes.

The purpose of this analysis is to estimate the probable impact that casino gaming—both cruising riverboat and stationary dockside scenarios—in Southeastern Pennsylvania and the Philadelphia areas would have on Atlantic City.

A RECENT HISTORY OF RIVERBOAT GAMING

A listing of states with some form of casino wagering as of early 1998 is represented in Table 1.

The explosion in riverboat casino gaming throughout the United States started in April 1991 when Iowa, which had approved the first riverboat legislation in March 1989, commenced riverboat casino operations. The industry then grew exponentially for the next four years as new jurisdictions came into play.

Table 2 represents the absolute revenue generated by riverboat gaming jurisdictions throughout the United States.

Since inception, riverboat casinos have generated almost $22.0 billion in gross casino revenues and will continue to grow as new jurisdictions are approved. Together with Class III gaming on Indian tribal lands, this growth in the newly created gaming locations will work to gradually erode the monopoly Atlantic City once had on gaming with the eastern United States.

TABLE 1
States with Some Form of Casino Gaming

State	Type	State	Type
Arizona	Indian	Montana	Indian, Slot Route Operations
California	Indian	Nevada	Land-based, Indian
Colorado	Mining Town, Indian	New Jersey	Land-based
Connecticut	Indian	New Mexico	Indian
Delaware	Race Track	New York	Indian
Illinois	Riverboat	North Dakota	Indian
Indiana	Riverboat	Oregon	Indian
Iowa	Riverboat, Indian, Race Track	Rhode Island	Race Tracks
Louisiana	Riverboat, Indian, Land-based (approved, not yet operating)	South Carolina	Slot Route Operations
Mississippi	Dockside, Indian	South Dakota	Mining Town, Indian
Michigan	Indian, Land-based (approved, not yet operating)	Washington	Indian
Missouri	Riverboat	West Virginia	Race Track
Minnesota	Indian	Wisconsin	Indian

CASINOS IN ATLANTIC CITY

Atlantic City commenced gaming operations on May 26, 1978 when Resorts International ushered in a new chapter in the history of casino gaming. Since then, twelve other Atlantic City properties opened—including the ill-fated Playboy/Atlantis casino.

The Atlantic City casino market, given its proximity to the major urban population centers of the Northeast, is by definition a day trip market. Atlantic City is, with Las Vegas and Orlando, one of the most frequently visited destinations in the United States, hosting more than 30 million visitors coming to the resort area each year.

Located only two hours away from the metropolitan areas of New York and within 90 minutes of Northern New Jersey and Eastern Pennsylvania, Atlantic City caters to a core of drive-in and bus passengers—a repeat visitation consumer market. It has been estimated that nearly 80% of all visitors who come to Atlantic City stay on average less than eight hours.

TABLE 2
United States Riverboat Gaming Revenue Performance (In $000s)

State	1991	1992	1993	1994	1995	1996	1997
Iowa	63,587	69,806	45,446	104,839	238,967	395,418	441,890
Illinois	14,293	226,608	503,598	979,549	1,178,312	1,131,491	1,054,573
Mississippi	0	121,808	789,836	1,469,924	1,721,109	1,866,231	1,988,769
Louisiana	0	0	16,234	603,686	1,051,440	1,209,524	1,244,568
Missouri	0	0	0	110,341	466,430	571,097	745,671
Indiana	0	0	0	0	6,203	372,008	961,936
Total	71,510	418,222	1,455,114	3,268,339	4,662,461	5,545,769	6,437,407
Growth in US		432%	248%	125%	43%	19%	16%

379

The remaining 20% of the visitors to the city comprise overnight hotel guests who stay on average less than two nights.

The primary trading area for Atlantic City consists of New Jersey, New York, Pennsylvania, Massachusetts, Maryland, Connecticut, Rhode Island, Florida, Delaware and Washington, DC. It is from these states, and Washington, DC, that Atlantic City draws nearly 98% of all its visitors.

The core market for Atlantic City is the four states of New Jersey, New York, Delaware and Pennsylvania. These states have a combined population base of approximately 39 million people. The actual gaming population potential from these states—approximately 26 million—is two-thirds of the total, with the balance of population being under age. This provides Atlantic City with a substantial local population base to which it can market its gaming products. It has been estimated from various governmental and tourism agencies that about 90% of total visitations to Atlantic City are derived from these four states.

The remaining portion of Atlantic City's visitations are derived from residents of Maryland, Virginia, Connecticut, Rhode Island, Delaware, Washington DC, Florida, and Maine. This information has been confirmed through proprietary casino research conducted by the authors at several Atlantic City properties over the past 10 years.

This information on the Atlantic City visitor profile has been obtained and verified by independent state and local governments, tourism agencies, and through sponsored research by the individual Atlantic City casinos. Given the proprietary nature of selected research information and to protect the confidentiality of information, we have offered a reasonable order of magnitude range of the number adults who visit Atlantic City each year from the four-state areas, their average number of annual visitations, and average casino win per visit for this analysis.

CASINO REVENUE PERFORMANCE OF ATLANTIC CITY

The immediate surrounding population base and growth of Atlantic City's casino industry supply of table and slot units have allowed Atlantic City to flourish. Atlantic City casino revenues climbed from a mere $325 million in 1979 to $1 billion in 1981 to over $3.9 billion in 1997. At the end of 1997, Atlantic City's gross gaming revenue of $3.9 billion was divided into approximately 70% slot revenues and 30% table revenues. Table game revenues, which once accounted for nearly 58% of the market in the early 1980's, now account for only 30% of the revenue mix.

The growth in slot revenues is a function of the increase in the number of units and in new slot product offerings (better pay-outs, video poker devices, etc.). Slot revenue growth caters to the aging marketplace of Atlantic City's day-trippers. With an average age of 55 and over during the midweek and with almost three-quarters of females playing slot machines as their favorite game, it is not surprising that this shift in behavior has occurred. The additional fact that video poker has increased in popularity over the past decade has also driven a number of male low-limit to moderate-limit table players to the video poker product.

In sum, understanding Atlantic City's primary market of New Jersey, New York, Delaware and Pennsylvania and the behavioral profile of the customer base one could possibly predict the potentially significant impact upon Atlantic City casino revenues, if some form of casino gaming was legalized in any of these nearby locations.

THE PROPOSED PENNSYLVANIA RIVERBOAT MODEL

In June of 1993, a first draft of House Bill 1883 calling for the legalization of casino gaming on navigable waterways within the State of Pennsylvania was presented to the General Assembly of Pennsylvania. The bill, in part, proposed an Act that would have authorized casino gambling on excursion riverboats. If approved by the state legislature, the bill would have been presented to the Pennsylvania Governor for signature or veto. This did not happen.

House Bill 1883 called for approximately twenty casino licenses strategically scattered throughout the state. The bill stated that the riverboats must cruise and no gaming activities shall take place until the boat has left the dock (with the exception of special circumstances). If it had been approved, riverboat gaming in western Pennsylvania—Pittsburgh, Erie, etc.—and central Pennsylvania (Harrisburg) would have had a minimal impact on Atlantic City revenues compared to gaming in the Southeastern part of the state—Philadelphia and its suburbs. Therefore, the balance of this analysis focuses on the proposed riverboat operations for the Southeastern Pennsylvania and Philadelphia areas.

THE SOUTHEASTERN PENNSYLVANIA AND PHILADELPHIA CASINO MARKET

Using the above cited bill as a benchmark, five or six casino licenses would have been issued within the City of Philadelphia with an additional one or two licenses in the nearby suburbs of Philadelphia (Bucks, Chester, and Delaware Counties). As noted earlier, the four-state area of New Jersey, New York, Delaware and Pennsylvania contributes about 90% of Atlantic City visitations. It is estimated that the Southeastern Pennsylvania and Philadelphia area residents account for about 25% of Atlantic City's annual visitations.

Examining the potential market for Southeastern Pennsylvania and

TABLE 3
Potential Dilution of Atlantic City's Casino Product

	Existing Atlantic City 1996–97	Estimated S.E. Pennsylvania 1996–97	Percent Dilution 1996–97
Casino Licenses	12	8	
Casino Square Footage	1,033,000	200–250,000	20–25%
Table Games	1,400	300–350	20–25%
Slot Machines	31,519	4,500–5,000	15–20%

Philadelphia area riverboat operations, the following areas would be considered the core trading area for the proposed casino riverboat operations:

- Philadelphia County, Pennsylvania—the immediate market
- Bucks County, Pennsylvania—to the north
- Delaware County, Pennsylvania—to the south
- Chester County, Pennsylvania—to the south
- Montgomery County, Pennsylvania—to the west
- Camden County, New Jersey—to the east
- Northern State of Delaware—to the south

These riverboats would be in direct competition with Atlantic City for casino visitors from these overlapping markets. The total of six to eight riverboat licenses in the immediate area could have potentially added an additional 200,000 to 250,000 square feet of casino gaming space to the current industry casino supply within the market, as well as an additional 300 to 350 table games and 4,500 to 5,000 slot machines. Table 3 shows the expansion of casino square footage and gaming devices as well as the dilution experienced by the Atlantic City casino industry.

ATLANTIC CITY'S PRODUCT OFFERING VERSUS SOUTHEASTERN PENNSYLVANIA AND PHILADELPHIA RIVERBOATS

The Atlantic City casino industry has a diverse gaming product to offer the discriminating casino customer. Atlantic City casinos have invested billions of dollars of capital for their casino hotel facilities and offer the consumer a complete gaming and entertainment experience.

Atlantic City can offer the casino gambler certain amenities that Southeastern Pennsylvania and Philadelphia riverboat operations would be unable to match. Direct access to hotel rooms, gourmet restaurants, and entertainment venues are several incentives offered to consumers by Atlantic City casinos. Also, from a service standpoint, Atlantic City has the most sophisticated and experienced casino gaming employees on the East Coast.

Because actual legislation in Pennsylvania never passed, for purposes of this analysis the authors assumed the types of riverboat casinos would be similar to existing riverboat operations in Illinois and Louisiana. This would make casino riverboat gaming in Pennsylvania, compared to Atlantic City's casinos, convenient with respect to proximity, but inconvenient in the sense of providing an artificially constrained environment for gaming.

Understanding how riverboat gaming currently operates in Illinois and Louisiana highlights several of the advantages Atlantic City would have over Pennsylvania. In order to go on a riverboat excursion, one must first purchase a ticket in advance for a predetermined cruise. The customer must then board the vessel, and wait until it leaves port to begin gaming. Customers are forced to remain onboard for the duration of the cruise. The typical riverboat cruise lasts around two to three hours, in which time customers are returned to the dock and must cease gaming activities. The dedicated consumer who enjoys recreational wagering and takes advantage of the variety of offerings at Atlantic City casinos may find this arrangement inconvenient and unsatisfying. Many of these consumers may eventually choose to return to Atlantic City because of these differences.

CRUISING RIVERBOAT SCENARIO

Financial Implications of Southeastern Pennsylvania and Philadelphia Riverboats on Atlantic City

An analysis of the market for Atlantic City, taken together with the immediate Southeastern Pennsylvania and Philadelphia riverboat market, provides an estimate of the market potential for the casino riverboats. The purpose of this exercise is twofold. First, it provides an order of magnitude for the market potential for the Southeastern Pennsylvania and Philadelphia riverboat industry. Second, it assists in forecasting casino revenues that would be cannibalized from current Atlantic City revenues. Two independent analyses were produced to provide internal verification as to the reliability of the revenue estimates.

A population-based model was developed to analyze the immediate population within the expected core market for the Southeastern Pennsylvania and Philadelphia area riverboats. For this model, it was assumed that Philadelphia and its outlying suburbs, Eastern New Jersey, and Northern Delaware would comprise the majority of visitors to the Southeastern Pennsylvania and Philadelphia riverboat operations. This was supported by the Illinois riverboat experience that indicates the direct market for these casino operations is primarily the local population base. Estimates were then made using known casino visitation patterns from other riverboat jurisdictions, as well as current visiting patterns of Atlantic City patrons from proprietary casino research information. This provided the estimate for the total casino revenue potential for the Philadelphia riverboat industry.

A critical secondary analysis examined the current player database of a major casino operator in Atlantic City. The database was segmented based upon geographic residency and examined the number of patrons who visit Atlantic City from the predefined Southeastern Pennsylvania and Philadelphia market. This took into account the total number of players from the proposed market area. These players were further segmented by type of player (table player or slot player) and by trip worth (based upon historical gaming activity). This information was then extrapolated to yield the projected number of patrons who visit Atlantic City from the Southeastern Pennsylvania and Philadelphia target market area. Additional estimates were made for the number of patrons who are members of other Atlantic City casino databases, the number of non-rated retail customers who visit Atlantic City from the area, and for a newly created customer base for riverboat casino operations. This provided a secondary estimate for the total potential for the riverboat industry, based upon actual proprietary information from the Atlantic City market.

These analyses yielded similar projected estimates of the total casino revenue market potential for the Southeastern Pennsylvania and Philadelphia cruising riverboat scenario. This forecast the total number of dollars that could be expected to be wagered in any Southeastern Pennsylvania and Philadelphia casino based upon population and consumer behavioral information. The resulting forecast for the Southeastern Pennsylvania and Philadelphia area riverboat casino industry for the first year of complete operations is $450 million to $500 million in casino revenues per annum. At maturity, riverboat casino revenues could exceed $750 million up to $1.0 billion per annum.

These preliminary estimates are internally consistent with the population based modeling scenario using demographic (population, age, income levels, etc.) and consumer behavioral information. These estimates of Southeastern Pennsylvania and Philadelphia gaming potential are consistent with projections on a win per visitation, per device (per table game and per slot machine), and per square foot for the riverboat gaming jurisdictions of Illinois and Mississippi. This forecast also implies an expected range of annual visits of 8.0 to 9.0 million; with an average casino win per visit of between $56 to $62.

Financial Impact of Southeastern Pennsylvania and Philadelphia Riverboats on Atlantic City

When forecasting the revenue impact upon Atlantic City casinos, assumptions were made regarding the number of customers from the various market areas and the types of customer who would visit the Southeastern Pennsylvania riverboats instead of Atlantic City. In simplistic terms, the prevailing belief was that the lower limit slot and table player would be the most likely candidate to patronize the casino riverboats. The majority of Atlantic City's existing mid-level and higher-end customer base would still patronize Atlantic City casinos as the service and experience levels would exceed those initially offered by the riverboats.

The internal analysis used to support the authors' position analyzed the player database of one of Atlantic City's casino operations. This analysis examined the players' demographic and behavioral information regarding type of player (table versus slots, length of play, average wager, etc.), the number of annual visits, the player's per trip worth, and the percentage mix of players across the gaming worth spectrum.

This information resulted in the estimates of a "hypothetical" transfer of gaming dollars from the Atlantic City revenue base to the newly created casino gaming market in Southeastern Pennsylvania and Philadelphia. Of the total projected gaming revenue generated by the Southeastern Pennsylvania and Philadelphia riverboat casino industry, it is estimated that between 80% to 85% would come at the expenses of Atlantic City casino revenues. This "hypothetical" transfer of gaming dollars from the Atlantic City casino industry to the newly created Southeastern Pennsylvania and Philadelphia riverboat casino industry amounts to approximately $375 million to $425 million in casino revenues per annum.

Impact on a Specific Atlantic City Casino Operation from Southeastern Pennsylvania and Philadelphia Riverboat Casino Operations

Total casino revenue loss to the industry is only the headline. From each of the twelve casino operators' viewpoints, the impact on the property's financial statements is a major concern.

Information was obtained from the year end financial statements for a typical Atlantic City casino for the year ending 1996. The effect of the decrease of Atlantic City's casino revenues attributed to the Southeastern Pennsylvania and Philadelphia riverboat casino industry was extrapolated on a per casino basis based solely on expected market share of gross gaming revenues. Table 4 shows the relative impact upon an individual casino property's gross gaming revenues given only a conservative 10% decrease in Atlantic City casino industry revenues.

Property's Market Share and Resulting Casino Revenues

Utilizing the above revenue forecasts, this information was then incorporated with historical expense information to show the potential reduction in gross operating profit and ultimately the effect upon a casino property's net income.

As noted previously, revenues were expected to decrease by 10% and it was assumed each individual property would lose its fair share of revenues.

TABLE 4

Projected Gross Gaming Revenues After Southeastern Pennsylvania
and Philadelphia Begin Riverboat Casino Operations

Reduction in Gaming Revenues 1996–97		Existing Atlantic City Revenues 1996–97*	Post S.E. Pennsylvania Operations 1996–97*
$425		$3,900	$3,470
Casino Market Share	$ Reduction in Gaming Revenues*	Casino Revenues Pre- S.E. Pennsylvania Operations*	Casino Revenues Post- S.E. Pennsylvania Operations*
13.5%	$57	$527	$469
13.0%	$55	$507	$452
12.5%	$53	$488	$434
12.0%	$51	$468	$417
11.5%	$49	$449	$400
11.0%	$47	$429	$382
10.5%	$45	$410	$365
10.0%	$42	$390	$348
9.5%	$40	$371	$330
9.0%	$38	$351	$313
8.5%	$36	$332	$295
8.0%	$34	$312	$278
7.5%	$32	$293	$261
7.0%	$30	$273	$243
*In Millions			

Expenses were forecast to decline, but less than revenues for a variety of reasons:

- Several expenses incurred, such as utilities, insurance, etc., are fixed expenses for casino operations. These costs are incurred independent of reductions of volume;
- A reduction in the number of employees will result due to the decrease in visitor volume;
- However, the potential cost saving from employee reductions may be limited as some positions are required by regulatory mandate, and may not disappear with the reduction in volume (i.e., security, surveillance, finance, compliance, etc.);
- Marketing costs will increase as Atlantic City casinos will be forced to strengthen efforts to attract and retain their existing customer bases against competition from Pennsylvania;
- Promotional allowances as a percentage of casino revenues will increase due to the competition from Pennsylvania and other Atlantic City casinos attempting to retain customers and cannibalize customers from other Atlantic City casinos by offering better value.

An example of a typical Atlantic City casino property with a 60,000–75,000 square foot casino, 8.0% casino revenue market share and the following operating income statement shows the effect upon a single "hypothetical" Atlantic City casino (see Table 5).

So far, this analysis shows the impact upon earnings from operations. Additional non-operating expenses such as debt service expense, income and related taxes, and capital expenditures will further erode the net income. It would become increasingly difficult for several Atlantic City casinos to meet their current debt service and other obligations given this estimated decline in revenues and income.

These projections are for the legalization of riverboat casino gaming in Philadelphia. If the legislation were to allow dockside casino gaming, the impact upon Atlantic City could be twice the estimates generated for the cruising riverboat model. Resulting revenue and income losses would require draconian decisions by management—a survival strategy for the weaker competitors. This topic is examined in the following section.

STATIONARY DOCKSIDE RIVERBOAT SCENARIO

Casino Revenue Projections of Southeastern Pennsylvania and Philadelphia Dockside Casinos on Atlantic City

Using the same methodology as for the cruising riverboat model, preliminary estimates of dockside casino gaming revenue estimates for the South-

TABLE 5

Projected Impact on Atlantic City Casino Properties After Southeastern
Pennsylvania and Philadelphia Begin Riverboat Casino Operations

	Prior to SE Pennsylvania* 1996	Post SE Pennsylvania 1996–97*	Change*
Casino revenue	$310	$275	($35)
Room revenue	20	17	(3)
Food & Beverage	45	40	(5)
Other	15	13	(2)
Total Revenue	$390	$345	($45)
Less: Promotional Allowance	$45	$45	$0
Net Revenue	$345	$300	($45)
Cost of Goods	$175	$155	$20
SGA	85	80	5
Prov. for D/A	5	5	0
Total Expenses	$265	$245	$20
Gross Profit	$80	$60	($20)
Gross Margin	20%	17%	(25% or 3 points)
*In Millions $			

eastern Pennsylvania and Philadelphia casino industry for the first year of
complete operations are $900 million to $1 billion in casino revenues per
annum. At maturity, dockside casino revenues could exceed $1.2 billion
per annum. Using the same methodology for calculating hypothetical
transfer of gaming dollars from the Atlantic City casino industry to the
newly created Southeastern Pennsylvania and Philadelphia dockside casino industry amounts to approximately $750 million to $850 million in
casino revenues per annum.

Impact on a Specific Atlantic City Casino Operation Resulting from Southeastern Pennsylvania and Philadelphia Dockside Casino Operations

Information was obtained from the year end financial statements for a
typical Atlantic City casino for the year ending 1996. The effect of the
decrease of Atlantic City's casino revenues attributed to the Southeastern
Pennsylvania and Philadelphia dockside casino industry was extrapolated

TABLE 6

Projected Gross Gaming Revenues After Southeastern Pennsylvania
and Philadelphia Begin Dockside Casino Operations

Reduction in Gaming Revenues 1996–97*		Existing Atlantic City Revenues 1996–97*	Post S.E. Pennsylvania Operations 1996–97*
$850		$3,900	$3,050
Casino Market Share	$ Reduction in Gaming Revenues*	Casino Revenues Pre- S.E. Pennsylvania Operations*	Casino Revenues Post- S.E. Pennsylvania Operations*
13.5%	$115	$527	$412
13.0%	$111	$507	$397
12.5%	$106	$488	$381
12.0%	$102	$468	$366
11.5%	$98	$449	$351
11.0%	$94	$429	$336
10.5%	$89	$410	$320
10.0%	$85	$390	$305
9.5%	$81	$371	$290
9.0%	$77	$351	$275
8.5%	$72	$332	$259
8.0%	$68	$312	$244
7.5%	$64	$293	$229
7.0%	$60	$273	$214
*In Millions			

on a per casino basis based solely upon market share of gross gaming revenues. Table 6 shows the relative impact upon an individual casino property's gross gaming revenues given a 20% decrease in Atlantic City casino industry revenues.

Property's Market Share and Resulting Casino Revenues

Utilizing the above revenue forecasts, this information was then incorporated with historical expense information to show the potential reduction in gross operating profit and ultimately the effect upon a casino property's net income.

The effect of dockside casino gaming on a "hypothetical" Atlantic City

TABLE 7

Impact on an Atlantic City Casino Property after Southeastern Pennsylvania
and Philadelphia Begins Dockside Casino Operations

	Prior to SE Pennsylvania* 1996	Post SE Pennsylvania 1996–97	Change
Casino revenue	$310	$245	($65)
Room revenue	20	15	(5)
Food & Beverage	45	30	(15)
Other	15	5	(10)
Total Revenue	$390	$295	($95)
Less: Promotional Allowance	$45	$40	$5
Net Revenue	$345	$255	($90)
Cost of Goods	$175	$130	$45
SGA	85	80	5
Prov. for D/A	5	5	0
Total Expenses	$265	$220	$45
Gross Profit	$80	$40	($40)
Gross Margin	20%	14%	(30% or 6 points)
*In Millions $			

casino property with a 60,000–75,000 square foot casino, 8.0% casino revenue market share with the following operating income statement is as shown in Table 7.

As with the previous analysis, additional non-operating expenses such as debt service expense, income and related taxes, and capital expenditures will further erode the net income.

With this scenario of dockside gaming and competition from Southeastern Pennsylvania, there would almost certainly be a reduction in the number of casinos competing in the Atlantic City marketplace. The resulting casino market revenue base would be thinly distributed between Atlantic City and Pennsylvania casino operations. Several of the less financially stable casino operations in Atlantic City would be forced to close their doors if the scenario of full scale dockside casino gaming were to be permitted in Pennsylvania.

HOW ATLANTIC CITY COULD MINIMIZE THE FINANCIAL IMPACT FROM LEGALIZATION OF PENNSYLVANIA CASINO OPERATIONS

From a strategic marketing standpoint, Atlantic City's strengths as a total gaming resort and entertainment product would have to be used in its marketing efforts to mitigate the amount of potential impact that Southeastern Pennsylvania casinos would have upon Atlantic City's casino revenues. This marketing position—fully supported by a united casino industry—would be difficult to obtain. A potential conflict of interest would arise from casino operators positioned to have casino operations in both Atlantic City and in Pennsylvania. The operators may not support such marketing and promotional efforts sponsored by the Atlantic City casino industry.

Atlantic City casinos would have to emphasize their strengths and competitive position over the Philadelphia operations. Atlantic City could focus on their existing casino facilities and tourism infrastructure, on the convenience of casino gaming versus riverboat style gaming, and on the diversity of their tourist product offering. They could also emphasize a more complete entertainment experience, their appeal to higher-end customers in light of the capital investment in their properties, complimentary support services—hotel, food and beverage, entertainment, etc.—and other resort offerings.

These efforts would help to mitigate the impacts of Pennsylvania casino legalization on the Atlantic City casino industry. However, there is no way the adverse competitive impacts of such actions could be fully neutralized.

SOURCES OF INFORMATION

The following sources were utilized in the preparation of this analysis:

Atlantic City Casino Chronicle
Casino Journal's *National Gaming Summary*
Greater Atlantic City Hotel & Motel Association
Greater Atlantic City Chamber of Commerce
Greater Atlantic City Convention and Visitors Bureau
Greater Atlantic City Hotel & Motel Association
General Assembly of Pennsylvania House Bill 1883 (1994)
Greater Atlantic City Tourism Marketing and Master Plan January 1990
New Jersey Casino Association
New Jersey Division of Travel and Tourism
Riverboat Gaming Report
South Jersey Department of Transportation

State of Illinois Gaming Board
Sate of Iowa Gaming Board
State of Mississippi Gaming Board
State of Louisiana Gaming Board
State of Missouri Gaming Board
State of Indiana Gaming Board

The Changing Southern California Market: Implications for the Southern Nevada Gaming Industry*

J. Kent Pinney, Lawrence Dandurand, and Mary Alice Maloney

The Southern Nevada gaming industry has relied heavily on the Southern California market for many decades. In 1976, research indicated that "Las Vegas obtain(ed) 82% of its gambler market from Southern California. . . . "(Pinney et al., 1976). Although the dependency on Southern Californians has dropped dramatically—down to 27% of all visitors to Las Vegas in 1992—this still represents a significant portion of visitors sustaining the industry (GLS Research 1991, 1992).

Much of the proportional decline of the Southern California market has been attributed to the changing nature of gaming, the local, domestic, and international gaming public, the local, domestic, and international infrastructures, Southern Nevada product markets, target markets, and market niches, and marketing, operations, and financial strategies. However, it is also affected by the changing demand structure of the Southern California market. Included in this change is the rapid growth in minority groups with their unique socio-demographics, lifestyles, values, and propensity to gamble. This, in turn, has had a major impact on the changing supply structure in Las Vegas as exemplified in the emerging marketing of the family destination image.

This paper examines the changing demographics of the Southern California market from 1980 through 1992, considers projected changes through 2000 and indicates the impact of these changes on the Southern Nevada gaming industry. The purpose of this paper is to identify those elements of the Southern California market that are undergoing dramatic

---

* *Editor's note*: The data in this paper focuses on the time period from the late 1980s through 1992 and the trends occurring at that point in time. This was an important time frame for Las Vegas in that it was the beginning of the refocusing of the gaming industry and the introduction of the mega-resorts.

changes and to describe how these changes may impact the Las Vegas gaming industry into the 21st Century.

Specific emphasis in this paper is placed on data research to determine whether or not the following conclusions can be substantiated:

1) The composition of the Southern California market is changing dramatically. These changes most assuredly will dictate the marketing strategies of Southern Nevada gaming properties well into the 21st Century.

2) These changing market conditions—specifically, rapidly growing minority groups with traditionally lower incomes, lower levels of education, and larger families—will dictate a change in the marketing strategies of Southern Nevada gaming properties.

3) There has been a net migration outward of both businesses and professionals from Southern California which will have a noticeable effect on the composition of the Southern California market and, consequently, will have an impact on the marketing strategies of many of Southern Nevada's gaming properties.

4) These ongoing changes in Southern California have been the basis, in part, for the emergence of family niche marketing of selected Southern Nevada gaming properties. The purpose of this paper is to review the available demographic data concerning this important demand sector and to provide some observations of how these demographic factors might alter the marketing strategies of Southern Nevada gaming properties.[1]

BACKGROUND OF GAMING IN SOUTHERN NEVADA

For many years the State of Nevada has enjoyed the exclusivity of being the only legalized casino-based gambling state in the country. For most of its existence, Southern Nevada—with particular emphasis on Las Vegas and, more recently, Laughlin—has survived, in large part, due to the repeated loyalty of the Southern California market. The close ties between Southern California's dynamic economy and its impact on the Southern Nevada gaming industry cannot be denied. A healthy Southern California economy has been a reliable source of support in gaming revenue for Las Vegas when other parts of the country would oscillate in and out of periods of recession. Unfortunately, reliability also meant dependence on Southern California as a primary source of economic survival.

A. The Changing Southern Nevada Gaming Industry

In 1969, the enactment of the Corporate Gaming Act allowed companies with publicly traded stock to invest in and operate casinos in Nevada. The impact of this legislation was the initiation of a totally new direction for Las Vegas and other communities in Southern Nevada such as Laughlin, Mesquite and Primm (formerly, Stateline). The emergence of gambling properties owned and operated by corporations rapidly took hold.

"The first big arrivals included Hilton and Holiday, which legitimized gaming for Wall Street and allowed such 'homegrown' companies as Circus Circus, Caesars, Mirage Resorts (formerly Golden Nugget) and others to reach the public market. Gaming became the engine of many of these companies. . . . Niche properties, appealing to a host of market tastes and needs, emerged in the two primary submarkets, the Strip and downtown" (Salomon Brothers 1992).

At the same time, the convention center was established to entice conventioneers to take advantage of Las Vegas convention facilities. The resulting growth created more jobs, causing a significant increase in the population. This now made Las Vegas more vulnerable to the effects of economic downturn, especially in Southern California.

In 1981, Las Vegas had a taste of the effects of a sour economy when overly optimistic real estate developers, coupled with avaricious casino property owners, exceeded the demand of their stale offerings. The label of "sin city," with its array of lounge acts, nude shows, cheap meals, and casino gambling, was becoming less of a draw for the average tourist. Spending by tourists grew less than 1% and visitor volume actually declined (*Wall Street Journal* 1990). "During the 1981–82 recession, real gaming revenues contracted by 6%. . . . "(Salomon Brothers 1992). This meant layoffs in the industry, something unaccustomed to Las Vegas. As stated by R. Keith Schwer, Director for the Center for Business and Economic Research, at the University of Nevada, Las Vegas, in an interview in the December 31, 1990 issue of the *Wall Street Journal:* "You must remember that the people who have been successful in this town have always had their feet on the gas pedal. . . . The movers and shakers have not been conditioned to deal with great economic downturns."

The response from Southern Nevada leaders was an attempt to diversify the Las Vegas economy in areas that would be unrelated to the gaming industry. In 1983, a law was passed in Nevada that allowed interstate banking which led to the establishment of a credit card distribution center owned by Citibank (*Wall Street Journal* 1990). While its opening created 2,000 jobs unrelated to gaming, no other major companies followed suit. In the meantime, the casino industry was not standing idly by.

True to the classic Las Vegas approach, when the going got tough, the tough got going. In the 1980s, plans for expansion of existing casino-hotels and related facilities accelerated. Hotel additions and casino renovations consumed the gaming properties like a virus. Among those which were bitten by the expansion bug included the Golden Nugget, Frontier, Flamingo Hilton, Tropicana, Bally's and the Dunes as well as three properties that included their own convention centers in the expansion—the Sahara, the Sands, and the Riviera. The community's own convention center began an expansion as well. The number of hotel rooms increased from 45,800 in 1980 to nearly 77,000 in 1991 maintaining between 85% to 89% occupancy level which was well above the 1989 national average of 67% (LVCVA 1990).

It was during this time that Las Vegas began evolving from its historical image as just a gambling town. Yet, the focus of this phase was in expanding the convention base to entice first-time visitors to return while continuing to use a very much adult-oriented array of product offerings. "Convention revenues and attendance grew at blistering annual compound rates of 30.7% and 9.5% per year, respectively, over the 1980–85 period" (Salomon Brothers 1992).

These changes not only gave the casinos a new lift, but the town itself began changing from one that was mostly transient into the true development of a community. The expansions caused the population to increase rapidly over that decade nearly doubling—from 450,000 to 830,000 by 1990—making Las Vegas the fastest growing metropolitan area in the country (Eadington 1992).

Equally, the 1980s were pegged as a decade of unprecedented growth in the gaming industry in Southern Nevada. For Clark County, gross gaming revenue showed an increase of $2.3 billion in the 10-year period 1982–1991. At the same time, gross gaming revenue for Las Vegas almost doubled by $1.6 billion. The growth in visitor volume went from 11.6 million in 1982 to 21.3 million in 1991, showing an increase of 9.7 million visitors over the ten-year period, while the range of average win-per-visitor went from $141 in 1986 to a high of $163 in 1990.

By the mid-1980s, another force in the gaming industry began to really take hold. Local casinos, namely, those gaming properties that catered to the local residents, began attracting attention through competitively priced food, gaming, and accessibility (Eadington 1992). The market demand for local casinos came about due to the tremendous population boom.

The emergence of the mega-casinos began in 1989 with the opening of The Mirage, located near the "four corners" of the famous Strip and Flamingo Avenue, at a price tag of $620 million. Its exorbitant price tag could be attributed to its unusual product offerings that included its exotic atmosphere and attractions such as a rare white tiger exhibit, a dolphin show and an eye-opening re-creation of an active volcano that erupted at scheduled intervals. One might argue the Mirage was the first gaming property to offer something of value for the entire family, certainly something new for a community known for its adult-oriented entertainment.

In mid-1990, the Excalibur, with its location further south on the Strip, became the second mega-resort to enter the market. Although its product offerings would not rival the attractions of the Mirage, Excalibur's medieval theme, prime location and reasonable rates created its own market niche, although it, too, offered the market place a more family-oriented environment and sources of entertainment. In October 1993, Treasure Island began the next wave of family-oriented attractions, followed by the MGM Grand Theme Park and the pyramid-shaped Luxor.

One should not conclude that this new surge in family-oriented attractions was an indication of the industry separating from its gaming base but, rather, was a response in large part to the influx of legalized gambling throughout the country and abroad. While Atlantic City has proven not to have had any real lasting threat to Las Vegas, the proliferation of various forms of gambling throughout the country has placed Las Vegas in contention with ever-increasing competitive gaming operations. More specifically, the passing of the Indian Gaming Regulatory Act of 1988, the proliferation of video lottery terminals, state lotteries, riverboat gambling, and the emergence of gambling in the European Community and elsewhere have had a major impact on both supply and demand statistics. However, one should also not conclude that what has happened in the past five years is not a major redirection of selected gaming properties. The changing market place has dictated a need on the part of Southern Nevada gaming properties to look to newly emerging market opportunities. By broadening their image as acceptable family resorts, these new mega-casinos hope to capture what is expected to be a lucrative marketing niche. The importance of the Southern California market and the major changes it is experiencing only reinforce this conclusion.

Finally, the community of Laughlin, which is located on the Colorado River at the Nevada/Arizona border, has only recently been recognized as a player in the Southern Nevada gaming industry. In 1980, Laughlin's gaming base consisted of one casino. By 1991, there were nine casinos with almost 8,000 hotel rooms and 11,000 residents employed in the gaming industry (Eadington 1992). The impact of increased competition in the Laughlin market can be measured by the incredible gain in gross gaming revenue from $62 million in 1982 to $463 million in 1991.

Its primary market is the large population of retirees in Phoenix and surrounding areas, as well as the retirement communities extending southward almost the entire length of the Colorado River. Laughlin is also popular with Canadians who travel to the area during the winter months, and Southern Californians who find it easily accessible (Salomon Brothers

1992). The product offering emphasizes slot machine play and low-stakes table games and relatively inexpensive hotel accommodations that average $25 per night.

Although Laughlin cannot rival the mega-resorts in Las Vegas, it too has found its marketing niche. With the addition of the Hilton, and the expansion and renovation of the airport, Laughlin is gearing itself for continued gains in the marketplace (Solomon Brothers 1992).

ANALYSIS OF THE SOUTHERN CALIFORNIA MARKET

The composition of the Southern California market—upon which Southern Nevada is extremely dependent—is changing dramatically. But one must be certain to distinguish between those changes which are symptomatic of problems and those changes which are the problems themselves. Regardless, these changes most assuredly will dictate many of the marketing strategies of Southern Nevada gaming properties well into the 21st Century.

A. Evidences of Change: The Symptoms of Emerging Problems

For many years, Southern California and Southern Nevada have enjoyed a relationship that seemed almost familial, with Southern California playing the role of the big brother supporting the endeavors of the less mature sibling. While Southern Nevada has flourished in its gaming operations, due largely to the loyal and repeated contributions from this network of support, Southern California has not faired well in recent years.

Southern California is going through radical transformations that have and will continue to reshape every environmental factor with which it is associated. Everything from its scenic coastal waters to its apron of opportunity and optimism continue to wane at an ever-increasing rate. Continued assaults that range from natural disasters to a critically wounded economic base, compounded by an overwhelmingly diverse population, has kept this giant market place debilitated.

Southern Nevada has already felt the adverse effects of Southern California's crippled economy in the drop of visitor volume, the decline of repeat visits, and a reduction in spending during visits to Southern Nevada.

The two major modes of transportation used by Southern Californians are airplane and automobile. Travel by automobile is used the most extensively at 59%, compared to 13% of those who travel by air (Market Opinion Research 1987–1990). In an analysis of the traffic flow through the Yermo Inspection Station on Interstate 15 (the main route from Southern California to Las Vegas) during the first three quarters of 1991, the decrease in traffic ranged from −.03% in January (indicating a decrease of 727 vehicles), to −15.6%, (a reduction 51,197 vehicles) in April. While the month of February showed a favorable gain as compared to the reductions in January and April, an overall decline of 2.1% was posted for the period (see Graph 1).

Laughlin's road volume from U.S. Highway 95 South as recorded by the State of Nevada Department of Transportation also indicated a decrease in traffic flow from Southern California during the same period. In comparison to the decline of traffic flow into Las Vegas, Laughlin's overall decrease for the same period was slightly larger, down by −2.8% (see Graph 2).

In interviews with Terrence Jicinsky of the Las Vegas Convention and Visitors Authority, he spoke of the Southern California market now representing less than 30% of the Las Vegas market. He indicated that the dependency on Southern California lies in a reduction of the historical repeat visits (Jicinsky, 1993). In comparing the number of repeat visits for Las Vegas in 1988 versus 1992, the lost percentage occurred in three or more visits annually. In comparing the gambling budget for the same years, the average gambling budget for Southern Californians dropped from $599 in 1988 to $364 in 1992 (Market Opinion Research 1987–1990). But these are just the symptoms.

B. Evidences of Change: The Problems

The problems of Southern California having direct or indirect impact upon Southern Nevada can be divided into two major subheadings: declining industrial activity (including divestments, unemployment, declining incomes, etc.), and a radically shifting demographic composition of the Southern California marketplace.

1. Industrial Decline California's employment base in the industries of defense and aerospace that accounted for one in every five manufacturing jobs since 1986, has seen the evaporation of 150,000 jobs, including those in related services (Roberts 1992). There has been a net migration outward of both professionals and businesses from Southern California. The professionals and businesses established in Southern California for years no longer view it as the land of opportunity. For them, the Golden State has laid an egg that is hollow and cracking. The image of a carefree, unrestricted lifestyle where opportunity abounds seems to have acquired more faults than the land in it. David Hensley, director of forecasting at the University of California, Los Angeles, says that ". . . by the year 2000, the departure of companies and workers could be a flood"(Stern 1990).

People are tired of commuting upwards of two hours to and from work.

GRAPH 1
Las Vegas Road Traffic
Through Yermo Inspection Station

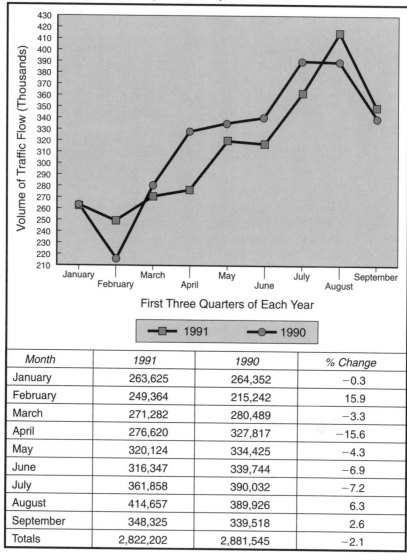

Month	1991	1990	% Change
January	263,625	264,352	−0.3
February	249,364	215,242	15.9
March	271,282	280,489	−3.3
April	276,620	327,817	−15.6
May	320,124	334,425	−4.3
June	316,347	339,744	−6.9
July	361,858	390,032	−7.2
August	414,657	389,926	6.3
September	348,325	339,518	2.6
Totals	2,822,202	2,881,545	−2.1

400

GRAPH 2
Laughlin Road Traffic
Through U.S. Highway 95 South

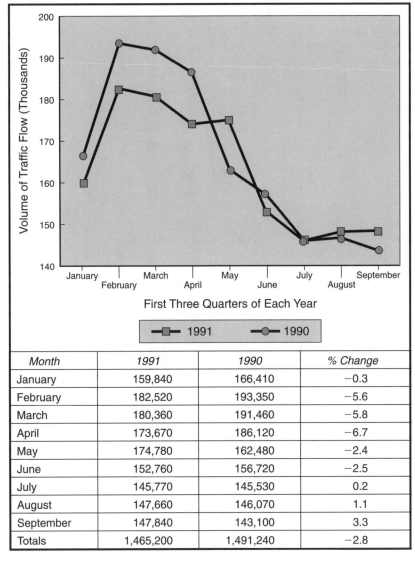

First Three Quarters of Each Year

Month	1991	1990	% Change
January	159,840	166,410	−0.3
February	182,520	193,350	−5.6
March	180,360	191,460	−5.8
April	173,670	186,120	−6.7
May	174,780	162,480	−2.4
June	152,760	156,720	−2.5
July	145,770	145,530	0.2
August	147,660	146,070	1.1
September	147,840	143,100	3.3
Totals	1,465,200	1,491,240	−2.8

They are fed up with the overcrowding, the high cost of living, taxes and pollution. There is no longer any time to spend on leisure activities between work and the travel time used to make a living. Everyone from doctors to architects, to those unemployed as a result of layoffs in the defense and aerospace industries, and closing of military bases, are leaving the state. Although there are numerous areas to where Southern Californians are relocating, the primary sights seem to be Washington (primarily Seattle), Arizona, Utah, Texas and Nevada.

Businesses are equally burned out. They feel requirements under laws have become unreasonable and they are equally disgusted with a system that seems to treat them with disdain. The attitudes among companies that have been in Southern California are changing. Instead of viewing alternative locations with a feeling of "why should I leave?," most are now taking an approach of "why should I stay?" (Stern 1990). Reluctantly, they are relocating out-of-state because of the exorbitant costs of land and energy; government inefficiencies and interference which cause extended project delays; stringent pollution requirements; and the burden of an unreasonable workmen's compensation program.

The cost of doing business, just from governmental compliance guidelines alone, is enough to create a difficult business environment for many companies. The ever expanding number of regulations and their complexity create countless delays. "Nowhere is this red tape more complex than in the four-county basin including Los Angeles that is governed by the South Coast Air Quality Management District. . . . The district has drawn up more that 120 regulations that govern everything from the consistency of glues and paints for the construction of jet planes to the use of charbroilers at Disneyland" (Stern 1990). Pollution standards set are felt to be unreasonable by businesses which feel that they are targeted to bear most of the costs when they are creating less than one-third of the pollution (Stern 1990). These businesses are not anti-environmental, but the cost of complying in the form of equipment conversions and the limits of production it creates for many companies is considered unreasonable. In addition, many question the effectiveness in the reduction of pollutants after the conversions.

The other major complaint businesses have is the workers' compensation program which is the most generous and flexible in the country. The primary differences between California's program and other states includes compensation for emotional stress, expensive medical checkups no matter how minor the physical injury, and the unlimited fee payments for vocational retraining: " . . . Employer insurance premiums are sixth highest in the nation . . . for every dollar received by an injured worker, employers pay another 74 cents to lawyers and insurers—overhead that exceeds the national average by 60%. . . . " (Roberts 1992). There is also a general feeling that the system allows for many fraudulent claims for which employers end up paying.

With these negative factors and the attraction and lure of other states, even the most reluctant of Southern California businesses are influenced to consider relocation. "Two percent of firms have left since 1980" (*Los Angeles Times* 1992). Places such as Rancho Rio, New Mexico are enticing businesses with economic packages and incentives that are hard to turn down. In fact, California lost the bid for Intel Corporation's $1 billion factory to Rancho Rio (*Los Angeles Times* 1993). Other states such as Utah, Nevada, Arizona, Idaho and Texas are soliciting businesses, as is Mexico.

Compounding this problem has been an out-migration of people in their most productive work years being replaced in the population through an increase of births (Bonfante 1991). "For the first time in 20 years, more licensed drivers left the state than moved in. California has become a land of disappointment for middle-aged residents, and the state is now experiencing a net outflow of workers in their highest-earning period, between ages 45 and 64"(Roberts 1992).

Nevertheless, some experts say that Southern California will rebound in the future and that the problems that plague it will eventually plague other states as well (Bonfante 1991). While these changes in the population of Southern California, in particular, and the state in general currently creates a multitude of problems, it is expected to bolster the economy in the future. The state is expected to excel in its trade with the fastest growing trade areas in the world, namely, the Pacific Rim and Latin America, and should benefit directly from the recent passage of the North American Free Trade Agreement among Canada, the U.S. and Mexico. In addition, California's resources in higher education, agricultural land and openness to opportunities should produce future generations that could ultimately lead the market globally.

2. Population Growth Southern California is experiencing unprecedented population growth which not only overshadows any other state's, but is also 3 million more than the entire population of Canada. As stated by California Governor Pete Wilson in an interview two years ago, "Delaware moves to this state annually" (Bonfante 1991). According to 1990 census figures, there were over 29.8 million residents of California and many say that is underestimated by at least another million.

There are two primary reasons for the rapid population growth in Los Angeles. First and foremost is the thousands of immigrants crossing the border illegally. And the second primary reason is attributed specifically to Los Angeles becoming " . . . the leading point of entry for legal immigrants to the United States" (Lockwood 1989).

In 1980, the white-anglo sector represented 76% of the total population. The 1990 U.S. census set the white-anglo sector at 57% which many say is overestimated due to the conservative count of minorities (Bonfante 1991). This population is so diverse that by the end of the century there will no ethnic majority in the State of California (Bonfante 1991). During the same period, the greater Los Angeles area accounted for 12.6 million of the entire population of the state of California. In Los Angeles alone, the population is expected to increase drastically to 16.4 million by the year 2000 and another two million within the next ten years thereafter (Lockwood 1989). The largest minority groups will consist of African-Americans, Asian-Americans and Latin-Americans. But they are not growing in direct proportion to their present numbers. It is estimated that by the year 2000, there will be only a 1% increase in the African-American population, for an additional 800,000; a 9.3% increase in the Asian population of almost one million; and an increase of 16% (from 24% to 40%) in the Hispanic population for an additional 4 million (Lockwood 1989).

3. Race   Southern California's changing market conditions, specifically, rapidly growing minority groups—with traditionally lower incomes, lower levels of education, larger families—will dictate a change in the marketing strategies of Southern Nevada gaming properties. In fact, they already have.

The racial composition is so diverse in Los Angeles alone, it is considered the largest metropolitan area for Mexicans, Chinese, Japanese, Koreans, Filipinos and Vietnamese outside their respective native lands (Lockwood 1989). Many have segregated themselves in or around the Los Angeles metropolis. For example, in Orange County, the towns of Westminster and Garden Grove are thriving districts filled with businesses run and patronized by Vietnamese. As of five years ago, "in the San Gabriel Valley, Alhambra's Asian population has tripled, from 12 percent to 36 percent of its total population of 71,300. . . . " (Lockwood 1989). In addition, the Asian middle class now represents over half the residents in Monterey Park.

In 1988, the top 1% of Iran's population fled the country, with 400,000 settling in Southern California. Most are relatively wealthy, having been their country's elite, and have remained in their professions by going back to school to get American licenses. Many have become successful entrepreneurs with most of the culture residing in or around Beverly Hills (Beauchamp 1988). Other, smaller, minority groups not already mentioned but part of the Southern California area include Nigerians, Guatemalans, Hungarians, Cubans and South Africans. This alone might have serious consequences for Southern Nevada gaming properties anxious to promote to and, in other ways, communicate effectively with these racially or ethnically based niche markets.

4. Income and Education   The changing demographics of Southern California describe an overall population that is becoming much younger and dominated by non-Caucasians. As previously mentioned, much of this is attributed to the influx of migrants, both legally and illegally, and the continued increase in domestic births to many unwed teenage mothers. But, it can also be attributed in part to the fact that in 1991, California experienced its first net outflow of Caucasians—mostly higher income and retired persons—in its entire history. This, too, will have a noticeable effect on marketing strategies of many of Southern Nevada's gaming properties.

Although many economists agree that immigrants will boost the economy in the long run, ". . . many come with low skills and large families and, in the short run, they place a strain on state resources" (Roberts 1992). Moreover is the impact of illegal migrants mainly from Mexico and Central America, who cross the border only to have their children born in the United States. Regardless, the evidence is emerging that both the average income and average level of education among the citizenry of Southern California are declining. These demographics might also impact upon Southern Nevada gaming properties and could dictate the various "prices" of rooms, meals, and even gaming options as well as the level of sophistication in promotion and other forms of marketing communication, given a potentially lower level of literacy.

SUMMARY ANALYSIS OF THE STATE OF CALIFORNIA

Southern California, as well as California in general, is going through a period of restructure. Tremendous change is occurring with respect to its people, its economy, and its identity.

The population continues to grow at an increasing rate. Even with a net migration outward of those who had already been established in Southern California, the influx of those migrating to Southern California and the rising birthrate are overwhelming the system. The diversity that exists in the population is currently segmented by culture, indicating a lack of unification among its residents. There is concern about the majority of the population being younger and the revenue generating part of the population shrinking. Providing for the imbalance in this population is a primary concern.

The residents leaving the state and relocating generally have higher degrees of education and income-earning ability than the ones replacing them. Most of the minorities replacing them differ as well in that their families tend to be larger and they generally are less educated and lack employment skills.

In addition, Southern California has incurred a great loss in its economic base in manufacturing. The federal government's restructuring in defense has had a ripple effect on its economy as well as the exodus of companies dissatisfied or unable to compete under the conditions that are mandated by the state.

Although the problems currently affecting Southern California are complex, finding alternative solutions is imperative so that its economy can be revived in the future. The potential for long-term gain is attainable if direction can be provided. Many of the problems, such as the cultural diversity and the immaturity of the population, are expected to be a wealth of resources in the future. But in order for this to take place, efforts to accelerate the integration process of the minorities are critical.

In addition, the opportunity to attract companies back to the state will become more viable as trade continues to open up. It is important that current conditions be altered to consider the needs of businesses so that they may grow in a competitive environment.

If these major areas can be addressed and leadership is effective, Southern California can regain its image of opportunity and vitality.

IMPLICATIONS FOR THE SOUTHERN NEVADA GAMING INDUSTRY

These continued changes in Southern California have been the basis, in part, for the emergence of "family niche" marketing of select Southern Nevada gaming properties.

The decline in visitor volume of Southern Californians demonstrates the adverse affects—although not severe—that can occur with the Southern Nevada gaming industry and the state's well-being.

The distribution among Southern California males and females visiting Las Vegas has averaged respectively with the exception of the fluctuation in the last two years of the 1980s. This distribution is expected to remain fairly constant for the remainder of the century with the exception of males out-numbering females by a slightly, ever-increasing margin.

The trend in marital status among Southern Californians visiting Las Vegas is noteworthy. While the majority of Southern California visitors in 1980 were married (88%), the projection for the turn of the century is a dramatic change with the percentages between married and single Southern Californians split almost equally (53%—M versus 47%—S).

There is a significant change in the distribution of the four major ethnic categories visiting Las Vegas from Southern California. Of these visitors, the white segment is decreasing significantly (dropping 23 percentage points) while the Hispanic and Asian groups are increasing (38 percentage points combined) as the next century approaches.

The trend in age distribution among Southern Californians visiting Las Vegas is also important with the greatest increases in the 21–29 age range (31%) and the category of "greater than 65" (36%) by the year 2000. A significant trend expected over the next six year period is a decline in the age groups of 50–59 and 60–64, keeping in mind that these are part of the highest income producing years for the majority of individuals in these age brackets.

The educational division among Southern Californians visiting Las Vegas is also of interest. The percentage of visits by Southern Californians with "some college" will continue to decline, representing only 15%, while the percentage of visits by Southern Californians who are "college graduates" is expected to steadily increase to 43% within six years.

The income distribution of Southern Californians visiting Las Vegas into the year 2000 is an important consideration in marketing. Graph 3 reflects that visits by those with incomes "less than $20,000" will constitute a larger percentage of visitors (29%), and the category of those visitors with incomes of "$20000–$39999" will show the biggest decline, ultimately only accounting for 13% of visitor volume in 2000.

The family niche strategy may actually serve a dual purpose for gaming properties in Southern Nevada. If pursuing the family niche is strategy-based, in part, on the demographic changes occurring in the Southern California market, it may also be considered a means to reduce dependency on that same market through the penetration of this marketing niche overall.

Reducing dependency of the Southern California market would soften the impact of an economic downturn in Las Vegas, where reliance on the industry for employment and economic survival is paramount. In order to continue to soften the dependency on Southern California, and to compete with other gambling operations across the country, the gaming properties of Southern Nevada, Las Vegas in particular, must continue to seek out other untapped segments in the market. As previously mentioned, attempts to diversify the economy of Las Vegas have not been successful and with the emergence of mega-casinos, the dependency on gaming is fully entrenched.

Southern California still represents a very important segment for Southern Nevada, contributing 27% of the visitor volume in Las Vegas. Southern Californians were also 74% more likely to visit Laughlin than other visitors visiting Las Vegas (Market Opinion Research 1987–1990). The primary concerns for Southern Nevada gaming properties are the current and future demographics of the population of California, the cities to which former Southern Californians are relocating, the expansion of

GRAPH 3
Southern Californians Visiting Las Vegas

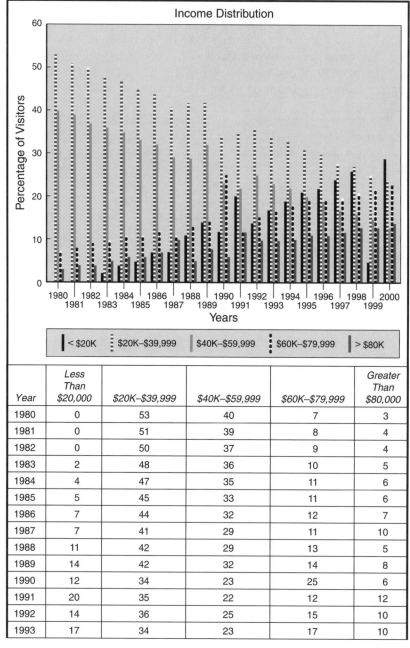

Year	Less Than $20,000	$20K–$39,999	$40K–$59,999	$60K–$79,999	Greater Than $80,000
1980	0	53	40	7	3
1981	0	51	39	8	4
1982	0	50	37	9	4
1983	2	48	36	10	5
1984	4	47	35	11	6
1985	5	45	33	11	6
1986	7	44	32	12	7
1987	7	41	29	11	10
1988	11	42	29	13	5
1989	14	42	32	14	8
1990	12	34	23	25	6
1991	20	35	22	12	12
1992	14	36	25	15	10
1993	17	34	23	17	10

(continued)

GRAPH 3
(*continued*)

Year	Less Than $20,000	$20K–$39,999	$40K–$59,999	$60K–$79,999	Greater Than $80,000
1994	19	33	22	18	10
1995	21	31	20	19	11
1996	22	30	19	19	11
1997	24	28	17	20	12
1998	26	27	16	21	13
1999	28	25	15	22	13
2000	29	24	13	23	14

gaming on Indian reservations, and the historic dependency on the Southern California market.

A. Population Changes

Consideration with regard to the Southern California population is two-fold: the way current conditions exist and how they will be changing long-term. As previously stated, the bulk of the population is younger. Strategies should be considered to accommodate different segments, with an emphasis on a population that will mature in years to come. Considerations should be given to factors such as the possible integration of minorities, especially the large Hispanic and Asian segments. The question is not whether this will occur so much as when it will occur. Also, it is expected that as integration of future generations takes place, an increase in educated, higher wage earning segments will surface once again.

B. Possible Growth of Gambling in Southern California

The growth of gaming in Southern California is considered the biggest threat to Southern Nevada gaming properties. According to Mr. Jicinsky of the Las Vegas Convention and Visitors Authority, the threat is not so much that the Southern California market will be eliminated but that repeat visits from that market will be drastically reduced.

Slot machines have become the most popular form of gambling and the highest revenue generator of all gaming products for Southern Nevada gaming properties. In particular, quarter slots provided the biggest win at $1.1 billion ending the fiscal year 1991 for Clark County.

But the introduction of video lottery terminals (VLTs) in Southern California, which are similar to slot machines, could have a significant impact.

Opinions about the degree of impact vary. They include the idea that VLTs will provide prospective consumers with a taste of the gambling that might be enjoyed more fully in Las Vegas, or that the impact from widespread VLTs will impact historically loyal repeat visitors from Southern California.

CONCLUSION

Planning and implementing alternative strategies such as the family market niche is expected to continue to give Southern Nevada a competitive edge. The infrastructure of Southern Nevada is very supportive to the gaming industry, something that many experts say is critical to the expansion and survival of gaming operations all over.

While Las Vegas' dependence on Southern California visitors has dropped more than half of what is was ten years ago, it is a market that has a critical impact on the Southern Nevada gaming industry. In the future, the viable market of Southern California can only increase, especially as its population comes of age. Developing Las Vegas more as a resort destination with an emphasis on gambling seems to be a positive direction for the future of Southern Nevada gaming properties.

---

1. The research conducted was primarily through extensive secondary sources. The data represents the most recent accessible findings from the various resources available at UNLV's James R. Dickinson Library (including tapes and documentation obtained in the Gaming Resource Center, its Special Collections Library), the Clark County Library, and the Las Vegas Convention Center and Visitors Authority. Interviews with Mr. Terrence Jicinsky of the Las Vegas Convention Center and Visitors Authority represent the sole source of primary data collected for this paper.

REFERENCES

Bonfante, Jordan (1989). "Californians Keep Out!," *Time,* vol. 134, November 13.

Bonfante, Jordan (1991). "The Endangered Dream," *Time,* vol. 138, November 18.

Beauchamp, Mark (1988). "Welcome to Teheran, Calif.," *Forbes,* vol. 142, December 12.

"California Economy Increasingly Shows Signs of Dragging U.S. Recovery Down" (1993). *Wall Street Journal,* January 29.

"Can Impact Fees Stunt a Town's Growth?" (1993). *The New York Times,* vol. 142, April 4.

"California Prospects TV Betting" (1993). *Christian Science Monitor,* vol. 85, no. 104, April 26.

"Casinos Coming to Tribal Land Amid Lax Regulation" (1991). *Los Angeles Times,* October 9.

"Catering to Consumers' Ethnic Needs" (1992). *New York Times,* vol. 141, January 23.

Christiansen, Eugene Martin (1991). *The Gaming Industry in 1995.* New York: Christiansen/Cummings Associates, Inc.

Dandurand, Lawrence (1985). *The Casino Gaming Phenomenon.* Las Vegas: UNLV.

Dandurand, Lawrence (1991). *Casino Gaming Game Preference and Correlated Profile Structures.* Las Vegas: UNLV.

"Doubling Down, Las Vegas Is Building Lavish Casinos in Bid to Defy Rivals, Slump" (1992). *Wall Street Journal,* West Coast Edition, New York, November 18.

Eadington, William R. (1992). "Recent National Trends in the Casino Gaming Industry and their Implications for the Economy of Nevada." Reno: Institute for the Study of Gambling and Commercial Gaming, University of Nevada.

Ernst and Young (1991). *Compilation of United States Gaming Data 1991.* Philadelphia: Ernst and Young.

GLS Research (1991). *1991 Las Vegas Visitor Profile Study.* NV: Las Vegas Convention and Visitors Authority.

GLS Research (1991). *Las Vegas Visitor Profile,* Southern California Version, Fiscal Year 1991.

GLS Research (1992). *Las Vegas Visitor Profile,* Southern California Version, Fiscal Year 1992.

"HIRING: Search First for New Jobs at Smaller Firms" (1992). *Los Angeles Times: Time 100 Supplement,* vol. 111, April 28.

Jicinsky, Terrence (1993). Marketing Research Administrator, Las Vegas Convention and Visitors Authority, Personal Interview, June 7.

Kenkelen, Bill (1990). "Church keeps California from building Babel," *National Catholic Reporter,* vol. 26, August 10.

Las Vegas Convention and Visitors Authority (1991). *Las Vegas Marketing Bulletin Third Quarter 1991 Summary,* vol. 18, no. 79.

Las Vegas Convention and Visitors Authority (1990). *Las Vegas: LVCVA Marketing Plan,* Fiscal Year 1990–91.

"Las Vegas Confronts Economic Crunch As Rapid Expansion Bumps Into Slump" (1990). *Wall Street Journal,* West Coast Edition, December 31.

Las Vegas Review Journal (1993). *Las Vegas Perspective: 1993.*

Lockwood, Charles (1989). "Los Angeles Comes of Age," *The Atlantic,* January.

Market Opinion Research (1987). *Las Vegas Visitor Profile,* Southern California Version. Nevada: Las Vegas Convention and Visitors Authority.

Market Opinion Research (1988) *Las Vegas Visitor Profile,* Southern California Version. Nevada: Las Vegas Convention and Visitors Authority.

Market Opinion Research (1989) *Las Vegas Visitor Profile,* Southern California Version. Nevada: Las Vegas Convention and Visitors Authority.

Market Opinion Research (1990) *Las Vegas Visitor Profile,* Southern California Version. Nevada: Las Vegas Convention and Visitors Authority.

1990 Consensus of Population and Housing, Summary Tape File 3A, November 1992 issue, UNLV James Dickinson Library.

Pinney, J. Kent and Powell, James D. (1976). "Marketing Segmentation of Casino-Type Gambling: A Case Study in the Application of the Marketing Concept." Paper presented at the Third National Conference on Gambling and Risk-Taking, Las Vegas.

Rand McNally (1986). *Rand McNally Zip Code Atlas.* Chicago: Rand McNally.

"Reason for California Business Loss Is on the Rio Grande" (1993). *Los Angeles Times,* vol. 112, April 27.

Reibstain, Larry (1992). "Where the Jobs Are," *Newsweek,* vol. 119, January 20.

Roberts, Steven V. (1992). "California Crumbling," *U.S. News & World Report,* vol. 113, September 14.

Schrag, Peter (1991). "30 Million and Groaning," *California,* vol. 16, September.

Salomon Brothers (1992). *United States Equity Research, Gaming,* "Las Vegas: The Mother Lode of Gaming," November.

"Start-ups in California Rise" (1992). *Los Angeles Times,* vol. 111, October 31.

State of California (1991). *Statistical Abstract.* Sacramento: Department of Finance.

"State's Regulators Laying a Gentler Hand on Business" (1993). *The Washington Post,* vol. 116, April 5.

Stern, Richard (1990). "Is the Golden State Losing It?," *Forbes,* vol. 146, October 29.

"Struggling to Strike the Right Balance" *Los Angeles Times,* April 28, 1992, vol. 111.

"2% of Firms Have Left State Since 1980, Report Says" (1992). *Los Angeles Times,* vol. 111, October 19.

"What's Wrong With Californians?" (1993). *Countryside and Small Stock Journal,* vol. 77, January–February.

Gambling and a Family Resort Destination?
John A. Schibrowsky

With the proliferation of commercial gaming throughout the country, Las Vegas is planning for the future by attempting to reposition itself as "The Gambling Family Resort Destination." While the sociology, ethics, and morals of mixing families and gambling must be considered, this paper investigates the issue from a business perspective. The decision is based on economic considerations. If it is profitable, the family resort destination strategy will continue. Virtually everyone in the city of Las Vegas, the State of Nevada, and the popular press (e.g., *Time* and *Newsweek*) believes it is a perfect plan for the future of the city. However, the plan has many pitfalls. These potential problems must be addressed.

First, the feasibility of repositioning a gambling destination as a family resort destination is discussed. Can Las Vegas reposition itself from "the Adult Disneyland" to "a family-oriented resort destination?" Second, the changes that the city and individual properties would need to make to accomplish the repositioning are examined. Third, the business implications are discussed. Currently, around 5% of visitors to Las Vegas bring their families. What happens when this number jumps to 40% or 50%? How much gambling is done by family members when they are in Las Vegas with their families? What will casinos do when per capita gambling expenditures are dramatically reduced?

Finally, the long run business implications of repositioning Las Vegas from a gambling destination to family resort destination with gambling are addressed. For example, when the number of minors is increased tenfold, how will casino security measures need to change to prevent minors from gambling?

While the specific case discussed in this paper is Las Vegas, the issue is extremely important for all gambling locations. As the novelty of gambling wears off, gaming locations will need to find ways to differentiate and position themselves to attract customers. Is the combination of gambling and a family vacation a feasible market to target?

A POSITIONING PRIMER

Positioning is the backbone of an organization's marketing plan (Dovel, 1990). It can be defined as "the act of designing the marketing offer and image so that it occupies a distinct and valued place in the target customer's mind" (Kotler, 1994). It is related to the concept of brand image except that it takes into account the competition (Aaker, 1991). As such, the development of a positioning strategy requires an understanding of the target customers, the competition, and the product/brand or service being positioned.

The "position" that a brand, product, or service possesses is the image, relative to the competition, that a brand holds in the mind of the consumer. It is important to note that a brand's position is in the mind of the customer. This point leads to two important implications. First, a brand's position may be different for each target customer, since it is based on the individual's experiences and other information remembered about the brand. Second, the position or image a brand possesses may not reflect the reality of the situation. For example, Caesars Palace is perceived by many locals as having tight slot machines. While Caesars argues that their slot machine mix is the same as other strip properties the image remains. If Caesars wants to change this perception, a long term communication campaign would be necessary. Before a positioning or repositioning strategy can be developed, an understanding of the current perceptions of the target customers is essential.

The competition also impacts the positioning decision by creating a frame of reference for positions. Valuable positions are those that differentiate a firm from the competition. Also, it is difficult to obtain a position currently being held by a competitor.

The most important factor in developing a positioning strategy is the product or service itself. Does the organization's advertising, pricing, distribution methods, and the product or service itself match the position that the firm is trying establish? Four questions about the product or service must be answered. What position is currently owned? Why? What position is desired? Does the organization match that position?

REPOSITIONING LAS VEGAS

Is it feasible for Las Vegas to reposition itself? Can Las Vegas obtain the position of "Family Resort Destination?" To answer these questions let's go through the basic repositioning questions.

A. What Position Does Las Vegas Currently Own?

Las Vegas has a solid position in the minds of most consumers. It is the "Gambling Mecca." Three other related positions exist: "Sin City," "The Adult Disneyland," and "The Entertainment Capital of The World."

B. Why Does Las Vegas Own That Position?

The position that Las Vegas has in the minds of consumers is based on the mental associations that individuals have with Las Vegas. These associations are the result of personal experiences and other information that individuals have heard or seen about Las Vegas. Major sources of information pertaining to Las Vegas include movies and television shows, magazine and newspaper articles, advertisements, and word of mouth communication.

It is easy to understand why Las Vegas is considered to be the Mecca of gambling. There is no place in the world like Las Vegas when it comes to gambling. The city was built on gambling. Virtually everything revolves around gambling. It is the focus of every casino/hotel, and in reality, the restaurants are for gamblers to eat, the hotel rooms are for gamblers to sleep, and the shows are designed to entertain gamblers. Las Vegas means gambling.

The Sin City and Adult Disneyland images of Las Vegas are grounded in both fact and fiction. They are due in part to the range of adult activities available in Las Vegas. Prostitution is legal in the surrounding counties. While Las Vegas itself does not allow prostitution, it certainly exists on a large scale. Also, the 24-hour-a-day atmosphere, free drinks for gamblers, risqué and off-color entertainment, and strip joints all help to build the image. In addition, the portrayal of Las Vegas in movies and on television reinforces this image. Las Vegas is typically portrayed as a glitzy, anything goes town. Recent movie portrayals include "Honeymoon in Vegas" and "Indecent Proposal."

Finally, the Entertainment Capital of the World image is based on the number and quality of shows that are offered by the casinos. This is good example of a position that has been developed over the years by consistently providing a quality service.

While the position that Las Vegas holds in the minds of consumers varies slightly from one individual to another, it is relatively consistent. Las Vegas means gambling, nightlife, and activities perceived by some to be immoral. Gambling, drinking, carousing, sex, nudity, immoral activity, gangsters, and glitz are typical associations that come to mind when Las Vegas is mentioned. While local residents and city officials will argue that this is an inaccurate stereotype, the perception exists.

C. What Position Does Las Vegas Want to Own?

City of Las Vegas officials, State of Nevada officials, the Las Vegas Convention and Visitors Authority, some casino operators, and the popular press (e.g., *Time* and *Newsweek*) seem to want to reposition Las Vegas as a "Family Resort Destination." Why?

First, realize that Nevadans are different from residents in other states with respect to gambling. In most states, gambling is viewed as an acceptable albeit immoral way of generating state revenues. Nevadans believe gambling is an acceptable form of entertainment and not an immoral activity. That's why there are slot machines in convenience stores, grocery stores, department stores, and the airport. Las Vegans do not understand why people have a negative opinion of gambling or the city. As such, Las Vegans desperately want to be considered as belonging to a legitimate city. Many individuals see the repositioning of Las Vegas as a family place a necessary and positive step in that direction.

Second, since 60% of the visitors to Las Vegas are on vacation, it seems that the future growth of Las Vegas is dependent on generating new vacationing customers (LVCVA, 1992). Families represent the largest vacation market and thus they are a logical target. While some families are already willing to vacation in the gambling Mecca, the percentage would increase dramatically if Las Vegas was perceived as a family resort destination rather than a gambling destination.

D. Does Las Vegas Match Its Desired Position?

Presently, Las Vegas does not match its desired position since for most people gambling and families don't mix. The major activity and form of entertainment offered in Las Vegas is illegal for minors. On the other hand, family resort destinations are wholesome, educational, and provide activities for the whole family to do together. Las Vegas has none of this. Most of the activity on the strip is not wholesome or educational. The entertainment activities provided by Las Vegas' casinos are not designed for family participation. In fact, unless children inside a casino are in transit to some other particular location, security will request parents to remove them. In addition, family resort destinations generally emphasize the children. The concept is that if the children are having fun so are the parents. Casino operators are not interested in children. They may be willing to tolerate them, but only if their parents are there to gamble.

E. Who Must Las Vegas Surpass to Gain the Desired Position?

The number one family resort destination is Orlando, Florida. While Orlando and Las Vegas are similar in terms of size and number of visitors, the similarity ends there. Orlando is on the opposite end of the spectrum from Las Vegas on almost every conceivable factor. Kids are king in Orlando. In Las Vegas, kids are only tolerated. Las Vegas will never be considered a family resort destination like Orlando. If Las Vegas wants to move in that direction they will have to do much more than set up a few amusement parks and arcades. They will have to change the focus of their business from adults to children.

F. What Are the Success Requirements?

Assume that Las Vegas wants to become a family resort destination with gambling. To accomplish this position, the casino hotels would have de-emphasize gambling and focus on family activities. This would require a change of philosophy from generating the bulk of the property's income from gambling to finding ways to generate revenues from family entertainment, meals, amusements, shopping, and lodging. In addition, those activities considered to be improper for a family atmosphere would have to be eliminated. These changes, however, seem unlikely.

G. What Are the Potential Dangers of the Repositioning?

Changing a successful position makes little sense and can be dangerous to the organization's financial health. There are three potential dangers associated with the repositioning of Las Vegas. First, it is difficult to establish a new position in the minds of consumers. This is especially true in the case of Las Vegas where the new position is virtually the opposite of the original position. The more individuals remember the first position, the more difficult it is to establish the second one (Rothschild, 1987). The net result is often confused consumers and a weak position or no position at all. The bottom line with positioning is that "You can't stand for two very different things."

When firms decide to establish a new position and go after new markets, they often "forget what made them successful" (Reis & Trout, 1972). In the case of Las Vegas this is crucial. The allure of Las Vegas has always been the gambling, nightlife, entertainment, carousing, and glitz. It has not been white tigers and theme parks. As Las Vegas becomes less gambling-oriented, it starts to look like many other resort destinations.

It is important to understand how the repositioning will influence current customers. For example, will the current customers find Las Vegas less appealing when the number of children vacationing here triples? Will the allure be gone? Will the ancillary services (e.g., restaurants) become so crowded with families that the gamblers are driven away. In addition, most gamblers like to be around other gamblers. Therefore, the danger is that potential gamblers will go to other gaming locations, rather than deal with the family crowds in Las Vegas.

The bottom line is that it is not likely that Las Vegas will ever be viewed as a family resort destination unless the general population's attitudes towards gambling change dramatically.

BUSINESS IMPLICATIONS

One feasible approach for growth is for some properties to market gamblers with families. Currently, only 7% of the visitors to Las Vegas bring children (LVCVA, 1992). This is up only slightly from 5% ten years ago (LVCVA, 1982). Since families constitute one of the largest vacation markets, the potential associated with this target is substantial. The remaining question is "How much is this market worth to Las Vegas?" To address this question, a investigation of the family market is in order.

The 1990 census figures indicate that 38 million (40.7%) households in America contain children under the age of 18. Of this group, 24.5 million are traditional two parent families (Waldrop & Exter 1990). However, family life-cycle research clearly indicates that parents tend to be more price conscience and to put a priority on spending money on their children (Derrick &Linfield, 1980; Murphy & Staples, 1979; Wells & Gubar, 1966). The implications of these findings for Las Vegas are straightforward.

The major problem with marketing Las Vegas as a family resort destination is that it would require an emphasis on non-gambling activities as sources of revenues. In essence a completely new approach to business will be necessary. It must be realized that once Las Vegas is marketed as a family resort destination with activities for the whole family, the result is likely to be an increase in the percentage of non-gambling adults. The percentage of non-gambling adult visitors to Las Vegas has increased from 3% in 1987 to 10% in 1992 (Las Vegas Convention and Visitors Authority, 1987, 1992). While a large proportion of these non-gamblers visited Las Vegas for trade shows or conventions, the point is clear. When you market Las Vegas as something other than a gambling destination, the percentage of non-gamblers increases.

As the number of families vacationing in Las Vegas increases, the number of non-gamblers also increases. Currently the combination of non-gambling adults and children result in a total of 15% of the visitors not gambling. If the percentage of visitors bringing children with them climbs to 25%, the percentage of non-gamblers increases to 33%, even if you assume that the parents are as likely to gamble as other Las Vegas visitors. This is a 120% increase in the number of non-gambling visitors. Add to this the fact that parents are less likely than the average Las Vegas visitor to gamble, and the percentage of non-gamblers could easily jump to 40%. That is nearly triple current percentages. With 40% of the visitors not gambling, the management of Las Vegas properties will need to change dramatically (Thompson, Pinney and Schibrowsky, 1996).

Those parents that do gamble are likely to have smaller gambling budgets. Table 1 shows the current trend in gambling budgets for Las Vegas visitors. Over the past ten years the average gambling budget per day per visitor has been cut in half. This trend is likely to continue when families are targeted as visitors to Las Vegas. Tables 2 and 3 provide additional evidence for this conclusion. Table 2 indicates that the percentage of families visiting Las Vegas doubles during the summer months. Table 3 shows the daily gambling budgets per person for each season. It is significant to note that gambling budgets decrease dramatically when the percentage of families increases. These conclusions are completely in line with other family life cycle findings.

Marketing to price sensitive segments requires careful price and cost management. Both Grand Slam Canyon and the MGM Theme Park have experience in this area and are now experimenting with creative pricing tactics.

In addition, families are much more likely to take advantage of traffic building specials such as 2-for-1 meals. With an increase in the number of families visiting Las Vegas, this is a potentially significant problem, as the purpose of these traffic building specials are to increase the number of gamblers in the casino, not the number of non-gambling families and children. If a traffic building special is inundated with families, the targeted gamblers are not likely to stand in line, and will probably leave the property dissatisfied.

Family life cycle findings that parents are more likely to spend money on their children than on themselves will require some rethinking. While some Las Vegas properties have developed methods to generate income from non-gambling activities, especially those targeted toward children, the importance of these sources of revenue will need to increase dramatically if families become an increased portion of the Las Vegas visitor mix. For an example, in Orlando the major sources of revenue for those properties are in family activities, particularly those activities primarily directed toward children. In Las Vegas, properties such as the MGM Grand have the right idea. Rooms, food and beverage, entertainment, and novelties must all be viewed as sources of revenue. The days of losing money on

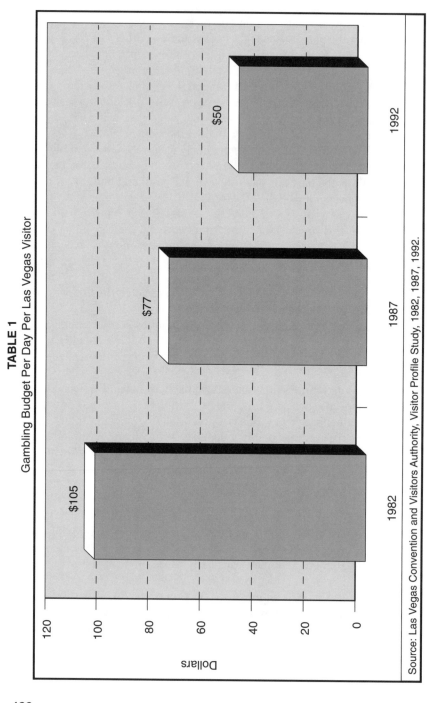

TABLE 1

Gambling Budget Per Day Per Las Vegas Visitor

Source: Las Vegas Convention and Visitors Authority, Visitor Profile Study, 1982, 1987, 1992.

422

TABLE 2

1992 Percentage of Visitors with Children in Their Party by Season

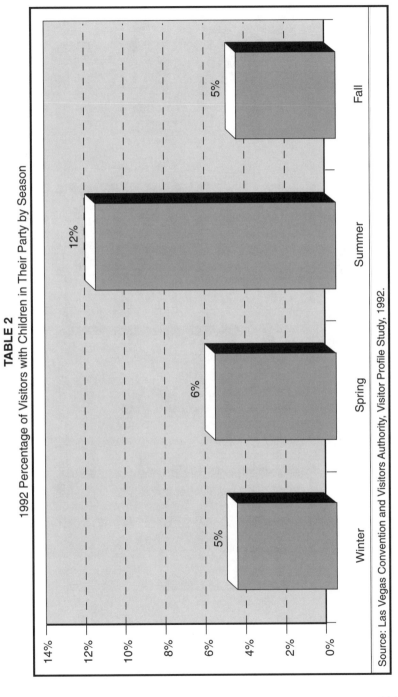

Source: Las Vegas Convention and Visitors Authority, Visitor Profile Study, 1992.

TABLE 3

1992 Gambling Budget Per Day Per Person by Season

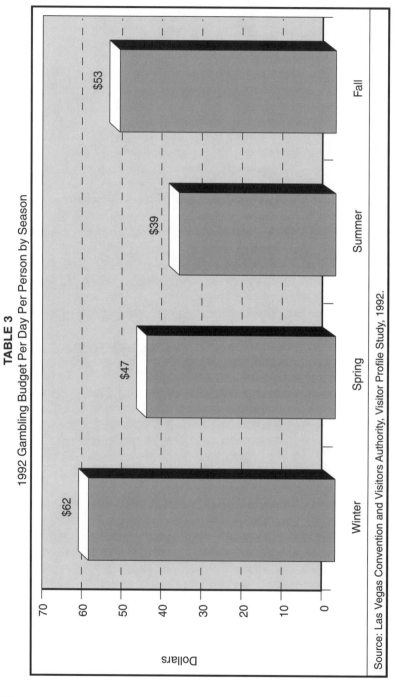

Source: Las Vegas Convention and Visitors Authority, Visitor Profile Study, 1992.

rooms and making it up in the casino will be over. Properties will have to manage all facets of their business. While it is true that not all properties will attract equal percentages of families, the impact will be felt everywhere, since families will search out room, meal, and entertainment values in all properties.

The variety of activities available for families will need to be expanded. If Las Vegas is marketed as a family resort destination, the city must be able to meet the expectations of families for family entertainment. Currently, most of the "family" activities are actually designed for children or young adults, but not for the whole family (Thompson, Pinney and Schibrowsky, 1996). While most casinos do not like the idea of creating activities that potentially reduce the number of hours that a gambler spends in the casino, the family market will demand them. The MGM's Grand Adventures Theme Park recently felt the reality of raising expectations without the ability to deliver (Palermo, 1994). As Tom Bruny noted, "The expectations of some people may have been too high. . . . MGM Grand Adventures was never meant to be a stand alone destination attraction." However, those are the type of expectations that come with Las Vegas positioning itself as a family resort destination.

Security problems generated by a doubling or tripling of the number of children in casinos is overwhelming. Casinos will not be able to hire enough security to police the problem of minors around gambling devices. In addition, what will properties do when a minor is caught gambling? Such a situation can only have a negative impact on the satisfaction of the family involved. The parents will either blame the casino, or the town in general. In any event, the chances of positive word of mouth recommendation or repeat visits are not likely. Properties will have to redesign their layouts to allow for families and especially unescorted children to navigate their way around a property without being stopped by security personnel. This is likely to be an expensive endeavor.

RECOMMENDATIONS

If one concludes that Las Vegas should not pursue a family resort destination position, what position should the city strive to obtain? Perhaps the answer lies in analyzing the position that Las Vegas already owns.

Las Vegas is regarded worldwide as the center of the "Gambling Universe." It would seem logical that the city should continue to build on this position. After all, it is the gambling ambiance and spirit that makes Las Vegas unique. If this approach is followed then all of the communication regarding Las Vegas as a resort destination should emphasize gambling and the fact that Las Vegas is the ultimate gaming resort destination. Currently, the approach has been to de-emphasize the gambling and over-

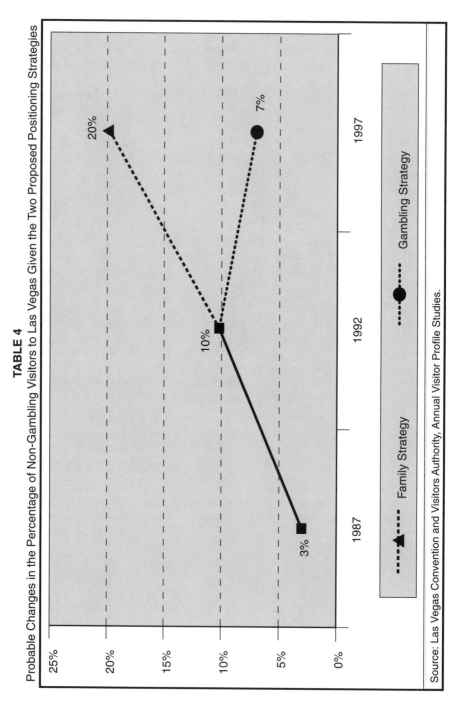

TABLE 4

Probable Changes in the Percentage of Non-Gambling Visitors to Las Vegas Given the Two Proposed Positioning Strategies

Source: Las Vegas Convention and Visitors Authority, Annual Visitor Profile Studies.

TABLE 5

Probable Changes in the Daily Gambling Budget per Person Given the Two Proposed Positioning Strategies

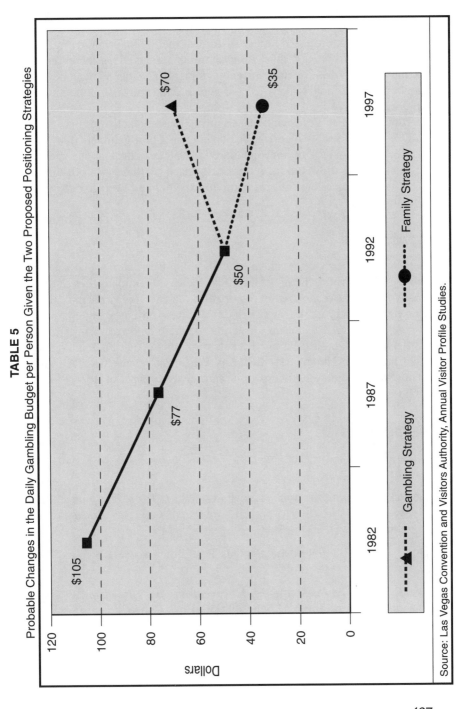

Source: Las Vegas Convention and Visitors Authority, Annual Visitor Profile Studies.

emphasize the non-gaming attractions. However, many casino/hotels in Las Vegas do not want non-gamblers and their families to vacation here.

The approach proposed here is to do the exact opposite and emphasize gambling in Las Vegas' marketing communications. This increases the likelihood that the city will attract gamblers. The percentage of non-gambling vacationers is likely to go down, and the daily gambling budgets are likely to go up.

However, if Las Vegas emphasizes attractions and activities other than gambling, it is likely to increase the percentage of non-gamblers that vacation here and reduce the average daily gambling budget of the visitors. Tables 4 and 5 show the likely results of each of these two positioning strategies on percentage of non-gambling visitors and average daily gambling budgets.

CONCLUSION

The local political and business officials should be commended on their foresight concerning the realization that increased competition will affect Las Vegas. Las Vegas cannot ignore the increase in gambling activity across the country or the impact that it will have on Las Vegas.

The focus needs to be on attracting gamblers and their families, not non-gambling families. Mirage Resorts spokesman Alan Feldman has the right approach. He suggests that Las Vegas market itself as "An adult (gambling) destination that people can easily bring kids to" (Pledger, 1993).

REFERENCES

Aaker, David A. (1991). *Managing Brand Equity.* New York, NY: The Free Press.

Derrick, Frederick W. and Alane E. Linfield (1980). "The Family Life Cycle: An Alternative Approach," *Journal of Consumer Research,* September, 214–17.

Dovel, George P. (1990). "Stake it Out: Positioning Success, Step by Step," *Business Marketing,* July.

Kotler, Philip (1994). *Marketing Management: Analysis, Planning, Implementation, and Control,* Eighth edition, Englewood Cliffs, NJ: Prentice Hall.

Las Vegas Convention and Visitors Authority (1982). *Las Vegas Visitor Profile Study.*

Las Vegas Convention and Visitors Authority (1987). *Las Vegas Visitor Profile Study.*

Las Vegas Convention and Visitors Authority (1992). *Las Vegas Visitor Profile Study.*

Murphy, Patrick E. and William A. Staples (1979). "A Modernized Family Life Cycle," *Journal of Consumer Research,* June, 12–22.

Palermo, Dave (1994). "No Disney World," *Las Vegas Review Journal,* March 19, 1E.

Pledger, Marcia (1993). "Las Vegas Changing Marketing Tactics," *Las Vegas Review Journal,* September 7, 1E.

Reis, Al and Jack Trout (1986). *Positioning: The Battle for Your Mind.* New York, NY: McGraw-Hill.

Rothschild, Michael L. (1987). *Advertising,* Lexington. MA: D.C. Heath and Company.

Thompson, William N., J. Kent Pinney, and John Schibrowsky (1996). "The Family that Gambles Together: Business and Social Concerns." *Journal of Travel Research,* vol. 34, no. 3, 70–74.

Trout, Jack and Al Reis (1972). "Positioning Cuts Through the Chaos in the Marketplace," *Advertising Age,* May 1.

Waldrop, Judith and Thomas Exter (1990). "What the 1990 Census will Show," *American Demographer,* January, 27.

Wells, William D. and George Gubar (1966). "Life Cycle Concepts in Marketing Research," *Journal of Marketing Research,* November, 355–63.

Economic Impact of Casino Expansion in the Reno Area

Robert R. Fletcher and George W. Borden

Managed economic growth
and sustainability has become a major topic of discussion for several western rural states and communities. Communities have increased efforts to attract and maintain basic industries that provide income and employment. This has raised several questions regarding the economic and community impacts related to changes in a community.

Nevada has been one of the fastest growing states in the nation, experiencing 75% increase in population from 1980 to 1993 (Nevada State Demographer's Office, 1993). The primary industry in Nevada—casino based tourism—has largely contributed to this growth with the construction of new casinos and the expansion of existing properties. With little indication of a slowdown in growth in many parts of the state, local communities are closely examining the economic impacts of gaming.

Economic impacts are measured in terms of total dollars generated, payroll and employee benefits, and the number of jobs supported. This information is important for state and community leaders to plan for population growth, housing requirements, infrastructure, and water consumption.

Water consumption is important to Nevada due to the arid conditions and dependence on outside sources. The Bureau of Reclamation (BOR) contracted with the Department of Applied Economics and Statistics, University of Nevada, Reno to estimate the economic impacts of water based recreation. Economic impacts were estimated under alternative scenarios for water storage and release flows in the Truckee River Basin (Macdiarmid, Stoddard, Harris, Narayanan, & Fletcher, 1993). The BOR was also interested in estimates for increased residential and commercial water requirements associated with casino expansion in the Reno area.

When this study was initially undertaken, downtown Reno was in the initial phase of constructing a 1,714 room multi-faced project that opened as the Silver Legacy in 1995. This project was a joint venture between Circus Circus Enterprises and the Eldorado Hotel Casino. By the late 1990s, other projects of comparable size were being actively discussed in the Reno area.

The purpose of this analysis was to estimate the economic impact on Washoe County, a subregion of the Truckee River Basin, from developing a project the size of the Silver Legacy in downtown Reno. The specific objectives were to:

1. Develop a casino sector in the input-output model for Washoe County;
2. Estimate the economic impact of the new casino in terms of direct output, indirect and induced effects, and total economic activity;
3. Estimate the impact components of personal income in the region generated by the proposed casino;
4. Estimate the number of new jobs that would be created in the area, and the effect these jobs would have on area population and demand for new housing units; and
5. Estimate residential and commercial water requirements that would be needed for commercial development and new residential housing units.

METHODOLOGY

Input-output (I-O) analysis was used to estimate the economic impacts generated by the casino industry for Washoe County, Nevada. An I-O model is a mathematical representation of the purchasing and sales patterns within a region, and it is a descriptive tool showing in detail the structure of an existing regional economy and how individual sectors interact within that economy. The I-O model is used to provide estimates of how a given economy will respond to changes in specific industries or sectors.

Secondary I-O models (i.e., Implan, Remi) are commonly used in estimating local and regional economic impacts. These models are developed around national I-O tables based on business Standard Industrial Code (SIC) classifications. Secondary I-O models, however, fail to accurately depict the purchasing and sales patterns specific to the casino sector. Such models include casino operations in the lodging sector, while business and employment activities are reported that are not directly related to the gaming portion of the casino sector. This required development of a casino sector was based on primary data to separate casinos from the lodging sector.

To develop an accurate casino sector for the Washoe County model, it was essential to define a typical casino operation in Reno that would represent anticipated income and expenditure patterns of the proposed new property. Primary data was collected from casinos in Reno during October 1993. A comprehensive questionnaire was used asking specific questions related to 1992 sales, wages and salaries, expenditures, and employment. As a follow-up to this questionnaire, personal interviews were conducted to verify responses and collect further information about individual operations. It is estimated that 16% of the total casino activity in Washoe County was surveyed.

It was determined prior to the development of the casino questionnaire that a typical casino operation had seven general cost centers. These cost centers included gaming, lodging, eating, drinking, entertainment, retail, and general administration. Each cost center operated as its own business enterprise, reporting sales, wages and salaries, expenditures, and employment. For the purpose of the Washoe County model development, all cost centers were aggregated to represent a Casino Sector.

MODEL CONSTRUCTION

Input-output modeling and analysis is centered around three basic tables: the transactions table, the direct requirements table, and the total requirements table. The development of the transactions table is considered the heart of input-output analysis, providing the basis for deriving the direct requirements and total requirements tables. It defines the purchases (columns) and sales (rows) between sectors in the economy.

The direct requirements table shows the regional requirements to produce one dollar of output. The endogenous portion of the direct requirements, including households, is the basis for calculating the total requirements table and how dollars are re-spent in the local economy. The total requirements table depicts the direct, indirect, and induced (with households endogenous) or total effects for a one dollar change in output for any given sector with the other sectors in the regional economy.

The total requirements table was adjusted to place the value 1.00 along the diagonal, the interaction within each sector. This allows an estimated output change for a given sector to be interpreted as a change in total output as opposed to a change in final demand. The total requirements table or matrix is the direct application to resource coefficients to estimate impacts of change. More technical discussion of input-output modeling can be found in Miller and Blair (1985).

A 16-sector Washoe County model was developed based on 1985 Implan direct requirements and household personal income coefficients. These coefficients were adjusted using 1987 business census data for the State of Nevada. Using data reported by the Division of the Bureau of Economic Analysis (BEA) for Washoe County, employment and personal income by sector were updated for 1992 (U.S. Department of Commerce,

Economic and Statistics Administration, Bureau of Economic Analysis, 1993). Sector output totals were estimated using reported BEA personal income divided by Implan direct income coefficients. Output totals for the casino sector were checked against total revenues reported by the Nevada Gaming Control Board.

The agriculture sectors were replaced with technical coefficients (direct requirements) developed from enterprise budget information. The agriculture sectors are on a commodity or enterprise basis and not based on SIC delineations. The casino sector in the State model was updated to more accurately reflect the gaming industry as casinos.

Casino sector transactions were replaced in the Washoe County model using primary data collected from casinos in Reno. One trade sector, a combination of wholesale and retail trade, is included in the model and marginalized at 25.5% to reflect only the mark-up on items sold in the local economy.

Appendix Table 1 shows the input tables used to estimate changes in employment, population, housing units, residential water consumption, and commercial water use. The output column represents the border totals used to develop the Washoe County transactions table. Income is the total personal income received by Washoe County households as reported by BEA. Employment in jobs is the total number of workers, as opposed to full-time equivalents (FTE), reported by BEA. Population estimates by sector are based on the ratio of Washoe County's total population to total jobs. Housing units were estimated as a ratio of Washoe County's total occupied housing units to total population. Residential water use is based on the projected water use by single and multi-family dwellings. Future growth was projected by the ratio between the two dwelling types. These numbers are not intended to accurately reflect current residential water consumption in Washoe County.

Estimates indicated that 65% of the families occupied single family residents in 1993, which consumed 0.70 acre feet or 228,096 gallons of water per year. The remaining 35% lived in multi-family structures or mobile homes and consumed 0.30 acre feet or 97,755 gallons of water annually. (Each acre foot of water is equivalent to 325,851 gallons.)

The projections for new housing resulting from casino expansion were 50% single family dwellings using 0.50 acre foot or 162,926 gallons annually. These projections reflected newly required water metering and projected use of smaller lots for new construction. Multi-family dwellings were projected to consume 0.30 acre foot or 97,755 gallons of water annually. Multi-family dwellings included estimates of outdoor and recreational use and mobile home parks. These estimates, provided in 1994 by Sierra Pacific Power Company, were used in arriving at the 0.40 acre foot estimate (or 130,340 gallons of water) required for an average new dwelling unit in the Reno area. Based on these average family annual water requirements, total residential consumption was estimated by sector.

Estimated commercial water use, provided by Nevada Division of Water Planning, was reported in gallons per employee per day for SIC classifications. This information was used to estimate total commercial water use and develop water coefficients in terms of gallons required to produce an additional one dollar of output.

The employment coefficient shows the number of jobs required to produce $100,000 of output for a given sector in Washoe County. The income coefficient shows the payments to households required to produce one dollar of output for a given sector in Washoe County.

ECONOMIC IMPACT ANALYSIS

Economic impacts were estimated for proposed expansion of the casino industry in the Reno area. Casino expansion is normally reported by the number of hotel rooms provided by either additions to an existing property or development of a new property. Although other measures could be used, such as the number of increased jobs, slot machines, or table games, hotel rooms were considered the most appropriate for this analysis.

Each additional casino hotel room in Reno was estimated to generate an additional $100,000 in revenue for the total casino operation. Table 1 gives the indirect and total economic impacts from the $100,000 of direct income shown in column 1. The indirect and induced effect is the $91,020, column 2 total. Of the $191,020 total economic impact shown in column 3, $47,065 (household row) is in the form of personal income. Each additional room would support 2.314 jobs in the local economy and add 3.070 people to the current population. These new residents would require 1.230 housing units consuming 159,951 gallons of water per year. The additional economic activity would demand 113,529 gallons of commercial water annually. Total additional water requirements per new casino room was estimated to be 273,480 gallons annually, with 159,951 gallons for residential use and 113,529 gallons for commercial use. Over 82% of the commercial use came from the casinos.

Table 2 shows the accumulative effect of adding 1,714 new casino hotel rooms to the economy. This is intended to represent the impact of the Silver Legacy. This project was estimated to generate $327 million in total economic activity throughout Washoe County including $81 million in personal income. New jobs created were estimated at 3,966, supporting an increased population base of 5,262 people. The new residents would require 2,108 additional housing units and consume 274 million gallons of water annually. Economic expansion would also require 195 million gallons of commercial water. A total of 469 million gallons or 1,439 acre

TABLE 1

Impact on Washoe County, Nevada of Additional Casino Rooms in Reno
Dollar Flows

Sectors	Direct Impact	Indirect Induced	Total Impact	Total Jobs
Livestock	0	0	0	0.000000
Other Agriculture	0	28	28	0.000916
Gold Mining	0	0	0	0.000000
Other Mining	0	0	0	0.000000
Construction	0	1,558	1,558	0.012812
Manufacturing	0	3,368	3,368	0.022559
Transportation & Communication	0	2,324	2,324	0.027408
Utilities	0	3,734	3,734	0.009885
Trade	0	5,231	5,231	0.105202
Casino	100,000	0	100,000	1.798872
Eat/Drink/Lodging	0	1,586	1,586	0.030718
F.I.R.E.	0	5,651	5,651	0.050708
Services	0	8,034	8,034	0.098842
Health	0	6,292	6,292	0.075609
Local Government	0	6,149	6,149	0.080264
Households	0	47,065	47,065	0.000047
Totals	100,000	91,020	191,020	2.313842

TABLE 2

Estimated Economic Impact on Washoe County, Nevada
of 1,714 Additional Casino Rooms in Reno

Total economic activity	($000)	$327,408
Total personal income	($000)	$80,670
Total employment	(Jobs)	3,966
Total population change	(Persons)	5,262
Total housing units required	(Dwellings)	2,108
Total residential water requirements	(Gallons)	274,156,014
Total commercial water requirements	(Gallons)	94,589,822
Total water requirements	(Gallons)	468,745,836
Total reduction in irrigated pasture	(Acres)	383
Total reduction in livestock sector	(Dollars)	97,665

TABLE 3
Impact On Washoe County, Nevada
of One Acre Reduction in Irrigation Pasture
Dollar Flows

Sectors	Direct Impact	Indirect Induced	Total Impact	Total Jobs
Livestock	−255	0	−255	−0.004818
Other Agriculture	0	0	−27	−0.000715
Gold Mining	0	0	0	−0.000000
Other Mining	0	0	0	−0.000000
Construction	0	−6	−6	−0.000047
Manufacturing	0	−12	−12	−0.000078
Transportation & Communication	0	−6	−6	−0.000070
Utilities	0	−5	−5	−0.000014
Trade	0	−18	−18	−0.000355
Casino	0	−3	−3	−0.000048
Eat/Drink/Lodging	0	−3	−3	−0.000059
F.I.R.E.	0	−21	−21	−0.000190
Services	0	−15	−15	−0.000188
Health	0	−6	−6	−0.000068
Local Government	0	0	−11	−0.000140
Households	0	−86	−86	−0.000000
Totals	−255	−218	−473	−0.006791

(continued)

feet of water would be required annually. Assuming the additional water requirements come from irrigated agriculture, which requires 1,225,200 gallons or 3.76 acre feet of water per acre annually, 383 acres of irrigated pasture would be taken out of production. This would have a negative $97,665 impact on the livestock sector.

Table 3 shows the distribution of the livestock sector impacts. Each acre taken out of irrigation would reduce direct farm income by $255. This reduction would have a ripple effect through the economy in a reduction of $473 total economic activity. Residential water consumption would decrease 503 gallons annually, while commercial water use would decrease 106 gallons annually.

Table 4 reports the total impacts for 383 acres reverted from irrigated pasture to dry pasture. This would reduce total economic activity by $181,159, including $32,938 personal income and 2.60 jobs. Population

TABLE 3
(continued)

Sectors	Population Increase Persons	Housing Units Number	Residential Water Gallons	Commercial Water Gallons
Livestock	−0.006846	−0.002743	−358	−75
Other Agriculture	−0.001016	−0.000407	−53	−11
Gold Mining	−0.000001	−0.000000	0	0
Construction	−0.000000	−0.000000	0	0
Manufacturing	−0.000067	−0.000027	−4	0
Construction	−0.000111	−0.000044	−6	−1
Transportation & Communication	−0.000100	−0.000040	−5	−1
Utilities	−0.000020	−0.000008	−1	−1
Trade	−0.000505	−0.000202	−26	−4
Casino	−0.000062	−0.000025	−3	−3
Eat/Drink/Lodging	−0.000084	−0.000034	−4	−2
F.I.R.E.	−0.000270	−0.000108	−14	−1
Services	−0.000267	−0.000107	−14	−3
Health	−0.000096	−0.000039	−5	−2
Local Government	−0.000199	−0.000080	−10	−1
Households	−0.000000	−0.000000	0	0
Total	−0.009644	−0.003864	−503	−106

would be reduced by 3.69 people and 1.48 housing units. Residential water consumption would be reduced by 192,649 gallons annually, and commercial water use would decrease by 40,598 gallons annually.

Reduction in irrigated pasture is only used as an example of negative impacts on Washoe County assuming agricultural water would have to be reallocated to municipal and industrial use to meet increased water demand for a new 1,714 room casino. This is one scenario that could result, assuming that total water allocation—residential and commercial—remained at its 1993 levels. However, if total water allocation to Washoe County was adequate to fully support the Silver Legacy, or other similar new projects, these negative impacts would not occur.

SUMMARY AND CONCLUSIONS

As Washoe County, Nevada experiences economic growth from its major export industry, there is a need to identify and understand the impacts this

TABLE 4
Economic Impact on Washoe County, Nevada from
383 Acre Reduction in Irrigated Pasture

Total economic activity	(Dollars)	−$181,159
Total personal income	(Dollars)	−$32,938
Total employment	(Jobs)	−2.60
Total population change	(Persons)	−3.69
Total housing units required	(Dwellings)	−1.48
Total residential water requirements	(Gallons)	−192,649
Total commercial water requirements	(Gallons)	−40,598
Total water requirements	(Gallons)	−233,247
Total reduction in irrigated pasture	(Acres)	383
Total reduction in livestock sector	(Dollars)	97,665

growth would have on the County. This study reports the projected impacts related to the 1995 opening of the Silver Legacy, a casino with 1,741 rooms, in terms of economic activity, personal income, jobs, population, housing, residential water consumption, and commercial water use.

In summary the main findings of this analysis indicated that the Silver Legacy would impact Washoe County by generating $327 million in economic activity, including $81 million in personal income, supporting 3,966 jobs. Using appropriate multipliers, such economic impacts would increase Washoe County population by 5,262 people, requiring 2,108 new housing units.

An important resource constraint in Washoe County is water since a large portion of the County's water comes from outside sources. It was estimated that this expansion would annually require an additional 469 million gallons of residential and commercial water.

This analysis provides a methodology and starting point for providing information to state and local planners and policy makers on how economic growth can impact an area. Additional work is warranted, addressing other issues that are important for states and communities to plan for expansion and growth. Among the questions that can be answered are:

- What impact will increased population and commercial business have on utilities?
- What impact will increased population have on school systems?
- What impact will increased population and business activity have on infrastructure demands and maintenance, or on local and state finances?

In addition, further input-output modeling can be performed, through business surveying, to include multiple counties, State of Nevada, and disaggregation of sectors under study (i.e., casino sector disaggregated to include separate sectors for each cost center identified during the surveys).

REFERENCES

Nevada State Demographer's Office (1993). Reno: Bureau of Business and Economic Research, College of Business Administration, University of Nevada, Reno.

Reno-Sparks Convention & Visitor Authority. *1993 Marketing Report.*

MacDiarmid, Thomas, Shawn Stoddard, Thomas Harris, Rangesan Narayanan, and Bob Fletcher (1994). *Methodology to Assess Economic Impacts Associated with the Proposed Truckee River Operating Agreement.* University Center Technical Report, July.

Miller, R. E. and P. D. Blair (1985). *Input-output Analysis: Foundations and Extensions.* Englewood Cliffs: Prentice-Hall.

U.S. Department of Commerce, Economic and Statistics Administration, Bureau of Economic Analysis (1993). Employment and personal income by major source of earnings by industry. Washington D.C.

Nevada State Gaming Control Board (1992). *Nevada Gaming Abstract.*

APPENDIX

New Casino Employment to Population Coefficient

1.42 persons in the population for each job in Washoe County.
40% of persons with new casino jobs will live in one casino job household = 1.42 persons in population for each new casino job.
60% of persons with new casino jobs will live in two casino job households = 1.21 persons in population for each new casino job.
Direct impact of new casino jobs to population = $(.40*1.42) + (.60*1.21) = 1.30$

Housing Coefficient

Total occupied housing units in Washoe County = 102,034
Total population in Washoe County = 254,667
Housing unit per person in Washoe County = 254,667 / 102,034 = .400657

Table 1
Input Table
Washoe County, Nevada

Sectors	Washoe Output ($000)	Washoe Income ($000)	Washoe Employment Jobs	Washoe Population Persons	Washoe Housing Dwellings
Livestock	4,234	685	80	114	46
Other Agriculture	54,564	22,857	1,385	1,968	789
Gold Mining	175,005	54,630	1,024	1,455	583
Other Mining	29,330	7,633	255	362	145
Construction	1,165,647	336,344	9,509	13,512	5,414
Manufacturing	1,432,310	382,202	9,595	13,634	5,463
Transportation & Communication	714,361	286,488	8,426	11,973	4,797
Utilities	746,526	93,645	1,976	2,808	1,125
Trade	1,505,271	740,387	30,271	43,014	17,234
Casino	1,460,193	471,350	26,267	37,325	14,954
Eat/Drink/Lodging	738,917	246,546	14,315	20,341	8,150
F.I.R.E.	1,523,739	211,367	13,673	19,429	7,784
Services	2,424,896	961,500	29,835	42,395	16,986
Health	1,056,370	495,108	12,693	18,036	7,226
Local Government	759,175	308,410	9,909	14,080	5,641
State Employees	192,130	5,975	8,490	3,402	
Federal Employees	139,893	4,032	5,729	2,296	
Totals	13,790,538	4,951,175	179,220	254,667	102,034

(continued)

TABLE 1

(continued)

Sectors	Direct Employment Coefficient FTE Per $100,000 of Output	Direct Income Coefficient Per $1 of Output	Commercial Water Coefficient Gallons Per $1 of Output
Livestock	1.889466	0.161863	0.294621
Other Agriculture	2.680000	0.418903	0.417887
Gold Mining	0.585126	0.312155	0.020909
Other Mining	0.869417	0.260177	0.033701
Construction	0.815770	0.288547	0.050648
Manufacturing	0.669897	0.263690	0.087707
Transportation & Communication	1.179516	0.401040	0.123044
Utilities	0.264693	0.125441	0.197303
Trade	2.011000	0.486901	0.242665
Casino	1.798872	0.322800	1.048900
Eat/Drink/Lodging	1.937295	0.333658	0.680172
F.I.R.E.	0.897332	0.138716	0.063933
Services	1.230362	0.396513	0.225260
Health	1.201568	0.422317	0.329456
Local Government	1.305233	0.371102	0.103429

(continued)

Direct Employment Coefficient

Direct employment / output * 100,000

Direct Income Coefficient

Direct income / output

Commercial Water Coefficient

Direct employment coefficient / 100,000 * gallons per employee per day * 365 days.

Residential Water Coefficient

50% single family housing units using 162,926 gallons or 0.50 acre feet of water annually.

TABLE 1
(*continued*)

Sectors	Total Residential Water Per Year Gallons	Total Commercial Water Per Year Gallons	Total Residential & Commercial Water Per Year Gallons
Livestock	5,936,465	1,247,570	7,184,035
Other Agriculture	102,775,048	21,596,028	124,371,076
Gold Mining	75,986,750	3,659,110	79,645,861
Other Mining	18,922,782	988,457	19,910,938
Construction	705,623,057	59,038,053	764,661,110
Manufacturing	712,004,757	125,623,017	837,627,774
Transportation & Communication	625,258,163	87,897,504	713,155,668
Utilities	146,630,683	147,291,633	293,922,315
Trade	2,246,284,105	365,277,130	2,611,561,235
Casino	1,949,164,038	1,531,595,936	3,480,759,974
Eat/Drink/Lodging	1,062,256,184	502,590,345	1,564,846,530
F.I.R.E.	1,014,616,054	97,417,390	1,112,033,444
Services	2,213,930,371	546,231,114	2,760,161,485
Health	941,894,359	348,026,828	1,289,921,187
Local Government	735,305,381	78,520,402	813,825,784
State Employee	443,379,721	47,346,796	490,726,517
Federal Employees	229,197,830	61,869,427	361,067,257
Totals	13,299,165,447	4,026,216,740	17,325,382,190

50% multi-family housing units using 97,755 gallons or 0.30 acre feet of water annually.
Annual gallons of water per average family unit =
(.50 * 162,926) + (.50 * 97,755) = 130,341 gallons
(.50 * .50) + (.50 * .30) = .40 acre feet

Commercial Water Use

Total commercial use = reported gallons per employee per day * employment * 365 days. Information provided by Nevada Division of Water Planning.

At the time that this study was conducted, Robert R. Fletcher and George "Buddy" W. Borden were Professor and Research Associate, respectively, with the Department of Agricultural Economics, University of Wyoming, Laramie. They are both presently affiliated with the University of Nevada, Reno.

SUCCESS IN THE GAMING INDUSTRY: A CASE STUDY OF TUNICA COUNTY

Jeff Wallace, John E. Gnuschke, and David H. Ciscel

In October 1992, the casino gaming industry began in Tunica County, Mississippi, with just one casino that employed a few hundred workers and faced what would appear to have been insurmountable obstacles to success. Necessary factors of production were virtually non-existent at the time in the area. Theories of comparative advantage would have predicted a relatively quick demise to this industry in Tunica County. Yet despite facing high odds of failure, by 1997 Tunica's casino industry developed into a half-billion-dollar-a-year industry with nine casinos employing thousands of workers. How is it possible that the casino industry could thrive in an area once labeled by political activist Jesse Jackson as "America's Ethiopia?" (Russell, 1995).

INTRODUCTION TO COMPETITIVE ADVANTAGE

The answer to the preceding question can be found by following the methodology laid out in Michael Porter's *The Competitive Advantage of Nations* (Porter, 1990). Although Porter's work was written to explain why nations are successfully competitive in specific industries, it can also be used as a guide in analyzing a budding industry or even a potential industry within any region of any country. Utilizing Porter's methodology as a guide will reveal the strengths of a region that will contribute to an industry's success and the weaknesses that must be overcome.

Porter found that success in any industry in any country is usually not attributable to only one basic factor, but instead to the complex interaction of a host of factors which can be grouped into four broad categories. As shown in Figure 1, the four basic determinants of why industries succeed in certain nations are: (1) factor conditions; (2) demand conditions; (3) related and supporting industries; and (4) firm strategy, structure, and rivalry. A thorough examination of a given industry in a given area using

FIGURE 1
Porter's Determinants of Competitive Advantage

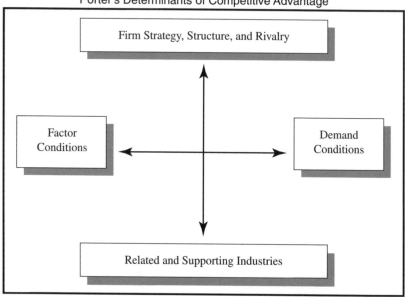

Porter's methodology will lead to an explanation of why certain industries in an area succeed or fail.

In accordance with Porter's determinants of competitive advantage, it will be shown that the casino gambling industry is a center of growth in North Mississippi due to strong inter-firm rivalry, dynamic and high-quality regional demand, the industry's innovative ability to overcome relative weaknesses in related and supporting industries, and factor conditions such as labor and infrastructure. Strong inter-firm rivalry forces the competitors to continually improve and upgrade their offerings in order to hold on to and expand their current market. Without the impetus provided by competition, an industry's offerings will become stagnant, with a diminishing ability to compete with firms from outside a small, localized area.

We first examine the external environment in which the Tunica casino industry operates. Firm strategy, structure, and rivalry have largely been influenced by casino regulations in the state of Mississippi. The state of Mississippi allows for an unlimited number of casino licenses provided that the casinos are located on a navigable waterway and meet certain other restrictions (UNLV, 1996; *Mississippi Code Annotated,* sec. 97-33-1 (1996)). While this policy is not as free-market oriented as the gaming industry in Nevada, it allows for greater competition and a greater number of competitors than are found in states with more restricted licensing such as Missouri and Illinois (UNLV 1996). Like Nevada, the competitive environment that has evolved in Tunica due to Mississippi's competitive licensing and low taxes provides the incentive for competitors to continually improve, thus allowing the industry to draw customers from a much wider geographic region than just the Memphis, Tennessee metropolitan area.

Porter states that, "Among the strongest empirical findings from our research is the association between vigorous domestic rivalry and the creation and persistence of competitive advantage in an industry"(Porter, 117). In other words, strong rivalry forces competitors to continually innovate and improve in order to survive. The effect of this rivalry can be seen by tracing the development of the Tunica casino industry.

The first casino opened in the Tunica County market in October 1992. Prior to this, the only local outlet for legalized gambling was at a dog track in West Memphis, Arkansas—directly across the Mississippi River from Memphis—and a horse track in Hot Springs, Arkansas—a three-and-a-half-hour drive from Memphis. This first casino, Splash Casino, operated for nearly a year without any local competition other than the dog track in West Memphis. It was essentially a floating warehouse crowded with slot machines and a few card-game tables. Initially, customers waited in line sometimes for hours to gain entrance to the casino, in addition to having to pay a $10 entrance fee (UNLV, 1996). This continued only as long as Splash held a monopoly on the regional casino market.

With the introduction of competing casinos in 1993, Splash dropped its entrance fee. Competition grew from one to four casinos in a matter of months, with each casino trying to outdo the others in an effort to attract customers. As shown in Tables 1 and 2, as competition increased, so did the size and amenities of the casinos. The local casinos went from cramped, poorly decorated, floating warehouses such as Splash and the original Lady Luck, to elaborate, spacious buildings that probably floated on water only during the construction phase.

The Tunica market changed considerably in its first five years in existence. Tunica County grew to as many as eleven operating casinos in 1994, and then declined to a low of seven in 1995, rebounding to a total of nine operating casinos in the summer of 1998.

The casinos that survived this early volatility had to innovate and upgrade to attract customers; and as they did, patrons' tastes were permanently upgraded and changed. No longer were customers willing to settle for gambling alone in a floating warehouse environment, such as the former Splash Casino. At this time, the casinos had to offer amenities such as hotel rooms, convention and meeting space, top-name entertainment, reduced food prices, a choice of several restaurants within the same estab-

TABLE 1

Tunica Casino Gaming Amenities

Casino	Opened (Closed)	Gambling Space (Square Feet)	Number of Slots	Number of Table Games
Splash	10-19-92 (05-24-95)	38,000	650	39
Lady Luck[1]	09-18-93 (04-24-94)	34,000	670	40
Harrah's	11-29-93 (05-19-97)	28,000	985	34
Bally's[2]	12-03-93 (02-09-95) 12-18-95	40,000	1,273	52
President	12-06-93 (07-08-94)	35,000	700	41
Southern Belle[3]	02-19-94 (08-31-94)	50,000	1,350	75
Treasure Bay	05-09-94 (05-23-95)	63,000	1,702	65
Sam's Town	05-25-94	94,000	1,900	81
Fitzgerald's	06-06-94	34,000	1,200	39
Sheraton	08-01-94	31,000	1,100	54
Hollywood	08-08-94	54,000	1,300	56
Circus Circus/ Gold Strike	08-28-94	60,000	1,451	66
Horseshoe	02-13-95	30,000	1,065	49
Harrah's Mardi Gras[4]	04-08-96	50,000	1,189	56
Grand Casino	06-24-96	140,000	3,175	161

Source: Author.
[1]Lady Luck moved and reopened in Coahoma County in June of 1994.
[2]Bally's orginally opened at Mhoon Landing prior to closing and reopening at Robinsonville.
[3]See note on Harrah's Mardi Gras.
[4]Harrah's Mardi Gras originally was the Southern Belle casino, which was purchased by Harrah's in 1995.

lishment, and even child-care. The increase in the availability of these non-gaming amenities would not have occurred without competition. This point is supported by the observation that the original Tunica casino—Splash—changed very little during the year in which it operated alone in the Tunica market.

In addition to offering a continuously growing number of amenities,

TABLE 2

Tunica Casino Non-Gaming Amenities

Casino	Child Care	Live Entertainment	Number of Restaurants	Hotel Rooms	RV Camper Spaces[5]	Convention/Meeting Space (Sq. Ft)
Splash	No	Yes	1	0	0	0
Lady Luck[1]	No	No	2	0	0	0
Harrah's	No	Yes	1	0	0	0
Bally's[2]	No	Yes	3	240	0	625
President	No	No	2	0	0	0
Southern Belle[3]	No	Yes	3	0	0	0
Treasure Bay	No	No	1	0	0	0
Sam's Town	Yes	Yes	5	860	0	33,882
Fitzgerald's	No	Yes	3	507	100	17,150
Sheraton	No	Yes	4	200	0	12,368
Hollywood	Teen Arcade	Yes	5	506	72	35,806
Circus Circus/Gold Strike	No	Yes	3	1,200	0	44,650
Horseshoe	No	Yes	3	505	0	0
Harrah's Mardi Gras[4]	Yes	Yes	3	200	0	13,464
Grand Casino	Yes	Yes	5	756	200	43,110

Source: Author.
[1] Lady Luck moved and reopened in Coahoma County in June of 1994.
[2] Bally's originally opened at Mhoon Landing prior to closing and reopening at Robinsonville.
[3] See note on Harrah's Mardi Gras.
[4] Harrah's Mardi Gras originally was the Southern Belle casino, which was purchased by Harrah's in 1995.
[5] While some casinos have dedicated RV slots with hookups, all casinos allow RV parking regardless of whether they provide hookups or not.

FIGURE 2
Casino Locations in Tunica County

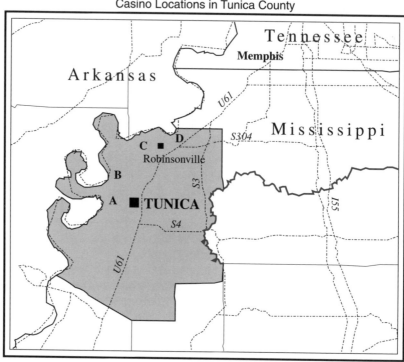

casinos are also competing differentially on location. As stated previously, the state of Mississippi allows for an unlimited number of casino licenses, provided the casinos are located on a navigable waterway and meet certain other restrictions, subject to voter approval within a given jurisdiction (MCA sec. 97-33-1 (1996)). According to state law, "navigable waters" has generally been interpreted to mean ". . . on or directly adjacent to the Mississippi River" (MCA sec. 27-109-1 (1996)). With the exception of a single Native American casino located inland in Philadelphia, Mississippi, and the casinos on the Mississippi Gulf Coast, this has resulted in the casinos locating exclusively along the Mississippi River.

There can only be one casino that is closest to Memphis. As a result, casinos have generally leap-frogged others in an effort to be the closest (Figure 2), culminating with the opening of Grand Casino Tunica just south of the Tunica County–DeSoto County border (POINT D), the closest to Memphis legally possible in 1997. When Splash Casino opened at Mhoon Landing (POINT A) in October 1992, it was the only casino in the Tunica market for nearly a year. Patrons from Memphis had to drive 35 miles or more just to get to the casino. Mhoon Landing thrived as a location for casinos as long as there was little or no competition closer to Memphis, and three more casinos opened there during the next two years (Lady Luck, President, and Bally's).

The casinos at Mhoon Landing began to decline once Harrah's Casino opened at Commerce Landing (POINT B) in November 1993, ten miles closer to Memphis. The decline accelerated with the closing of Lady Luck Casino in April 1994, of the President Casino in July 1994, and of Bally's in February 1995, leaving only Splash Casino at Mhoon Landing. Both Lady Luck and Bally's casinos were subsequently moved and then reopened. Lady Luck reopened just south of Tunica County in Coahoma County at the U.S. Highway 49 bridge in an effort to position itself as the closest to the feeder market of Little Rock, Arkansas. Bally's reopened at Casino Center (POINT C) in an effort to be closer to the Memphis feeder market. Splash Casino closed its doors permanently in May 1995.

A major lesson that was learned during this time was that competition forced the Tunica casino industry to continually improve and upgrade its offerings, resulting in an increasingly greater selection of entertainment alternatives for gaming and non-gaming consumers alike. No longer must gaming consumers settle for the likes of a "Splash Casino," with a few slot machines and table games crowded into what was essentially a floating warehouse. Instead, competition forced the Tunica casinos to expand their offerings, thus meeting the needs of both local and non-local consumers. Continued expansion of non-gaming offerings in the Tunica area will lessen the industry's dependence upon local demand, thereby providing for even greater success in the future.

RELATED AND SUPPORTING INDUSTRIES

The dearth of related and supporting industries in the Tunica area was another obstacle that local casinos had to overcome in order to be successful. This obstacle was, however, rather minor in light of the abundance of related and supporting service-sector industries in Memphis. As shown in Table 3, Tunica County had virtually nothing to offer to the casino industry in the way of related and supporting industries. While nearly all of Tunica's service-sector industries have shown significant levels of growth, the Tunica industries by themselves are not of sufficient size to be able to supply the casino industry with all of its needs.

On the other hand, as shown in Table 4, Shelby County (Memphis), Tennessee, has an abundance of well-developed service-sector and retail industries. Not only have these industries given casino operators existing supplier networks from which to draw (i.e., advertising, hotel/motel suppliers, restaurant/food-service suppliers, and hospital suppliers), but also a well-developed pool of labor.

TABLE 3
Establishments and Employment by Industry
Tunica County 1991 and 1995

Industry	Average Number of Firms		Percent Change	Annual Average Employment		Percent Change
	1991	1995		1991	1995	
Retail Trade	41	48	17.1	268	339	26.5
Eating/Drinking Establishments	7	13	86.0	53	95	79.2
Services	52	79	52.0	437	9,541	2,083.3
Hotels/Lodging	N/D*	16	—	N/D*	4,787	—
Health Services	3	4	33.3	21	132	529.0
Business Services	N/D*	N/D*	—	N/D*	N/D*	—
Banking Institutions	3	3	0.0	20	55	175.0

*N/D=Not Disclosable.
Source: Mississippi Employment Security Commission, 1992 and 1996.

TABLE 4
Establishments and Employment by Industry
Shelby County 1991 and 1995

Industry	Average Number of Firms		Percent Change	Annual Average Employment		Percent Change
	1991	1995		1991	1995	
Retail Trade	3,659	3,434	−6.1	74,375	84,016	13.0
Eating/Drinking Establishments	970	817	−15.8	23,926	29,763	24.4
Services	6,769	7,284	7.6	97,244	122,845	26.3
Hotels/Lodging	124	124	0.0	8,346	7,727	−7.4
Health Services	1,435	1,391	−3.1	35,393	38,540	8.9
Business Services	1,161	1,167	0.5	26,206	35,328	34.8
Banking Institutions	146	149	2.1	7,569	7,563	0.08

Source: Tennessee Department of Employment Security, 1992 and 1996.

The large near-by cluster of related and supporting service-sector industries is one of the main reasons the Tunica casino industry is thriving. With perhaps one exception, growth within related and supporting industries in Shelby County has allowed Memphis area businesses to supply the needs of both the local area and the Tunica casinos. The one exception has been the sector of hotels and lodging establishments, which lost employment within Shelby County probably because of the growth of the hotel and lodging industry within Tunica County. In the early stages of the Tunica casino industry, hotel rooms in Tunica County were virtually non-existent. As the casinos added their own hotels and attracted other hotel developments, they lessened their dependence upon the Memphis area for lodging for casino patrons.

CONCLUSION

Utilizing Porter's model as a guide has revealed strengths that are contributing to the Tunica casino industry's success and weaknesses that the casinos have had to overcome. Because of the near-total absences of supporting industry, theories of comparative advantage would have predicted a quick demise to the casino industry in Tunica County, but this obviously did not come to pass.

One of the most important observations to be made in this analysis is that vigorous competition has been a major driving force in the continual improvement and expansion of the casino gaming industry in Tunica. Without competition, Tunica would be left with perhaps nothing but small, cramped, floating warehouses with a few slot machines and table games, drawing upon a small, local market. Mississippi's relatively open licensing of casinos and low taxes on casino gaming revenue created a competitive environment which provided incentives for casinos to continually improve, thus allowing the industry to draw customers from a much wider geographic area than just Memphis.

Through a combination of strong, inter-firm rivalry, dynamic and high-quality regional demand, the industry's innovative ability to overcome relative weaknesses in related and supporting industries, and factor conditions, the casino gaming industry in Tunica County quickly became a center of growth in an area that was once one of the poorest counties in America.

REFERENCES

Mississippi Code Annotated (MCA), sec. 97-33-1 (1996).

Mississippi Code Annotated, (MCA), sec. 27-109-1 (1996).

Porter, Michael (1990). *The Competitive Advantage of Nations.* New York: Free Press.

Russell, William (1995). "Ten years ago . . . Tunica was visited by catastrophe." *The Tunica Times,* 9 February, B1.

University of Nevada Las Vegas (UNLV), International Gaming Institute (1996). *The Gaming Industry.* New York: John Wiley & Sons, Inc.

Market Behavior of Gaming Stocks: An Analysis of the First Twenty Years©

Leonard E. Goodall
and William J. Corney

Gaming stocks have now been publicly traded on the stock exchange for about twenty years. This study looks at the price movement patterns of gaming stocks compared with the broader market for six stock market cycles between 1973 and 1992. The study suggests that gaming stocks tend to be more volatile than the market as a whole and that this has been true throughout the twenty year period. It also shows that gaming stocks have risen in price during this period at a rate much greater than that for the general market. Special events, such as the establishment of gaming in New Jersey, can cause the gaming stocks to move in a direction opposite to the general market. Finally, the findings indicate that gaming stocks are especially susceptible to stock market declines which are related to concerns about the price or availability of oil.

One approach to evaluating the development of an industry is to look at the stock market behavior of those companies in the industry which are publicly traded. The gaming industry provides a unique opportunity for this research approach because it is possible to define rather specifically the period during which gaming companies have been publicly owned and traded. Most industries (computers would be a good example) have many small companies which come to the market at different times, and it is difficult to identify exactly when that industry began to be publicly traded.

The gaming industry, in contrast, can identify fairly specifically when public ownership and trading of companies in the industry began. Since casino gaming was restricted to Nevada until 1976, the early history of U.S. gaming is really a history of Nevada gaming companies. From the time of the legalization of gaming in 1931 through the 1960s Nevada's

©1994 Human Sciences Press, Inc. This article was previously published as: Goodall, L. E. (1994). Market Behavior of Gaming Stocks: An Analysis of the First Twenty Years, *Journal of Gambling Studies,* Vol. 10(4), Winter. Permission to reprint has been granted by the author and publisher.

rapidly growing gaming companies were privately owned, often family owned. There was a very practical reason for this. Nevada gaming regulations established strict licensing requirements for casino owners. There was no way that a publicly owned company, with thousands of shareholders, could get all of its "owners," i.e. its shareholders, licensed. It was not until changes by the 1967 and 1969 legislative sessions that it became possible for gaming companies to be publicly owned (Eadington, 1982).

Following the 1969 legislature, several Nevada gaming companies began to explore the possibility of public ownership of their stock. Also, some companies which were already publicly owned, Hilton for example, expressed an interest in buying into the Nevada gaming industry.

The purpose of this paper is to analyze the stock market behavior of gaming stocks during the first twenty years of their public ownership. The study looks both at individual stocks and the industry as a whole. It compares their price behavior with that of the general market during six stock market cycles between 1973 and 1992.

EXPECTED PRICE BEHAVIOR

Based on research on general stock market price behavior patterns, it could be expected that at least three patterns might be found in the gaming stocks. First, the gaming stocks could be expected to be more volatile than the general market, especially in the early years of trading. It is well established that the stocks of smaller companies tend to experience greater than average volatility (Malkiel, pp. 48–56; Dreman, 1982, pp. 168–73). This appears to be partly because they are not well known or as well researched by investors and analysts as larger stocks (Corney, pp. 216–217; Dreman, 1977, pp. 99–124).

Second, it could be expected that, over the longer term investment horizon, three to five years or longer, gaming stocks would increase in prices at a greater rate than the broader market. Known as the "small stock effect," researchers have shown that lower priced stocks tend to grow in value at above average rates (Auriana, pp. 5–7; Ibbotson, pp. 10–11; Markese, pp. 34–37). For example, it has been shown that the average twelve month price increase of the smallest twenty per cent of companies on the New York Stock Exchange, as measured by total capitalization, tends to exceed that of the broader market almost every year (Dreman, 1982, p. 170).

Third, it would be expected that as gaming companies grow and mature, their market behavior would come to more nearly parallel that of the general market. Increasing size and investor acceptability would be expected to bring the gaming industry more into line with the rest of the market and the economy.

TABLE 1
Major Stock Market Cycles
1973–1992

Jan. 11, 1973–Dec. 6, 1974	−45.1%
Dec. 6, 1974–Sep. 21, 1976	+75.7%
Sep. 21, 1976–Aug. 12, 1982	−23.4%
Aug. 12, 1982–Jul. 16, 1990	+286.1%
Jul. 16, 1990–Oct. 11, 1990	−12.2%
Oct. 11, 1990–Jan. 3, 1992	+21.6%

STOCK MARKET CYCLES

From 1973 to 1992 the stock market experienced six well defined major price movements, three downward and three upward (Brown, pp. 94–113). Gaming stocks began to appear on the stock markets by 1970. This study begins with the first clearly identifiable stock market cycle of the 1970s, the sharp downturn of 1973–74. Using the Dow Jones Industrial Average (DJIA) as an index for the market, the price patterns are shown in Table 1. The Dow Jones Industrial Average is the best known indicator of the market. The pattern would not be appreciably different if the Standard and Poor's 500, the New York Stock Exchange index or other major indicators were used. The average price of gaming stocks used in the study is an unweighted average, with each company regardless of size contributing equally to the average.

The price movements are at least partially explained by economic and political events. The 1973–74 downturn, the worst since the 1930s, reflected the market's distaste for uncertainty. Through much of 1973 the markets were shaken by the Watergate news, and this was followed by disastrous economic news—the Arab oil boycott—in the fall of 1973. The resulting inflation and higher interest rates continued the downward pressure on the market in 1974.

The rising market in the 1974–76 period was at least in part simply the bounceback from the sharp downturn preceding it. It was a period which one writer called the "bad earnings, good market" era. Brown argues that stocks had overreacted to bad news and moved so low that they had "discounted the end of the world" (Brown, p. 162). The Federal Reserve discount rate was also cut four times in early 1975, providing the market with what it likes best, declining interest rates.

From September, 1976 to August, 1982, the DJIA fell back by 23.4%. 1977 was a bad year for the economy, with increasing budget and trade deficits, rising inflation and six increases in the discount rate, beginning in May. The period from 1978 to 1982 saw some volatility, but the indices ended the period about where they began. The DJIA, which was trading at 742.12 at its low in February 1978, closed at 776.92 on August 12, 1982.

It may be worth noting in an article on gaming and chance that the longest peacetime bull market in the nation's history began on a Friday the 13th. After hitting its yearly low on Thursday, August 12, 1982, the market moved up slightly on Friday. The following week the Federal Reserve announced a basic change from an inflation-fighting tight money approach to an easier monetary policy, and the market began its long surge upward. On August 18, the New York Stock Exchange traded 133 million shares, the first time in history it had traded more than 100 million shares in a single day (to compare, 250–300 million share days are not uncommon today).

The upward direction of the market continued throughout the 1980s. Except for a slight decline in 1984, the market experienced price increases every year until 1990. Even 1987, the year of the infamous "Black Monday" in October, saw a slight increase as prices rebounded in November and December. The stock market in the 1980s appeared to be helped by declining interest rates, lower income tax rates, increasing corporate profits and a generally expanding economy.

The market experienced a brief but sharp downturn between July and October, 1990. By mid-year in 1990 most economic indicators had turned negative, and the long bull market of the 1980s ran out of steam and turned downward after hitting a high in July. A month later Iraq's invasion of Kuwait had placed a burden of uncertainty on the market, adding impetus to the downward movement. The market fell 12.2% in that brief three month period.

After hitting a low in October, 1990 the market turned positive and was up 21.6% by January, 1992. The optimism accompanying the end of the Gulf War helped restore confidence in the market during this period. The 1990–92 upturn provides a good point at which to conclude this study. It represents the close of the first twenty years of the public trading of gaming stocks. The following year ushered in a new era for gaming stocks, with new riverboat companies and several formerly privately held Nevada companies initiating public trading.

The price quotations used in the study come primarily from *Value Line* reports for the prices of stocks in the 1970s. From 1981 to the present the prices come from Dow Jones News Retrieval by computer data retrieval.

STOCKS IN THE STUDY

This study includes those gaming stocks which were publicly traded during the periods studied. All gaming stocks were included which traded publicly for all or nearly all of the period. Prices are adjusted for stock splits and stock dividends. Stocks were excluded only if they went through re-structurings or bankruptcies which made it impossible to make meaning-ful comparisons of the stock price movements.

From 1973 to 1982, the study covers five stocks: Caesars, Golden Nug-get, Hilton, Resorts International and Showboat. Resorts International actually traded as a gaming stock during the 1960s because its gaming interests were in the Bahamas but the stock traded in the U.S. Hilton traded publicly before 1970s, but it was not a gaming company at that time.

The 1982–1990 period was one of major expansion for gaming stock activity. Six new stocks were added to the study for this period: Bally's, Circus Circus, International Game Technology, Jackpot, Holiday Inns and United Gaming. Resorts International was dropped for this period because its legal and financial difficulties led to extensive corporate re-structuring. By the end of this period Golden Nugget had changed its name to Mirage. During the 1980s other gaming stocks began to trade, but they did not trade through the entire period so they are not included. With the addition of six new stocks and the omission of one, the study included ten stocks for this period.

Four new stocks were added to the study for the July-October, 1990 period: Aztar, MGM, Rio and Sahara. Holiday reorganized and its gam-ing activities traded under the name, Promus by this period. MGM was not added to the study earlier because its reorganization in the 1980s, including separate gaming and non-gaming interests, causes earlier figures to be non-comparable. Aztar came to the market as the company which operates the gaming properties formerly owned by Ramada Inns. During this period there were two publicly held companies carrying the "Sahara" name. Sahara Casino Partners is the operating company for the Las Vegas based properties of the company. Sahara Resorts is the parent company and primary stockholder of Sahara Casino Partners. This study includes Sahara Resorts as the representative of the Sahara interests.

No new stocks were added to the study for the 1990–92 period. There were also no omissions or name changes, so the list of stocks in the study remain unchanged for this period.

PRICE MOVEMENTS

The price movements of gaming stocks are compared here to the move-ments of the general market, as measured by the DJIA, for each of the stock market cycle periods identified above. For the January, 1973 to De-cember, 1974 period, the figures are shown in Table 2. During this period, the sharpest market downturn since the 1930s, the gaming stocks as a group declined significantly more than the broader market, 65.3% com-

TABLE 2
Price Changes
January, 1973–December, 1974

Caesars	−58.3%
Golden Nugget	−50.0%
Hilton	−79.6%
Resorts International	−81.3%
Showboat	−57.1%
Gaming Average	−65.3%
DJIA	−45.1%

pared with 45.1%. Also, each individual stock dropped more than the market average.

At least three factors may have influenced the gaming stocks in this period. First, in the early 1970s these stocks were still unfamiliar to most investors, including the large institutional investors. Second, ethical considerations were also important at that time in causing many to avoid gaming stocks, further reducing the number of potential buyers. Third, this period reflects a pattern confirmed later, which suggests that gaming stocks are especially vulnerable to economic and political events which threaten the availability and price of oil. Most observers agree that the Arab oil boycott was a major factor in the stock market decline of 1973–74.

The market recovery of 1974–76 was an impressive one, with the DJIA rising over 75% from its December, 1974 low. Table 3 shows the pattern in this period. The gaming average in this period is skewed by the dramatic price movement of Resorts International. Even omitting that company from the average, however, gaming stocks still outperformed the general market by a wide margin. There is no obvious explanation for this pattern during that time period, but this upward movement, considered along with the 1973–74 downturn, is the first indication that gaming stocks would tend to be more volatile than the market as a whole.

In the period from 1976 to 1982 gaming stocks confirmed the old adage that Wall Street is a "market of stocks" rather than a "stock market." The market turned downward from 1976 to 1978. Then, in spite of a brief upward move in 1980, the DJIA in August, 1982 was about where it had been four years earlier. For the six year period from September, 1976 to August, 1982, the decline for the DJIA was 23.4%. Gaming stocks moved quite independently of the general direction of the market during this time. As Table 4 shows, gaming stocks moved upward during this time while the overall market declined. Any attempt to explain why gaming stocks moved in the opposite direction from the market during this period

TABLE 3

Stock Prices

December, 1974–September, 1976

Caesars	+140.0%
Golden Nugget	+200.0%
Hilton	+427.3%
Resorts International	+1266.7%
Showboat	+90.4%
Gaming Average	+424.9%
(without Resorts)	+214.4%
DJIA	+75.7%

TABLE 4

Stock Prices

September, 1976–August, 1982

Caesars	+700.0%
Golden Nugget	+680.0%
Hilton	+18.9%
Resorts International	+268.3%
Showboat	+25.9%
Gaming Average	+338.6%
DJIA	−23.4%

must probably take into consideration the coming of gaming to Atlantic City. The expansion of gaming to the east coast not only offered the gaming companies new markets, it also gave them new visibility in the financial community. With many financial analysts and brokerage firms located in New York City, the presence of gaming in that region made it much more difficult for the financial community to ignore the industry.

As noted above, the long period of economic expansion and upward movement for the stock market began in August, 1982, with help from the Federal Reserve. During this period there were more gaming stocks trading and as a group they rose sharply. Table 5 shows the long upward trend of the 1980s.

The gaming stocks outperformed the rest of the market by a wide margin during this period. Even omitting the dramatic rise in United Gaming, gaming stocks were up 341.6% compared with a 286.1% rise in the DJIA. One gaming stock fell during this time. Most of the decline in Ballys came near the end of the period, in 1988 and 1989. The company was hit hard at that time by several financial reverses, and it went through a bankruptcy

TABLE 5
Stock Prices
August, 1982–July, 1990

Ballys	−68.1%
Caesars	+190.6%
Circus	+845.0%
Hilton	+298.6%
Holiday Inn	+152.2%
IGT	+447.3%
Jackpot	+361.5%
Mirage	+824.2%
Showboat	+22.7%
United Gaming	+2203.0%
Gaming Average	+557.7%
(without United Gaming)	+341.6%
DJIA	+286.1%

and financial restructuring. The saying, "a rising tide lifts all boats" applied well to nearly all stocks on the stock market in the 1980s. The tide appears, however, to have lifted the gaming stocks more than most others.

The market fall of 1990 was brief but sharp. The drop began in July and, with impetus in August from Iraq's invasion of Kuwait, the market fell over 12% in just three months. As noted above in connection with the decline of 1973–74, gaming stocks react strongly to crises related to the availability and price of gasoline, and this pattern was demonstrated again in 1990, as seen in Table 6.

The gaming stocks were down an average of 51.1% during this period. Stated another way, the gaming stocks lost about half their total value in this three month's period. The gaming stocks as well as the broader market showed an ability to bounce back in the 1990–92 period (see Table 7). The sharpest decline in interest rates in over 20 years helped move the stock market to new highs. As a group the gaming stocks (omitting IGT) rose 114.9% while the general market gained 21.6%. Only Sahara did not participate in the upturn.

The stock market fluctuations shown in Tables 2 to 7 are unweighted. A small company like Jackpot affects the averages as much as larger companies like Hilton or Holiday Inn. It is reasonable to ask whether the fluctuation patterns would be different if they were based on weighted rather than unweighted averages. Table 8 compares the unweighted averages with weighted averages for the same time periods. The weighted aver-

TABLE 6
Stock Prices
July, 1990–October, 1990

Aztar	−61.9%
Ballys	−61.6%
Caesars	−45.7%
Circus	−49.5%
Hilton	−52.0%
IGT	−54.9%
Jackpot	−39.6%
MGM	−34.1%
Mirage	−68.9%
Promus	−64.8%
Rio	−42.3%
Sahara	−33.3%
Showboat	−22.2%
United Gaming	−85.2%
Gaming Average	−51.1%
DJIA	−12.2%

ages are based on total capitalization (share price times number of shares) for each company.

The table shows that the general price movement patterns remain the same, but the impact of the larger companies on the weighted averages is noticeable. In the 1976–82 time period, for example, the weighted average was much less volatile than the unweighted. This is influenced by the fact that, as Table 4 indicates, the largest company in the group, Hilton, was the least volatile in that time period. In contrast, the 1982–90 period shows great differences in the unweighted averages depending on whether United Gaming is included or excluded. In the weighted averages, however, United Gaming makes little difference because it is so small compared to other companies in the group. It appears, therefore, that the general volatility patterns in the study are similar whether one uses weighted or unweighted averages, but the larger companies do have the expected impact on the weighted averages.

DISCUSSION

Generalizing about patterns of stock price movements is a tentative process. Some would argue that such movements are essentially random and

TABLE 7

Stock Prices

October, 1990–January, 1992

Aztar	+178.6%
Ballys	+125.7%
Caesars	+232.7%
Circus	+92.1%
Hilton	+70.1%
IGT	+2280.4%
Jackpot	+98.5%
MGM	+26.5%
Mirage	+117.8%
Promus	+239.3%
Rio	+40.0%
Sahara	−23.6%
Showboat	+97.1%
United Gaming	+198.6%
Gaming Average	+269.6%
(without IGT)	+114.9%
DJIA	+21.6%

TABLE 8

Gaming Stocks Price Movements: Weighted and Unweighted Averages

	Unweighted	Weighted
1973–74	−65.3%	−70.5%
1974–76	+424.9%	+308.7%
(without Resorts)	+214.4%	+226.9%
1976–82	+338.6%	+109.4%
1982–90	+557.7%	+228.7%
(without Un. Gam.)	+341.6%	+227.2%
7/90–10/90	−51.1%	−52.3%
1990–1992	+269.6%	+133.4%
(without IGT)	+114.9%	+94.0%

FIGURE 1

Price Fluctuations of Gaming Stocks and Dow Jones Industrial Average

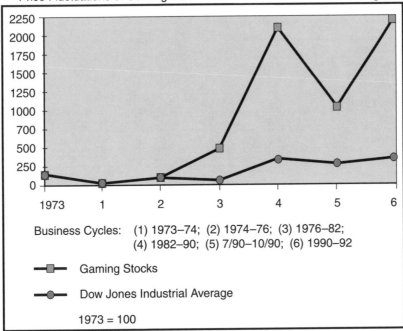

Business Cycles: (1) 1973–74; (2) 1974–76; (3) 1976–82;
(4) 1982–90; (5) 7/90–10/90; (6) 1990–92

—■— Gaming Stocks

—●— Dow Jones Industrial Average

1973 = 100

that past movement patterns have no predictive ability for the future. Nevertheless, based at least on the six periods studied here, four patterns seem to have emerged during the first twenty years of gaming stock trading.

First, gaming stocks appear to be more volatile than the broader market. Whether in up or down cycles, these stocks as a group moved farther than the DJIA. Figure 1, which shows the data in Tables 2 through 7 as a chart, shows the greater volatility of the gaming stocks. In some cycles, every individual gaming stock had a greater movement than the broader market. One likely reason for this is that stocks of smaller companies generally are more volatile than stocks of larger ones. Certainly in the 1970s, and to a large degree even today, gaming stocks are small when compared to the industrial giants that dominate the market averages. Widespread ownership of stocks by institutional investors, such as pension funds, mutual funds and bank trust departments, also can help reduce volatility. Institutional investors are only recently buying gaming stocks in large amounts. This is because of an earlier lack of familiarity with the stocks and in some cases probably also because of ethical considerations.

The above average volatility of gaming stocks is also confirmed when

TABLE 9
Beta Values of Gaming Stocks

	1982	1992
Ballys	1.15	1.60
Caesars	1.35	1.55
Circus	1.15	1.25
Hilton	1.50	1.15
Promus[1]	1.60	1.85
IGT	NA	NMF
Jackpot	1.20	1.100
Mirage[2]	1.15	1.35
Showboat	.80	1.25
United Gaming	NA	NA

Source: *Value Line Reports*
[1]Promus, 1992; Holiday Inn, 1982
[2]Mirage, 1992; Golden Nugget, 1982
NMF—no meaningful figure (designation is *Value Line's*)
NA—not available from *Value Line*

measured by the *beta* values for the individual stocks. *Beta* measures the volatility of a stock against the stock market as a whole (as measured by some index such as DJIA or the SP500), with a *beta* of 1.0 representing the general market. A *beta* of 1.2, for example, indicates that a stock is 20% more volatile than the general market. When the stock market moves up or down by 10%, a stock with a *beta* of 1.2 would be expected to move by 12%. A stock with a *beta* of .8 would be expected to move only 8%.

Table 9 shows the *beta* of those stocks included in the study during the last ten years of the study. *Beta* values can change over time, but the values shown suggest that gaming stocks have had higher than average volatility going back to the time when only a few of the stocks were publicly traded. Table 9 suggests that gaming stocks are as volatile today as they were over a decade ago.

Second, in spite of greater volatility in both upward and downward directions, over the 1973–92 period the average return on gaming stocks far exceeded that of the broader market. Based on the price movements shown in Tables 2 through 7, a hypothetical investment of $100 in the gaming industry in 1973 would have grown to $2,196 in 1992. This calculation is based on the unweighted averages of gaming stocks using the conservative numbers which omit the sharp price increases of Resorts International (1974–76), United Gaming (1982–90) and IGT (1990–92). It also omits any potential impact from dividends, taxes or transaction costs. A hypothetical investment of $100 in the DJIA for the same period would have grown to $305. Based on these numbers, the average annual return for the 1973–92 period was 17.7% for the gaming stocks and 6.1% for the DJIA.

In retrospect, we might surmise that the higher return of gaming stocks results not just from the fact that smaller stocks tend to provide higher than average returns, but also because we can look back and see that the gaming companies were providing a service for which demand was much greater than supply. For most of the period of our study, casino gaming activities were available mainly in Nevada and New Jersey. The dramatic success in recent years of newer casinos in South Dakota, Colorado, on the riverboats and on Indian reservations suggests that there was a great pent-up demand for casino gaming. The fact that a monopoly or near monopoly situation existed in gaming, and that there was a major unsupplied demand for the service, helps explain the high return on gaming stock investments as the industry expanded to respond to the demand in the marketplace.

A third observation is that gaming stocks do occasionally move in directions at variance with the general market in response to specific events. This is not surprising because other stock groups do the same. In early 1993, for example, while the general market was rising, the stocks of health related companies fell in response to fears about the Clinton administration health care proposals. The period from 1976 to 1982 was such a time for gaming stocks, which rose in price while the rest of the market was drifting lower. It is very likely that the expansion of gaming to New Jersey was a major impetus in causing these stocks to move against the trends during this time.

Fourth, it appears that the gaming industry is especially vulnerable to stock market movements which are related to the price and availability of oil. These issues affect the supply and availability of gas, which impact directly on tourism. Most market analysts would agree that oil was a factor in the market downturns of 1973–74 and 1990. In both periods gaming stocks fell sharply.

One of our original hypotheses proved not to be valid—at least not yet. The greater volatility of these stocks suggests our hypothesis that the price movement patterns of gaming stocks would come to resemble those of other stocks with the passing of time has not yet proven valid. Perhaps twenty years is not long enough, or perhaps gaming stocks are truly different. Only time and future studies will tell.

Although this study concludes in 1992 it is worth noting that the major trend since then has been the number of new gaming stocks which have come to market. Many of them are based in new states or the riverboat areas and have little connection to Nevada or New Jersey. Some have casinos on Indian reservations. The gaming industry has become much more heterogeneous in the 1990s, and that is reflected in a growing number of companies in the industry. That, however, is a story for another time.

REFERENCES

Auriana, Lawrence (1989). "Small Stock Fund Focuses on Reality, Not Hope," *American Association of Individual Investors Journal,* Vol. XI, No. 5, 5–7.

Brown, John Dennis (1991). *101 Years on Wall Street.* Englewood Cliffs, NJ: Prentice Hall.

Corney, William J. (1986). *Dynamic Stock Market Analysis.* Homewood, IL: Dow Jones Irwin.

Dremen, David J. (1977). *Psychology and the Stock Market.* New York: Warner Books.

Dremen, David J. (1982). *The New Contrarian Investment Strategy.* New York: Random House.

Dow Jones News Retrieval. A computer data retrieval service.

Eadington, William R. (1982). "The Evolution of Corporate Gambling in Nevada," *Nevada Review of Business and Economics,* Vol. 6, No. 1, 13–22.

Ibbotson, Roger. (1990). "When is 'Cheap' a Bargain?" *American Association of Individual Investors Journal,* Vol. XII, No. 3, 8–11.

Malkiel, Burton G. (1975). *A Random Walk Down Wall Street.* New York: W. W. Norton.

Markese, John (1990). "Transacting in Small Stocks," *American Association of Individual Investors Journal,* Vol. XII, No. 1, 34–37.

Value Line Reports (weekly). New York: Value Line, Inc.